The Social Democrats in Imperial Germany

The Social Democrats in Imperial Germany

*A Study in Working-Class Isolation
and National Integration*

Guenther Roth

Preface by REINHARD BENDIX

 The Bedminster Press • Totowa, New Jersey • 1963

TO MY PARENTS

Acknowledgments

This study originated in research on class relations in industrializing countries, as part of the Inter-University Project on Labor and Economic Development financed by the Ford Foundation. It was conducted under the direction of Professor Reinhard Bendix in the Institute of Industrial Relations at the University of California, Berkeley, during the years 1955–58. By 1960 it had become my Ph.D. dissertation in the Department of Sociology at the University of California. Since then the study has changed considerably to assume its present form. At various stages of completion it was furthered financially by the University Research Board of the University of Illinois at Urbana and by the Columbia University Council for Research in the Social Sciences.

I wish to thank Professors Lewis Feuer, Seymour Martin Lipset and Paul Seabury of the University of California, Berkeley, and Professors Juan Linz and Hans Zetterberg of Columbia University for their willingness to discuss or read the emergent analysis in part or as a whole. The critical editorial sense of Professor Daniel Bell and of Mr. Claus Wittich (both of Columbia University) was very welcome in the last stage of the work.

My greatest debt is to Reinhard Bendix, his counsel and his scholarship.

Contents

Preface

A future historian will give more weight than contemporaries usually do to the impact of events upon the development of ideas. This applies with special force to modern social science. World War II and its consequences, the Cold War and the massive involvement of Americans with events all over the world, have redirected the attention of many American social scientists. Increasingly, they have become concerned with the complex changes variously designated as industrialization, democratization, and modernization. The consequent proliferation of studies shows the earmarks of earlier intellectual orientations, especially the dual emphasis on fact-finding *and* theorizing at a very general level, which owes much to the still earlier emphasis on social evolution. These legacies, together perhaps with an undercurrent of moralism that has characterized American approaches to other civilizations, have given an optimistic and go-getting slant to much literature on the problems of the "developing areas," and this slant is notable also in the positivism with which some social scientists have approached these same problems.

It is in this context that the present study by Professor Guenther Roth makes a genuine contribution and provides a much needed corrective. Avoiding the fallacy of "retrospective determinism" the author analyzes in detail the pattern of action and reaction that represents the cumulative opportunities and liabilities of class-relations in Imperial Germany. He shows that some of the political problems encountered today in the "developing areas" had to be met in their own way in the "developing areas of yesterday." However, he makes clear that at this level there is no easy way of generalizing from one case of development to another, and that those who have generalized have also tended to neglect in varying degrees the impact of ideologies, institutional legacies, and international events. Though in this probing and perceptive study Dr. Roth confines himself to the limitations of a single case, his approach raises major questions with which studies of industrializing societies will have to deal in the future.

REINHARD BENDIX
Professor of Sociology
University of California, Berkeley

The Social Democrats in Imperial Germany

I
Introduction

1. *Recurrent Problems of Democratization and Industrialization*

In recent years public interest in the relationship between political liberty and material well-being has greatly increased. This interest has two major sources: The Western and the Communist world compete for the allegiance or benevolent neutrality of many newly independent countries which are uncertain about their political choices but committed to rapid industrialization; and the two worlds compete directly with regard to their own social and economic achievements. Scholars have responded to this state of affairs by conducting an increasing number of inquiries into the relationship between economic growth, class relations and political change.

One way of exploring recurrent problems of political organization, social change and economic growth consists in taking a long step back into an age when most of Europe was economically underdeveloped in comparison with England. Such an extended perspective makes it possible to overlook a time span in which industrialization advanced under different forms of government. Theoretically, a critical starting or contrast point for the examination of the relationship between political and economic processes has been provided time and again by Marxism. It has become customary to point out that with advancing industrialization labor movements do not typically gain the importance that Marxism and Socialism envisaged as inevitable and, correspondingly, that Marxism turns out to be appealing or successful in the less-developed rather than in the more developed countries.[1] Left-wing radicalism is seen as declining with successful economic development, which, in turn, appears positively related to democratic two-party and multiparty systems.[2] The Marxist thesis has therefore been modified to apply to the early phases of industrialization; labor protest reaches a peak early and then declines as a revolutionary threat. This view, which was succinctly formulated by a prominent group of writers in the mid-fifties, was recently elaborated by them and even further removed from the original Marxist thesis.[3] They now consider labor protest to be less important in the course of democratization than had been assumed previously; labor organizations are seen essentially as reflections of the societies in which they develop, and instead the political and industrial elites emerge as crucial forces.[4] But this theory insists that despite the differences in elite strategies, political structure and historical legacies, there is a "logic of industrialism" eventually resulting in a "web of rules"—industrial relations sys-

[1] For recent statements of this thesis, see W. W. Rostow, *The Stages of Economic Growth: A Non-Communist Manifesto* (Cambridge University Press, 1960), esp. "Communism: A Disease of the Transition," 162 ff; and Adam Ulam, *The Unfinished Revolution* (New York: Random House, 1960), esp. Ch. IV.

[2] On the relationship between left-wing radicalism and economic development in various European countries, see S. M. Lipset, *Political Man* (Garden City: Doubleday, 1960), 61 f. See also Val R. Lorwin, "Working-Class Politics and Economic Development in Western Europe," *American Historical Review*, LXIII:2, Jan. 1958, 338–51. On the limited validity of the hypothesis that economic development and political competitiveness are positively correlated, see G. Almond and J. S. Coleman, eds., *The Politics of the Developing Areas* (Princeton University Press, 1960), 544.

[3] See Clark Kerr, Frederick H. Harbison, John T. Dunlop and Charles A. Myers, "The Labour Problem in Economic Development," *International Labour Review*, LXXI:3, March 1955, 1–15; and, by the same authors, *Industrialism and Industrial Man* (Cambridge: Harvard University Press, 1960). The authors wrote as directors of the Inter-University Study of Labor Problems in Economic Development; their joint publications are partly programmatic, partly based on the accumulated research of the project.

[4] The authors distinguish five ideal types of industrial-political elites: dynastic, middle-class, colonial, revolutionary-intellectual and nationalist.

tems in which bureaucratic skirmishes rather than class conflicts are the rule and in which the importance of ideologies declines. Thus, despite the inversion of Marxist theory, industrialization is still conceived to have determinate political consequences. Most social scientists do not accept Marx's specific rationale, based as it was on his concept of alienation and his linkage of political power with private property of the means of production. However, quite a few continue to assume universal political consequences of industrialization.

These widely held views are increasingly challenged and modified by another view which maintains the relative "neutrality" of industrialization toward the social and political character of the early industrial work force.[5] Industrialization, according to this view, tends to facilitate mass emancipation from traditional ways of life, but sometimes also contributes to their partial preservation by providing the requisite material means. It creates the social basis for a labor movement, but it also swells the ranks of the new middle classes usually hostile to organized labor. In the course of industrialization the repressive power of the state, the political ascendancy of big business, the survival chances of the agrarians and the revolutionary appeals of dissident intellectuals have sometimes been strengthened and sometimes been weakened—thus raising the issue of intervening variables.

Such political developments can be more readily explained if they are viewed in the context of democratization: the entry of the lower classes, on formally equal terms, into the political process

[5] In a theoretical statement, Herbert Blumer recently rejected the prevailing view of industrialization, which is based largely on the English case, Marxist class analysis, anthropological theory on culture contact, and psychological theory on frustration and aggression. He argued that the "objective" nature of the work situation cannot explain protest phenomena; he acknowledged the frequent occurrence of labor protest during early industrialization and explained it as a coincidence with situations of intense social change. See H. Blumer, "Early Industrialization and the Laboring Class," *The Sociological Quarterly,* I:1, Jan. 1960, 5–14.

from which they have been traditionally excluded. Democratization has been associated too grossly with industrialization. The reason for this lack of differentiation has to be sought in an older perspective shared by Marxists and many non-Marxists. They consider politics an epiphenomenon of social and economic processes. Industrialization and democratization are consequently seen as more or less one process. This perspective grows out of the history of Western Europe since the 18th century, where, in a meaningful sense, a middle-class society came to control the state. There the rising middle classes induced massive political change in the course of industrialization. But in other areas of the world, during the last decades, masses of people previously excluded from the political process have been activated and political revolutions have occurred because of and in spite of the absence of a strong middle class and before large-scale industrialization got under way. Therefore, Reinhard Bendix has recently proposed that democratization and industrialization should be recognized as two distinct processes, although they are sometimes closely interrelated.[6]

Democratization was initiated ideologically in the 18th century when liberal and absolutist representatives of the Enlightenment postulated fundamental rights for all men. This led to a prolonged debate in Europe about the possibility and desirability of the integration, through universal citizenship, of the lower classes into the new political entity of the sovereign nation state.[7] In the en-

[6] See Reinhard Bendix, "The Lower Classes in the Age of Democratic Revolution," *Industrial Relations*, I:1, Oct. 1961, 91–116, esp. 105 f. See also id., "Social Stratification and the Political Community," *Archives Européennes de Sociologie*, I, 1960, 181–210.

[7] The distinctiveness of this historically new political phenomenon is easily understood if it is compared to "predemocratic" political systems, which were not national communities but were composed of a plurality of quasi-sovereign corporate bodies with their own reciprocities of rights and duties. Correspondingly, older forms of lower-class protest were different from the fight for political equality, which was made possible because of the equalitarian institution of citizenship in the modern nation state. On these differences and especially on "predemocratic" types of unrest, see R. Bendix, "The Lower

suing struggles social classes arose as agents of collective action: organizational cohesion came to rest on the shared social and economic characteristics of large numbers of persons in contiguous social strata, thus overriding past and contemporary differences.[8] The first protests of the emergent industrial work force usually took the form of an endeavor to regain some of the privileges of preindustrial guilds and the benefits of patriarchal relations. Once it was clear that there was no return to a more or less idealized past, workers turned toward the attainment of the new political equality.

Under the threat of losing their predominance or of being annihilated altogether, ruling groups had to devise policies that would deal with the demands of the lower classes. Historically, two extreme developments can be distinguished: the class conflict may be resolved by a far-reaching integration of the lower classes into the national community, through a granting of formal political equality and social recognition, or a class cleavage may develop which, after an accumulation of aggravating factors, results in a total, revolutionary reorganization of society. England is the most prominent European example of the success of a dominant system in retaining the allegiance of the masses. In contrast, Imperial Russia failed in her insistence on the complete subordination of the masses and in her efforts to check the rise of independent popular movements. Thus, democratization may lead to constitutional government and a pluralist society or to totalitarianism, which also derives its legitimacy from the consent, however manipulated, of the masses.[9] In between the extremes are more or less protracted cases of class cleavage and partial integration extending beyond the early stages of industrialization.

Classes . . . ," *op. cit.,* and R. R. Palmer, *The Age of Democratic Revolution* (Princeton University Press, 1959).

[8] Cf. T. H. Marshall's definition of class in his essay, "The Nature of Class Conflict," in R. Bendix and S. M. Lipset, eds., *Class, Status and Power* (Glencoe: Free Press, 1953), 81–87.

[9] Cf. J. L. Talmon, *The Origins of Totalitarian Democracy* (New York: Praeger, 1960), 1–6 and 257–59.

One such intermediate type is characterized by negative integration: a political system permits a hostile mass movement to exist legally, but prevents it from gaining access to the centers of power; this contrasts with the institutionalization of conflict among genuinely legitimized interest groups in such countries as England and the United States. A radical mass movement constitutes at least a potential source of instability, but if it can be legalized without sharing in governmental power it may contribute to the stability of the dominant system by leaving intact the latter's basic structure and by developing vested interests in its own legal status. From the viewpoint of the historical participants this phenomenon may primarily appear as a matter of purposive isolation or of self-containment, but from the viewpoint of the observer it can be recognized as a form of integration. The negative integration of radical labor movements has been important in France from the Third to the Fifth Republic, in Italy before the First World War and after the Second World War, and in the case with which I shall be concerned, Imperial Germany.[10]

2. Class Conflict and Negative Integration in Imperial Germany

In Imperial Germany an authoritarian state, rather than a governing middle-class elite, was confronted with the threat of democratization under conditions of rapid industrialization, and the labor movement was isolated as a subculture and negatively

[10] On France, see E. Drexel Godfrey, Jr., "The Communist Presence in France," *American Political Science Review*, L:2, 1956, 321–38; on Italy, see M. E. Neufeld, *Italy: School for Awakening Countries: The Italian Labor Movement in Its Political, Social, and Economic Setting from 1800 to 1960* (Ithaca: Cornell University Press, 1961), Chs. VI–VIII and X.

integrated into the dominant system.[11] Imperial Germany is a complex intermediate case between the parliamentary system of Victorian England and the autocratic system of Imperial Russia, which was only attenuated after the Russian Revolution of 1905.[12] Imperial Germany had a large, articulate and self-conscious bourgeoisie which was committed to nationalism, liberalism or both, but could not defeat an authoritarian regime maintaining its strength through a combination of permissive and repressive policies. This regime was for the most part constitutional, adopted parliamentary institutions and permitted an independent labor movement. It also accepted responsibility for promoting the rise of industry and for improving the lot of the workingman. However, it successfully kept the liberal bourgeoisie and the labor movement in check by preventing the national parliament (*Reichstag*) from gaining control over the government, which was only responsible to the crown; it steadfastly refused the political and social recognition for which the Social Democratic working class fought. The net effect of this granting and withholding of substantial con-

[11] Kerr *et al., Industrialism* . . . treat Imperial Germany illustratively as one of their major examples of the "dynastic elite." I prefer the term "authoritarian" because it identifies more clearly the constitutional setting. The term refers in this analysis mainly to the ideology and practice of a dominant system in which the government is responsible not to an elected parliament but to a sovereign ruler. The context will make clear whenever the term "authoritarian" also refers to individual attitudes and to intra-organizational practices.

[12] This comparative perspective is suggested by Reinhard Bendix' *Work and Authority* (New York: Wiley, 1956), in which Anglo-American and Russian ideologies of management are analyzed as indices of changing class relations; the work does not consider Germany, with the exception of using Communist Germany as a case of Soviet managerial ideology and practice. I will not deal with managerial ideologies proper, but with political ideologies and organizational manifestations as indices of class relations. For a comparative study of English and German miners, focussing on the different historical legacies and the different ideological setting, see Gaston Rimlinger, "The Legitimation of Protest: A Comparative Study in Labor History," *Comparative Studies in Society and History*, II:3, April 1960, 329–43.

cessions was the perpetuation of a deep class cleavage through the development of a large isolated subculture.

The political preoccupations of the German labor movement have always been recognized and often been contrasted with the economic emphasis of the English and American labor movements of the time. The German case has usually been explained in terms of economic and political "underdevelopment," which forced the labor movement to fight for fundamental political rights. Probably the one factor which has been most frequently cited is the failure of the middle-class revolution in Germany in 1848/49. This failure has been related to the early stage of economic development, which had not yet sufficiently strengthened the middle classes. For the Marxists, Germany was socially backward as long as she was industrially far behind England; once she had become an industrial power, they saw her as an advanced capitalist country and discounted the authoritarian monarchy as a long outdated remnant of a feudal stage. Some Marxists even came to consider her as historically more advanced than capitalist England because of her state-socialist tendencies. Westerners considered Germany backward, even after her industrialization was well under way, since she still remained in the "transitional stage" of monarchic constitutionalism; implicitly they assumed a correlation of industrialization and parliamentary government. The delay appeared to them as something of a cultural lag.

I intend rather to consider the authoritarian system as a case *sui generis* and to look at labor protest in a political rather than an economic context. In doing this, I do not overlook the fact that direct economic interests played a significant part in making journeymen and factory workers turn to politics. Economic interest representation was, after all, severely handicapped by the authoritarian state. However, vocational groups have always tried to advance their material interests, and lower-class groups have always been exposed to deprivations: these interests and frustrations do not determine the specific form of political protest. The origins of the political alienation of the labor movement will be sought in ideological class antagonism preceding the period of rapid industrialization, the persistence of this alienation in the clash with an authoritarian state which endeavored to control and suppress class conflict. The authoritarian monarchy had an old social base in the landed aristocracy and the professional civil servants, but as a power center the government and its bureaucracy played an important independent role vis-à-vis the class relations of the industrializing society.

I shall analyze the ideological manifestations and the structural and organizational features of the German case. First, I shall deal with the factors accounting for the emergence of an independent, class-conscious labor movement and for the attendant cleavage between the labor movement and the bourgeoisie. Next, I shall turn to the structure of the authoritarian state and the ideological clash between government and labor movement, giving particular attention to the mixture of antagonistic and affirmative elements in the Social Democratic attitudes toward the dominant system, on the grassroots level and among party spokesmen. Related to this will be a discussion of the extent to which the Social Democratic subculture was opposed to and yet part of the dominant culture. Lastly I shall consider the peacetime stability of the Empire and the labor movement, their positive integration, crisis and disintegration as a result of the war, and the vexing problem of historical alternatives.

The ideological aspect will be approached on two levels: (1) the level of explicitly formulated class ideology as it is articulated by the spokesmen of the respective groups; [13] (2) the level of the less articulate and more diffuse grassroots attitudes and sentiments in the middle and lower classes. I shall be concerned with the ideological dimension, since a group's ideology reflects the flexibility or

13 Ideology is here understood as any aggregate of ideas in so far as it is revelant for collective action or group-determined political behavior; on the ideological level it is irrelevant whether the ideas are systematic or false or true in an empirical or philosophical sense.

rigidity with which it confronts other groups in the face of a changing social structure. This approach assumes that ideologies are not only rationalizations of the present self-interest of a group, but that they are also shaped by historical legacies.[14] If this argument is accepted it requires an historical as well as a structural approach to the analysis of societies and their social integration.

The level of formal political theory and social philosophy will be considered only when it seems necessary to elucidate its impact on ideologies.[15] The latter, which are continuously formulated and reformulated by the spokesmen, contain an image of other groups as well as a collective self-image. These conflicting group images are one aspect of reciprocal class relations. In the present context they form the framework for the great national debate about the social reconstruction necessitated by the advance of industrialization and democratization.

The social philosophizing of the spokesmen of broad strata fuses, at the grassroots level, with the less articulate attitudes and sentiments of masses of people. This is the most elementary level of class relations and it is also important for the private behavior of individuals, especially for direct relations with members of a different class. These grassroots attitudes and perspectives are partly in harmony and partly in conflict with ideological appeals of the spokesmen. The latter constantly manipulate the allegiance of their groups by alternately indoctrinating them with their views and by

[14] On the rationale for treating ideologies as an index of social structure and on the wide-spread tendency of social scientists to search for "hidden forces" rather than to analyze ideologies on a phenomenological level, see Reinhard Bendix, "Industrialization, Ideologies, and Social Structure," *American Sociological Review,* 24:5, Oct. 1959, 618 f.

[15] Cf. H. S. Hughes' distinction between three levels of studying ideas: (1) The enunciation and development of ideas, left out by me; (2) the ethico-political level, on which ruling minorities and their rival minorities operate; and (3) the level of "retrospective cultural anthropology," on which the diffusion of ideas among the masses takes place and on which they are popularly comprehended. See Hughes, *Consciousness and Society* (New York: Knopf, 1958) 9 f.

adjusting to grassroots opinions as the situation demands. It is here that intraorganizational factors become relevant which influence group action in addition to, and sometimes contrary to, ideological commitments.

The place where the spokesmen of different groups came face to face with one another was the parliament. Therefore, the protocols of the Reichstag (1871–1918) and, prior to that, of the North German diet (1867–70) were used. Here the debates on specific issues provide an opportunity to identify the images of the opponent and the collective self-image—images that were an important part of the antagonistic class relations. The bourgeois grassroots perspective of the labor movement and the authoritarian regime was approximated by analyzing the published views of educated men, which views, to be sure, were more sophisticated than those of average educated middle-class men, but which still appeared to be basically representative of them. The convention protocols of the Social Democratic party and the Socialist unions were used especially for the ideological self-clarification of the Social Democratic spokesmen and for their image of the labor movement and the dominant system. But these protocols and the party literature in general are insufficient for the identification of grassroots beliefs and, in particular, for the identification of the meaning that the labor movement and the dominant system had for the rank and file. The leaders either took this meaning for granted or, as far as it was not easily reconcilable with the official self-image of the movement, they did not verbalize it. The meaning to the rank and file can be better deduced from autobiographies of former workers and from a few unusually perceptive and reflective writings of other participants or close observers.

The data of an historical study are limited to the existing primary sources and the secondary literature. There is a wealth of literature on Imperial Germany and the Social Democratic labor movement, but most of it does not have a sociological orientation. As primary sources are often nonexistent, inaccessible or too cumbersome to use, much of the secondary literature has had to be treated as providing the "raw data" of research. Historical monographs had to be frequently cited in order to reconstruct relevant historical facts; sometimes double quotations were inevitable. The concrete subject matter of this study falls into the area of several academic disciplines and therefore has to contend with their various orientations. Some sociologists might prefer a more abstract level of generalization which might be applicable to a larger number of cases in the same problem area or even in quite different ones; some historians might want to see more primary data or more of the "total picture"; some political scientists might wish for a more complex institutional analysis; and some labor economists and students of economic growth might desire a closer analytical relation to industrialization. It is difficult to serve more than one master; the one most clearly recognized here is political sociology. In his review of the state of political sociology in the nineteen fifties, Seymour Martin Lipset's most urgent plea was for a more balanced study of the integrative and nonintegrative aspects of political institutions, combining the structural-functional emphasis on integration with the political sociologist's traditional interest in cleavage and conflict.[16] My treatment of the German case is intended to contribute toward the establishment of such a balance.

The level of this sociological analysis was determined by my judgment of an adequate relationship between historical complexity and generic relevance. A case study cannot really confirm or disprove generalizations about democratization and industrialization, but it can deal with specific historical resolutions of a generic problem, thus exploring the range of alternatives in the relationships be-

[16] See S. M. Lipset, "Political Sociology," in R. Merton *et al.*, eds., *Sociology Today: Problems and Prospects* (New York: Basic Books, 1959), 112 ff; see also L. Coser, *The Functions of Social Conflict* (Glencoe: Free Press, 1957) and R. Dahrendorf, *Class and Class Conflict in Industrial Society* (Stanford University Press, 1959). For the treatment of conflict in the field of industrial relations, see H. L. Sheppard, "Approaches to Conflict in American Industrial Sociology," *British Journal of Sociology,* V:4, 1954, 324–41.

tween political and social structure, cultural legacies, elite strategies and lower-class response.

Studies with an historical subject matter have to reconstruct pertinent historical facts for the reader who is not a historian or area specialist. Historical description and sociological analysis cannot really be separated fruitfully, but some historical data which are mainly relevant for general orientation can be dealt with by way of introduction. The following section is a bare outline of 19th-century German history, as far as it is relevant for national unification and industrialization, for those readers who are relatively unfamiliar with it. Others for whom it is still a meaningful reality are advised to proceed *in medias res*.

3. An Historical Background

When the French Revolution broke out, Germany was composed of many sovereign principalities along with the two outstanding political powers of Austria and Prussia. Both of these states had been under the rule of an enlightened absolutism which stressed central administration, a large efficient civil service and a strong, combat-ready army. Austria and Prussia had carried through military, legal and administrative reforms under a comprehensive *raison d'état,* partly under the direct influence of the Enlightenment.[17] Under Joseph II (1765–90), for example, Austria undertook legal reforms, abolished serfdom, permitted free movement and freedom of trade, secularized the monasteries and issued an edict of tolerance. Since these met only very limited success, the state was not strengthened against the French revolutionary threat. While the influence of the ideas of the French Revolution was great

[17] On the emergence of the bureaucracy and its influence on public policy, see Hans Rosenberg, *Bureaucracy, Aristocracy and Autocracy: The Prussian Experience: 1660–1816* (Cambridge: Harvard University Press, 1958).

on the intellectual life of Germany and resulted in the rise of liberalism as an intellectual power [18] the actual political (and especially the military) events had a greater immediate impact on Germany. The advance of the revolutionary troops and later of Napoleon's armies brought about a far-reaching political and social reconstruction. For 25 years state lines changed rapidly, and republics, duchies, kingdoms, and empires rose and fell. In the process, the old Holy Roman Empire was dissolved. This was a social no less than a political revolution of the first magnitude. More than a hundred states or estates, including all ecclesiastical principalities, were abolished. Nearly all free cities and the freeholds of all abbeys and cloisters were mediatized. Hundreds of aristocrats, who had been "subordinate" only to the emperor and whose property had been subject only to imperial constitutional law, fell under the rule of the remaining territorial princes. This was, in part, directly the result of French policies; in part, it was owing to the policies of the stronger states, above all Austria and Prussia, of finding compensation for the extensive losses of territory west of the Rhine river. This territory remained French for nearly a quarter-century with the support of large parts of its middle and lower classes. Some areas permanently retained the *Code Napoléon,* the superior French civil law of 1804. The consolidated states on the right side of the Rhine river (among them the new kingdoms of Württemberg and Bavaria and the new duchies of Hesse-Darmstadt and Baden) took over many of the French legal and administrative innovations.

Both Austria and Prussia embarked on new major internal reforms after 1805 following several military and diplomatic defeats. The means chosen were those of the Revolution: the *levée en masse* and the appeal to patriotism. The intent was—in contempo-

---

[18] Cf. Alfred Stern, *Der Einfluss der französischen Revolution auf das deutsche Geistesleben* (Stuttgart: Cotta, 1928); also G. P. Gooch, *Germany and the French Revolution* (London: Longmans, 1920).

rary language—"to militarize the nations and to nationalize the armies." [19] Thus, patriotism of the Austrian and Prussian variety was promoted and fused, not without many contradictions, with the emergent, all-German nationalism furthered by the Romantic movement. Austria reorganized her standing army along French lines; in 1808 the *Landwehr* (second reserve) was created, into which burghers were recruited. But Austria was defeated decisively in 1809, two years after Prussia's position as a major power had been broken by Napoleon. The Prussian reforms began after the military catastrophe of 1806/7. The government abolished serfdom, introduced an extraordinarily liberal self-administration for the cities, instituted freedom of trade and reaffirmed religious tolerance. The primary and secondary school system was reformed; in 1810 the University of Berlin was founded in order to create a national intellectual center. In 1812 the Jews were emancipated. These reforms were carried through by liberal or rationalist aristocrats who were under the influence of the French and English Enlightenment and of the German idealism of Kant and Fichte. They took over many accomplishments of the French Revolution, but did so mostly with a view to uniting the people, who had been apathetic or even pro-French after Prussia's defeat, behind a thoroughly reformed and liberal monarchical system. Most important for the *rapprochement* between the crown and the people was the military reform at the end of which, in 1814, universal draft was introduced. The military reform was based on the idea of a union of nation and army and the concept of the citizen-soldier who was motivated by his own ethos toward civic and military duties, who was no longer treated with the traditional brutal discipline of the absolutist standing armies. The officers' corps was made less exclusive, and a *Landwehr* was created which was officered largely by middle-class reservists. The military reformers themselves, who

[19] Cf. Emil Daniels, "Ein vergessenes Dokument zur Geschichte der Freiheitskriege," *Preussische Jahrbücher*, Vol. 144, 1911, 260.

were brilliant military organizers and strategists, participated in elaborating schemes of social and even German national reconstruction.[20]

The self-administration of the cities was intended as a first step by Baron vom Stein, a former Imperial knight with a broad national vision, who headed the Prussian government after the military debacle of Jena in 1806. Self-government as the major instrument of political education was to start at the bottom, culminating finally in national representation. These plans did not materialize; even rural self-government was not realized until the seventies.[21] However, the urban middle classes had permanent local self-government, and a generation of liberals grew up which was trained in local self-government or which had at least been exposed to it.

The term "liberal" referred to the sovereignty of the people and their equality before the law under a constitution. Sovereignty of the people did not usually imply either extended suffrage or the denial of legitimacy of the traditional rulers, but rather the regulation of relations between ruler and ruled through a constitution accepted by both. Despite the fact that many middle-class people were not liberal and many aristocrats were, liberalism became the political ideology par excellence of the bourgeoisie, because it aimed at the political and social recognition of the economically rising middle classes and at the limitation of the power of the state in favor of the individual. The dilemma of liberalism was that many of its reformist intentions were carried through by Napoleon,

---

[20] For two excellent treatments of the political implications of the military reform and the reasons for its success and failure see Gordon A. Craig, *The Politics of the Prussian Army, 1640–1945* (New York: Oxford University Press, 1956), pp. 37–81; and Gerhard Ritter, *Staatskunst und Kriegshandwerk: Das Problem des "Militarismus" in Deutschland* (Munich: Oldenbourg, 1954), esp. pp. 99 f. On the downfall of the whole reform movement, see Walter Simon, *The Failure of the Prussian Reform Movement, 1807–1819* (Ithaca: Cornell University Press, 1955).

[21] Cf. H. Heffter, *Die deutsche Selbstverwaltung im 19. Jahrhundert* (Stuttgart: Koehler, 1950).

a Caesarist conqueror whose power had to be broken before a free constitutional life became possible. However, his defeat would inevitably restore the power of the old authoritarian military states of Austria, Prussia and Russia. This is exactly what happened in 1814/15. In the hour of all-out mobilization of the people against Napoleon, constitutions were promised to the German people, but once these dynastic powers had won the "Wars of Liberation," with the decisive help of nationalist and liberal popular support, they instituted the period of Restoration under the Holy Alliance.

A very loosely connected German Federation of 30 autonomous states, under Austria's leadership, was created, which lasted for about half a century. For the future it was important that Austria retreated from its former possessions to the right and left of the Rhine river (Belgium, Breisgau, parts of Bavaria), while Prussia acquired, through the Congress of Vienna (1815), large and commercially as well as industrially important parts of western Germany. The new Prussian territories had a substantial Catholic and liberal population which had been thoroughly exposed to French influences, yet this incorporation greatly strengthened Prussia, not the militarily powerless liberals. The great liberal reforms had always been under severe attack by the legitimistic and conservative aristocratic landowners of East Elbia, who still formed the backbone of the Prussian army and exercised full political and administrative control over the countryside. The liberal emancipation of the peasants actually resulted in their proletarianization, since their holdings were added to those of their former lords. Thus the military state of Prussia, which was still based on the semicolonial German and Polish provinces of East Elbia, continued in its old ways. In 1819 the rationalist Prussian prime minister, Prince Hardenberg, and Wilhelm von Humboldt, the great liberal humanist and minister of education, lost their fight for a Prussian constitution because of the direct intervention of Metternich, the Austrian chancellor and diplomatic genius of the Holy Alliance, with the King of Prussia.

Some southern and central German states (Baden, Bavaria,

Hesse-Kassel and Sachsen-Weimar) adopted limited constitutions, but this did not change the fact that the trend toward greater participation of the bourgeoisie had been arrested effectively. The majority of the middle classes was satisfied with the return of "normal" conditions after a quarter-century of turmoil, but there was also much disillusionment and disappointment about the standstill of constitutional advances and the lack of progress toward national unification. The repression of the press and the universities, the introduction of universal censorship, the dissolution of patriotic student clubs and the outlawing of the gymnastics clubs, which had played a conspicuous role in kindling the national enthusiasm of the people, produced much dissatisfaction, which first broke through in the wake of the French July Revolution of 1830. Although Saxony adopted a constitution and liberalization took place in other parts of Germany, oppression soon became prevalent again. But liberalism grew stronger as an ideological force by the middle of the century; the decisive showdown occurred in 1848 when industrialization, with a few exceptions, had scarcely begun. The German revolution, which followed the French Revolution in February, was aimed at establishing constitutional political life and national unification. But the unification of the country under a constitutional government and the liberal reconstruction of the individual states failed because the legitimist monarchs of Austria and Prussia could not be forced into accepting them.[22] In contrast to England, the German middle classes were faced with two powerful

[22] During the revolution of 1848 a few weak labor organizations emerged which belonged politically to the left wing of the middle classes and which were later suppressed with it. The handful of communist intellectuals and workers, among whom were Marx and Engels, remained without more than limited local influence or gained some influence only by avoiding public identification with communism. Too late for consideration came a major study of the "Universal Brotherhood of Workingmen," the largest workingmen's association during the revolutionary period: Frolinde Balser, *Sozial-Demokratie 1848/49–1863* (Stuttgart: Klett, 1962), 2 vols.; this study is important because of its emphasis on regional variation and its wealth of source materials reprinted in vol. II.

centralized monarchies whose large standing armies were responsible solely to the sovereign.

The counter-revolutionary repression lasted through the fifties, but the enforced tranquillity on the domestic scene was disturbed by the very ruling groups which were interested in its preservation. The governments were unable to maintain the peace which Europe had enjoyed since Napoleon Bonaparte's political exit. First there was the Crimean War of 1854–56; next, the Italian War of 1859 between France and Austria brought Italian unification under way and also made the unification of Germany again a public issue. Austria's defeat led to some domestic liberalization which also extended to other German states. The liberalization in Prussia resulted in a comeback of liberalism and the last major middle-class challenge to the authoritarian monarchy, during the constitutional conflict from 1862 until 1866.[23] The King of Prussia had imposed a constitution in 1850 which gave parliament general budgetary rights. Repression was relaxed after Prince William of Prussia became regent in 1858 because of the mental illness of Frederick William IV. Though this was the very same man who had crushed the democratic-republican uprising in southwest Germany in 1849, many democrats and liberals decided to enter politics again in order to make the best of the existing constitution. Democrats cooperating with the liberals avoided, as much as possible, any identification with the democratic traditions of 1848.

In August 1859, liberals from different German states founded the *Nationalverein* (National Association), which was to play a great role in promoting unification of the country through Prussia. In 1861 the Progressive party was founded in Prussia by a coalition of democrats and liberals. It insisted on the right of parliament to detail the military budget and fought the government's reorganization of the army along more efficient, but less liberal lines. The

---

[23] On the prehistory of the Constitutional Struggle, see Eugene N. Anderson, *The Social and Political Conflict in Prussia: 1858–1864* (Lincoln: The University of Nebraska, 1954).

militarily most important part of the bourgeois, and frequently liberal, *Landwehr* was incorporated into the troops of the line and thus was brought under the political control of the army and the king.

At the beginning of the Constitutional Conflict the liberals held the absolute majority in the Prussian diet: they received large majorities in the cities, as well as strong support from Catholic farmers in the Rhine provinces and Protestant farm areas in East Elbia.[24] William I, King of Prussia since 1861, was at the point of abdicating when he was prevailed upon by military and conservative circles to refuse any compromise. In 1862 Bismarck was appointed prime minister and started a vigorous unconstitutional rule, disregarding the budgetary rights of parliament. His policies were aimed primarily at retaining undisputed control for the king over the army and at reorganizing the army for the wars of the near future. As in the fifties, civil servants and deputies were persecuted and the government interfered again in the elections.

The authoritarian monarchy emerged victorious in the Constitutional Conflict when Bismarck embarked on a policy of national unification from above and the Prussian army succeeded through spectacular campaigns. With the Prussian and Austrian victory over Denmark in 1864, the liberals began to lose ground. Austria and her German allies were crushed in the war of 1866, fought over the issue of national unification under Prussia without Austria. Five states were incorporated into Prussia: the kingdom of Hanover, the principalities of Hesse-Kassel, Nassau, Schleswig-Holstein, and the Free City of Frankfurt. Thus Prussia established not only a geographical connection with her Rhenish provinces, but also a very large unified area. The remaining North German principalities were linked with Prussia in the North German Federation.

During the war of 1866, the liberals suffered a resounding de-

[24] For a revealing statistical breakdown see Arthur Rosenberg, *The Birth of the German Republic: 1871–1918* (London: Oxford University Press, 1931), 28 f.

feat because they had demanded, in their electoral program, that parliament refuse military appropriations as long as Bismarck was unwilling to respect the budgetary rights of parliament. Afterwards many liberals accepted Bismarck's *fait accompli* of a unified Northern Germany, as they gave priority to national unification over constitutional issues, either for ideological or tactical reasons. A group of Progressives founded the National Liberal party, which remained the dominant right-wing liberal party until 1918. The party was founded in order to create a basis of cooperation with Bismarck, who needed liberal legislative support since the conservatives were still numerically weak and partly disapproving of his destruction of dynasties. The Prussian National Liberals were joined or supported by many liberals, often members of the *Nationalverein,* in the new areas seized by Prussia and in other regions of Germany. Ever since Napoleon's intervention in the Italian War of 1859, realizing the military weakness of Germany, they had been afraid of a Bonapartist invasion. The South German liberals were also confronted with new alliances of their state governments with the Catholic church and orthodox Protestantism. Despite the Constitutional Conflict, many liberals, inside and outside of Prussia, were more afraid of Austria than of the Prussian king. Prussia appeared as the smaller evil since it was at least a constitutional state. All over Germany, Bismarck's successful ruthlessness impressed many liberals who did not care for another clash with the superior power of the Prussian monarchy and who did not want to lose the chance of positively influencing the political, legal, and economic reconstruction of Germany. The notion of *Realpolitik* gained wide currency as they began to take a more pragmatic position.

National unification under Prussian dominance was accomplished in 1871 after the defeat of Napoleon's empire by the allied North and South German states. Prussia constituted about two thirds of the new Reich. The Prussian kings became hereditary emperors, and the chancellor of the Reich was usually also the Prussian prime minister. The rulers of the 25 remaining federated states were represented in the Federal Council headed by the chancellor. The Federal Council proposed legislation to the Reichstag and had the right to reject the latter's legislation. The members of the Reichstag were directly elected by the people on the basis of universal, equal and secret suffrage; they did not exert parliamentary control over the government.

The 43 years of peace in Central Europe which followed German unification were accompanied by relative domestic tranquillity in Germany, at least compared with the domestic disturbances in many other European states. The period of general liberal cooperation with the Prussian and Imperial government ended late in the seventies. From 1878 until 1890 the antisocialist legislation attempted to destroy the Social Democratic labor movement. At the same time the liberals were decisively weakened by a conservative restoration, the so-called "Era Puttkamer." [25] After the rise of modern interest groups—industrial, agrarian, petty-bourgeois—in the eighties, a *rapprochement* took place in the nineties between the big business interests of the West and the aristocratic agrarian interests of East Elbia. This alliance became highly important for the domestic balance of power which was not changed significantly by the greater flexibility of party alignments after the turn of the century.

4. Some Features of German Industrialization

German industrialization was shaped by the sometimes antagonistic and sometimes harmonious cooperation between bourgeoisie, land-

[25] It was so called after the Prussian minister of cultural and religious affairs (1879–81) and minister of the interior (1881–88), who was entrusted with the execution of the conservative restoration. Puttkamer was fired during the 99 days rule of the relatively liberal Frederick III, the son of William I (King of Prussia from 1861 until 1888 and German Emperor from 1871 on) and the father of William II (King of Prussia and German Emperor from 1888 until 1918).

owning aristocracy and the authoritarian state.[26] They had in common a "reactive nationalism" which went back to the Napoleonic wars and which became a major noneconomic motivation for Germany's economic development. At the least, they shared an interest in making Germany strong enough to withstand military attacks. The upheavals of the Napoleonic period retarded economic development, but Napoleon's simplification of the political map of Germany facilitated economic development in the long run. However, there were still some 30 sovereign states left after 1815. Eventually both Austria and Prussia endeavored to create large unified customs areas. Prussia succeeded by 1834 in establishing a German Customs Union. After the kingdom of Hanover joined in the early fifties, the union comprised most of the area of the future German empire. Austria, the Free City-states of Bremen and Hamburg and some minor principalities remained outside the union. Its customs policies were moderate, but highly effective since they increased the bargaining powers of its members vis-à-vis England and France. In 1850 the tariff barriers between Austria and Hungary were abolished, but Prussian resistance defeated an Austrian attempt to create a vast customs union between all German states and the Double Monarchy.

Purposive though restrained state intervention and early economic concentration were distinct features of German industrialization. In contrast to England, joint stock credit banks, first emerging in the fifties, played an extraordinary role in German industrialization. In contrast to the United States, cartelization met no obstacles. Cartels emerged during slumps as well as booms. They were first established in heavy industry during the seventies and then expanded into other industries, often with the help of the banks.

[26] For a brief account of German industrialization, see Gustav Stolper, *German Economy: 1870–1940: Issues and Trends* (New York: Reynal & Hitchcock, 1940). Most recognized among the older literature is A. Sartorius von Waltershausen, *Deutsche Wirtschaftsgeschichte: 1815–1914* (Jena: Fischer, 1923), 2d ed.

About the turn of the century these habits of entrepreneurial co-operation facilitated the growth of employers' associations which could fight the unions effectively.

After a free trade period, government, agrarians and heavy industrialists became increasingly protectionist from the late seventies on, but even then many important tariffs remained relatively moderate. The tariffs hurt the workers as consumers, but the economy continued to grow rapidly, a development which also benefited the workers. Despite the tariffs, Germany was second only to England in world trade by 1914.

In terms of W. W. Rostow's theory of economic growth, Germany began her take-off period shortly after the economic recovery from the revolution of 1848.[27] The take-off period was completed in 1873 when the boom which resulted from the Franco-Prussian War and the establishment of the Empire collapsed. Germany reached her stage of economic maturity during the last peace years of the Empire, about 1910. In comparison, England had passed through her take-off period by 1802 and had reached maturity by 1850; France and the United States began and ended their take-off periods earlier than Germany, between 1830 and 1860; however, they reached maturity only at about 1910 and 1900 respectively. While cotton textiles were the major industrial factor for the take-off in England, railroad expansion seems to have been the initiating factor in France, Germany and the United States. Military buildup and military modernization were also important in Germany, as later in Russia and Japan. Steel and its varied applications became

---

[27] W. W. Rostow defines the take-off as the stage when economic growth becomes a "normal" condition, when investments rise from about five per cent of the national income to ten per cent or more, and when there is a high growth rate in at least one large manufacturing industry. This stage is followed by the drive to maturity, which is reached when the society has succeeded in applying advanced technology to most of its resources. The stages should be considered heuristic distinctions. See W. W. Rostow, *op cit.*, esp. Chs. IV and V.

the most significant indicator for the period after the take-off in Germany, France and the United States.

From an economic viewpoint I am dealing with the German labor movement from the last years of the take-off period, when it came into being, until the beginning of the economic stage of maturity.

II
The Rise of the Independent Class-Conscious Labor Movement

1. Liberalism, Bourgeois Class Consciousness and Equal Suffrage

Long before labor protest arose as an independent force and large-scale industrialization got under way, major conditions for the rise of a class-conscious labor movement were created by the class consciousness of the liberal bourgeoisie and by the nature and outcome of its struggles for a liberal constitution. Liberalism was a major force of democratization by advocating universal rights of man, but it did not favor a full-scale political mobilization of the lower classes. Ideological commitments, material interests and strategic imperatives made the liberals ambivalent and often hostile toward extensive democratization. In order to explain these complex interrelationships, I will first deal very briefly with the liberal struggles, in the context of the historical developments from the 1840's to the 1860's.

A revealing index of the bourgeois class consciousness is the liberal attitude toward universal and equal suffrage. Suffrage, the major means of mass participation in the political process of the national community, is an issue important for the analysis of class consciousness because democratic suffrage demands were bound to provoke an ambivalent reaction on the part of the liberal bourgeoisie. On the one hand, equal suffrage was a radical conclusion of the universalist tendencies of liberalism; on the other, it did not recognize any political prerogatives in the social distinctions of the bourgeois class. The political and social position of the liberal bourgeoisie and aristocracy seemed to be threatened by it, and the resulting discussions and controversies helped to articulate the liberal self-image as well as the liberal image of the lower classes. In Germany, the suffrage issue led to a prolonged national "debate," which lasted, with intermissions, for about a century, until the First World War. This national debate reached a first climax in the parliamentary suffrage debate of the Constituent Assembly of 1848, which had been elected under universal and equal suffrage as a result of the revolution.

Although no large industrial work force existed at the time, the working classes were a prominent subject in the parliamentary discussions of the suffrage system to be incorporated into the planned federal constitution. Since industrialization was only incipient, the speakers usually did not make a clear distinction between industrial workers and petty-bourgeois craftsmen, but used the term "working class" in a comprehensive sense. Seventy-five per cent of the deputies were members of the self-employed and employed intelligentsia, including higher-ranking civil servants; only between three and four per cent were merchants and manufacturers. Property and education were the social and ideological base of the middle classes in all Western countries, but in Germany *Bildung* (humanist education) had a particularly high prestige. Historically, the high estimation for educational and administrative pursuits was largely due to the origin of a significant part of the middle classes in the civil service of the principalities and to the link between the middle classes and the universities. In 1848 the educated liberals could still speak for many businessmen who shared their emphasis on *Bildung*.[1]

[1] On the social composition of the Frankfurt parliament, see Karl Demeter, "Die soziale Schichtung des Deutschen Parlamentes seit 1848," *Vierteljahrschrift für Sozial-und Wirtschaftsgeschichte,* Vol. 39:1, 1952, 1–29. On the social and regional composition of the factions in the Frankfurt parliament and for comparative statistics of the Frankfurt and the Prussian National Assembly of 1848, see Gerhard Schilfert, *Sieg und Niederlage des demokratischen Wahlrechts in der deutschen Revolution 1848/49* (Berlin:

In the Constituent Assembly, there was a wide range of opinions from outright restorative to ultra-leftist.[2] However, there were trends of opinion shared by the majority of educated and propertied bourgeois; this majority was convinced that the bourgeoisie was morally justified, because of its education and property, in being politically autonomous and in taking a position of leadership. Interests in the acquisition of property and in the intergenerational welfare of one's own family were seen as prerequisites for the ability to carry political responsibilities. Since the masses did not seem to have

---

Rütten, 1952), 401–8. On the prevalence of intellectual values militating against business careers see the contemporary account by Wilhelm Riehl, *Die bürgerliche Gesellschaft* (Stuttgart: Cotta, 1930). The book was written between 1847 and 1851. It was mainly after the rise of heavy industry, decades later, that a business mentality became articulate which was contemptuous of *Bildung*. For example, Alfred Krupp made this forthright statement shortly before his death in 1887: "I have no need to ask Goethe or anyone else in the world what is right. I know the answer myself and I don't consider anyone entitled to know better. I don't care how great a philosopher Goethe may have been nor how many other people dispose of overwhelming amounts of worldly wisdom and respect for society and the dominant masses. It does not make the slightest difference to me. Those who deliberately reflect and judge like fools, no matter how highly placed they may be, make guttersnipes of themselves and that is how I regard them. I pay no attention to anyone when I am acting on my own behalf. I always go my own way and never ask anybody what is right." Quoted in Gert von Klass, *Krupps, the Story of an Industrial Empire* (London: Sidgwick and Jackson, 1954), 178. It should be added, however, that this mentality was even then balanced by the pride in *Bildung* on the part of the higher civil servants and the professions and by the popular reverence for higher education.

2 The protocols of the Constituent Assembly of 1848 were not available to me, but recent monographs on the central suffrage issue made it possible to reconstruct the class-conscious liberal image of the lower and middle classes. See Schilfert, *op. cit.,* and Walter Gagel, *Die Wahlrechtsfrage in der Geschichte der deutschen liberalen Parteien, 1848–1918* (Düsseldorf: Droste, 1958). On the suffrage issue before 1849, see also Heinz Boberach, *Wahlrechtsfragen im Vormärz: Die Wahlrechtsanschauung im Rheinland 1815–1849 und die Entstehung des Dreiklassenwahlrechts* (Düsseldorf: Droste, 1959); see also Hans Dietzel, *Die preussischen Wahlreformbestrebungen von der Oktroyierung des Dreiklassenwahlrechts bis zum Beginn des Weltkriegs* (Ph.D. dissertation, University of Cologne, 1934).

these interests, their desires and appetites were often feared more than the power of the old dynastic and feudal upper classes. Moreover, many liberals were still influenced by the idealist philosophy of the state, and not yet strongly by laissez-faire doctrines, and therefore assigned the dominant role in solving social problems to the state. A vociferous democratic minority of middle-class deputies fought for the point of view, which gradually won out in England, that equal suffrage for all would preserve social peace or at least prevent a full-scale lower-class revolutionary threat.[3]

Despite the liberal ideological inclinations and conservative opposition, universal and equal suffrage was finally adopted in the Constituent Assembly because situational pressures proved stronger than ideological propensities. The opponents were divided as to the kind of suffrage that should be adopted. Their most important handicap was the popularity of universal and equal suffrage as well as the fact that the deputies had been elected by it. The constitutional committee had originally come up with a definition of social independence excluding a considerable number of people. This tactically weakened the position of those who wanted to restrict

---

[3] An antagonistic middle- and working-class consciousness was, of course, older in England than in Germany. During the Chartist period of the thirties, a working-class consciousness spread inside and outside the Chartist movement. Some Chartist leaders rejected the overtures of the Anti-Corn Law League, not because they disagreed with its direct objectives, but because of its middle-class policies which were considered discriminatory against labor. On the other hand, many middle-class leaders, like Peter Gaskell, rejected working-class organization as—in his words—"an 'Imperium in imperio' of the most obnoxious description." But this did not vitiate the overall trend toward accommodation. Class terminology was revived again in the sixties, but the exacerbation of class conflict was attenuated by the passage of the Second Reform Bill in 1867. See Asa Briggs, "The Language of 'Class' in Early Nineteenth-Century England," in id., ed., *Essays in Labor History: In Memory of G. D. H. Cole* (London: Macmillan, 1960), 63 and 73. For a portrait of the typical moderate trade union leader who strove for the integration of a "respectable" trade union movement into the national community see Asa Briggs' description of Robert Applegarth in his book *Victorian People* (Chicago: University of Chicago Press, 1955), pp. 168–96.

the suffrage. The influential liberal historian Rudolf Haym, a member of the assembly's right center, complained of this motion revealingly: it "excluded quite honorable classes from the right to vote with a recklessness which was not at all objectively defensible. Therefore, it had all the odiousness which the people see in the contrast between the workers with the 'callous fist' and the 'gentlemen with soft hands.' The unacceptability of this motion must be considered very unfortunate." [4]

The historical "accident" of the adoption of equal suffrage was to remain without major consequences. [5] It might have greatly changed the subsequent relationship between the middle classes and the labor movement; it might have meant the beginning of the integration of the lower classes under a successful "middle-class elite." However, the constitution adopted by the Constituent Assembly never went into effect because the King of Prussia was unwilling to become emperor of a united Germany by the grace of the people. Thus, universal and equal suffrage did not exist in Prussia when the labor movement was permanently established in the early 1860's. In contrast to England and the United States, where a permanent labor movement emerged only after universal suffrage had advanced substantially, the German labor movement had to fight for fundamental political freedom. From 1849 until 1918 a three-class suffrage, solely based on the criterion of taxable wealth, remained in effect for state and municipal elections in Prussia; and after 1866 Prussia constituted two thirds of Germany. [6] The three-

[4] Rudolf Haym, *Die deutsche Nationalversammlung* (Frankfurt: Jügel, 1849), 293.

[5] It can be argued, of course, as Conservative opponents did, that the liberal acceptance of universal and equal suffrage proved the ultimate ideological compatibility between liberals and democrats and that the "material" interest in political survival prompted the liberal acquiescence in further democratization. However, a hiatus often remains between sociological explanations derived from social structure and ideology and the uniqueness of historical "accidents."

[6] The electoral law of May 1849, which imposed the three-class suffrage in Prussia, and the Prussian Constitution of January 31, 1850, established a

class suffrage became the most important political symbol of the second-class citizenship of the workers.

Without the institutional counterweight of universal suffrage, the bourgeois class representation was likely to resist a consideration of specific labor interests at the time of the first workers' attempts to again organize themselves.[7] More important than this inclination, however, was the actual course of events which prevented a liberal coalition with working-class interests. The exigencies of the Constitutional Conflict and of its aftermath reinforced the liberal aversion to equal suffrage at the very moment that a few radical workers demanded it. The liberals even refused membership in the *Nationalverein* to workers. Schulze-Delitzsch, the prominent sponsor of the cooperative movement, pleaded with workers in Berlin to recognize the importance of the "middle estate" for their own interests: "On the German *Mittelstand* rests the development of the true German national character [*Wesen*]. . . . You serve yourself best if you correctly interpret your position within

---

general, indirect suffrage for both municipal and state elections. The voters were divided into three classes according to their tax payments. Each class voted for the same number of electors who elected the parliamentary deputies. Thus, a very small number of millionaires had as much voting power as hundreds of professionals, higher civil servants and businessmen, who, in turn, balanced the votes of tens of thousands of workers. This system was adopted at the suggestion of David Hansemann, a liberal Rhenish businessman, who took over a ministry shortly after the outbreak of the revolution. Hansemann, representative of the industrially most advanced province of Prussia, had been in favor of a similar system as early as 1830 and took as a model for the three-class suffrage the municipal suffrage of the Rhineland. Though this system was imposed by a king leading a successful counter-revolution, it actually served also the interests of the grand bourgeoisie. Cf. Gagel, *op. cit.*, 18 and Gustav Schmoller, "Die preussische Wahlrechtsreform von 1910 auf dem Hintergrunde des Kampfes zwischen Königtum und Feudalität," *Schmollers Jahrbuch,* vol. 34, 1910, 1261–79; reprinted in id. *Zwanzig Jahre deutscher Politik: 1897–1917* (Munich: Duncker, 1920), 67.
[7] A few workingmen's associations were founded in the wake of the 1848 revolution; they disappeared with the defeat of the revolution. See fn. 22, p. 20.

the great development of bourgeois society." [8] A correct interpretation would lead them to save money in their own economic interest and not to spend it on political action. In doing so they could regard themselves honorary members of the *Nationalverein*. The latter argument addressed to workers in Leipzig—after Berlin, the significant industrial center at the time in Germany—failed to impress many of them.

The liberals were afraid that universal, equal and direct suffrage would only help the government and the conservatives. Because Prussia was still a predominantly agrarian state, with patriarchal relations prevailing in the countryside, the industrial workers could not have balanced the increase of conservative votes. Furthermore, not even the urban masses were much interested in constitutional issues. The bourgeoisie feared that the rural and urban lower classes, if given equal and universal suffrage, might support a Bonapartist solution.[9]

Bismarck proposed universal, equal and direct suffrage for tactical reasons of domestic and foreign policy in 1866, and one year later he introduced it for the federal elections in the North German Federation; in 1871 it was incorporated in the constitution of the Empire.[10] In 1866 Bismarck moved first in the *Bundestag* (the

[8] Quoted in Gagel, *op. cit.*, 36.

[9] These liberal fears had already been great in 1848 when Louis Napoleon was elected under universal suffrage. Cf. H. Gollwitzer, "Der Cäsarismus Napoleons III. im Widerhall der öffentlichen Meinung Deutschlands," *Historische Zeitschrift*, Vol. 173, 1952, 23–75.

[10] The liberals were also afraid of the direct election method; the system of electors had fortified bourgeois power. Under the new system, the liberal parties had to adjust to the requirements of mass agitation. This was very difficult for the liberal notables who were accustomed to address themselves to a small body of independent, educated electors. Pastors, teachers, burgomasters and *Landräte* (government-appointed county commissioners or district heads) replaced the electors as political opinion and decision makers. To be sure, many electors held such positions, but now an institutional support was withdrawn from those who had had no other office than that of an elector.

consultative organ of the German states), in Frankfurt, for the convening of a national assembly. This assembly, to be elected by universal and equal suffrage, was to reform the *Bund* of the German states. Thus, Bismarck gained a great tactical advantage over the liberals by making himself the champion of national unification and by advocating a more democratic suffrage than they favored. Bismarck hoped for a conservative mass vote against the liberals, especially in the countryside.[11] In his memoirs, however, he justifies himself mainly on the grounds of foreign policy: [12] the demand for universal suffrage was a warning to Austria and other countries that Prussia might support nationalist and revolutionary forces within their territories; it also prevented Napoleon III from gaining a pretext for intervention on the side of Austria against Prussia, since his power had been established by universal suffrage. When he wrote his memoirs in the nineties Bismarck still considered universal and equal suffrage justified, although he vigorously opposed the secret ballot, which had been adopted under a liberal motion: it "is incompatible with the best characteristics of Germanic blood."

Bismarck was supported in his attack upon the three-class suffrage by the polemics of Hermann Wagener, the social welfare expert of the conservatives, who attacked it along with other tax-based suffrage as plutocratic: "This electoral system is nothing but the representation of money capital with the deceitful pretense that it is a representation of the people. It leads to the rise of a modern

[11] In the sixties Bismarck had thought that indirect and class suffrage furthered the revolutionary movement more than direct and equal suffrage. Therefore he introduced the latter. He reasoned that the great majority of the common people in Prussia would vote for the King's party and repudiate the liberal bourgeoisie. Bismarck recognized, however, the danger of universal, equal and direct suffrage once revolutionary sentiments would spread among the people. See his letter to the Prussian minister in London, Count Bernstorff, April 19, 1866, in Hans Rothfels, ed., *Bismarck und der Staat: Ausgewählte Dokumente* (Stuttgart: Kohlhammer, 1953), 326.

[12] The following is a summary of Bismarck's arguments as presented in his *Gedanken und Erinnerungen* (Stuttgart: Cotta, 1898), Vol. 2, 59 f.

moneyed aristocracy. . . . Compared with such a dreary system we consider the general suffrage a genuine advance." [13] Like Bismarck, Wagener believed at the time that the opposition to the Crown was most likely to come from well-to-do people. Therefore he resorted to the argument that universal and equal suffrage was necessary in order to balance the social inequalities of society. The outstanding historian and National Liberal deputy, Heinrich von Sybel, replied that equal political rights were only justified once all social inequalities had been eradicated. [14]

Both sides obviously emphasized arguments according to tactical convenience. However, the tactical component should not be overestimated. The commitment of the liberals to the three-class suffrage which once had been imposed upon them was accompanied by an ideological re-evaluation in keeping with major historical trends of German liberalism. Many liberals of the sixties still adhered to the idealist philosophy of law and state. They were concerned about the intrusion of society into the realm of the state and did not want politics to become a conflict arena for social groups and class interests; this awareness of danger had been awakened largely by Lorenz von Stein's analysis of class developments in France. [15] The new theory of the relation between political rights and social position stipulated that the latter should be determined by political functions, not personal wealth; however, wealth would be the basis on which these functions were performed. The theory enabled the liberals to justify a limited suffrage and to demand anew the predominant position in the state for the propertied

[13] H. Wagener, "Wir fahren fort," in the *Neue Preussische Zeitung*, April 18, 1866, quoted in Joachim Knoll, *Führungsauslese in Liberalismus und Demokratie* (Stuttgart: Schwab, 1957), 51 f.

[14] Cf. Gagel, *op. cit.*, 56 ff.

[15] Cf. Lorenz von Stein, *Geschichte der sozialen Bewegung in Frankreich von 1789 bis auf unsere Tage* (Darmstadt: Wissenschaftliche Buchgesellschaft, 1959), 3 vols. The volumes were originally published in 1849–50. A selected English edition translated and introduced by Kaethe Mengelberg will be published in the near future by the Bedminster Press.

and educated classes. It rejected the egalitarian tendencies of democracy in favor of a principle of stratification according to political function.[16]

The liberals were embittered that, at the same time in which they were involved in a showdown over the preservation and enlargement of parliamentary rights, a class-conscious labor movement arose to attack them from behind.[17] The liberal bourgeoisie, distinguished by property and education, could indeed claim that it was the only social and political power that could fight, with some chance of success, the absolutist and conservative-aristocratic forces. The liberals felt that they had the right to expect the allegiance of the masses because they were fighting for the whole people; they did not understand that in focussing on constitutional issues and in championing increasingly laissez-faire doctrines they were fighting more for their own interests than for those of the working class. Liberalism was vulnerable to a political class cleavage because its strength depended largely on the acceptance of the bourgeois leadership by the lower classes. Therefore, the liberals opposed the incipient independent labor movement, since this

16 The suffrage system finally lost much of its importance as an issue between liberals and conservatives. The Progressives lost many votes in the old Prussian provinces under both the three-class system for the Prussian diet and the universal system for the North-German diet; however, the newly formed National Liberal Party did very well in the new provinces. As a result, the liberals no longer objected so strongly to the universal suffrage of the North-German Federation and the conservatives were no longer eager to abolish the three-class suffrage of the Prussian diet. National Liberals and Progressives began to accept, with some reservations, the universal suffrage and used its establishment as an opportunity to press for greater liberalization of political institutions. They demanded, especially, an administrative reform of the counties because the conservatives derived strong advantage from the self-administration of the big estates in the Eastern provinces. The conservatives retained their dominance after the introduction of these reforms in the seventies because now the small farmers turned to them: one of their major grievances had been removed through liberal efforts.

17 See, e.g., an article by the Progressive, A. Streckfuss, in the Berlin *Volkszeitung* (Oct. 22, 1862), reprinted in Ferdinand Lassalle, *Gesammelte Reden und Schriften,* Eduard Bernstein, ed. (Berlin: Cassirer, 1919), Vol. 3, 16 f.

movement considered, as one of its Lassallean slogans said, "the idea of the working class as the dominant principle of society."

Later tactical adjustments of some liberal leaders who recognized the socially conservative function of equal suffrage [18] could not prevent the deepening of the cleavage which developed in the sixties between the bourgeoisie and the incipient labor movement as a consequence of ideological commitments strengthened by strategic considerations. At the same time, the forces of liberal intransigence against the authoritarian monarchy were decisively weakened. A new liberal disaster, due to the military victories of the Prussian monarchy, could be turned into partial success when the government offered the liberals a chance to participate in the unification of Germany. This necessitated a close political alliance with the monarchy and the adoption of a cautious policy of compromise as the only remaining means of reform. Under these conditions, the liberals were not interested in securing working-class support by appealing to its politically most active and also most radical part, which appeared, in the balance of power, as a *quantité négligeable*.

2. *Working-Class Interests and Democratization*

The developments of the 1860's left the incipient working class on its own. Class-conscious organization appeared to some politically interested workers, mostly energetic journeymen in small-scale industries, as the only alternative; in contrast, the English working class could for decades support the liberal bourgeoisie in the ex-

---

[18] Schulze-Delitzsch finally came out for equal suffrage because he wanted political, but not social equality. He feared that political freedom would be lost in the process of attaining social equality, since the latter could only be realized through the revolutionary intervention of an all-powerful absolutist or socialist state. Cf. Gagel, *loc. cit.*

pectation of gradual democratization. Despite the Constitutional Conflict, however, the 1860's were a decade of improving political conditions for German workers. Limited rights of association and universal and equal suffrage on the federal level were granted before democratization was blocked at the end of the decade. A crisis of aspiration in an improving situation is a well-known phenomenon. During the repressive decade of the fifties, in 1856, Alexis de Tocqueville observed: "Experience teaches us that, generally speaking, the most perilous moment for a bad government is one when it seeks to mend its ways. Only consummate statecraft can enable a king to save his throne when after a long spell of oppressive rule he sets to improving the lot of his subjects. Patiently endured so long as it seemed beyond redress, a grievance comes to appear intolerable once the possibility of removing it crosses men's minds." [19] Tocqueville had in mind the *ancien régime* and the French Revolution, but his generalization was also to apply to German developments of the near future. Prussia had a statesman, possessing "consummate statecraft" who instituted revolutionary changes from above—national unification, universal and equal suffrage, laissez-faire principles in economic policy—which fortified rather than weakened the supreme authority of the monarchy.

The liberal crisis of aspiration was strong enough to challenge the dominant regime for a while. The workers were too weak to pose a threat to the government, but a few thousand urban workers raised their level of aspiration to the point of seizing opportunities to improve their lot through adult education and organization. The resurgence of political life sensitized them to their second-class citizenship. In the fifties, journeymen and workers had been completely passive politically. Their status was low. "Married journeymen were rare and such marriages were frowned upon," recalls Vahlteich, one of the first proletarian labor leaders. "Male factory

[19] Alexis de Tocqueville, *The Old Regime and the French Revolution* (New York: Doubleday Anchor, 1955), 176 f. By permission of the publisher.

workers were held in low esteem; female workers were subjected to prejudiced contempt. This does not mean that journeymen were particularly respected either." Vahlteich acknowledges that the relationship between masters and journeymen was often cooperative and that many masters considered it a point of honor to help their journeymen in bad times. However, discrimination was keenly felt through the existing "legislation and thus through the courts, the police and the hospital administrations." [20] On the other hand, many workers and journeymen often indulged in behavior which inevitably aroused the moral censure of middle-class persons.

Workers' associations were outlawed until the early sixties. This prevented the development of an articulate political consciousness among a large number of workers; a few workers, however, managed to develop it. Just as industrialization was not an entirely indigenous process in any country apart from England, so labor protest was also influenced by the first responses in England and France. Some workers absorbed liberal ideas about self-help, borrowed from England, and socialist ideas about independent working-class organizations, which had trickled into Germany from France.

The first organizational opportunity for workers became available through nonpolitical organization within the liberal movement. Liberal intellectuals who, with the exception of Schulze-Delitzsch, did not belong to the top leadership of the Progressives began to found workers' educational associations as subdivisions of bourgeois organizations. They were either motivated by liberal ideas about the importance of education and self-help as major means of improving the lot of the workers or by tactical considerations arising from the struggle with the conservatives. When a workers' educational association was founded by liberals in Leipzig in February 1861, Vahlteich, one of the few workers who had read some socialist literature in the fifties, pleaded immediately for equal

20 Julius Vahlteich, *Ferdinand Lassalle und die Anfänge der deutschen Arbeiterbewegung* (Munich: Birk, about 1902/3), 16.

rights and political independence of the workers, before 400 persons who had accepted the public invitation to form the association.[21] He rejected the emphasis on education and argued that this should be the task of the public schools, not of an association of adults. Young August Bebel, who was to become the greatest spokesman of the Social Democratic labor movement, still sided with the liberals against the proposal of independent labor associations, but he was greatly impressed by the vigor with which Vahlteich and Fritzsche, another worker, stood up to the educated liberal gentlemen and wished that he could do the same.[22] Social and political problems were not yet in the foreground of the interests of the Leipzig association; however, a faction more closely concerned with the promotion of specific workers' interests emerged. It was headed by two democratic intellectuals and Vahlteich and Fritzsche, both of whom were later to become Reichstag members. In 1862 Vahlteich went a step further and demanded universal suffrage. Eventually the liberalization of political conditions made it possible to establish an association, *Vorwärts,* which devoted itself to agitation and the organization of mass meetings. The move toward independent working-class associations was not possible without antagonizing devoted friends of labor who could not understand why the workers should want to have their own associations.

The Progressives managed to win the majority of politically interested workers; they failed to control the minority, which adopted some socialist ideas. This minority combined with a few democratic middle-class intellectuals, who rejected the liberal constitutional and unification policies as too moderate, to establish an independent labor movement. Both groups existed at the very margin of the political life of the emergent nation; they were the only ones interested in radical democratization.

[21] The association was established as a branch of the bourgeois Polytechnical Society in order to avoid police interference. On Vahlteich's role and the history of the Leipzig organization, see *op. cit.,* 12 ff.

[22] Cf. August Bebel, *Aus meinem Leben* (Berlin: Dietz, 1946), Vol. 1, 56.

The first independent national labor organization was founded by Ferdinand Lassalle (1825–64), whose style of life was romantic heroism and idealistic exaltation. He was the son of a well-to-do Jewish merchant, a brilliant student of philosophy and law, and a democratic tribune with aristocratic affinities. He joined the left in 1848 and spent six months in prison in 1850/51 for allegedly advocating armed resistance against officers of the state. From 1846 until 1854 he litigated successfully, though with dubious means, for the interests of Countess Hatzfeldt in a divorce and property suit which attracted national attention and ranged the liberal against the conservative public. The fight for the countess, who became his life-long and politically influential friend, was for him a battle against feudal injustice, in which he could play a conspicuous and chivalrous role. Marx and Engels, who were absorbed in the class struggle and hostile to universal ethics, considered the defense of an aristocratic lady by a radical democrat and socialist an embarrassing and irrelevant pursuit. In the fifties and early sixties Lassalle wrote voluminous philosophical, legal, economic and dramatic works. He entered politics again during the Italian War of 1859, advocating Prussian predominance over Austria. In contrast to Marx, he did not consider foreign politics an extension of domestic politics, and he was not averse to an alliance with Bismarck and the conservatives against the liberal bourgeoisie. Lassalle leaned heavily on Marx's analysis of capitalist society, but the two men were personally and politically too different to get along well. Their precarious friendship lasted until 1862, when Lassalle started his working-class agitation against the liberals; this tactic was contrary to Marx's evolutionary scheme, which necessitated working-class support for the middle classes in order to precipitate the bourgeois revolution.[23]

---

[23] Lassalle died fittingly in a duel with an aristocrat over the latter's fiancée, whom he tried to marry, imploring the support of the Catholic church. His collected works were published in 12 vols. by Ed. Bernstein, *op. cit.*, 1919/20 and by Gustav Mayer in six vols., *Nachgelassene Briefe und*

Lassalle created the labor movement explicitly as a means of democratization by mobilizing working-class interests. For him, the middle class was following "no longer the banner of a democratic movement," it was governed not only by "the fear of government, but also by the fear of the people. . . . Our liberal bourgeoisie cannot smash the military state, cannot win political freedom." [24] Lassalle's motive for turning to the workers was rooted in his awareness of the powerlessness of the democratic intellectuals. He exclaimed that only "myself and about one thousand ideologists in Germany" are fighting for "political freedom," sup-

---

Schriften (Stuttgart: Deutsche Verlagsanstalt, 1921–25); the most important German biography is by Hermann Oncken, *Lassalle* (Stuttgart: Deutsche Verlagsanstalt, 1920), 3rd ed.; for a good English biography, see David Footman, *Ferdinand Lassalle: Romantic Revolutionary* (New Haven: Yale University Press, 1947); for comparisons between Lassalle and Marx see Franz Mehring, *Die deutsche Socialdemokratie: Ihre Geschichte und ihre Lehre* (Bremen: Schünemann, 1878), 2nd ed., 55 f, Footman, *op. cit.,* and Carl Landauer, *European Socialism* (Berkeley and Los Angeles: University of California Press, 1959), Vol. I; on Lassalle's legal and social philosophy, see Thilo Ramm, *Ferdinand Lassalle als Rechts-und Sozialphilosoph* (Vienna: Westkulturverlag, 1953).

[24] Ferdinand Lassalle, "Arbeiterlesebuch," *op. cit.,* Eduard Bernstein, ed., III, 273. The following Lassalle quotations are from pp. 279–87. The "Arbeiterlesebuch" consists of two speeches delivered at Frankfurt/Main on May 17 and 19, 1863, before a Workers' Day of local workingmen's educational associations. A few days earlier Dr. Louis Büchner, a South German democrat and the author of the famous materialist best-seller *Kraft und Stoff* (and brother of the revolutionary dramatist Georg Büchner), had taken a stand against a separate working-class organization, but he had urged the workers to listen to Lassalle's case. Lassalle repeated, in an unprecedented four-hour speech, his economic ideas and proposals without impressing the majority of his audience; but he did impress them greatly with his attack on the Progressives in his second speech and with his appeal to the workers to carry the banner of democracy. Lassalle knew that his South German audience would be predisposed toward such an appeal; he wrote to Rodbertus that he would "shake his old revolutionary mane," but this tactical element does not negate the fact that democratic rather than specifically socialist appeals gained him mass support.

ported by perhaps ten to fifteen thousand people scattered throughout Germany but not by the interests of any one class.

It is in the greatest interest of political freedom to mobilize a class interest, a social interest and, in particular, the interest of the propertyless classes which predominate in sheer numbers and [potential] power. . . . I have to reject the misunderstanding that I want to establish a separate movement merely of the working class. The banner which I have raised is the democratic banner. . . . I am turning against the sleepy and feeble movement which the bourgeoisie promotes as a class and can only promote as a class, the liberal-progressive movement. . . . It is a general democratic movement of the people, not a mere class movement, for which I call.[25]

In order to play the role which Lassalle attributed to them, the workers had to become independent from the liberals and aware of their own class interests. Therefore, Lassalle set out to establish an independent proletarian party which was to revolutionize the political and social order. However, Lassalle propagated an idealistic notion of revolution which, in contrast to Marx's, did not assert the inevitability of class struggle and violent change and which stressed the possibility of class conciliation and of the peaceful victory of "principles." Lassalle's idealism had, of course, some tactical components. In view of the strength of the government and his prosecution by police and courts (for example, for having advocated "class hatred" in his *Arbeiterprogramm*), he had to stress

25 Lassalle was not against the middle classes as such and against their accumulation of wealth, but he rejected the political class prerogatives which the bourgeoisie wanted to arrogate to itself by virtue of its economic position. See his "Arbeiterprogramm," *op. cit.,* II, 174. This was a lecture delivered to predominantly Progressive workers in Berlin on April 12, 1862. It was the first introduction to historical materialism presented before workers; but it was also idealist and non-Marxian in that Lassalle said, "We are all workers insofar as we have only the will to be useful in some way to human society" (186), and insofar as he assigned to the state "the function of advancing freedom, the development of the human race towards freedom" (197). The workers were reportedly unimpressed. Later, however, the lecture became very popular within the labor movement.

the nonviolent aspect of his revolutionary intentions. Furthermore, he wanted to keep alive the slim chance that the Prussian government might come to terms with him by conceding universal and equal suffrage and offering economic aid for producers' cooperatives.[26]

The demands for universal and equal suffrage and state-supported producers' cooperatives were the basis of Lassalle's agitation, expressed for the first time in his most popular and influential writing, the *Open Address* (*Offenes Antwortschreiben*) of March 1863. The demand for producers' cooperatives was sure to find vociferous opposition from many quarters, liberal and socialist; but at least it could be presented under the given political conditions. Lassalle was primarily interested in establishing the principle of state help on a large scale and in giving the workers an irresistible reason to press for universal and equal suffrage, both as a politically and economically indispensable condition of their advancement. As long as the workers were not running their own producers' cooperatives, Lassalle argued, the "iron law of wages"—which maintained that the average wage of the workers would always gravitate about the subsistence level socially necessary for survival and reproduction—could not be abolished. He maintained that this was the "normal condition of the whole working class" and that welfare schemes could not obliterate it; therefore, the workers should not concentrate their attention on welfare plans, but take a much more comprehensive perspective: "The working class (*Arbeiterstand*) must constitute itself as an independent political party and embrace the universal, equal and direct suffrage as its principal slogan. . . . The representation of the working class in the legislative bodies of Germany is the only means of satisfying its

---

[26] Bismarck was quick to recognize, after Lassalle's plea for state intervention, that a small labor movement could attack the liberals from the rear, while it was not large enough to endanger the government. In 1863/64 Bismarck and Lassalle talked together about welfare policies and universal suffrage.

legitimate interests politically." In this way the state will become "the great association of the poorer classes." [27]

Lassalle started his campaign with the *Workers' Program* of 1862, which came to the attention of Vahlteich and his few class-conscious fellow workers in Leipzig. They got in touch with Lassalle and agreed with him on the convening of the first general assembly of the General German Workingmen's Association in Leipzig. Despite Lassalle's vigorous agitation, through his *Open Address,* only 14 people came together on May 23, 1863, representing about 400 people in 11 cities. By early 1864, Lassalle's organization numbered not yet 1,000 members; he had hoped that he could organize 100,000 workers within a year or so and that the popular response to his address would be similar to the people's reaction to Luther's theses of 1517.

The situation was particularly difficult for the Lassalleans in Berlin, where the Progressives controlled most of the politically engaged workers. Lassalle's address, *To the Workers of Berlin,* in the winter of 1863 had little impact; his followers were continuously exposed to the threat of physical force at the hands of Progressive workers. Only conservatives, wearing black and white cockades on their top hats, supported the Lassalleans against the liberal workers by attending their meetings.[28]

Lassalle set out resolutely to further his democratic interests by organizing the workers in an authoritarian fashion. His authoritarian tendencies grew stronger once he found out how difficult it was to win workers for his cause. His authoritarianism was also encouraged by certain working-class characteristics of his followers. Traditional status consciousness persisted side by side with the new class consciousness and facilitated the subordination of work-

[27] Lassalle, "Offenes Antwortschreiben," *op. cit.,* III, 47 and 81.
[28] Cf. Vahlteich, *op. cit.,* 27. As late as 1869, Bebel asserted in the North German diet that "certain groups in the Prussian government" see the advantage of using the split between the bourgeoisie and the workers for their own purposes. See *Reichstag Protocols,* March 18, 1869.

ers to educated men.[29] More important, however, was the fact that even the most active workers were young, without sufficient experience in politics and organizational matters, without more than elementary education, and without financial resources. Thus, even those critical of his authoritarian tendencies depended, at least for some time, on his intellectual brilliance, his learning and his political skill, as well as on his considerable financial means, if they wanted to succeed in establishing a nation-wide labor movement.

Lassalle vigorously combatted ideological competition by closing uncontrolled channels of communication between bourgeois intellectuals and workers. All intellectuals who applied for membership in a local had to be cleared by party headquarters. Lassalle, the bourgeois with aristocratic manners, and his most important successor, Johann Baptist von Schweitzer, scion of an old aristocratic family, succeeded in welding together the nucleus of a class-conscious labor movement which was held together by two means: intensive indoctrination and organizational isolation. Schweitzer's exit, in the early seventies, did not change this policy, as can be seen from the following statement by the major Lassallean newspaper:

Reconciliation is an insult to the worker, if it is to be approached on the basis of the present society. Therefore, the awakening of class consciousness, the separation of the workers from the rest of society, is

[29] An example of traditional status consciousness and the high regard of educated men is a Reichstag speech in 1869 by Försterling, a member of the Lassallean General German Workingmen's Association—a splinter group which Countess Hatzfeldt, Lassalle's aristocratic friend, sponsored after his death for the sake of the "pure" Lassallean program. Försterling demanded the release of the association's president, Mende, who had just been arrested even though he was a Reichstag deputy. He pointed to the class difference between himself, a *worker,* and Mende, an *educated man.* He complained that Mende was put together with other prisoners and was not allowed to pay for his own maintenance; he considered this a particular hardship since Mende belonged to the "educated classes." He added that he would not have cared so much if it had happened to him. See *Reichstag Protocols,* April 28, 1869, 645.

the first step to victory; and this separation is accomplished by the preaching of Lassalle's doctrines and by the tight-knit organization of the General German Workingmen's Association, in which the worker feels that he belongs to the [closed and] united working class.[30]

Although Lassalle and Schweitzer's centralist methods were effective, they also produced severe strains. A minority of Lassalleans left the party because of its centralist organization and cult of the dead Lassalle, but without giving up their class-conscious attitude.[31] The Lassallean belief in the necessity of a class-conscious labor movement survived these strains as well as the breaking up of the General German Workingmen's Association into various competing groups after Lassalle's death in 1864. The Lassalleans, within and without the Lassallean associations proper, impressed the need for political class organization on other workers and thus forced their democratic and socialist opponents, under Bebel and Liebknecht, to speed up the separation from the bourgeois left in the late sixties.

[30] *Der neue Sozialdemokrat*, 1871, 77, quoted in Richard Schuster, *Die Social-Democratie, nach ihrem Wesen und ihrer Agitation quellenmässig dargestellt* (Stuttgart: Steinkopf, 1875), 141. The phrase *geschlossene Arbeiterklasse* means conventionally "the united working class," but *geschlossen* literally means "closed"; thus the choice of the term clearly expresses the progressing class separation of the labor movement.

[31] Among these members was Vahlteich who had been class-conscious before meeting Lassalle. As the latter's secretary, he was one of the first to take a stand against his authoritarian tendencies and proposed decentralization of the Workingmen's Association. Lassalle, shortly before his death in 1864, tried to eliminate Vahlteich. At the time, Vahlteich's break with Lassalle was delayed by A. Vogt, who wrote a letter dispatched with Liebknecht's consent urging Vahlteich to yield in favor of another attempt to control Lassalle—by uniting the "party Marx and comrades" with Lassalle's organization. Vahlteich notes that the "party Marx," as it was called in the letter, consisted of only two persons, Vogt himself and Liebknecht. This is indicative of the lack of influence Marx had at the time. Vahlteich finally went over to Liebknecht and Bebel. See Vahlteich, *op. cit.*, 80–84.

3. The Self-Isolation of the Labor Movement

The second labor party which emerged in the sixties was also founded by a basically democratic intellectual, Wilhelm Liebknecht (1826–1900). Liebknecht's family descended from Martin Luther. His ancestors were higher civil servants and university professors. He received an academic education but did not feel any inclination to pursue an academic career in the Germany of the forties. In Switzerland he had his first contacts with organized German workers in 1847. He participated in the two abortive military campaigns of Republican volunteers in Baden, who hoped to save the 1848 Revolution. From the fifties on, he put his faith in mass propaganda rather than revolutionary action by a minority. For 13 years he lived in exile in London, where he joined the Communist League and became an intimate friend of Marx's family. After getting an amnesty, he went to Berlin in 1862. Three years later he was expelled from Prussia and went to Leipzig in Saxony where he won August Bebel (1840–1913) for radical democracy.[32] Bebel, the

[32] In contrast to Lassalle and Schweitzer, there are, to my knowledge, no major biographies of Liebknecht and Bebel, for decades the two most prominent leaders in the German labor movement. For Bebel's description of his early relationship with Liebknecht, see his autobiography, *op. cit.,* I, 114–18; for a comparison between Liebknecht and Bebel's views in the sixties, see Gustav Mayer's excellent biography, *Johann Baptist von Schweitzer* (Jena: Fischer, 1909), 150; for an invidious contrast between the "Prussian hater" and "Communist" Liebknecht and the "simple, honest" working-class leader Bebel, see Mehring, *op. cit.,* 84–87. Mehring, a middle-class intellectual, joined the Social Democrats in the eighties and became their most brilliant editorialist; in his history, still written from an outsider's viewpoint, he condemned Liebknecht and Bebel's anti-Prussian and "internationalist" line and regretted the decline of the positive Lassellean attitude toward state and nation. He was not aware of the ideological and tactical differences between Liebknecht and Marx-Engels. Bebel acquired some knowledge about socialism by reading Lassalle with polemical intent; he had no theoretical

son of a noncommissioned officer, was orphaned early and lived through years of poverty but rose to become a master turner. Through him Liebknecht gained influence on the non-Lassallean workers' associations, which were loosely linked with the liberals. Bebel was at the time chairman of the liberal Leipzig workers' educational association and also of the permanent committee of the Union of German Workingmen's Associations, which had been founded in Frankfurt in 1863.

Liebknecht was ostensibly Marx's representative in Germany, an agent of the International, who fought the Lassalleans. However, he differed from Schweitzer mainly with regard to national unification and the relation between democratization and industrialization. In fact, Schweitzer was better schooled in Marxism than Liebknecht, who never gained as thorough an understanding of Marxian theory as his Lassallean opponent; Schweitzer was also the first to present an outline of the Marxian analysis of capitalist society to the Reichstag on March 17, 1869. It is not surprising in view of his Catholic aristocratic background that he was primarily concerned with the effects of industrialization on the individual and with the economic reorganization of society. For the middle-class intellectual Liebknecht, the fight for democratic liberties and against the "feudal classes" was paramount.[33] Schweitzer's greater interest in fighting

---

discussions with Liebknecht on Marx and Lassalle. Bebel's turn toward socialism and Marxism was typical, in its slowness, of the most active members of the labor movement. See Robert Michels' necrologue, "August Bebel," *Archiv für Sozialwissenschaft,* Vol. 37, 1913, 675. The gradual advance of Marxism is treated in Ch. VII. For a Revisionist biographical essay on Bebel, see Hellmuth von Gerlach, *August Bebel* (Munich: Langen, 1909).

[33] Both Liebknecht and Schweitzer maintained the inseparableness of democratic and socialist ideals, but Schweitzer held that "the question of ownership, the question of absolute poverty and of limitless wealth is the only really important question of this century. With its solution, all other problems will be solved; and if it is not solved, every other solution will be pretty irrelevant." *Reichstag Protocols,* March 2, 1870, 145. Mayer added: "Whereas Liebknecht was more inclined to consider socialism as a func-

the evils of capitalist society, rather than in fighting Prussia, made it easier for him to be pragmatic. He supported the imminent unification of Germany by Prussia as the only realistic solution. Liebknecht hoped until the late sixties for a federated nation state which would include Austria.[34] When the Prussian victory over Austria and Saxony in 1866 buried the last hopes for a major bourgeois democratic challenge of the authoritarian monarchy, Liebknecht founded the Saxonian People's party, which rallied the "democratic, petty-bourgeois, anti-Prussian elements." [35] It was made up of small businessmen, craftsmen and workers.[36] Vahlteich observes in his memoirs that the same districts in Saxony (left of the Elbe River) that voted for the left in 1848 also voted two decades later for Liebknecht's party.[37] Liebknecht and Bebel believed, as did Lassalle in the early sixties, that the chances of democratization depended on the mobilization of the working class. Political democracy would have to become social democracy; it would have to encompass the economic and social interests of the working class. "Democratic and socialist are for me identical terms," said Liebknecht in his programmatic speech at the 1868 convention of the non-Lassallean Union of German Workingmen's Associations in Nuremberg; and one of his supporters, a delegate of the South

---

tion of democracy, Schweitzer inclined to the reverse evaluation of the relationship. . . . Liebknecht considered it the major task of his party to prevent the *Junkers* from exploiting the class struggle between the proletariat and the bourgeoisie for their own selfish purposes. This he thought to accomplish by dissolving the 'artificially created and nourished distrust' [i.e., created by the Lassalleans] against the 'so-called bourgeois democracy' and by trying hard to keep the petty bourgeoisie at the side of the working class in their common political struggle against Reaction." Mayer, *op. cit.,* 299 and 306.

[34] For a detailed exposition see G. Mayer, *op. cit.,* Ch. VII, 147–172.

[35] Vahlteich, *op. cit.,* 40.

[36] Cf. Gustav Mayer, "Die Trennung der proletarischen von der bürgerlichen Demokratie," *Archiv für die Geschichte des Sozialismus,* II, 1912, 24.

[37] Vahlteich, *op. cit.,* 6.

German People's party, added: "Democracy must become social democracy if it honestly wants to be democracy." [38]

Liebknecht and Bebel wanted to win over the working class without losing the democratic lower middle-class groups they had organized. However, they came under the pressure of class-conscious workers, and Liebknecht was motivated by them at the Nuremberg convention to push through a program supporting "the endeavors of the International Workingmen's Association." [39] Sixtyone associations voted for the program; 32 voted against it. Under continued pressures Liebknecht and Bebel finally founded the Social Democratic Workers' party at Eisenach in 1869. Its members came to be called the Eisenachers. Liebknecht only hesitatingly accepted the name "Workers' Party" at the insistence of ex-Lassalleans. He later denied that the name was limiting the socialist movement to the working class, and he interpreted the term "work" in an idealistic fashion as "application of humanity"—"Arbeit ist Betätigung des Menschentums." [40]

Marx and Engels were often exasperated with Liebknecht's democratic and federative aims. "I dislike Liebknecht's tabloid to the highest degree. Nothing but hidden South German federalism," wrote Engels about his *Demokratisches Wochenblatt* to Marx in 1868. He was dismayed that Liebknecht wanted to run the paper as an organ not only of the Saxonian People's party but also of the

---

[38] Protocol of the Fifth Convention of the Union of German Workingmen's Associations in Nuremberg, Sept. 1868, reprinted in Wilhelm Liebknecht, ed., *Der Hochverratsprozess wider Liebknecht, Bebel, Hepner* (Berlin: Vorwärts, 1894), 782 f. Until its merger with the Progressives in 1910, the South German People's party founded in 1868 represented South German republicanism and preserved the democratic heritage of the 1848 revolution.

[39] *Loc. cit.*

[40] Protocol of the 1875 Gotha convention, 35, quoted in Kurt Brandis, *Die deutsche Sozialdemokratie bis zum Fall des Sozialistengesetzes* (Leipzig: Hirschfeld, 1931), 29. Brandis is at pains to show that, contrary to older interpretations, the Eisenachers were essentially no more Marxist than the Lassalleans were. I agree with this view (cf. Ch. VII) without sharing the polemical interests of the author, a revolutionary Marxist.

International—"the German petty bourgeois (*Spiessbürger*) and the European workers." Particularly ridiculous to Engels and Marx was the statement "that bourgeois society or, as he says, 'the social' is determined by 'the political' and not vice versa. Naturam si furca expellas, etc. Nearly every article is full of nonsense." [41] Until after the beginning of the Franco-German War, they approved of Liebknecht and Bebel's opposition to Bismarck's unification and war policies. They realized that their moralistic pathos accounted for much of their appeal among anti-Prussian groups, but they feared that the insistence on principles and the fervent stand for a democratic and federative solution of German unification would, in the long run, prevent them from pursuing a realistic policy. [42]

Liebknecht and Bebel's round-about opposition to the Franco-German War at first dismayed many Eisenachers; but the continuation of the war against the French Republic kindled their indignation and also effected a *rapprochement* with the Lassalleans, whose representatives had at first voted for the war credits. When Liebknecht and Bebel were prosecuted for their stand, they became martyrs in the eyes of many workers, and their fame and extraordinary position within the labor movement were guaranteed. [43]

[41] Engels' letters of Feb. 2, 1868, July 6, 1869, Oct. 14, 1868, in V. Adoratsky, ed., *Marx-Engels Gesamtausgabe* (Berlin: Marx-Engels Verlag, 1931), III:4, 19, 202, 111.

[42] Cf. Engels' letter of Oct. 22, 1867, Marx's letter of Dec. 17, 1867, *op. cit.*, III:3, 438 and 464; Marx's letters of Aug. 17 and Sept. 2, 1870, III:4, 369 and 375. Eduard Bernstein agreed decades later with Marx and Engels that the moralistic basis on which Liebknecht and Bebel refused to vote for the war credits in the North-German diet could have been shared by any bourgeois pacifist and democrat. Cf. Bernstein, "Von der Sekte zur Partei," *Zeitschrift für Politik*, Vol. 3, 1910, 513.

[43] Liebknecht and Bebel's position appeared as an opportunity to the Saxonian government, prompted by Bismarck, to prepare a trial against them for high treason. After considerable legal and political difficulties, the government finally succeeded, in 1872, in sentencing them to two years confinement in a fortress. Cf. Paul Kampffmeyer and Bruno Altmann, *Vor dem Sozialistengesetz* (Berlin: Der Bücherkreis, 1928), 68–76. The Leipzig trial gave Lieb-

Though Liebknecht was so deeply involved in the issue of unification that, as Gustav Mayer said of him, "for several years socialist aims were of secondary importance to him," [44] he was not demoralized by the unification of Germany through Bismarck as so many South German democrats were. He and Bebel now fell back on Marx and Engels' conviction that the social and economic developments following unification would necessarily further the cause of the Social Democrats. "The future belongs to us," wrote Bebel in November 1870, because "our greatest enemies, against their will, further most . . . the development of things." [45] The patriotic enthusiasm about the military victories and unification slowed down, at first, the expansion of the two Social Democratic parties, but postwar developments worked in their favor. The precarious situation of the industrial workers, even if they succeeded in raising wages during the boom of the early seventies, and the persistent interference of the authorities with party and union organization tended to neutralize the patriotic feelings of many workers after 1871.

The unification of Germany removed the major issue between the

---

knecht and Bebel an opportunity to propagandize their views before an audience larger than they could have had without the trial. The public took a great interest in the trial which lasted for two weeks—an extraordinarily long duration for a trial at that time. The prosecution cited many pamphlets, articles, letters and speeches in the presentation of its case; it read the whole Communist Manifesto and dealt especially with the defendants' relation to Marx and the First International. This gave Liebknecht and Bebel a chance to define the nonviolent revolutionary aspirations of their party, a position to which the Social Democrats adhered from then on. Liebknecht immediately published an edited version of the trial manuscript (ca. 600 pp.); it became one of the major pieces of Social Democratic literature and played a significant role in mobilizing sympathies among workers for Social Democratic leaders. The second edition (1894, *op. cit.*) also contains about twenty additional manuscripts (convention protocols, proclamations, reports, party programs, etc.) which had been used as evidence by the prosecution and the defense. This swells the volume to 942 pages.

[44] Mayer, *Schweitzer, op. cit.,* 150.
[45] Mayer, "Die Trennung," *op. cit.,* 65.

Eisenachers and the Lassalleans. Much antagonism, however, persisted until the increasing persecution by the government after the 1874 elections and internal dissensions of the Lassalleans produced a situation which broke down resistance to a merger in 1875. Before the merger the Eisenachers severed their ties with the bourgeois democrats. The first break had occurred in 1869, when the party was founded. At that time a prominent early sympathizer of labor, Sonnemann, the owner of the left-wing *Frankfurter Zeitung* and leader of the South German People's party, turned away from the Social Democrats.[46] The bourgeois adherents of the South German People's party had furthered the Workingmen's Associations from which the Social Democratic Workers' party emerged; the People's party recognized many demands of the Social Democrats and fought the laissez-faire credo of the outstanding Progressive leaders Richter and Bamberger. The same type of republican who belonged to the People's party in southern Germany often joined the Social Democrats in northern Germany for lack of a better alternative. For a time many of these democrats and republicans belonged to both parties before they were forced to make a decision, when the Eisenach congress of 1873 adopted a motion requiring all members with dual membership to make a choice.[47] Thus the dividing line between the South German People's party and the Social Democrats was not laissez-faire, as with the other liberal parties, but it was created by the socialist insistence on organization along class lines.

There were more intellectuals among the Eisenachers than there were among the numerically and organizationally superior Lassalleans. Eduard Bernstein recalls from the early seventies that the Eisenachers, to which he belonged, were sometimes called a "general staff without soldiers." The majority of the members in Berlin, for example, were workers, but intellectuals dominated the discus-

---

[46] Cf. Paul Massing, *Rehearsal for Destruction* (New York: Harper, 1949), 156, 184, and 252 f.

[47] Cf. Wilhelm Schröder, *Geschichte der sozialdemokratischen Parteiorganisationen in Deutschland* (Dresden: Kaden, 1912), 18 f.

sions, and this predominance retarded the increase of working-class membership.[48]

Bernstein points out an organizational phenomenon which was partly due to the perseverance of the democratic mentality of the 48ers: The Berlin Eisenachers came together only once a month for a Social Democratic party meeting, but three times for meetings of the older Democratic Workingmen's Association (*Demokratischer Arbeiterverein*). A fight for reorganization ensued which became a struggle between the attitudes of two generations. The opposition—the members under 30 years of age—argued that the name Democratic Workingmen's Association gave rise to the misunderstanding that the association was not a truly socialist organization but only an appendage of some bourgeois-democratic party. The South German Ignaz Auer, who had been a worker and who was rapidly rising within the party, warned that workers coming from southern Germany into Berlin would not join the association because of its name and would join the Lassalleans instead.[49]

[48] Cf. Eduard Bernstein, *Sozialdemokratische Lehrjahre* (Berlin: Bücherkreis, 1928), 9 f. Actually, there were just enough intellectuals and businessmen to help the labor movement establish itself. Among those who stuck to the labor movement despite its increasing class consciousness was Karl Höchberg, a wealthy bourgeois and ethical socialist. He published later the first theoretical journal of the party, *Die Zukunft,* and after its suppression the *Jahrbuch für Sozialwissenschaft und Sozialpolitik* in Zürich. Only few newspapers drifted into the Social Democratic camp; one of them was the *Demokratische Zeitung* in Berlin; cf. Bernstein, *loc. cit.,* and Adolf Held, *Die deutsche Arbeiterpresse der Gegenwart* (Leipzig: Duncker, 1873), 86–94.

[49] In defence of the organization's name, the chairman of the Democratic Workingmen's Association, Theodor Metzner, used an argument similar to Marx's argument objecting to the term "social democratic." Metzner considered the proposed name Social Democratic Workingmen's Association "an accumulation of equivalent notions which must be avoided in the interest of clear thinking" (Bernstein, *op. cit.,* 10). The opposition won out. The younger members took over the organization which soon became strong competition for the Lassalleans. The political strength of the Berlin Eisenachers increased particularly when they gained control over vocational associations such as the Saddler Journeymen's Association. Ignaz Auer was elected chairman of the association's executive committee in the early seventies. On

By the middle of the seventies, the separation of the Social Democrats from the remnants of the democratic bourgeoisie was completed. However, the socialist insistence on class-conscious organization remained linked with democratic "bourgeois" ideology. This was recognized by Marx in his critique of the 1875 Gotha program draft of the united Socialist Workers' party (renamed Social Democratic party in 1890):

Its political demands contain nothing beyond the old democratic litany familiar to all: universal suffrage, direct legislation, popular rights, a people's militia, etc. They are a mere echo of the bourgeois People's party. . . . Even vulgar democracy, which sees the millennium in the democratic republic and has no suspicion that it is precisely in this last form of state of bourgeois society that the class struggle has to be fought out to a conclusion—even it towers mountains above this kind of democratism, which keeps within the limits of what is permitted by the police and not permitted by logic.[50]

Marx knew well Liebknecht's democratic inclinations, but he did not sufficiently realize that there were no major theoretical differences between the Lassalleans and the Eisenachers, many of whom had been educated in the Lassallean organizations. Marx assumed that the Lassalleans had triumphed over the Eisenachers, but Bernstein recalls that Liebknecht was responsible for much in the program which Marx attributed to the Lassalleans.[51] Liebknecht simply suppressed Marx's critique; even Bebel does not seem to have known it at the time. Not before 1891 did the party become aware of Marx's letter when Engels published it before the Erfurt program was adopted.

Marx and Engels' criticism of the term Social Democratic, at the time when Schweitzer chose this name for his newspaper, see their letters of Nov. 16 and 18, 1864, in *Marx-Engels Gesamtausgabe, op. cit.,* III:3, 203 and 205.
[50] Lewis Feuer, ed., *Marx and Engels: Basic Writings on Politics and Philosophy* (Garden City: Doubleday Anchor, 1959), 128. By permission of the editor.
[51] Cf. Bernstein, *op. cit.,* 46.

After the First World War, revolutionary Marxists and left-wing critics like Brandis, Korsch, Lukacs and Rosenberg rediscovered that before and after their unification the Social Democrats adhered to many features of radical democratic ideology.[52] What Lukacs stated about Lassalle was also true of the Eisenachers: "The whole conception of revolution, despite all of its proletarian details, remains within the ideological realm of bourgeois society." [53] Brandis, too, was right in concluding that the Lassalleans as well as their opponents did not make a complete break with the "bourgeois world of ideas" because "they did not shed the ideology of bourgeois democracy." Therefore "the separation from it remained organizational." [54] From the viewpoint of the total revolution, the Social Democratic ideology had to appear as a failure to arrive at the "correct" class consciousness, but we must add that for the authoritarian state as well as for the overwhelming majority of the middle classes "bourgeois democracy" was as unacceptable as a proletarian-revolutionary ideology. Since the labor movement became the major advocate of extensive democratization, the fight for this goal was bound to result in an intensification of the class struggle and sooner or later in a major clash with the authoritarian monarchy.

[52] For Korsch and Rosenberg, see Ch. VII, 167.
[53] Georg Lukacs, "Die neue Ausgabe von Lassalles Briefen," *Archiv für die Geschichte der Arbeiterbewegung,* XI, 1925, 414.
[54] Brandis, *op. cit.,* 36 f.

III

Bismarck and the Spectre of Revolution

1. The Incompatibility of Parliamentarism and the Labor Movement with Bismarck's Reich

The labor movement was regarded in leading government circles as a permanent revolutionary potential within the Reich because it could have been satisfactorily integrated only if the very structure of Bismarck's edifice had been greatly modified. Foreign policy, domestic policy and the constitutional history of the Prussian state must be seen together in order to understand the particular form which Bismarck gave Germany in 1871 and in order to comprehend his policies and attitudes toward the labor movement. Bismarck approved of the German middle-class aspiration to unify Germany because he considered this to be in the interest of Prussia, as well as of the other parts of Germany, Austria excepted. Until the early fifties he had supported Austria; then he realized her inability, as a state of many nationalities, to effect German unification. He concluded that the only solution was an alignment of the Prussian military aristocracy with the militarily powerless German middle classes. The Prussian aristocracy would organize the military power required to establish and defend a united Germany; and the middle classes would contribute their intellectual, commercial and industrial resources. He managed to convince the King of Prussia and to get sufficient though not complete support from the Prussian aristocracy. Also he could count on the support of the majority of the German liberal bourgeoisie.

Bismarck established the Reich as an authoritarian regime. In order to understand this particular authoritarianism it is necessary to look briefly at the constitutional history of Prussia.[1] The enlightened absolutism of Prussia evolved after 1850 into monarchical constitutionalism. Its essence was the rule of the king through a responsible minister, appointed by him without parliamentary confirmation. The constitution which was imposed in 1850 did not stipulate clearly the form of this responsibility, but it was largely self-responsibility of the minister in the sense that he was free to decide whether his conscience and political evaluation agreed with the policies of the monarch or of the parties.[2] All bills passed by parliament and signed by the king were countersigned by the prime minister who thus took constitutional responsibility for them. The responsible minister had a mediating role which made his position more delicate than that of a parliamentary minister.

Under monarchic constitutionalism, the king retained his ultimate authority, and the crown did not derive its position from a contract with the people. In fact, in a sense, the people did not exist as a political entity proper; the constitution recognized the people only as civil society (*bürgerliche Gesellschaft*), represented by parties in a parliament which was not the supreme institution of the political society—the latter was formed by the authoritarian military state. As a military entity, the people were the personal instrument of the king. The army did not take a loyalty oath to the constitution, and the relations of the king to the army and the church were beyond the realm of ministerial responsibility and parliamentary participation. The king was the supreme commander and the head of the Protestant state church.

It is important to understand that monarchic constitutionalism

[1] The discussion of monarchical constitutionalism follows the brilliant comparative analysis by the historian Otto Hintze in "Das monarchische Prinzip und die konstitutionelle Verfassung," *Preussische Jahrbücher,* Vol. 144, 1911, 381–412.

[2] The constitution satisfied the demands of the more moderate liberals by recognizing the equality of all citizens before the law and by providing for the joint exercise of legislative power through the king and the two chambers.

was not just an "imperfect" transition to parliamentarism, as it often appeared to English and French observers and to German liberal adherents of parliamentary government; it was an institution consistent with the heritage of the absolutist Prussian state which had developed from patrimonialism to "state consciousness": that means, the monarch subordinated himself to the totality of the state interest or "the idea of the state" (*Staatsidee*) without, however, really giving up his absolutist powers. The Prussian state was based squarely on the ultimate authority of the military monarchy by virtue of "the historical right of the dynasty." In 200 years the crown had created a powerful Prussia from a conglomeration of territories and in view of this accomplishment and Prussia's role in German unification, no power and no argument could change her preeminence.

Monarchic constitutionalism became the Prussian-German system of government. There was no contemporary parallel to it in Europe. France had had it from 1814 until 1830. Russia was slowly approaching monarchical constitutionalism but had not yet realized it. The Dual Monarchy had parliamentary rule in Hungary as well as "parliamentarized" ministerial government, as it was called, in Austria; that is, members of parliament were in the government, but the civil servants predominated. England had been a parliamentary monarchy since 1835 when the parliamentary majority leaders definitely took over the government. The eminent constitutional historian Otto Hintze argues that the decisive difference between England and Prussia was the predominance of society in the former and of the state in the latter:

The modern state in England has been based on the ruling social classes —agrarian and industrial—not on the crown. Society has here, so to speak, swallowed the old monarchical state; it has politicized itself and has become a "political society"; the crown functions as a conservative emblem. . . . The parliamentary system corresponds to the tendency towards the formation of that industrial type of state which Herbert Spencer praised as the highest form of civilization; the monarchic-constitutional system, however, is based on the characteristics of the military type of state which prevails on the Continent. Insular security, on the one hand, and the need for military preparedness, on the other, characterize the different existential conditions to which the governmental forms adjusted here and there. In England the socially ruling classes, first the agrarian and then the industrial classes, have taken over leadership and reconstructed the state according to their interests and needs; and they have made, step by step, the concessions to which they were forced by the lower strata. [In Prussia] the old authoritarian state (*obrigkeitliche Staat*), which arose out of the arts of war, has retained the leadership and *engages now in subordinating social class conflict to the interests of the state*. . . . In the age of absolutism . . . the authoritarian military state had nearly swallowed up society and its economic interests; only the reforms of Stein and Hardenberg again emancipated society from the state; and [monarchic constitutionalism] meant an organic association of society and state in which, however, the latter remained dominant.[3]

Liberal and conservative theoreticians of the first half of the 19th century, including Hegel, did not differentiate clearly between the monarchical and parliamentary principle in a constitutional regime. The conservative theoreticians showed little interest in elaborating a distinction between their own country and conservative England, since they were more interested in fighting the principles of the French Revolution. But when England clearly developed into a parliamentary regime, the leading conservative theoretician of the Prussian cause, Friedrich Julius Stahl, came for-

[3] *Op. cit.,* 387 f. My emphasis.—Hintze's comparison appears to me compatible with the view that in Anglo-Saxon countries, too, the state increasingly acquired a mediating function in the course of democratization and industrialization; witness Lloyd George's reforms at the end of the period. The point is that in some Western countries the state became, so to speak, an instrument of the industrializing pluralist society for the balancing of diverse class and group interests. Governmental bureaucracies develop vested interests, but American higher civil servants, for example, do not form a status group as did the Prussian civil service. Cf. Reinhard Bendix, *Higher Civil Servants in American Society* (Boulder: University of Colorado Press, 1949); cf. also Max Weber's critique of the German bureaucracy in my Ch. XI, 299 ff.

ward with the purposively distinct principle of monarchic constitutionalism.[4] The Prussian constitution of 1850 implicitly followed this principle, and the policies of Frederick William IV certainly corresponded to it, though he would rather have been a more personal absolute ruler. The principle became decisive for German historical development when Bismarck came into power and affirmed it as the basis for his self-image as chancellor and prime minister.

Bismarck considered monarchical constitutionalism an appropriate form for Prussia and the Reich in view of the heterogeneity of both. In addition to the important regional cleavage between East Elbia and Prussia's western provinces, there were great regional differences in the Reich. The religious cleavage was more pronounced in the Empire than in any other European country. Besides the political cleavages attendant to the regional and religious differences, there were party differences independent of them. Since the Reichstag was constitutionally excluded from responsibility for government policies, the parties were socio-economic and religious pressure groups rather than political organizations responsible to the whole nation (as was possible under parliamentarism).[5] Bismarck encouraged the development of parties

[4] F. J. Stahl (1802–61) opposed the status quo in the thirties and lost his professorship, but after the 1848 revolution he became the most effective conservative spokesman. His philosophy of state derived the state from the Divine order of the world and vigorously maintained the Divine right of kings. As staff member of the important conservative *Kreuz-Zeitung* he played a great role in public opinion. He was highly regarded by the romanticist Frederick William IV and influential in shaping the Prussian constitution of 1850 along conservative lines.

[5] For Hintze the existence of the great cleavages precluded parliamentarism in Prussia, the Reich and, on the highest level, in the Double Monarchy, since parliamentary government required a considerable degree of homogeneity in a country. He referred to Switzerland and the United States as other examples of very heterogeneous countries unable to afford this form of government. Cf. *op. cit.*, 381 and 400 ff. It should be added that Hintze personally preferred the system of monarchic constitutionalism over parliamentarism, as did most other academicians. He hoped that the "monarch,

as interest groups. This permitted the government to rule by the principle of *divide et impera* and by the compromise policies of *do ut des*. In practice, however, the government could only work with a coalition of conservatives and Catholic Center or conservatives and moderate liberals, since the left-wing liberals and the Social Democrats were interested in changing the system of monarchical constitutionalism into a parliamentary monarchy or even a republic.

Bismarck did not hesitate to use the constitutional imperatives, as he defined them, against the king and against the popular representation. Twice, in 1857 and 1866, he prevailed on the king not to change the constitution in the crown's favor. The second time, Bismarck was interested in mitigating the conflict with the liberals because of his foreign policy plans. In the mid-sixties, he ruled unconstitutionally by disregarding the budgetary rights of parliament to enable a reorganization of the army; however, he was also willing to compromise, if the same purpose was served. Without an army capable of victory over Austria and France, he could not hope to unify Germany.

In 1882 Bismarck gave the Reichstag a lecture on the reasons why a strong king and army, not a strong parliament, had been necessary for unification. This was an attack on the parliamentary conceptions just propounded by Hänel, a prominent progressive. Bismarck reminded the deputies that the king of Prussia "had been in complete possession of power, in legislative and in every other respect, when the constitution was given" in 1850. He considered it very fortunate that the king's successor, William I, had not consented to a parliamentary form of government in the early sixties: If William I had selected the ministers according to the liberal majority and had followed its foreign policy precepts, the army would not have been reorganized. Bismarck concluded:

---

as a representative of the idea of the state" rather than of the "legitimistic-religious idea," would be able to cope with the "democratic tendencies of the present period" (*op. cit.,* 412).

The gentlemen in parliament had such a limited understanding of the political possibilities in Europe that they did not recognize that if they wanted German unification the first requisite was a strong Prussian army and the signature of the king of Prussia.[6]

When Bismarck established the Reich in 1871, he was confronted with the problem of balancing the demands of the middle class with those of the aristocracy, since he believed it necessary for the stability of the Reich to have a strong army as well as a prosperous middle class. The army was needed for the protection of the new Empire, surrounded by major powers (Russia, Austria, France); and it served as a guarantee of domestic peace. The liberal middle classes were needed for carrying out the legislative work of unification through the Reichstag. Bismarck incorrectly anticipated that the ruling houses of the other German states would try to slow down unification. Representatives of the middle classes could work in parliament on legislation and discuss all political issues, but they could not determine the domestic and especially the foreign policy; they could vote on military appropriation, but the army was directly and completely an instrument of the king and emperor. The showdown of the early sixties had proven that even the parliament's refusal to grant military appropriations could not weaken the power of the king and army.

Bismarck used the power of his office and of the constitution to suppress the cleavage embodied in the domestic enemies of his specific setup of the Reich: the Prussian conservatives, the Catholic Center party and the Social Democrats. The old conversatives were the pillar of the Prussian monarchy, but when their social and material interests were infringed upon they often turned against the Reich and, not infrequently, against the Prussian crown. They adhered first to dynastic and specifically Prussian values, rather than national values, and later they concentrated most successfully on

[6] Bismarck in the Reichstag on Jan. 24, 1882, reprinted in Rothfels, ed., *op. cit.*, 280.

agrarian pressure-group policies. At first their power was based on institutional prerogatives, which gave them a dominant role in the army and administrative control on the village and county level in East Elbia. When the small towns and peasants gained self-administration in the early seventies, antagonism against the aristocratic landowners diminished and the conservatives picked up many rural votes. Bismarck clashed with the conservatives several times and held them at bay. Only a strong chancellor of the Reich and minister-president of Prussia or a personally strong monarch could keep them in check. Thus the system of monarchical constitutionalism failed to insure automatically the predominance of the government. The Prussian government never became wholly a government of the Conservative party; the party, however, often exerted a veto power. After Bismarck's dismissal in 1890, neither his successors nor William II were able to restrain the conservative landowners from the single-minded pursuit of their political and economic group interests, nor were they able to wring from them political concessions deemed necessary for the survival of the Reich.[7] The three-class suffrage functioned to keep the conservatives permanently in power, once they had gained control of the Prussian diet in the wake of the National Liberal collapse of the late seventies.

During the first years of the Reich many Prussian aristocrats resented the profits of the urban middle classes from unification and French reparations. For decades the East Elbian landowners continued to oppose industrialization because of the rapid social changes it brought about. Their opposition was shared by the Center party, the second great opponent of Bismarck's Reich, which united federalist groups from all strata—aristocrats, priests,

[7] Bismarck's first successor, Caprivi, was under strong pressures from the conservatives because of his liberalization of protective tariffs. Hohenlohe maneuvered cautiously and sometimes won on political issues. Bülow resigned in 1909 when the conservative refusal to accept inheritance taxes for increased military expenditures destroyed his conservative-liberal coalition. Bethmann-Hollweg was unable to initiate suffrage reforms in Prussia.

farmers and workers, most of them Catholics. These groups were against the economic rise of the middle classes and against the political predominance of Prussia. The different class interests were so strongly accentuated that many Catholic middle-class persons in the Rhineland and southern Germany continued to support Bismarck and the National Liberals, despite the conflict with the Catholic church.[8] Bismarck resented the Center party especially because of its alliance with the Catholic Polish provinces and its agitation among the workers. The Catholic church and the Center party encouraged a labor movement independent of the liberal bourgeoisie, but dependent on them. Class cleavage was particularly severe in areas where the workers were predominantly Catholic and the managers Protestant, such as in Upper Silesia.

In the seventies the third political opponent of the Reich, the Social Democratic labor movement, was much less strong than the others but even less compatible with the structure of the Reich. Because of his fight against the Center party and the conservatives and his fear of a Catholic coalition between France and Austria, supported by south German Catholics, Bismarck viewed the Social Democrats, in the short run, as a minor threat. However, he considered them a great potential danger to the social and political order of the Reich; he saw the paramount danger to his system and to European society in cumulative tendencies toward a lower-class revolution, basically perceived in the image of the French Revolution rather than of Marx's proletarian revolution. He was

[8] Bismarck and the liberals fought the so-called *Kulturkampf* against the Catholic church from 1872 until 1887. It began after the new papal dogma of infallibility had resulted in a split within German Catholicism. The government recognized the small independent German Catholic church; this was the beginning of protracted struggles leading to the expulsion of the Jesuits and the arrest of bishops. The church and the Center party eventually emerged as the winners; from then on the party was willing to support the government in exchange for extensive concessions. Only three measures of the *Kulturkampf* survived: the supervisory right of the state over clerical affairs, state supervision of schools, and civil marriage.

convinced that the two supreme dangers to the Reich were an international war, uniting Germany's neighbors against her, and an international revolution; a revolutionary situation in Germany and other countries was most likely to arise after a concerted attack of major European powers on Germany. Bismarck tried to coordinate his diplomacy and domestic policy in order to forestall such a possibility.[9] However, as in his fight against the Catholic church and the Center party, he exaggerated foreign policy motives in his advocacy of antisocialist legislation. He emphasized the support such a legislation would provide to the precarious position of the Tsar in his struggle with social and pan-Slavic revolutionary forces.[10] As Hans Rothfels has pointed out, it would be wrong to consider this argumentation as evidence for the thesis, adhered to by many German historians, of the primacy of foreign policy.[11] Bismarck often hid his domestic intentions behind arguments of foreign

[9] Rothfels, ed., *op. cit.,* XLVII.

[10] This weakness of Tsarism was not recognized by the labor movement. In their *rapprochement* with nationalism after the turn of the century, the Social Democrats were strongly influenced by what they perceived as the deadly threat of Tsarism. They took the appearance of overpowering strength of the Russian regime at face value. In a memorandum to William II, in Feb. 1918, the Prussian minister of the interior, Drews, linked the strong impression which the Russian revolution of 1917 made on the Social Democrats with their overestimation of the power of the Tsarist regime. Cf. Erich Volkmann, *Der Marxismus und das deutsche Heer* (Berlin: Hobbing, 1925), reprint in the appendix, 309 f.

[11] Cf. Rothfels, *loc. cit.* The idea of the primacy of foreign policy which gained currency, as a normative and empirical concept, because of the events leading up to German unification was explicitly rejected by Drews. He explained to the Emperor that domestic issues in Germany were more crucial than foreign issues, in contrast to other countries where parliamentary majorities could be formed on the basis of agreements in foreign policy. Linked to domestic cleavages, struggles over issues of foreign policy were bitter in Germany. Drews charged that the right-wing parties were responsible for delaying the suffrage reform in Prussia, which would have to be carried through by the crown, if consensus on foreign policy was to be preserved. Thus, to the very end of the Reich the irreconcilable cleavage between right and left continued which made the authoritarian regime so vulnerable to the domestic consequences of outside military defeat. Cf. Volkmann, *loc. cit.*

policy, since he could in this way more easily manipulate public opinion. The fight against the Catholic church and the Social Democrats was primarily a domestic matter.

Bismarck believed that the government could not offer enough to the Center party, the Social Democrats and also the Progressives to commit them permanently to the Reich as he had established it.[12] As he had feared, these three groups were to unite in the hour of military defeat to establish the parliamentary republic. He hoped that a strong authoritarian system could indefinitely prevent the revolutionary potential from becoming active; he considered it much too dangerous to make concessions to the masses, trying to integrate them into the political process. This was one of his reasons for refusing to grant even the moderate demands of the liberals for more parliamentary rights. He judged the bourgeoisie incapable of holding its ground against the lower classes. Because of its lack of military power and its universalist ideals existing side by side with its particularistic convictions about the importance of property and education, the bourgeoisie had a tendency to make concessions when hard pressed. To Bismarck every step in the direction of genuine mass participation in politics meant a strengthening of the revolutionary force which would first produce chaos and then Caesarist dictatorship. He was correct in assuming that greater bourgeois participation would probably be followed by more concessions to the labor movement, but he failed to recognize that this might stabilize the Reich rather than precipitate its downfall.

Although Bismarck had a basic difference with the liberals, he shared many of the prevailing liberal ideas. He believed that the educated and propertied classes were the real support of the state; through their influence the agitation of ambitious demagogues and the appetites of the masses could be controlled; the masses were not responsible for themselves and easily fell prey to dictatorship.

[12] Cf. Bismarck, *Gedanken, op cit.,* Vol. 3, 1921, 131.

He did not want Germany to run "the French circle." [13] After his dismissal by William II in 1890, he emphasized the importance of a free press and modern parliament in providing a countervailing power against the ruling monarch and his bureaucracy. He felt that the best intentions of the most idealistic monarch can bring ruin if there is no effective check on his power. But as long as he was chancellor, he did everything to prevent the rise of such a countervailing force. On the other hand, he was clearly aware of the dangers of a permanently dissatisfied bourgeoisie. In some of his many speeches from retirement he stated that he feared the dissatisfaction of the educated and propertied classes more than dissatisfied masses which, he believed, could be pacified by material improvement or crushed by the army.[14]

In another of these speeches he maintained that stable government was possible only "if we manage to refrain from extremes and if we concentrate on those opinions which are represented by the educated bourgeoisie." [15] He regretted the appeal for votes from the lower classes and reiterated his policy of uniting the moderate conservatives and the National Liberals in order to create a stable majority in the Reichstag. Compromise, he said, is an essential element of a constitutional state. He criticized the parties for believing that each might eventually win an absolute majority, and urged the "merger of the moderate parties which represent the educated bourgeoisie." [16] This makes it clear that he well-nigh equated

[13] This paragraph summarizes Bismarck's arguments in *Gedanken, op. cit.,* Vol. 2, 59 f.

[14] Cf. address before 700 secondary schoolteachers in Friedrichsruh, April 18, 1895, in H. Kohl, ed., *Die politischen Reden des Fürsten Bismarck* (Stuttgart: Cotta, 1905), Vol. 13, 326 f.

[15] "Ansprache an die Südwestdeutschen," Kissingen, July 24, 1892, in Kohl, ed., *op. cit.,* 110 f. This speech was addressed to a relatively liberal middle-class audience of 5,000 southwest Germans, including bank directors, lawyers, factory owners and their families. As in the case of the address to secondary schoolteachers, his emphasis may have been influenced somewhat by the composition of his audience.

[16] *Loc. cit.*

"educated" with "moderate," the latter implying acceptance of the political framework he had set up.[17]

There was, then, little room in Bismarck's Reich for the direct participation of the bourgeoisie in government, except through the mediation of the chancellor or through personal relations with the emperor, as in the later case of William II. If Bismarck's system was to work, there was no place for an independent working-class movement. He could not accommodate a potential mass movement which would strengthen the forces of parliamentarism. Arthur Rosenberg's conclusion that "the structure of the Empire did not, indeed, permit anything but the repression of the working class," [18] is correct if we also include isolation under repression. After an abortive attempt at direct suppression, isolation became the major means of keeping the labor movement in check.

2. *Bismarck's Attack Upon Parliamentarism and Social Democracy*

Bismarck consistently acted on his understanding of the balance of forces necessary for the preservation of the Empire. In the late seventies he began to attack the liberals. Economic developments played a considerable role in Bismarck's policy change. In the early seventies the government outdid the liberals in its laissez-faire trade policies. Its attitude changed, however, when the postwar boom was ended by the international depression of the mid-seventies and foreign industrial and agricultural competition increased sharply. In the decade after 1867, Bismarck had a successful working agree-

---

[17] Bismarck did not, of course, mention that he had broken the liberal majority in the Reichstag. He preferred a compliant coalition of liberal and conservative parties or a liberal-conservative government party to an independent majority party.

[18] Rosenberg, *op. cit.,* 21 f.

ment with the National Liberals. Through it, a vast number of legislative and administrative problems of unification, ranging from a code of civil and commercial law to the reform of currencies and measurements, were solved. Since Bismarck needed liberal support for higher taxes and for the *Kulturkampf,* the liberals opportunely asked for extended parliamentary rights—in particular for greater budgetary rights in the Prussian diet. Confronted in the late seventies with the alternatives of making more concessions to the liberals or to the conservatives, Bismarck resolutely decided in the latter's favor, and a new era of restoration began. He used the issues of tariffs and of antisocialist legislation to destroy his old liberal majority. He also hoped that the new tariff income would make the Reich independent of the financial contributions of the States and even allow him to give money to them. This exchange would have weakened the position of the States vis-à-vis the Reich and adversely affected the budgetary control exerted by the Reichstag and the State parliaments.

Until 1877 the National Liberal party had a strategic position in the Reichstag; it was able to form a majority with the conservatives as well as with the Progressives. Until the mid-seventies, National Liberal relations with the progressives were good; they deteriorated when antagonism between Bismarck and the Progressives over the military appropriations became more intense. In the elections of 1877, the two parties fought each other and emerged weakened in relation to the conservative parties. The National Liberals failed to win enough seats to retain their strategic position between right and left, but despite their increasing weakness, the liberals continued to refuse passage of antisocialist bills. Many liberals did not care to strengthen the government beyond the extraordinary powers that they had given it for fighting the Catholic church. Even after the first attempt on the life of William I in 1878, the Reichstag voted, 243 to 60, against the proposed legislation; but when the second attempt occurred, Bismarck used public hysteria and bourgeois fear of the "red danger" to dissolve the parliament. He saw his chance to split the National Liberals: the left wing was for free trade and against antisocialist legislation, while the right wing wanted to follow the trends in bourgeois public opinion and to compromise with the government. Bismarck weakened the liberals in the elections, especially the left wing of the National Liberals. The National Liberal party was now ready to consent to antisocialist legislation, although it considerably softened the government's proposal. The final bill passed with 221 to 149 votes; it outlawed all permanent Social Democratic organizations and nearly all unions, but it permitted campaign activities before elections and the sending of Social Democratic deputies into the Reichstag. This attenuation undermined much of the long-run effectiveness of the antisocialist law.[19]

The defeat in 1878 of the National Liberals and the Progressives was a turning point in German history. Soon afterwards, in 1881, the National Liberal party split over the tariff issue. Its left wing was firmly committed to laissez-faire principles, as were the Progressives. In seven years, 1874 to 1881, the party sank from the dominating position of 152 seats to 45 seats. The liberal majority was definitely destroyed and liberalism divided into several factions. Bismarck skilfully took advantage of the rise of industrial and agrarian interest groups. In 1874 Reichstag representatives from the industrial regions formed an inter-party association for protective tariffs. Then the *Verein der Steuer-und Wirtschaftsreformer* (Association of Tax and Economic Reformers) was founded; and in 1876 the *Zentralverband deutscher Industrieller* was founded by the leader of the Free Conservatives, von Kardorff. When Bismarck turned against the National Liberal notables they proved particularly vulnerable to the attack because they often had no party machine or interest group to support them. For the same reason,

[19] The major provisions of the law are reproduced in Bertrand Russell, *German Social Democracy* (London: Longmans, Green, 1896), 100 ff; too late for consideration came Wolfgang Pack, *Das parlamentarische Ringen um das Sozialistengesetz Bismarcks 1878–1890* (Düsseldorf: Droste Verlag, 1961).

the educated liberal deputies from the cities lost their rural districts to the conservatives.[20] Until the eighties the liberals drew considerable strength from the Protestant countryside. Then the conservatives appealed to strictly agrarian interests and built up farmers' organizations, which proved to be very efficient interest groups.

After the exodus of the left wing of the National Liberals, the dividing line between left and center no longer ran through the party. The liberal left formed the Advanced Liberal party (*Freisinn*) in 1884, to which most of the prominent liberals belonged: Richter, Rickert, Hänel, Virchow, Bamberger, Schrader and others. This was a large group of 106 deputies. Bismarck set out immediately to destroy them. He kept the public continuously disquieted about the Social Democratic party and again exploited the bourgeois fear of the "red spectre." Friedrich Naumann points out that from the perspective of 1910, it is hardly comprehensible how much concern the small Social Democratic party evoked; it had only about 30,000 members in 1875 and from 9 to 12 deputies in the Reichstag between 1874 and 1881.[21] Before the elections of February 1887, half of the seats in the diet were held by the Center party, the Social Democrats, and the advanced liberals. Bismarck dismissed the old diet after they vigorously opposed his demand for appropriation of the military budget for seven years. He formed an alliance of the two conservative parties and the National Liberals: the so-called "cartel." The campaign was the most vigorous organized up to that time; Bismarck whipped up public hysteria again

---

[20] Cf. Rosenberg, *op. cit.*, 14; for statistics on the decline of liberalism in rural districts, 29. In contrast to the liberals, the Center party could fall back on the organizational strength of a universal church and the religious commitments of its followers in its struggle with Bismarck. Bismarck had hoped to weaken the party by ending the *Kulturkampf* at the same time that he smashed the National Liberals. But from 1874 until 1912, the party held between 91 and 106 seats. Since Bismarck destroyed his own liberal majority in 1878, he frequently had to rely on the Center party's support from that time on. With the exception of the period from 1887 to 1890, the Center retained its strategic position until 1906 and resumed it again in 1909.

[21] Cf. Naumann, *op. cit.*, 34 ff.

and finally got the kind of governmental Reichstag he wanted. The total vote was larger than ever before; from this time the established pattern brought defeat to the left whenever the right made an all-out nationalist appeal against the enemy inside and outside of the Reich. Bülow was later to repeat this strategy in the "Hottentot" elections of 1907, so called because of the greatly exaggerated importance of colonial issues. A new record turnout occurred in these 1907 elections.[22]

The great hope of the advanced liberals, and one explanation for their frequent ideological and tactical rigidity, was the prospect that Crown Prince Frederic would side with them when he succeeded William I as emperor.[23] Because of the authoritarian structure of the Reich, a liberal on the throne, or at least a man sympathetic to the liberal cause, would best be able to facilitate the development of parliamentarism. Bismarck was much concerned about this possibility; he managed to weaken the advanced liberals so rapidly that the Crown Prince felt compelled to move toward the right in order to insure satisfactory public support once he should become emperor. Frederick III had no chance to prove himself; he died three months after William I, in 1888.

Despite the recklessness with which Bismarck fought the liberals, he did not, in these later years, harbor the intense hostility against them that he did against the politically isolated Social Democrats. By 1878, he considered it possible that the labor movement might, in the long run, become a greater revolutionary threat than the liberals had ever been. From the very beginning of the labor movement, there had been no lack of interference by the police and other governmental agencies, but until the mid-seventies

[22] From 1871 to 1884 participation of those entitled to vote increased from 51 per cent to 60.6 per cent; in 1887 it suddenly rose to 77.5 per cent; in 1907 it jumped to 84.7 per cent.

[23] In a famous letter of 1863, the Crown Prince had advised Bismarck against violating the constitution. Reprinted in Robert Saitschick, *Bismarck und das Schicksal des Deutschen Volkes* (Basel: Reinhardt, 1949), 85 f; for other quotations on the liberalism of the future Frederick III, see p. 86., *op. cit.*

the government of the Reich did not attempt nation-wide suppression. During the middle of the sixties, when Bismarck played with the idea of using Lassalle against the liberals,[24] police and courts remained active against the labor associations. The laws on association, promulgated during the counter-revolution of the fifties, made it nearly impossible for a labor organization to escape conflict with the authorities. The Lassallean organization in Berlin was first dissolved by the police in July 1865; and Bernhard Becker, Lassalle's first successor, was banished from the capital.

The uprising of the Paris Commune in the spring of 1871 seemed to socialists and the public to be a major manifestation of a trend toward a proletarian revolution in Europe. The governments were greatly concerned about the Commune and the First International, even though the latter was very weak and planned no direct overthrow of any government. Diplomatic exchanges and international conferences took place among the major governments.[25] Bismarck began to consider major legislation against the antipatriotic and internationalist Social Democrats. He did not want a Social Democratic mass vote added to that of the Center party and the Polish Nationalist party, groups which already disturbed the smooth working of his system. The 1874 election returns showed a marked increase of socialist votes. In 1871 the two socialist parties had obtained 102,000 votes and one seat in the Reichstag; in 1874 they drew 352,000 votes and gained nine seats. Bismarck was now ready to resort to extensive repression: The Prussian police stepped up its policy of harassing the labor movement. In March 1876 the recently united Social Democratic party was suspended in all of Prussia.

Bismarck's federal antisocialist legislation of 1878 had its desired effect upon the liberals by disuniting them, but he was not satisfied with its effect upon the Social Democrats. One of the most

[24] Cf. Gustav Mayer, "Der Allgemeine Deutsche Arbeiterverein und die Krise von 1866," *Archiv für Sozialwissenschaft,* Vol. 57, 1927, 167 f.
[25] Paul Kampffmeyer and Bruno Altmann, *op. cit.,* 76–92.

severe measures, the expulsion of Social Democratic functionaries from their place of residence, had an unforeseen consequence. The displaced Social Democrats went to areas where the party was weak and started successful organization drives and campaigns. Compared to contemporary Russian practice and later historical examples, the antisocialist legislation was moderate repression. There was no deportation of "undesirable elements" as in Russia; there was no Siberia. Although Bismarck wanted to expatriate and deport functionaries, he failed to persuade the liberals to make antisocialist legislation more strict. The liberal belief in the *Rechtsstaat* was strong; many liberals also remembered the treatment received from Bismarck during the sixties. As long as the Social Democratic movement did not increase by leaps and bounds, Bismarck was willing to accept the limitations of the law. In 1890, however, a situation arose in which the complete suppression of the Social Democrats or the eventual destruction of the Reich appeared to him as the only alternatives.

After some fluctuations in the early years of the antisocialist legislation, the Social Democrats nearly doubled their vote—from 763,000 in 1887 to 1,427,000 in 1890. Instead of eleven seats in 1887, when "the Social Democrats were scarcely more strongly represented in the Reichstag than was the Polish Nationalist party," [26] they now had 35 seats. Bismarck lost his majority of 1887. He considered the situation critical; the votes of all opposition groups—including the Center, Poles, Alsatians, Danes and Guelphs—had risen, in a time of peace and prosperity, to 40 per cent of the total vote. Bismarck began to advocate a revision of the electoral law through a legal change of the constitution or through a *coup d'état*. Both were difficult to accomplish. First, a Reichstag majority that would curtail its own powers could not be found. Second, the ruling monarchs were not inclined toward radical constitutional changes. As early as 1884 Bismarck let the Federal Council declare

[26] Rosenberg, *op. cit.,* 20 f.

that the Empire was a federation of ruling monarchs who could dissolve it at will. However, such a radical "legal" move would have been indistinguishable from a *coup d'état*. Bismarck conceded that his proposals could be interpreted in different legal ways. However, he stated in his memoirs, in a passage which remained unpublished for a long time and which reveals his exalted interpretation of the minister's role under monarchic constitutionalism:

I have never doubted that, in a severe crisis, a minister must advise his monarch to stage a *coup d'état,* and then be personally responsible for the consequences, rather than let his fatherland succumb to anarchism and the state perish before his eyes. I would not let the sentence come true, "C'est la légitimité qui nous tue," but would disregard legitimacy. If this should fail, then fighting it out is still more decent and less irremediable than sinking into a moral morass. . . . A state which fights for its very existence does not make its decisions dependent upon the advice of law faculties.[27]

Such a determined minister needed a compatible monarch, and this William II was not, neither in temperament nor in age. Shortly before the latter ascended the throne, Bismarck wrote him a programmatic letter in which he exhorted the man who was to abandon his throne 30 years later:

I perceive the most solid support of the monarchy in a ruler who is ready not only to participate actively in the affairs of state in quiet times, but also to die for his right in critical times, falling with the sword in his hand on the steps of his throne rather than to yield. Such a ruler no German soldier will desert; and the old rhyme of 1848 remains true: "Gegen Demokraten helfen nur Soldaten." (The only appropriate weapon against democrats are soldiers.)[28]

[27] Otto von Bismarck, *Die gesammelten Werke.* Gerhard Ritter and Rudolf Stadelmann, eds. (Berlin: Deutsche Verlags-Gesellschaft, 1932), Vol. 15, 449 and 637.

[28] Bismarck added, with venom against Court Chaplain Stoecker and his attempts to woo the workers and the lower middle classes with his Christian Social Program: "Priests can spoil much in this regard and are of little use;

Bismarck tried to convince William II that "the Social Democrats produced, more than foreign countries, a danger of war for monarchy and state, and that they should be viewed by the government in terms of a military and power problem, not a legal problem." [29] The young emperor, however, was not interested in a military showdown, but in the enhancement of his popularity. He even hoped, for a short time, to win the workers by a substantial extension of welfare legislation. Conservative ministerial officials introduced, in the wake of the antisocialist legislation, comprehensive welfare legislation to prove to the workers that the Crown did not oppose them as workers, that it was serious in fulfilling its patriarchal obligations, neglected in the governmental laissez-faire period. Bismarck was correctly skeptical about the desired effect on the political attitudes of the workers; he feared that the welfare legislation might interfere with business interests. Despite his switch to a limited tariff policy, he continued to share some of the views of laissez-faire liberals. He objected to the Imperial Address on social welfare legislation of 1890, arguing that workers should not be forbidden by law "to control freely their own working-time and work opportunities and those of their families." [30] But he differed from the laissez-faire liberals in his insistence that positive social reforms could only be carried out by the king and his officials, not by voluntary associations. He added that voluntary associations were good only "as weapons for the attack on and destruction of the existing conditions, not for their preservation and improvement." [31]

---

the countries most pious towards priests are also the most revolutionary; in 1848 all clergymen supported the government in religious Pomerania, but the countryside voted socialist: all day-laborers, innkeepers and small merchants." From a letter to Prince William on Jan. 6, 1888. The letter warned him of committing himself to Stoecker's program. *Gedanken und Erinnerungen, op. cit.,* Vol. 3, 16 f.

[29] *Op. cit.,* 42.

[30] *Loc. cit.*

[31] *Op. cit.,* 21.

Bismarck maneuvered for a stiffer antisocialist law, but achieved only a lapse of the old law by default: the majority of the Reichstag was in favor of retaining antisocialist laws, but the liberal left did not want a stricter law, and the right wing rejected the old law as too lenient. Bismarck planned a *rapprochement* with the Center, which displeased William II at the time, and he finally fell by opposing new welfare legislation.[32]

However, William II was very soon disappointed with what he saw as the workers' ingratitude and moved closer to Bismarck's position, but he did not seriously consider a *coup d'état* for fear of having to call Bismarck back. Other German monarchs gave him negative advice about the *coup d'état*.[33] Bismarck tried to advance his plans through newspapers which were loyal to him and through parliamentarians such as the Free Conservative leaders Kardorff and Stumm-Halberg. He considered a constitutional crisis his best chance to stage a come-back. Inextricably fusing genuine concern and tactical exaggeration, he told Kardorff in December 1895 that it must be "a matter of course for serious, practical politicians . . . to counteract the eventual desires of socialist majorities to turn the Reichstag into a Convention" à la 1793.[34] However, many offi-

---

[32] On the fall of the antisocialist legislation against Bismarck's will, and for his clash with William II, see Bismarck, *op. cit.,* Vol. 3, Ch. 5. In his memoirs, Bismarck severely criticized William's attempt to reconcile the Social Democrats, "the worst enemy," and perceived the struggles over his relation to the Emperor and over social welfare legislation as resulting from an improper influence of "intrusive advisers such as Hinzpeter, Berlepsch, Heyden, Douglas . . . and career-minded generals" (*op. cit.,* 130). See also the memoirs of the leader of the Free Conservatives, *Wilhelm von Kardorff,* S. von Kardorff, ed. (Berlin: Mittler, 1936), 208–24, and of Friedrich von Holstein, *The Holstein Papers,* Norman Rich and M. H. Fisher, eds. (London: Cambridge University Press, 1955), 146–49.

[33] Cf. Bismarck, *op. cit.,* 79, and the 1895 memorandum to Hohenlohe by Philipp Eulenburg on a conversation with William II, in *Fürst Chlodwig zu Hohenlohe-Schillingsfürst,* A. von Müller, ed. (Stuttgart: Deutsche Verlagsanstalt, 1931), 99 ff, cited henceforth as Hohenlohe.

[34] Quoted in Fritz Hellwig, *Carl Ferdinand Freiherr von Stumm-Halberg* (Heidelberg: Westmark Verlag, 1936), 511.

cials were more concerned with the implications of interrupting the established governmental process than with the great *Kladdera-datsch,* as the potential lower-class revolution was colloquially called. They accepted the system of monarchic constitutionalism as Bismarck had set it up and resisted his attempts to tear it down with his own hands. This acceptance and the fear of Bismarck's revenge, if he should return to power, aligned many influential officials, including Holstein, the "grey eminence" of the foreign office, against a *coup d'état.*

Throughout the nineties chancellors Caprivi and Hohenlohe insisted on strict legality. They were twice under strong pressure from the Emperor, the Prussian Minister of the Interior, big business and the right-wing parties to pass new laws against the Social Democrats. Big business was angry about the resurgence of strikes;[35] the Emperor and the public were shaken by a wave of anarchist terror in 1894, which claimed the life of Carnot, the President of the French Republic.

At the time, the Emperor was increasingly receptive to the influence of Stumm-Halberg, the industrial tycoon who was one of the most vociferous champions of managerial paternalism and of the absolute authority of the state. After Carnot's assassination, Stumm-Halberg addressed a letter to Chancellor Caprivi explaining that the government's lack of vigor had resulted in its loss of prestige within "broad circles of the nation's best elements"; he hoped that the favorable moment of public excitement would not be missed for imposing antisocialist legislation.[36]

Chancellor Caprivi answered this remarkably blunt epistle with a no less remarkably cautious reply on July 8, 1894:

It seems to me that we have serious reasons for not introducing bills, while accepting their rejection or being content with the *diligentia*

[35] See the correspondence between the coal and steel magnates Fritz Krupp and Stumm-Halberg, *op. cit.,* 493 ff.
[36] *Op. cit.,* 500.

praestata—as was done in the seventies and eighties. The conditions of the Empire and of the state are too grave for such a policy. Once the government has made it clear through proposing a bill that the existing laws are insufficient, that much more rigorous ones are necessary, it cannot accept the rejection of such a proposal. Then it must be ready to dissolve the Reichstag and, if necessary, to take the most serious steps. Before deciding on such a move, the government must consider whether to take such steps at all or how to take them concretely. I do not want to mention the general difficulties for such extreme measures in the pluralist (*vielköpfige*) Empire. But the question cannot be avoided: If laws against the anarchists or Social Democrats are rejected, if new elections do not produce a better Reichstag, would we not merely promote the business of Social Democracy, increase dissatisfaction and produce new Social Democratic followers? These are very serious problems which have to be recognized clearly before one takes the first step.[37]

The government responded to the pressures exerted upon it by sporadically vigorous application of the *existing* laws. In the wake of Carnot's assassination, the Prussian Minister of the Interior, Botho Graf zu Eulenburg, unsuccessfully proposed the *Umsturzvorlage* (Antisubversion Bill). Caprivi and Eulenburg fought to a draw, which the exasperated Emperor attempted to remedy by dismissing both and by appointing the aging Prince Hohenlohe as a chancellor who would presumably be more pliant.[38] But the latter did manage to defeat the last attempt to impose new antisocialist legislation in 1898, the so-called *Zuchthausvorlage* (Penitentiary Bill). This was also a decisive defeat for Stumm-Halberg, whose influence on the Emperor declined because he had drawn him personally into the party struggles about social reform and Social

[37] *Op. cit.,* 501 f.

[38] Botho zu Eulenburg had energetically executed the antisocialist legislation between 1878 and 1881, when he resigned after a conflict with Bismarck. His predecessor was Friedrich Graf zu Eulenburg, who unsuccessfully asked the Reichstag in 1875 for legislation against the Social Democrats (see Ch. V, p. 107 f). He also resigned after a clash with Bismarck. The third Eulenburg, Philipp Graf zu Eulenburg, was the go-between for William II and the government, before he fell into disfavor.

Democracy. Monarchic constitutionalism, however, prescribed an indirect role to the emperor. William II's repeated attempts at personal rule failed because they intensified conflict among the very groups most committed to the authority of the monarchy. Prince Hohenlohe keenly perceived the requirements for the stability of the dominant system: "Only if a people is convinced, as it is in England, that its liberties will not be tampered with, will it be ready to vote conservative. The fear of Social Democracy must be greater and weigh more heavily than that of a *coup d'état.*" [39]

There were, logically, three alternatives for the government in the 1890's: (1) The complete repression of the Social Democrats, if necessary by a *coup d'état,* that is, by the abolition of the Reichstag or by the imposition of a new restrictive electoral law; (2) Democratization—by first giving the middle classes a greater share in government and by subsequently integrating the Social Democrats into the national community; (3) Continued isolation of the

[39] Hohenlohe, *op. cit.,* 99. The last time rumors of a *coup d'état* were in the air was during the *Daily Telegraph* Affair of 1908—so called after the publication of some views of William II on England and Germany. This time the supposed *coup* was directed against the Emperor. However, the most famous statement ever made in the Reichstag in favor of a *coup d'état* was unrelated to any concrete plan and merely a highly emotional declaration of allegiance to the monarch. In a debate on the desirability of greater parliamentary control of the army in 1910, Oldenburg-Januschau, the incarnation of the Prussian Junker, declared that the officers' corps was "an estate personally linked to the Supreme War Lord; the public has no business concerning itself with it. ('Very true' on the right, shouts on the left.) Yes, gentlemen, this too is an old Prussian tradition; that you don't like this tradition, I readily believe. The king of Prussia and the German emperor must be able at any moment to say to a lieutenant: Take ten men and close the Reichstag. (Great and lasting amusement. Unrest and shouts on the left, 'very true' on the right, repeated stormy shouts and unrest on the left.)"

For Oldenburg-Januschau this was not equivalent to the advocacy of a *coup d'état,* because the King of Prussia had affirmed in 1861 that he could give any order to the army without the consent of the minister of war who was constitutionally responsible. Appropriately enough, Oldenburg-Januschau broke down after his speech and wept. See *Reichstag Protocols,* 1910, 898 C, and Oldenburg-Januschau, *Erinnerungen* (Leipzig: Koehler, 1936), 108–13.

Social Democrats. Bismarck failed in his attempt at the first alternative before and after his dismissal. The second alternative was beyond the vision of William II and of his officials. The Emperor and the government elected the easiest course; they continued to isolate the labor movement while not blocking its expansion among the working class. This policy was persistently adhered to until the First World War, facilitated by the relatively constant strength of the German left between 1893 and 1906, when the Social Democrats made their advances partly at the expense of the advanced liberals, who also lost heavily to parties further to the right. In the short run, this policy of isolation was convenient; in the long run, it was bound to be dangerous in times of external crisis.

IV

Bourgeois and Social Democratic Attitudes Toward Revolution and Patriotism

With the increasing governmental policy of repression in the seventies the cleavage widened between the small but growing labor movement and the large bourgeois public, which was proud of the achievements of national unification and intolerant of any basic criticism of it. This chapter contrasts Social Democratic perspectives with those of general public opinion. As far as the evidence permits, I will distinguish the attitudes of articulate opinion-leaders from those of their public. I will select examples of the most extreme statements of the period in order to make clear what kinds of statements aroused intense hostility and also in order to indicate the degree to which they were largely rhetorical and, on balance, even restrained.[1] The issues of patriotism and revolution and, slightly less so, of idealism and materialism established a clear dividing line. The divergent attitudes will be illustrated in some detail in order to facilitate the reader's understanding of the highly charged political atmosphere.

1. The Issue of Revolution

Within the political setting of the sixties and the new national structure of 1871, the Social Democrats were radicals because of their democratic aspirations and socialist ideals—not because of any

[1] Chapters VI, VII and VIII, will also deal with moderate as well as unpublicized and inarticulate attitudes.

specifically Marxist tendencies, which played an insignificant role in the early years of the socialist movement.[2] A vague ideology of democratic and socialist reconstruction perturbed the conservative as well as the liberal public. Even if the Social Democrats had renounced all revolutionary rhetoric, as most unions actually did,[3] their social-democratic aims alone were bound to produce hostility on the part of a government committed to the perpetuation of the power structure of the Reich, and on the part of the conservative and liberal bourgeoisie. However, the Social Democrats did not eschew quasi-revolutionary rhetoric, though they tried to tone it down sufficiently to escape prosecution. They also adhered to their own patriotic values. Thus, hostility on both sides was aggravated by widely divergent attitudes toward unification and the Reich.

Friedrich Naumann remembers that the Social Democrats were considered dangerous because many of them, as well as a large part of the public, believed in the eventual possibility of a proletarian revolution.[4] Bismarck did his best to exaggerate the revolutionary danger of the labor movement. He viewed the uprising of the Commune with genuine concern as to its long-run implications, but, in the short run, he valued the tactical advantages accruing to him from this uprising. He observed with satisfaction in 1872 that the impact of the Commune had driven many Germans toward the right on the political continuum:

No attentive observer could fail to notice how extensive and massive the conversion from red to moderate liberalism has been in Germany, from moderate liberalism to conservative attitudes, from doctrinaire opposition to a feeling of interest in the state and of responsibility for it, since the *experimentum in corpore vili* which was carried through

[2] See the detailed discussion of this problem in Ch. VII.
[3] In order to avoid suppression by the police and the courts and in order to attract more members, many of the small unions of the seventies tried to be nonpolitical. Nevertheless, most unions were dissolved by the authorities in the late seventies.
[4] Cf. Naumann, *op. cit.,* 24.

by the Commune before Europe. France serves usefully as a deterrent example. If she were to play yet another act of the interrupted drama for Europe—I do not like to wish for that out of humane considerations—this would contribute even more strongly to the illumination of the benefits of a monarchic constitution and to the attachment to monarchic institutions in Germany.[5]

In 1878, when he manipulated the public hysteria about the two attempts on the life of William I, Bismarck told the Reichstag that he had fully recognized the dangers of the Social Democrats to state and society when its spokesmen "praised the Commune as a political model and openly embraced the gospel of those murderers and incendiaries." [6] Both the Eisenachers and the Lassalleans defended the uprising of the Commune and predicted that this suppression of the proletarian vanguard would precipitate more vigorous efforts of self-liberation on the part of the rising European proletariat. Bebel made a passionate address in the North German Reichstag on May 25, 1871, after the Commune had been bloodily suppressed:

You should be firmly convinced that the whole European proletariat and everyone who has still within him a feeling for freedom and independence looks to Paris. And though Paris is suppressed at the moment, I would like to remind you that the battle in Paris is merely a small skirmish of outposts, that the decisive events are still to come, and that within a few decades the battle cry of the Paris proletariat— "War on the palaces, peace for the huts, down with misery and idleness"—will be the battle cry of the whole European proletariat.[7]

The major Lassallean journal, the *Neue Socialdemokrat,* wrote on the Commune and on its implications for the future:

The mighty uprising of the proletarians, the June battle [of 1848], was followed by the mightier uprising of the Paris Commune; and the

[5] From a directive to the ambassador in Paris, Graf von Arnim, Berlin, Dec. 20, 1872; see Rothfels, ed., *op. cit.,* 269.
[6] Kohl, ed., *op. cit.,* 1893, Vol. 7, 267.
[7] *Reichstag Protocols,* May 25, 1871, 921.

latter will be followed by the mightiest uprising of the people for the social emancipation of the fourth estate. (1872, 98) . . .

. . . .

We German socialists must fight no less hard than our brothers, the proletarians of the other civilized countries (*Kulturländer*). Neither the heroic battle of the Paris Commune has been equaled elsewhere nor its glorious downfall, when it buried itself under the smoking ruins of Paris after being repressed with abominable atrocity by the Versailles henchmen. Now a movement is gripping the proletariat of the whole world. This movement will bring about new struggles with the same terrible effect until the class struggle will end with the victory of the fourth estate, with the triumph of socialism. (1873, 34) [8]

This Social Democratic attitude toward the Commune further antagonized the remnants of the democratic bourgeoisie.[9] The shock of middle-class persons about the Commune paralleled the horror which the terrorism of the French Revolution had evoked, and hurt socialism for some time in much the same way as it had liberalism. On the other hand, the Commune was bound to be an encouraging event for many a Social Democrat who morally rejected the existing society and vaguely hoped for an ultimate overthrow of the ruling classes. Nearly all of them realized, however, that the emergence of the powerful Bismarckian empire forestalled any revolution for some time to come.

The clash between bourgeois and Social Democratic attitudes can be documented particularly well through two contemporary books by bourgeois writers on the Social Democrats.[10] The authors, Reverend R. Schuster, a Protestant, and A. Held, a professor of

[8] Quoted in R. Schuster, *op. cit.*, 159 f. It should be added that many of these rhetorical outbursts suffer from considerable syntactical inadequacies which impede the translation.

[9] Cf. G. Mayer, *Schweitzer, op. cit.*, 415.

[10] See Schuster, *Die Social-Demokratie,* nach ihrem Wesen und ihrer Agitation quellenmässig dargestellt, 1875, *op. cit.* and A. Held, *Die deutsche Arbeiterpresse der Gegenwart,* 1873, *op. cit.*

political science and *Kathedersozialist,*[11] were representative of the most sophisticated bourgeois opinions; but their indignation and antipathy were shared, in similar and often aggravated form, by the bourgeoisie in general. Both authors quote extensively from the leading Lassallean and Eisenacher journals, the *Neue Socialdemokrat* and the *Volksstaat,* and from other Social Democratic publications; in fact, about half of Schuster's 232 pages are quotations. This has the advantage of placing the antagonistic attitudes and group perspectives next to one another, the authors' comments being a direct reaction to Social Democratic statements challenging the government and the bourgeoisie.

Most Social Democratic leaders were cautious in the choice of their radical vocabulary. However, the two most prominent radicals, the ex-student Wilhelm Hasselmann, a Lassallean, and Johann Most, an Eisenacher, indulged freely in colorful imagery and attracted particular attention from worried bourgeois observers.[12] In order to demonstrate the subversive intentions of the Social Democrats to his readers, Schuster quoted some of the revolutionary and military imagery of the *Neue Socialdemokrat,* edited by Hasselmann. The revolutionary climax is here envisaged as the advance of the "workers' battalions" who shout Lassalle's name as their battle cry:

The avalanche is rolling. We hope that it will grow bigger and bigger. Lassalle himself had heard the heavy steps of the workers' battalions. He visualized his avengers. Now the anticipated hour draws nigh. Already our enemies tremble at the mere sound of Lassalle's name: they tremble when the factory slave mutters his name with a heavy sigh; they tremble when the people in the street, drunk with enthusiasm,

[11] On the academic social reformers, the so-called "socialists of the chair," see Ch. VI, 136 ff.

[12] In the nineties both became prominent anarchists in the United States. Cf. Max Nomad, "Johann Most, Terrorist of the Word," in his *Apostles of Revolution* (Boston: Little, Brown, 1939), 256–301.

call it with glittering eyes; they tremble because they fear the great reckoning, they fear that some day hereafter the call to arms will be heard in the streets and the thundering cry—Lassalle—will rise from the phalanx of the proletarian battalions. Let us move ahead undismayed. Forward with Ferdinand Lassalle. (1871, 62) [13]

Hasselmann follows Lassalle's tactic of predicting a violent revolution *if* the ruling classes continue their old policies.[14] He quotes, for example, the old French revolutionary song "ça ira" and makes some threatening remarks about violence, but then he qualifies his statement:

Ah ça ira, ça ira
Les aristocrates a la lanterne.
Ah ça ira, ça ira.
Les aristocrates, on les prendra. . . .

When the people began to sing this fierce song, they did not just sing it. The men of the revolution were quick to act, and soon, here and there, the body of an aristocrat or cleric would hang from a lamp-post. This ça ira is a true warning. If the bourgeois felt their hearts beat and had a moral hangover from hearing this song during the struggle of the Paris Commune, we will not regret this. On our part, we would like them to consider that the fierce popular revenge of 1793 took place because the ruling classes interfered, through force and conspiracy, with the lawful development of the revolution. The French people would never have resorted to axe and rope if the treacherous aristocracy had not used force first. Only if the people find a peaceful way to their sacred rights blocked, will they hang and behead all traitors of the people without giving pardon. (1873, 13) [15]

[13] Quoted in Schuster, *op. cit.,* 160.
[14] This remained a standard Social Democratic argument. In a passionate speech on March 27, 1908 (*Reichstag Protocols,* 4351), Bebel warned that the revolution would be inevitable if the ruling classes refused to adjust themselves to the social changes which had produced a proletariat "which, in terms of political education and insight into the character of the state and of bourgeois society, has a greater sophistication than the bourgeoisie had fifty or sixty years ago."
[15] Quoted in Schuster, *op. cit.,* 161.

Another "if-statement" reaches its climax in the following metaphor: "If the ruling class does delay the peaceful, lawful social revolution for too long, the social revolution will break through violently with wildly streaming hair and iron sandals on her feet" (1871, 54). Schuster acknowledges that the revolution is made dependent on the "compromising or resistant attitude of the other social classes," but he considers this merely an attempt to shift responsibility to the latter according to the "ordinary gangster logic which makes the victim's resistance responsible for the harm done to him." [16] Schuster seems to believe seriously that the party leaders are aiming at a violent revolution, whereas the rank and file are ignorant about the real intentions of their leaders. As evidence for the revolutionary aspirations of the leadership he quotes from the *Proletarian Song-Book* (*Proletarier-Liederbuch*) edited by Johann Most. Among the examples he cites are the Workers' Marseillaise which was sung at the end of meetings, a revolutionary rephrasing of the famous Lutheran song "Ein' feste Burg ist unser Gott" and a "Proletarian Song" whose first verse may be approximately rendered in the following way:

A call resounds from land to land,
The poor should clasp each other's hand,
And call a halt to tyranny
And stop the slave's agony.
The drums are beaten dully,
The red flags flutter briskly:
   Let us live working or die fighting.[17]

[16] Schuster, *op. cit.*, 156.
[17] Quoted in Schuster, 162. The rephrasing of religious songs for political purposes must have offended many people besides parsons like Schuster. His political and religious sentiments were particularly offended by the following parody of the Lord's Prayer, describing the relationship between Bismarck and the National Liberals:
   Prince Bismarck who art in Varzin,
   Hallowed be thy name,
   Thy session come,

The quotations from Hasselmann's *Neue Socialdemokrat* and Most's *Proletarier-Liederbuch* exemplify the most radical appeals, made by leaders who were at least regionally influential among the workers. For Schuster they reveal a "most brutal fanaticism," "revolutionary passion" and "open preaching of bloody revolution." [18] They indeed show that a glowing image of revolution, arising from the historical examples of 1789, 1848 and 1871, appealed to Hasselmann, Most and a few others; but by their complete lack of concreteness, they also indicate the purely rhetorical character of this type of revolutionary threat. There was no mass base for such revolutionary sentiments. Held concludes in his analysis of the Social Democratic press in 1872 that revolutionary rhetoric and passion diminished in relation to the distance from party headquarters. [19] However, he notices a "general revolutionary spirit of bitterness" expressing itself in "a tendency to tackle practical problems energetically." The workers, he thinks, follow the Social Democratic leaders primarily because they are flattered by them and see them as their most active friends. [20]

In addition to revolutionary imagery, Hasselmann also used anti-Semitic rhetoric extensively. Most, who once defeated Court

---

Thy will be done in the [Prussian] deputies chambers as it is in the
  Reichstag.
Give us today our daily lesson,
And forgive us our speeches
As we forgive those of the [Prussian] Upper House;
Lead us not into temptation with legislation
But deliver us from all serious progress,
For thine is the *Reich,* and the glory and the power,
  Amen.

Quoted in Schuster, 43 and Held, 75, from the *Dresdener Volksbote,* 1872, 291, a paper of the Eisenachers.

[18] Schuster, *op. cit.,* 164.

[19] According to Schuster, there were about fifteen socialist newspapers before the merger of the parties in 1875. They appeared at least once a week. There were also eleven more or less socialist trade union papers. *Op. cit.,* 233 f.

[20] Held, *op. cit.,* 72 f.

Chaplain Stoecker in an open dispute before a mass meeting of workers,[21] engaged more than any other leader in antireligious propaganda to make workers officially abandon their church affiliation. To Reverend Schuster, as well as to most middle-class persons, this rhetoric was repulsive and sounded openly subversive. Therefore, they favored strong action by the government. Schuster was incensed about what he called the "anti-German activities" of the Eisenachers and heartily approved of the court sentences for Liebknecht and Bebel.[22] He saw in the Reich a guarantee against any revolutionary danger and asserted, with some justification, that the intransigence of the Eisenachers was partly due to their realization that the unification of the nation through Prussia had destroyed all short-run prospects for the revolutionary establishment of a democratic republic.[23]

The academic observer Held was more detached in his approach than Schuster. The same was true of the liberal leaders in the Reichstag in their relation to the bourgeois public. These leaders refused several times before 1878 to heed the government's plea for a comprehensive antisocialist legislation, justified by similar rhetorical evidence.[24] However, Held and the liberal party leaders did not necessarily have less bitter feelings about the Social Democrats than middle-class persons who were not politically sophisticated or committed to standards of academic objectivity. For example, Ludwig Bamberger, a liberal leader and banker, flatly called Hasselmann and Most "beasts" in an invidious comparison with the more congenial type of functionary prevailing in subsequent years, when the party no longer appeared a revolutionary danger to him.

Anyone who knew the Reichstag at the time when such beasts as Hasselmann, Most and their consorts were raging in its chambers, can scarcely recognize their successors in the deputies who, as reporters or

[21] Cf. Massing, *op. cit.,* 24 f.
[22] Cf. Ch. II, 53.
[23] Schuster, *op. cit.,* 23, 25, 29.
[24] Cf. Ch. V, 107.

chairmen of commissions cooperate in a friendly and *gemütliche* fashion with their colleagues to make small changes, for better or worse, in the bourgeois world. . . . Certainly, they have not abjured their belief in the wickedness and untenableness of present-day society but they have become too intelligent to believe any longer that the German state can be overthrown on the barricades and that, even if this were possible, barricades would really do away with [private] property.[25]

In general, the Eisenachers seem to have been less venomous and more cautious in their rhetoric than the Lassalleans. This may be seen from a comparison of Bebel's speech on the Commune with the general tone of Hasselmann's articles. For Professor Held and Reverend Schuster, however, the Eisenacher leadership was no less revolutionary, and the leaders themselves did not want to appear less revolutionary than the Lassalleans. Both Held and Schuster quote as proof of revolutionary mentality the concluding address of Chairman Geib at the first convention of the Social Democratic Workers' party at Eisenach in 1869:

There is a tree which bears golden fruit, but if those who planted it reach for the fruit it withdraws. A snake, guardian of the fruit, is wound around the tree. This tree is today's society; the snake stands for the present conditions which deny to us the enjoyment of the golden fruit. Gentlemen! We are determined to enjoy the golden fruit, to drive away the snake. If this is not possible in a peaceful fashion, we—as men who do not shrink back from action—will fell the old tree and plant a new, strong one. How can we best reach our goal? By implanting the spirit of brotherhood and liberty into the hearts of the workers and by clasping hands [i.e., by uniting] with our brothers in all parts of the world.[26]

This was certainly not a clear call to revolutionary action, addressed as it was to "gentlemen" (*meine Herren*). Also indicative of this is the fact that Geib dropped the metaphor when he came

[25] Ludwig Bamberger, *Wandlungen und Wanderungen in der Sozialpolitik* (Berlin, 1898), 18, quoted in Massing, *op. cit.,* 192.
[26] Convention protocol, p. 75, quoted in Schuster, *op. cit.,* 155 f. and Held, *op. cit.,* 19.

to the means to be employed, speaking merely of the international solidarity of the workers.

In order to bolster their case, Schuster and Held employ an auxiliary argument, frequently used at the time, that the Social Democrats had to be revolutionary even if they denied it or did not want it. *"Democracy* has no chance to achieve its goal peacefully since *society* [sic!] will not voluntarily submit," Schuster says, revealingly emphasizing the democratic rather than socialist character of the labor movement and identifying "society" with the middle and upper classes.[27] Held, too, contrasts democracy and middle-class interests:

If Lassalle asks in his *Open Address,* "What is the state?" and answers, "The great association of the poorer classes"—then this means that mass rule is to replace the now dominating influence of the educated and propertied classes. Since these classes will never voluntarily yield, this can only be achieved through a *democratic* revolution.[28]

The Eisenachers were vulnerable to this charge, since Liebknecht repeated again and again in the early seventies that the Social Democrats expected nothing from parliamentary activities, that they used them only for the purpose of agitation. Schuster quotes from Liebknecht's famous speech on this position and from an article in the latter's *Volksstaat,* in both of which the revolutionary character of the party was affirmed and parliamentary politics repudiated.[29] Of course, behind this emphasis on agitation stood also

[27] Schuster, *op. cit.,* 155, my emphasis.
[28] Held, *op. cit.,* 18, my emphasis.
[29] "The Social Democratic party is a revolutionary party; if it is lured onto the level of parliamentarism, it will cease to be revolutionary—to exist at all. We participate in the Reichstag elections and send deputies into the Reichstag exclusively for the purpose of agitation. The strength of our party rests in the people; there is our realm of activity; we should talk from the rostrum of the Reichstag only in order to address the people. If we move away from the revolutionary origin and character of our party, if we lose only for a moment the contact with the revolutionary people, we are up in the air and will be pitilessly strangled like that giant of antiquity [Antaeus]. [The Social Demo-

the realization that the party was too weak to be influential in parliament and that the Reichstag was constitutionally weak in relation to the government and the crown: "The Reichstag is powerless and merely hides the absolutism of the government." [30] For decades the Reichstag remained a sounding board for the party's agitation, but Liebknecht quickly dropped the revolutionary argument and affirmed the reformist and parliamentary character of the party when the antisocialist legislation approached; the party never returned to its earlier position.

Liebknecht's antiparliamentarism was based, to a large extent, on his bitter opposition to the Prussian solution of German unification. The problem of unification linked the issues of revolution and patriotism.

2. The Issue of Patriotism

From the very beginning of the Reich, the Social Democrats of both persuasions violently attacked the nationalist values embraced by a majority of the people. Until the outbreak of the First World War, the Social Democrats appeared to the great majority of the middle and upper classes not only as a potential threat to the established order but also as utterly unpatriotic, despite their protestations of their own kind of patriotism. The achievement of unification was considered as something so great by the majority of the middle classes that any fundamental opposition to the particular

---

cratic deputies] cannot be effective within the Reichstag, only outside of it; [they cannot be successful] through legislation, but only through agitation. The Reichstag should be only a means, not an end for them, not their area of activity, but a visible platform from which to address the people and to enlighten them about the true character of society, from the center of class domination." Liebknecht in the *Volksstaat,* 1874, 50, quoted in Schuster, *op. cit.,* 153 f.

[30] Id., 1874, 112, quoted in Schuster, *loc. cit.*

form of the Empire was perceived as a lack of patriotism. During the first years after unification, the differences in outlook and evaluation were articulated with special regard to the Reich, Bismarck, the military leaders and the Franco-German War.

Liebknecht's attacks in the *Volksstaat* were relentless, mixing historical truth and involved satire. Schuster's reactions reveal the exalted affirmation with which South German educated men viewed the Reich, Bismarck and the Prussian army during these years. The following synopsis contrasts the irreconcilable views:

Schuster's views:	*The views of the "Volksstaat":*
"The feeling of one's own worth at long last awakened in the breast of *every good German,* and the joy about the glorious and honorable history of our dear fatherland."	"150 per cent patriotism."
"The men who sacrificed goods and blood for the love of their fatherland and those who hold the fallen martyrs in high honor, those who are proud of the victories bought with their sacrifices and who consider the love of the fatherland the first virtue of the citizen."	"Murderous patriots."
"The attitude which the 'organ of the Social Democratic Workers' party' takes toward the events of the war and their effects, so *very advantageous* for the German fatherland, offends every German heart most deeply."	"The war became necessary because of Bismarck's policies of conquest." (1871, 84) "Diplomatic tricks à la Ems dispatch and as a last means blood and iron—this is the whole recipe of Prince Bismarck." (1872, 66) "Bismarck prepared the war long in advance; he played out the candidacy for the Spanish crown at the very moment when success seemed most assured." (1873, 74)

"Moltke, whose name is the most celebrated among the German army leaders, has, among many others, *for all times* a just claim to the gratitude of the German nation."

"Holy Moltke whether he writes voluminous volumes, as he has done, or 'keeps voluminous silence,' as it is alleged; Moltke whose value is to be sought in the speed of slaughter, the quantity and quality of the slaughtered; 'holy Moltke,' the nine-centimeter canon mounted on his skull, the Mauser rifle clenched in his teeth, the shrapnel detonators in his nostrils, the 'efficacious' sabre bayonet and the 'elegant' Uhlan lance in one hand, the endowment purse filled with captured funds in the other; this 'holy Moltke' is the queer enlightening figure of the 19th century." (1874, 35)

"Through all annual sets of the *Volksstaat* up to this day, the pervasive endeavor to deprecate the honor of the German arms is to be seen."

"The victory ecstasy has been cooled with a pail of water—and this the most amusing side of it —from a source whence one did least expect it: the Great Prussian General Staff, which best knows how the 'victories' were gained. From the book just published by the general staff we can glean two facts which are expressed there in meagre words: (1) that Prussia was already prepared for the war with France in 1869, and (2) that France was not prepared for the war with Prussia at the inception of the 'holy war.' The defeat of an unprepared, numerically inferior army—this is an accomplishment for which neither particular 'genius' nor bravery are necessary and which does not justify the chubby-faced fanfares of Bismarck's

G-r-r-reat national trumpeters."
(1872, 58) [31]

The quotations from the *Volksstaat* are not directly indicative of the attitudes of the Eisenachers toward the Reich and Bismarck but of the position with which Liebknecht confronted the readers of the major party journal sent to all members. At most, a few thousand Lassalleans and Eisenachers may have shared Liebknecht's intransigence in the early seventies. However, among them were hundreds of very active members who later influenced many thousands of workers. Furthermore, the increasing governmental repression facilitated, in the second half of the seventies, the spread of some of Liebknecht's attitudes and emotions.

Underlying the opposition of the Social Democrats to the Reich were patriotic values often articulated by their spokesmen. In 1889, for example, Liebknecht told the representatives of the other parties in the Reichstag that they were not the fatherland and that they were wrong in asserting that the workers loved their country less than they did. He argued that the Social Democrats were "a thousand times more patriotic" than the ruling groups because they wanted a "reasonable, comprehensive social reform" which would turn "Germany into the fatherland of happy and free men." [32]

Though Liebknecht's position derived from his experience as an intellectual, it may be assumed that workers liked to hear that they were better patriots than the ruling classes because they fought for social and economic improvements. Such an argument was most important, since the ruling groups typically expected the labor movement to bear the proof that their aspirations and activities were not detrimental to the national interest. Liebknecht's patriotism was determined by the perspective of intellectuals like himself, Marx,

---

[31] Schuster, *op. cit.*, 26–35. My emphasis. For another quotation from the *Volksstaat* on the last subject and for Held's reaction see his book, *op. cit.*, 64.
[32] *Reichstag Protocol*, Nov. 5, 1889, 137.

Arnold Ruge and Edgar Bauer, to whom large-scale social reconstruction appeared the only means of bringing the social and political conditions of German society up to the level of its cultural
achievements. They suffered deeply from this discrepancy and were
prone to vacillate from depression about the social and spiritual
conditions to exaltation over the cultural achievements. A little-
known story may illustrate the tensions of Marx, Bauer and Liebknecht, even if the location, an English pub, may indicate a
"human, all too human" element to which everyone can easily succumb. Liebknecht was in London

. . . together with my two companions "without a country." . . .
Edgar Bauer, hurt by some chance remark, turned the tables and ridiculed the English snobs. Marx launched an enthusiastic eulogy on German science and music—no other country, he said, would have been
capable of producing masters of music such as Beethoven, Mozart,
Händel and Haydn, and the Englishmen, who had no music, were in
reality far below the Germans, who had been hitherto prevented only
by the miserable political and economic conditions from accomplishing
any great practical work, but who would yet outclass all other nations.
I had never heard him speaking English so fluently. For my part, I
demonstrated in drastic words that the political conditions in England
were not a bit better than those in Germany . . . the only difference
being that we Germans knew our public affairs were miserable while
the Englishmen did not know it, whence it was apparent that we sur-
passed the Englishmen in political intelligence.[33]

The particular patriotic tension which plagued intellectuals like
Marx and Liebknecht was not recognized by Held. He conceded—
and probably not many German professors were willing to do that
—that Marx

. . . is undeniably the most eminent personality in today's Social
Democratic party. . . . He is critically the most astute and at the

[33] Marx and his friends fled the pub. They stoned several street-lamps and
ran from the police. See Wilhelm Liebknecht, *Karl Marx* (Chicago: Kerr,
1904), 147–49.

same time most scholarly man the party has. . . . This man lacks all national feeling. . . . The tendency to have only a smile for German national pride has remained with him. This spirit has been transmitted to the German Social Democrats. . . . The enthusiastic devotion to the nation state which our propertied classes have preserved despite the materialism of our time has completely disappeared among the Social Democrats, who see in the war of 1870/71, just as Marx does, only the beginning of the repression of the Commune by the armies of both sides in the interest of the bourgeoisie.[34]

It was the sentiments rather than the actual political behavior of many Social Democrats which remained intransigent toward the Reich. Schuster complains in 1875 that "the 18th of March, the anniversary of the uprising of the Paris Commune, is for the German Social Democrats a holiday which they oppose to the second of September, the national holiday of the German people." On this day Napoleon III surrendered at Sedan in 1870. "Every year on the 18th of March all Social Democratic associations, at the instigation of the party executive, commemorate the Paris Commune." [35] After 1918 Sombart could still say that "there are probably few convinced proletarian socialists to whom the heroes of the June battle [of 1848] and of the Paris Commune do not mean more than the heroes of Gravelotte and Tannenberg mean to the Germans [sic!]." [36] By contrasting, perhaps inadvertently, "convinced proletarian socialists" and "Germans," Sombart indicated the depth of the rift which continued to divide German society.[37]

[34] Held, *op. cit.,* 50 f. Held's statement would be incorrect if it implied that Marx was a major influence in shaping the contemporary anti-Prussian attitudes of the Eisenachers and their opposition against a Reich united by Prussia. Cf. Ch. II:3 and VII:3.

[35] Schuster, *op. cit.,* 159.

[36] Werner Sombart, *Der proletarische Sozialismus* (Jena: Fischer, 10th ed., 1924), Vol. 2, 34.

[37] This antagonism may be related, on the highest intellectual level, to the irreconcilability of the perspectives of two great adversaries, Marx and Ranke. While Marx looked at contemporary history in terms of the chances for a revolution, Ranke considered history only meaningful if it was a con-

3. The Issue of Idealism versus Materialism

The issue of idealism versus materialism may be briefly discussed as the third major issue between the labor movement and the bourgeois public. To educated observers, even those favoring social reforms such as Schuster and Held, the Social Democrats of both parties appeared as a particular threat to ideal values. By the time Schuster and Held felt prompted to write their books, the Social Democratic agitation lacked the sophisticated argumentation with which Lassalle had addressed himself to the workers as well as to the educated. The idealized aspect of Lassalle's conception of the revolution could no longer be realized. It had depended on the support of the educated classes, but they were horrified by his appeal to the interests of the working class. The Social Democratic agitation was now indeed more vulgar; there was increasing emphasis on the class struggle; nearly all agitators were self-educated men.

For Held the most dangerous aspect of Social Democracy was its lack of idealism (*Idealität*). He explains this as a result of a revolutionary movement that is no longer led exclusively by educated men. Only if the Social Democrats were idealists would they have something in common with the "higher classes."

I would be inclined to declare that all the democratic hobbies are a harmless byproduct of the energetic drive for higher wages, and even to consider the perpetual invectives against the propertied and against

---

tinuous progress uninterrupted by revolutions. He even said that he would not have written his work on world history without a "great deed of Providence," the victory of the forces of order over "revolutionary Caesarism." He meant by this the victory of Prussia over France in 1870. See Karl Kupisch, *Vom Pietismus zum Kommunismus* (Berlin: Lettner Verlag, 1953), 193.

every government action as merely the aimless pathological intensification of the enjoyment of political opposition, if the hatred against the
contemporary social and political order would not have degenerated
into flat, anti-state mentality and crass materialism. . . . Lassalle addresses himself successfully to those workers in whom the feeling of
being suppressed pariahs and disinherited proletarians has become the
dominant sentiment, those who have lost the urge to rise gradually
through hard work . . . who seek the responsibility for their misery
exclusively outside themselves and for whom it is the greatest satisfaction to revenge themselves on those powers they consider enemies.
. . . Among workers in the large industries, this type of dissatisfaction
is a mass feeling. . . . This combination of impassioned dissatisfaction about social conditions with the ideas of political revolution was
preconditioned by the history of the German labor movement which
received its first intellectual impetus from France.[38]

Related to the emphasis on idealist values was an adherence to
the ideal of the cultured and highly educated individual by generations of liberals. The socialist emphasis on collective values consequently horrified them. Friedrich Naumann explains the antagonism between the older generation of liberals and socialists as
having been largely a clash between two groups each of which
believed itself to be more progressive than the other. He knew from
personal experience that many educated and well-meaning liberals
could not understand why the workers did not better appreciate
their new freedom, won through liberalism. These liberals failed
to understand the workers' everyday deprivations, which made
them interested in collective ideals and action.[39] This was not just
a blind spot. The older liberals' humanistic outlook was unrelated
to much of the political and social reality of the time. Therefore,
many educated persons abandoned it or made it even more abstract when the chance arose to take part in political and economic reconstruction. After 1870, the younger bourgeois generation turned increasingly to the social and economic opportunities

[38] Held, *op. cit.*, 49 f and 15 f.
[39] See Naumann, *op. cit.*, 95 ff.

of industrialization, embraced more "realistic" values, and more frequently seized chances to fuse with the old upper class.

The same humanistic values that made many older liberals turn against socialist ideals were also adhered to by many Social Democrats, who combined both and who played them out against the turn of the bourgeoisie to more "realistic" values. During the height of the postwar boom in 1872, a Social Democratic journal attacked "the general corruption" which made the educated akin to businessmen in the pursuit of "material interests."

To be sure, there are within the so-called "better classes" groups which keep aloof from the general corruption. But they have no influence; they do not stand out in comparison with the Mammon and in comparison with those adaptable intellects which follow "the trend of material interests." The German spirit, tired of forming theories and ideas, is today intent on becoming "practical." Our historians are proud to defend without any "sentimentality" Sulla's proscriptions as well as the *coups d'état* of modern saviours of society. They consider action, active intervention, and the success resulting from it to be the highest achievement; they think it ridiculous to measure a successful action in terms of morality. The spirit of our Treitschkes comes to the fore in our speculators. It is the same ingenuity—the petty-bourgeois would call it insolence or shamelessness—which seizes profits with a quick hand. The language is somewhat different, the scholar expresses himself in a slightly different manner from the jobber, but the closeness is revealed even in the style. Some of the advertisement for shareholding companies may very well have been written by a scholar.[40]

Though the Social Democrats were generally in favor of technological progress and rapid industrialization, their moralistic position and adherence to older humanistic values, as in this journal, may have supported attitudes inimical to industrialization. Irrespective of

[40] *Demokratische Blätter. Zeitschrift für politische und soziale Fragen,* 1872, 8–9; S. Kokosky, ed., quoted in Held, *op. cit.,* 95 f. The journal was published for educated readers and presented a "liberal democratic" or "social democratic" protest against the political and economic developments of the time. According to Held, the article was typical of the journal's perspective.

the adherence of some Social Democratic leaders to these values, they were class ideals based on higher learning. The kind of knowledge esteemed in the institutions of higher learning militated most of the time against serious attempts to understand the social problems of industrialization, the ideology of the Social Democrats, and the mentality of the workers attracted to it. At the time, Held and Schuster were among the few educated persons familiar with Social Democratic literature. Even though most educated people were ignorant about socialism and the Social Democrats, they were against them and feared them. The former Austrian minister of finance, Albert Schäffle, who wrote the first German academic treatise on Marx's *Kapital* in 1874, regretted the widely held misconceptions about socialism:

In opposition to all contrary views, which have been very widely spread, it must be emphatically stated that socialism does not universally exclude either property in general, or private property in particular. . . . Even educated people betray a scandalous ignorance on the question of "negation of property," which is already clearly perceived by thousands of workmen and is readily ascribed to the malevolence of the upper classes.[41]

In subsequent years the academic social reformers did much to further the understanding of the social problems of industrialization, but the public was slow to become more sophisticated.

[41] Albert Schäffle, *The Quintessence of Socialism* (London: Sonnenschein, 1890), 101 f. Cf. also Tönnies on Schäffle's critique of the ignorance of the "propertied and educated classes." See Ferdinand Tönnies, *Kritik der öffentlichen Meinung* (Berlin: Springer, 1922), 479. Educated people read about the labor movement in the partisan bourgeois press. Held quoted sympathetically from a Social Democratic article which complained that the bourgeois press never bothered to view the demands of striking workers objectively. *Op. cit.,* 69 f.

V

The Antagonistic Discourse Between the Spokesmen of the Government and the Labor Movement

From the beginning until nearly the end of the Reich, many of the arguments that the spokesmen of the government and the labor movement used against one another remained the same. This was so largely because Bismarck's system necessitated at least an isolation of the labor movement. Thus, the high-pitched rhetoric of the government continued under Bülow after 1900 when there was growing awareness that the policies of the Social Democratic party and the unions were reformist. The Social Democratic spokesmen were intransigent in attack and defense and, since they had no way out of their isolation, stuck to their highly aggressive rhetoric even after the party and the unions had become more and more involved in reformist activities through municipal, state and federal institutions. Only the expressions of patriotism and the plea for social recognition underwent some moderating changes. The fact that strategic requirements forced both sides into mutual all-out rejection does not mean, of course, that the emotional antagonism was not genuine, based as it was on very different value orientations. However, there was often a disparity between the public and private views of the spokesmen involved and, on both sides, a purposeful exaggeration of certain qualities in the opposing party. Although the private views were sometimes milder than the public ones, or the public views more severe than the public actions, as in the case of William II, the net effect of the public images presented was the perpetuation of the deep cleavage between the labor movement and the dominant system.

The most important forum for the great national debate, where these images were evolved, was the Reichstag. Here the spokesmen of the government and the labor movement came together, face to face. Therefore, the present chapter will give particular attention to Reichstag speeches. It will use other materials in so far as they are relevant to bring out the private views and public rhetoric of higher civil servants and of the Emperor himself. Where possible, direct exchanges have been selected to bring out the divergent perspectives.

1. High-Ranking Government Officials on the Social Democrats and a Social Democratic Rejoinder

After the electoral gains of the Social Democrats in 1874, police and courts stepped up their activities, and Bismarck began maneuvering for more stringent repressive legislation. The government knew that it could not immediately achieve its objectives, but it wanted to discredit the liberals in the eyes of those who wanted such legislation and to go on record as proposing legislation against the Social Democrats. A government bill was defended by the Prussian Minister of the Interior, Count Friedrich zu Eulenburg, on January 27, 1876, before the Reichstag; it was poorly prepared.[1] Eulenburg presented the official position of the Prussian government to the public. He knew that he would not be able to convince the majority of the Reichstag. The speaker for the liberals, Lasker, told him afterwards that he had presented nothing new to his listeners. One passage in Eulenburg's speech became famous and was used for decades by the Social Democrats as evidence of the determination of the Prussian ruling class to resort to physical force at an opportune time. Eulenburg stated that if strong measures were not taken now, the present weak provisions of the law

[1] See *Reichstag Protocols,* Jan. 27, 1876, 941–54.

would have to be used as a makeshift until "the guns will shoot and the sabres strike." Underlying this statement was his conviction, real or pretended, that the Social Democrats would one day resort to force although they were presently careful to keep within legal limits. He reasoned logically rather than realistically that civil war was inevitable because the Social Democrats would never gain a parliamentary majority, because "society" would not voluntarily allow itself to be "equalized." [2]

On this score Eulenburg's reasoning is similar to that of Schuster and Held. There are further parallels between the arguments of the three men, and they refer partly to the same evidence. Eulenburg, for example, mentioned three articles that Schuster also discussed in his book. Because of the scarcity of informative books on the Social Democrats, it appears quite likely that Eulenburg's advisers knew the two books. The fact that the three men refer to the same articles may mean that this was the worst evidence against the Social Democrats that could be found. Indeed Held had shown that most of the party papers, especially the union papers, were more restrained and more occupied with practical problems than were the two major Social Democratic journals. At any rate, the similarity of arguments and evidence indicates an area of shared perception and thinking on the part of government officials and educated men from other fields.

Eulenburg tried to show that the insistence of an article in the Lassallean *Neue Socialdemokrat* of 1871 on the inevitability of the class struggle contradicted the emphasis on legality which Social Democratic speakers usually professed at the end of their speeches. He also quoted the Eisenacher *Volksstaat* to the effect that the Social Democratic Workers' party is revolutionary and considers parliamentary activities only from the viewpoint of agitation,[3] that the revolution is inevitable with or without a parliamentary framework, and that Christianity is a hindrance to social progress. Eulen-

[2] As with Schuster, the term "society" excludes the workers. Cf above, p. 95.
[3] Cf. above, *loc. cit.*

burg presented an historical sketch of the development of the two labor parties which had merged only a year before in Gotha. He read the whole Gotha program and commented that it betrayed much but that no organization inimical to the state would openly admit its real intention for two reasons: in order to avoid conflict with the law,[4] and in order to attract followers before gradually indoctrinating them. For Eulenburg the *real* aims of the Social Democrats are the "red republic," "communism" and "atheism." Because of these aims, repressive measures appeared necessary to him.

Hasselmann undertook the defense of the party. Under the circumstances he had to restrain his usual aggressive rhetoric. However, the speech has interest as a summary of the defensive arguments of the party and as an example of the irreducible elements of opposition against the dominant system. His major argument was that social conditions give the workers a right to protest against the existing social order and that moral indignation is continually spreading among them. He insisted on the possibility of peaceful social progress and on the Social Democrats' resolution to propagate Socialism within the confines of the law. He rejected the "eternal accusation" that the Social Democrats were *Reichsfeinde* (enemies of the Reich). He tried to defend the economic views of the party with references to Adam Smith, Ricardo, Rodbertus and Schmoller. Interpreting the Gotha program's demand for socialization of the means of production, he pointed to Bismarck's projected nationalization of the railroads as a first step by the government in the same direction. On religion he stated that the Social Democratic program declared it a private matter, while the pro-

---

[4] Here is another parallel between Eulenburg and Schuster: Eulenburg's suspicion about the real intentions of the Social Democrats is shared by Schuster, who presents extracts of an article from the *Volksstaat* defending the necessity of a cautious statement of aims (*Volksstaat,* 1874, 33, quoted in Schuster, *op. cit.,* 16). Schuster comments that this "confession" makes it impossible to take the Gotha program at face value. This is the same argument as Eulenburg's.

posed repressive bill aimed at persecuting atheists. Also, he did not fail to link a denial that the Social Democrats were champions of free love with the party's protest against prostitution and commercially contracted marriages. Hasselmann's speech is a good example of what was later called "vulgar materialism" by advanced Marxists. However, there were few among the 350 odd agitators and even fewer among the 30,000 odd members of the united party—Eulenburg's estimate for August 1875—who could attain a higher level of comprehension and tactical skill.

Eulenburg's three themes—the real goals of the Social Democrats as the Red Republic, communism and atheism—were standard arguments. These were indeed the ideal goals of many a Social Democrat; but the government usually went so far in picturing the depraved characteristics and horrible dangers of Social Democracy, that it was relatively easy for Social Democratic agitators to deny them. Typical of the tone of such governmental pronouncements to warn the public, especially workers, is the following statement, which the head of the regional Prussian government in Schleswig published in the official government paper (*Amtsblatt*) in July 1872:

Everyone should know what to think of party emissaries who do not hesitate to glorify the bloody crimes perpetrated by the Commune in March of 1871—robbery, plundering, extortion, murder, gluttony, arson. Their aim is to overthrow everything that is venerable, sacred and dear to us—fatherland, throne, altar, custom and law— and to replace the hearth at home with the ale-house-bench, to dissolve property and possessions and to turn labor, which is the preserver and nourisher of the nations, into a tool of ambitious party leaders. The Red Republic is the goal of the Social Democrats. . . . Since the leaders know that under the given conditions they cannot achieve these goals, since they realize that the intelligence of the population and the strong arm of the state block their way, they try to dissolve the bonds which unite the population. Therefore, hatred is preached against the propertied class, therefore the public order is undermined, the moral code is relaxed, the Christian religion is exposed to scorn and mockery.

But above all, work and making a living are deprecated, the trust between employers and workers is destroyed, dissatisfaction is aroused and kindled through strikes, the inclinations to indulge in slothfulness, to frequent pubs, to join seditious, fruitless associations are furthered. The cry "Hand over the capital" is intended to make simple workers believe it possible to secure work and income without capital, and to make them believe the foolish assertion that capital is the enemy of labor.[5]

The *Arbeiterfreund,* the only major contemporary bourgeois journal concerned with social reform, criticized the approach of this governmental warning as being hardly suitable for the purpose. It considered it wrong to accuse the Social Democrats time and again of glorifying the crimes of the Commune. In reality, the great majority of Social Democrats desired the communist republic without its criminal excesses, which would at best be excused as unfortunately inevitable by-products.[6]

The ardor to repress the Social Democrats increased among those higher civil servants who were dismayed to discover that a rising standard of living would not necessarily pacify the workers. In 1876 William I was greatly impressed with the repressive tactics of the police chief of the Bavarian capital, von Feilitzsch, and wanted them applied in Prussia.[7] Feilitzsch's rationale was the following:

Practical experience has repudiated the theory, often propounded, that the workers will be most satisfied when they have high wages, that then the activities of the Social Democrats will lose their justification,

[5] From a reprint in the *Arbeiterfreund,* 1872, 248 f. The journal pointed out that Social Democratic agitation was very active in Schleswig-Holstein, despite the region's lack of industry. It explained the receptiveness to this agitation as being due to a general activation of political interest and a general dissatisfaction. These appear to be results of the uncertain political future of the province, before its definite incorporation into Prussia in the sixties, of the long period of partial or complete martial law and of the failure to satisfy the workers' urge for *Bildung* or to improve their social position and conditions.
[6] *Loc. cit.*
[7] See Kampffmeyer, *op. cit.,* 122 f.

that the agitation will come to an end. The higher the wages, the more the Social Democrats prosper. If wages are high, workers work less; the individual worker has time to attend the meetings of the agitators and to listen daily to their siren songs. His dissatisfaction is aroused by the demands and fallacies propounded there. He has enough money to pay dues, to support the agitators, to buy socialist literature. Not sophisticated enough to recognize the truth, he throws himself into the arms of his leaders, becomes a dissatisfied person, a bad worker, and according to the *mot d'ordre* of the agitators he is not supposed to accumulate savings. . . .

If the worker has only a moderate income, he must work every day to satisfy his daily needs and to support his family; he has not enough money or time, therefore he will be more satisfied with what he has and will try to keep his job through industry, temperance and good behavior; the agitators themselves have to take a job; strikes will be impossible or will fail.[8]

Many higher civil servants seem to have retained for decades the image of the Social Democrats which was formed in the seventies. As late as 1908 a former liberal mayor gave the following polemical account of the views of higher civil servants in northern Germany:

In northern Germany it is possible to become an aged higher civil servant without hearing of Karl Marx. But it is fashionable in Prussia to know Lassalle, though only for his duel and his affair with a lady of high birth. The goals, trends, ideals and justifications of socialism are unknown among many educated persons. They are familiar with a few phrases: "to divide everything," "free love," "religion is a private matter," "the increasing misery of the masses," "property is theft," "[the socialist state will be a] great penal institution," "republic." This is the approximate image which quite a few judges and nearly all higher administrative officials have of socialism. Some still talk of the great *Kladderadatsch* [i.e., the catastrophic collapse of society] and of the "great expropriation." They have in mind the hazy notion that they might one day not only lose their jobs, but also that they might be forced to hand over their laboriously accumulated savings to a few ex-convicts, probably of Jewish descent. These unsympathetic persons

[8] Quoted in *ibid.,* 149 f.

would then compel them to work as prisoners without compensation and to live on food from public soup-kitchens. This is the conception of socialism of the Prussian higher civil servants. That socialism only aims at the socialization of the means of production is repressed. This ignorance about socialism which creates fear is artificially bred. The state skilfully insures that science and its representatives do not carry too much knowledge into the ranks of the educated. It is already cause for suspicion to write about socialism.[9]

2. William II's Private and Public Views and Their Divergence from His Actions

When William II realized, soon after the introduction of his extensive social welfare legislation in 1890, that the effect of the anti-socialist legislation could not easily be obliterated, he became one of the most vociferous spokesmen against the Social Democrats and followed his general tendency to indulge in images of violence. It is true that he did not act on these images. Either he knew better himself, or he was advised by friends not to act, or the imperial and state governments opposed action. Joseph Schumpeter tried to defend William II by pointing to this divergence of word and action.

He was no insignificant ruler. Moreover, he was fully entitled to the comment made upon him by Prince Bülow, in the most unusual defense ever made for a monarch in a parliament: "Say what you will; he is no philistine." If he quarreled with the one man who could have taught him the technique of his craft, critics of his behavior to Bismarck should not forget that the quarrel was mainly about the persecution of socialists which the emperor wished to discontinue, and about the inauguration of a great program of social legislation. If one disregards talk and simply tries to reconstruct intentions by following the emperor's act from year to year, one cannot help arriving at the conclu-

[9] Lothar Schücking, *Die Reaktion in der inneren Verwaltung Preussens* (Berlin: Hilfe, 1908), 17 f.

sion that he was often right in his views about the great questions of his time.[10]

By 1895, however, William II hesitated to act strongly against the Social Democrats *because* of his previous quarrel with Bismarck. He no longer continued to quarrel with him over the treatment of the socialists, as he had done in the Imperial Privy Council on January 24, 1890, the clash that resulted in Bismarck's dismissal.[11] In any case, his rhetoric was bound to contribute to the perpetuation of the high tension between the Social Democrats and the dominant system, just as his many impetuous speeches on other subjects were bound to produce perplexity and antagonism abroad. His public utterances thus reduced the chances of a gradual *rapprochement* between labor movement and dominant system.[12]

[10] Joseph Schumpeter, *Capitalism, Socialism and Democracy* (New York: Harper, 1947), 343. By permission of the publisher.

[11] Cf. Wilhelm von Kardorf, *op. cit.,* 214; also the report of Philipp Eulenburg, the go-between for Emperor and government, to Chancellor Hohenlohe, in Hohenlohe, *op. cit.,* 97 f. Eulenburg remarked that William would not go all-out against the Social Democrats without the consent of the people, that means the Reichstag, as long as Bismarck was alive—for fear of playing his game. Hohenlohe added that the major driving force behind the suggestion to pass new laws against the Social Democrats was the Bismarck press, which urged the government "to use the enthusiasm of the 25th anniversary of our victories, against the Social Democrats. Perhaps [Bismarck] merely agitates in order to make the government, which does not accept his advice, appear weak."

[12] Eckart Kehr once suggested that the Social Democrats had no less a sense of Prussian honor than the aristocrats and their overlord who so often spoke of it: "At the time when the naval armament bills were passed the state [showed the Social Democrats] with the proposed 'Penitentiary Bill,' which was only the most consequent result of the *Sammlungspolitik,* that it did not want to accept them into the nation. The Prussian sense of honor, very much alive among Social Democrats, was offended and at a decisive moment it was once more directed against the state and its policies." Eckart Kehr, *Schlachtflottenbau und Parteipolitik 1894–1901* (Berlin: Ebering, 1930), 341. Kehr was a brilliant Marxist historian and one of the best students of the eighteen eighties and nineties; he died very young in the early nineteen thirties. On the *Sammlungspolitik,* see my Ch. VI, p. 145.

The Emperor's attitude toward the Social Democrats and the typical divergence of word and deed may be seen in the 1895 attempt at extensive repressive legislation. When the 25th anniversary of the victory of the German army over Napoleon III at Sedan was enthusiastically celebrated, on September 2, 1895, the Social Democrats again ridiculed the values that were of great importance to a large part of the population, and they made some aggressive remarks about William I. Thereupon, William II indulged in suggestions of violence and hoped that mounting public indignation would make it possible to pass a new law against the Social Democrats. One of his proposals for a new law contained a paragraph stipulating jail sentences for those who "defame the memory of dead German ruling princes." [13] Another proposal would have prohibited all Social Democratic meetings, as had been done in Saxony. More William II did not want, but this much was too much for Hohenlohe. The new Prussian Minister of the Interior, von Köller, a typical *Junker,* presented four drafts to Hohenlohe and commented bluntly:

The outcry that this is an exceptional law does not mean much because, in the last analysis, every penal law is an exceptional law. We must be determined to treat the Social Democrats not as a party but to fight them with means of coercion as revolutionaries against state and order.[14]

Philipp Eulenburg conveyed Hohenlohe's resistance to the court and pointed to the possibility of the chancellor's resignation. This was enough to make William II yield to the opposition of his "dear uncle," as he addressed Hohenlohe, who was forty years his elder, in his letters. The Prussian Minister of the Interior had to resign. Thus, despite his uncontrolled verbal reactions, William II did not support the extreme views of the Prussian government and the

[13] Cf. Hohenlohe, *loc. cit.*
[14] *Loc. cit.*

right-wing parties. In a talk with Philipp Eulenburg, William II first blurted out that the old adjutants of William I "should have hit Bebel and his gang over the head in the offices of the *Vorwärts*." Then "the patriotically aroused people would have smashed up the printing shop and frightened the Social Democrats for the first time." After this outburst he referred to the King of Saxony, who "just like he, the Emperor, was by all means against an *Umsturzgesetz*"—that is, against new comprehensive legislation. William wanted the prohibition of Social Democratic meetings in order to break "the terrorism of socialist leaders" against workers who attended involuntarily. He hoped that the people would give him the means to protect "the quiet elements in the state from attempts on their lives." [15] Eulenburg maintained that his real motive was fear for his wife and children. If the people would not support him, William said, he would be forced one day to act alone, ignoring their protests.

An example of the intransigent public rhetoric of William II is the Emperor's Speech of 1907—the traditional address on the occasion of the first meeting of a new Reichstag.[16] Chancellor Bülow had succeeded in bringing about a liberal-conservative coalition, which won a great electoral victory by an appeal to nationalist sentiments; the Social Democrats lost 50 per cent of their seats even though their votes increased.

William II asserted that the Social Democrats had done nothing for the workers or "the progress of culture." They negate "everything that is good and healthy in the existing conditions," and they are "against the steady peaceful development of state and society." Social welfare legislation would continue because it "rests on the principle of the social obligation toward the working classes." [17]

[15] *Op. cit.*, 98–101.

[16] See *Reichstag Protocols,* February 19, 1907, 2.

[17] Welfare legislation, however, was not continued. Little more than one year before this speech, on the occasion of the Morocco crisis, William II urged Chancellor Bülow to prevent a war, because army and navy were not yet sufficiently prepared and reorganized and the socialists were preaching open

In his reply to the Emperor, Bebel stated cautiously that the Emperor's Speech was "objectively untrue"; then he launched a broad attack on the political and cultural backwardness of Prussia, "the incarnation of cultural stagnation" and the country with "the worst and most miserable of all electoral systems." [18] He quoted foreign and German scholars and politicians on the *Kulturfeindlichkeit* (hostility to culture), brutality, Caesarism, militarism and feudalism of Wilhelminian Germany and Prussia.

3. Chancellor Hohenlohe Answers the Social Democrats

Prince Hohenlohe was a Bavarian aristocrat who considered himself a moderate liberal. In the late sixties he was very active, as Bavarian prime minister, in promoting the unification of southern and northern Germany. He was one of the staunchest South German supporters of Bismarck. He took over the chancellorship from Caprivi in 1894 and held it until 1900. Hohenlohe was not averse to new legislation against the Social Democrats nor to a constitutional reform restricting equal suffrage in the Reich, but he refused to work against the majority in the Reichstag. Because of the pressure of the Emperor, the Bismarck press and other right-wing groups, on the one hand, and the Reichstag's unwillingness to provide the means for the legal suppression of the Social Democrats, on the other, he could be expected to resort at least to sharp rhetoric against the Social Democrats. He did this, to some extent, but he publicly retained the reserve of the experienced diplomat and the dignity of the grandseigneur.

revolt. With typical logical and grammatical jerkiness, he added in this non-public communication: "First deter the socialists, behead them and render them innocuous—if necessary through blood bath—then declare war on the outside. But not before that and not *a tempo*." See Gerhard Ritter, *Der Schlieffenplan: Kritik eines Mythos* (Munich: Oldenbourg, 1956), p. 131.

[18] *Reichstag Protocols,* February 26, 1907, 51 f.

An example of a statement which is at the same time defensive toward the conservatives and the Emperor and aggressive toward the Social Democrats is his Reichstag speech of December 10, 1895. He rejected the conservative criticism that the government lacked initiative and pointed out that it did not command a firm majority in parliament. He condemned the Social Democrats and reaffirmed his determination to fight them—within the limits of the existing laws. This was an indirect rejection of the attempts of the Emperor and the right wing to institute new antisocialist legislation. Hohenlohe contrasted the Social Democratic view of the fatherland and the national celebrations on the anniversary of the French army's surrender in 1870 with the perspective of the "peaceful citizen," to whom Social Democratic activities appeared anticultural, antinational and unpatriotic.

The Social Democratic party now protests, through its press, the present application of the laws; I would like to point out that they are themselves responsible for this. When during this summer the German nation commemorated the great achievements and the victory of the year 1870/71 and remembered gratefully and proudly the venerable Emperor, to whose courage and wisdom we owe the establishment of the German Reich, the party and the Social Democratic press ridiculed this national movement in accordance with the belief of its leader that the fatherland, in our sense, is an anticultural (*kulturwidriger*), reactionary notion. . . .

All of this was very offensive and I have often been asked how long we would tolerate it. The gentlemen of the Social Democracy must not forget that the principles underlying the systems of collectivism, communism and similar systems do not impress the peaceful citizen as matters of scientific discourse. The peaceful citizen perceives in them anticultural, antinational and unpatriotic endeavors (*kulturwidrige, vaterlandswidrige, vaterlandslose Bestrebungen*). Quite a few people do not see in the future state of the Social Democrats a state of law and order, but a robber state. It is natural that this diminishes the sense of security and that, therefore, people look to the state for protection. If we have tightened the reins of government somewhat since last summer, it is in correspondence with the feelings of all people of good will in the German Reich.[19]

Hohenlohe's diplomatic reserve, clearly evident in this statement, did not indicate moderate private reactions against the Social Democrats. In a private letter, dated December 23, 1898, he called Bebel "the shameless loud-mouth" (*den unverschämten Schreier*).[20] He was also physically affected by Gerhart Hauptmann's play *Hannele,* which he termed "social democratic":

A terrible, wretched piece of work, social-democratic-realistic, full of pathological, sentimental mystics, affecting the nerves, really horrible. Afterwards we went to Borchard in order to return to a human mood with champagne and caviar.[21]

4. The Rhetorical Duels Between Bülow and Bebel on Patriotism and Revolution

The rhetorical battle between the spokesmen of the government and the Social Democratic party continued under Hohenlohe's successor, von Bülow, who held the chancellorship from 1900 until 1909. The rift in German society as well as the intransigent rhetoric persisted,[22] but the dangers of new comprehensive antisocialist

[19] Speech in the Reichstag, December 10, 1895, see Hohenlohe, *op. cit.,* 141.
[20] *Op. cit.,* 475.
[21] Diary, December 14, 1893, quoted by Kampffmeyer in his introduction to Friedrich Ebert, *Schriften* (Dresden: Reissner, 1926), 55. Borchard was the name of a famous restaurant in Berlin.
[22] Pinson states correctly that Bülow verbally attacked the Social Democrats as violently as Bismarck had done in the seventies and that the Social Democrats retorted in the same fashion: "In the session of February 25, 1907, Bülow called them 'the party of hostility to Christianity,' 'the deadly enemy of the national state and bourgeois society,' a party, 'born out of hate' and

legislation and of a *coup d'état* against parliament subsided. Internally, Germany continued to be more peaceful during these years than many other European countries.

Every year, on the occasion of the discussions of the budget, the public awaited the "duel" between Bülow and Bebel. Their speeches were rhetorical highlights of the Reichstag debates; they were not typical of the majority of speeches, which were concerned with more concrete problems, such as details of a pending bill. Apart from the ideological battle, the power struggle was carried on over taxation to meet the ever expanding military expenditures: What groups should be privileged or subsidized at the expense of what other group? The federal taxes were mainly indirect and, therefore, burdened the workers relatively more than the higher strata. Year after year the Social Democrats would point to this and particularly denounce the tariff policies that favored the landed estates at the expense of the common man, who had to buy food at higher prices. They also had frequent reason to complain in the Reichstag about petty interferences of the authorities with Social Democratic activities.[23] Bebel and other leading deputies would use these details for their general critique of conditions in the Reich.[24]

Since the government was interested in keeping the Social Democrats isolated, Bülow had to go on asserting as his predecessors had done, that the party was unpatriotic and revolutionary. He

---

like an 'Indian tribe on a war path.' Socialist leaders, for the most part, did not care to bridge this gap. In theory, at least, they would have none of the capitalist state, or capitalist culture. An almost caste-like attitude was developed among the Socialist workers which bound fathers and sons to their party but which looked askance at all others." Koppel S. Pinson, *Modern Germany, Its History and Civilization* (New York: Macmillan, 1955), p. 211. By permission of the publisher.

[23] For example, the government refused permission to Jean Jaurès in 1905 to come to Berlin and make a speech. Bülow defended the government's position against Bebel on December 9, 1905, *Reichstag Protocols,* 194 f.

[24] See the details on military expenditures, foreign trade, tariffs, and the living costs of workers in Bebel's budget speech on December 7, 1905, 156–61.

therefore continued to use the old vocabulary, according to which the Social Democrats were *vaterlandslos, unpatriotisch, fanatisch* and *kulturwidrig*.[25] The following were some of Bülow's tactics and recurrent arguments: He utilized theoretical literature, newspaper articles and convention speeches of the party to attack the party's position in the Reichstag.[26] He maintained that in contrast to the internationalist German Social Democrats, foreign socialists were patriotic,[27] that the revolutionary Jacobins, for example, had been ardent patriots while the Social Democrats merely shared their fanaticism and dogmatism.[28] He accused the Social Democrats of continuously contributing to the misunderstandings abroad about the intentions of the German government.[29] He distinguished between the workers and the party and maintained that the great majority of the German workers, even of the Social Democratic workers, were patriotic and would do their duty in the event of war.[30] He was careful to point out that the government's fight was not directed against the workers, but against "the political and revolutionary Social Democratic party."[31]

In his "duel" with Bebel in 1907, Bülow repeated his plea to the Social Democrats "to stop offending the sentiments which are sacred to the great majority of the German people."[32] Social Democratic papers indeed offended these feelings again and again with their attacks on the Prussian military traditions. In 1905, when a Social Democratic paper (*Münchener Post*) labeled the "hero's death" a simple act of slaughter, many people were probably as genuinely disgusted as was Schuster in 1875, when he complained that

[25] February 26, 1907, 66.
[26] December 9, 1905, 195 f., and December 14, 1905, 317–19.
[27] December 9, 1905, 195 D.
[28] December 14, 1905, 319 D.
[29] December 9, 1905, 195, and December 14, 318 f.
[30] December 14, 1905, 318 D.
[31] February 26, 1907, 67 B.
[32] February 26, 1907, 66 B.

. . . the attitude that the "organ of the Social Democratic Workers' Party" takes toward the events of the war and their effects, which are so very advantageous for the German fatherland, offends every German heart most deeply.[33]

Bülow made the most of this article and linked it to the controversy between Jean Jaurès and Bebel at the Amsterdam congress of the Second International in 1904, where the latter had spoken about potential salutary effects of military defeat. Bülow concluded by saying:

This forms the deepest rift between you and us, this constitutes the greatest cleavage between you and us: this lack of understanding for the vital interests of the nation, for those demands without which the nation cannot maintain itself in the world.[34]

Three years later Bülow again referred to the Amsterdam speech, which was often cited against the Social Democrats in newspapers, and Bebel answered him.[35] Bebel reasoned that military defeat had led to salutary reforms in Prussia in 1806 and to the establishment of constitutional or republican regimes in Austria in 1866, in France in 1870 and in Russia in 1905.[36] Underlying this controversy between Bülow and Bebel was the recognition that a military defeat was the supreme threat to Prussian predominance and the internal security of the Bismarck Reich.

The historical role of Prussia and the Prussian three-class suffrage were particularly controversial issues between the Social Democrats and the government. On March 26, 1908, Bülow re-

[33] See Ch. IV, 97, above.
[34] December 14, 1905, 319 D.
[35] March 27, 1908, 4355.
[36] However, the Social Democrats continued to dread a defeat at the hand of Tsarism because they were convinced that this would mean the destruction of the Reich as well as the labor movement. Bebel's account of his difference of opinion with Jaurès also brought out again the problem of the disproportion between the numerical strength of the party and its inability, because of the constitutional setting, to democratize Germany.

affirmed the government's intention to modify the Prussian three-class suffrage, but he refused "a revolution from above" or a *coup d'état* in favor of "the revolution from below." [37] Provoked by a speech of Bebel, he highly praised the role of Prussia in bringing about and sustaining the Reich. He emphasized the mutual importance of the Reich and Prussia and particularly stressed the following: the peaceful aspects of unification, Bismarck's readiness to ask the Prussian diet for indemnity (which ended the Constitutional Conflict), the South German states' voluntarily joining Prussia in the Reich, and the Prussian determination to respect their constitutional rights and to accept their equality. The following day Bebel answered Bülow that

. . . when Bismarck took on the task of German unification and realized it according to the precepts of the Right, this was only in the interest of Prussia, so that the constitution and all else would depend on Prussian power. . . . Ten million good Germans [i.e., Austrians] were thrown out of Germany. . . . If you view history in this way, the judgment on the role of Prussia will be different from the one you habitually present. There is no doubt Prussia is today, as it always was, the incarnation of reaction, the drag-chain of progress.[38]

Characteristic of the very strong democratic component of Social Democratic ideology is the disappearance of nearly all specifically socialist terminology, with the exception perhaps of a term like "class" in some of Bebel's most important speeches before the Reichstag. Instead, a humanitarian and democratic credo is professed, which has the following goals: to attain "the highest possible development of the physical, intellectual and political *Bildung*

[37] March 26, 1908, 4290. With the refusal of "a revolution from above" or a *coup d'état,* Bülow meant that he was not willing to impose a suffrage reform on the Prussian diet. Because of the conservative domination of the Prussian diet, the government never managed to effect a reform. The last negotiations about a suffrage reform were outpaced by the revolution of November 1918.

[38] March 27, 1908, 4355.

of the people," "to enable the last of the citizens to be a *Kultur-mensch,*" to create "a state which stands on the pinnacle of *Kultur,*" and to make "Germany highly respected in the world and a model for all other states." Complementary to these tenets is the conviction that there cannot be genuine cultural and political progress in Germany as long as the *Junkers,* "the most reactionary class in the world," go on ruling.[39]

Bebel's rhetorical strategy scarcely changed during Hohenlohe's and Bülow's tenure. His basic arguments were the following:

(a) The Social Democratic party was not a revolutionary party but rather a reform party which actually dissipated the revolutionary potential in the working class.

(b) It was not actually unpatriotic because it wanted finally a freer and more beautiful fatherland.

(c) The dominant groups were not genuinely patriotic because they imposed the burden of military expenditures mainly on the workers, whose patriotism they distrusted and to whom they would not grant equal rights and social recognition.

(d) The real revolutionaries were the big industrialists.[40]

Two examples may be given: During the Russian revolution of 1905 Bebel reminded the ruling classes of the revolutionary potential accumulating in the working class, but he went on to say that

[39] These are phrases from Bebel's great speech before the Reichstag on February 26, 1907, 63, when he had to perform the difficult task of rehabilitating his party after it had lost fifty per cent of its seats, even though it had gained more votes, in the nationalist "Hottentot elections" (so called because of the exploitation of the colonial issue). The tactical contingency, however, does not make Bebel's declaration less genuine, as can be seen from a comparison with many other Reichstag speeches.

[40] Bebel apparently had in mind not the consequences of large-scale organizations, but the uncompromising opposition of big industrialists like Stumm, Krupp and Heyl against the party and the unions. See August Bebel, *Akademiker und Sozialismus,* second ed. (Berlin: Verlag der sozialistischen Monatshefte, 1906), 24. On the same page, Bebel also defined the patriotism of the workers: "He wants a fatherland in which he can live freely as a citizen and under conditions worthy of a human being."

the Social Democrats were actually dissipating this force.[41] He declared that the workers could no longer be expected to fight for the fatherland without worth-while reasons for doing so.

Georg von Rheinbaben, Prussian Minister of Finance, answered Bebel, saying that he did not care for the help of the Social Democrats in controlling revolutionary tendencies and that he preferred to rely on the authority of the state. He condemned Bebel for suggesting that a majority vote of workers and not the call of the Emperor should decide in the future whether or not the fatherland would be defended.

Two years later Bebel demonstrated the reformist character of the party by quoting the famous passage in the 1867 preface to Marx's *Kapital* on the "economic laws of modern society which cannot be disregarded."[42] He maintained that the Social Democrats never introduced a bill in parliament directed against the basic social and political order, and he called socialism "the leaven which forces bourgeois society ahead." The beneficent influence of Lassalle, Engels and Marx and the labor movement in general on the German universities was one way in which Socialism served this function. The *Kathedersozialisten* and the *Verein für Sozialpolitik* were no longer an object of ridicule for Social Democratic leaders as they had been in the seventies.[43]

On several issues, the views of the opponents were diametrically opposed, while the terms of the charges leveled against one another were identical. For William II, Bülow, and Bassermann, the leader of the National Liberals,[44] Social Democracy was (a) an obstacle to cultural progress, (b) a danger to national security, (c) disrup-

[41] December 7, 1905, 162.
[42] From the seventies on, Social Democrats used Marx's supposedly scientific recognition that a society "can neither clear by bold leaps nor remove by legal enactments the obstacles offered by the successive phases of its normal development" as a defensive argument. See Ch. VII:3 for an elaboration. Cf. Karl Marx, *Capital* (New York: The Modern Library, 1936), 14 f.
[43] On the *Verein für Sozialpolitik* see the next chapter.
[44] Bassermann, February 25, 1907, 32 f.

tive to the basic unity of interest between workers and employers.[45] For the Social Democrats, (a) and (b) were also true of the imperial government, the personal regime of the Emperor, the Prussian ruling class and the employers. For Bülow, Germany's continuously increasing military power was the basis of her economic prosperity and the best means of preserving peace.[46] For Bebel, the naval armament program was absurd.[47] The main argument of its defenders was that Germany's large overseas trade needed the protection of a powerful fleet; Bebel argued that Germany traded mainly with states that it would have to fight on land (France, Russia) or states whose power would readily defeat Germany (England, United States).

These perspectives seem irreconcilable, and they largely were. However, Bülow was not as fierce an opponent of the Social Democrats as his Reichstag speeches seem to indicate. Since he had to exaggerate, for tactical reasons, the gap between the Social Democrats and the government, he pronounced Revisionism dead [48]— this after it had spread widely within the party and the trade unions. In private, however, he seems to have been well aware of the differences within the party and somewhat sympathetic toward the revisionists.[49] Outwardly, national solidarity remained Bülow's criterion. Therefore, in 1915, he could say about the Social Democrats after their decision of August 1914 to support the government:

If the most radical of the Social Democrats were to come to me and offer his help, I should accept it in full confidence, so genuine is their

[45] Bülow, February 26, 1907, 67 C: "In the last analysis the interests of the employers and the workers are identical."
[46] December 9, 1905, 194 ff.
[47] December 7, 1905, 156–59.
[48] February 26, 1907, 66.
[49] See Harry Marks, "The Sources of Reformism in the Social Democratic Party of Germany, 1890–1914," *Journal of Modern History*, XI:3, 348.

feeling of national solidarity. But in other quarters, unhappily, how much there is of egoism, pettiness, envy and jealousy.[50]

5. The Fight Against Second-Class Citizenship in the Reichstag

In the Reichstag the quest for social recognition was addressed to the ruling powers, while outside, the party tried to awaken in millions of workers the feeling that the withholding of universal and equal suffrage was an insult to their dignity as citizens. For the Social Democrats, social recognition of the workers was a necessary consequence of the evolution of modern society, especially of democratization. The Lassalleans as well as the Eisenachers attributed paramount importance to equal suffrage as a major means of achieving political equality. In 1869, for example, Bebel attacked a bill pending before the North German Reichstag that would deprive, in his words, "a great number of quite honorable citizens, through no fault of their own, of their highest right," the right to vote, if they are, or were during the preceding year, on poor relief. "Humanity and justice demand that the poor have the opportunity to exert their influence through voting in order to change those conditions which most oppress them." He anticipated the argument that "most workers will not be interested in exercising their political rights because they are so apathetic . . . but this would be for me only one more reason not to exclude them from the right to vote; if they voluntarily renounce it, then the misuse and the dangers . . . which some of you fear, will not occur." [51] The bill was passed.

[50] Theodor Wolff, *Through Two Decades* (London: Heinemann, 1936), 27. Bülow said this at a time when he entertained plans to regain the chancellorship with the help of the Social Democrats. Thus considerations of expediency played a role in his positive as well as his negative statements.

[51] *Reichstag Protocols* of the North German Federation, March 19, 1869, 169.

On the Lassallean side, Försterling, a deputy of the splinter group sponsored by Countess Hatzfeldt, declared that "we, the workers, want to solve the social question peacefully and legally on the basis of the general, equal and direct suffrage." [52] However, he did not consider the universal, equal and direct suffrage of the North German Federation general and equal enough since the labor representatives neither receive daily allowances nor are they permitted payment by their organizations. Thus the workers are handicapped in sending their leaders to parliament. The workers, however, have become conscious of their "general human rights," and this must be recognized by the powers-that-be.[53] Statements like this are typical of the tendency of the Social Democratic representatives to consider themselves the spokesmen of the working masses. For a long time, of course, they spoke only for a small minority. Bebel acknowledged this limitation of representativeness in 1875, when he distinguished between three groups of workers: the first is hostile toward the *Reich,* the second is already distrustful, and the third still has sympathies for the government and puts hope in legislation.[54] He expected that eventually most workers would belong to the first group.

Bebel put the demand for social recognition in an evolutionary perspective. He told parliament that the workers fought a battle similar to that which the bourgeoisie once fought against feudalism.[55] In a debate on more repressive controls over workers' sickness funds, he pointed out that the bourgeois guilds were considered political at one time and therefore were often outlawed by emperors and patricians.[56] The evolutionary theme was particularly emphasized in a speech of 1890, in which Bebel exposed the "historical irony" that no one had done more than the liberals to

[52] April 28, 1869, 644.
[53] May 5, 1869, 815.
[54] November 5, 1875, 80.
[55] December 14, 1905, 304 D.
[56] February 3, 1876, 1124 f.

awaken a sense for equality among the people, the equality
now refused to the workers. "We have advanced so far in the meantime with regard to political education as well as general culture,
that even the lowliest citizen has a strong need for equal rights." [57]
"The whole German working class, as far as it is independent," has
for twelve years been made to feel that it is made up of "second-
class citizens." Bebel assured his parliamentary colleagues that the
awareness of being outlawed will be reflected in the attitudes of
the workers toward the existing political and social order. "Nothing can enrage the individual citizen more than to recognize that
he is not treated as someone else who, as a human being, is completely his equal." [58]

Eventually the Social Democrats developed a pluralistic theory
to press their demand for social recognition. The standard argument that the workers did not want privileges but freedom and
equality for all was a stepping stone toward such a theory.[59] Related to this was the argument that the ruling groups were condemning the Social Democrats and the unions for trying to defend
the economic interests of the workers when they themselves were
protecting their own economic interests. The veteran Social Democratic leader Frohme told the Reichstag in 1889 that the dissatis-

---

[57] At about the same time the prominent law historian Rudolf Sohm attacked
the inconsistency and insufficiency of the liberal attempts to stop the development toward democratization initiated by liberalism itself. Sohm then played
a political role as contributor to the *Allgemeine Konservative Monatsschrift*.
"The ideas which now carry the flaming torch into the masses and incite the
fourth against the third estate originated within the latter. What was written in
the books of the educated and the scholars, this and nothing else is now
preached in the streets. . . . The *Bildung* of the 19th century preaches its
own downfall. As did the *Bildung* of the 18th century, the *Bildung* of the 19th
carries the revolution under its heart. If it gives birth, then the child who was
nourished with the mother's blood will murder her." Quoted in Eckart Kehr,
"Das soziale System der Reaktion in Preussen unter Puttkamer," *Die Gesellschaft*, 1929, 2, 254 ff.
[58] January 25, 1890, 1227.
[59] Cf. Bebel's speech of February 3, 1876, 1124 f.

faction of the workers is still interpreted by the governmental press as the result of agitation.[60] Thus the legitimacy of their dissatisfaction, which Frohme felt was primarily caused by rising food and housing costs, was denied. On the other hand, the ruling groups considered their dissatisfaction with economic developments legitimate enough to establish high tariffs and to appropriate more money for the household of the monarch. The attempts of the unions, however, to improve the economic conditions of the workers are denounced as spurious and "actually" aimed at revolution (*Umsturz*). The laws are not only used against "revolutionary" activities of workers' associations, as the government maintains, but against all their activities. Every trade union meeting, every meeting of executive and strike committees has to be announced in advance to the police and is subject to surveillance.[61]

Bebel himself finally elaborated the demand for equal rights into an explicit pluralist scheme. Employers and workers should have equal chances to fight for their interests. For example, in 1905, he compared the pressure of workers on strike breakers with the pressure of employers' associations on deviant employers. In order to win approval for the workers' actions, he conceded to the employers the right to pressure other employers and to fight the workers— "C'est la guerre"—but capital and labor should have equal chances, and the state should set the rules of the game. For the present he recognized that the employers were more organized than the workers and that they had stronger means of enforcing conformity. For the rest of his lengthy speech Bebel followed the familiar pattern, using pending bills or government and employers' practices as so many examples of the lack of social recognition. He pointed to the

[60] November 4, 1889, 109.
[61] These interferences must have contributed considerably to the alienation of the workers from the government. The workers were continually reminded of their tutelage by the ubiquitous presence of policemen, usually sitting next to the chairman or the speaker of a meeting and declaring it closed if something was said that they considered a violation of the laws.

economic hardships of the workers, the lockouts, and the political inequality and concluded that these strengthened the class consciousness of the workers and would result in the further expansion of the labor movement. He exclaimed that "the worker will no longer tolerate his treatment as a pariah." [62]

Bebel and other Social Democrats [63] clearly accepted the theory that social recognition would diminish working-class protest. In the same speech Bebel explained to the parliament that the Social Democratic movement had up to now made less progress in England than in Germany because "the English bourgeoisie has been reasonable enough for decades to meet the wishes of the English workers in every way" and because it has been paying more taxes than the German bourgeoisie.[64]

[62] December 14, 1905, 303–7. The speech was also typical in its determinaistic parts: Capitalism inevitably strengthens the Social Democrats by enlarging the proletariat. A revolution will be "a necessary reaction" if the ruling classes continue their old policies. In his answer to Bebel, Chancellor Bülow replied with the demand for equal rights for Germany in her comparative position toward England and other countries: "How often have the Social Democrats declared that our world policy is responsible for ill-feeling, especially in England. How often have I said that we understand nothing else under world policy but the demand for the same consideration all other countries have in regard to trade, industry and shipping and that we want to stand on a footing of equality with the whole world." December 14, 1905, 317.
[63] Frohme, for example, asserted in the speech mentioned above that recent strikes in Silesia and Westphalia would not have happened if the employers had been willing to grant equal rights. *Loc. cit.*
[64] Accepting an inverse relationship between social recognition and revolutionary mentality, a number of observers of the German labor movement such as Jaurès and Sombart suggested that the lack of revolutionary spirit among German workers had to do with the early granting of universal suffrage. See W. Sombart, *op. cit.*, 367, also there on Jaurès. For the late sixties it seems indeed true that nationalist enthusiasm and the granting of universal suffrage on a federal level induced in many workers a positive attitude toward the existing political system, while their predominantly traditionalist attitudes inclined them in the same direction. Even organized workers came to accept the dominant system, especially because Lassalle's major demand had been universal suffrage. See Gustav Mayer, "Trennung," *op. cit.*, 27. But the granting of equal suffrage for the Reichstag was soon offset by prosecu-

A logical result of the pluralism acknowledged by Bebel was the development of the quest for social recognition into a theory of solid bargaining with the dominant system. The revisionist Richard Calwer wrote, at the same time that Bebel made his pluralist confession, that

. . . the workers strive for political power and recognition: They are willing to take responsibilities, but they also want the corresponding rights. The opponents of the labor movement, above all the government, show not the slightest intention of compromising with workers' demands for political equality. In a difficult battle the workers are forced to advance slowly, step by step. And now it is seriously expected of the workers to mobilize their parliamentary influence in the Reichstag without any compensation, without any guarantees, in order to expand the army and navy. Perhaps we could talk about this if the organization of the army and navy were more in the interests of the people, if the purpose of the army were only to fight the external enemy, if the costs for the defense of the country were less of a burden to the workers. But what is the situation at present? The Social Democratic movement is considered the domestic enemy, the army the bulwark against the advance of the labor movement, and the treatment

---

tion and persecution and, in the long run, by the government's refusal or inability to change the three-class suffrage in Prussia. This was the root of the opposition spirit of masses of workers against the government, a spirit which had originally been rather weak in the Lassallean movement. See Schröder, *Geschichte, op. cit.,* 8. Federal universal and equal suffrage and a precarious right of combination, which did not apply to agricultural workers, seamen, state employees in administrations and government industries, could not "satiate" the workers, contrary to what Jaurès and Sombart suggested. The three-class suffrage in the two most industrialized states, Prussia and Saxony, became the symbol for the unwillingness of the dominant system to accord social recognition. (In Saxony a more liberal suffrage was replaced from 1896 to 1909 by the three-class suffrage, thus eliminating a sizable Social Democratic activity. The Social Democrats were helpless vis-à-vis this change because they were committed to election campaigns as their major means of political action. The suffrage was also changed in order to thwart the Social Democrats after 1890 in Hamburg, Lübeck and parts of Thuringia.

of the common man in the army does not meet in the least the demands which German workers are entitled to raise.[65]

Some revisionists equated socialism with the attainment of equal rights. Thus the revisionist Heinrich Peus told parliament in 1906 that workers become Social Democrats because they want equal rights. "This is the core of all our aspirations, the rest is mainly a consequence of automatic economic and technological development." This reliance on automatic development made it possible for him to say that once "equality is obtained, the Social Democratic party will be superfluous, and democracy and socialism will be the dominant principles of society." [66] The revisionists could plead without mental reservations for social recognition and criticize the government with genuine indignation for refusing it. Despite their conviction that parliamentarism was a step on the path toward socialism, orthodox Marxist believers were sometimes ambiguous in their attitude toward social recognition of the workers within the existing system. They vociferously demanded equality of rights, but they also expected or hoped that this recognition would not be forthcoming. They thought that objective tendencies—that is, the continuous growth of the proletariat and the objectively determined inability of the ruling groups to make genuine concessions—would finally result in a revolutionary situation and insure ultimate victory. As usual, Bebel expressed both tendencies. For decades, he pleaded for the social recognition of the workers and warned the ruling groups that they would be responsible for a revolution if they refused equality of rights. And in his speech to students in 1897, he granted that a multitude of measures was conceivable to make possible a gradual transformation of society. However, he thought that these would not be taken

[65] Richard Calwer, "Englands Absichten und die deutsche Sozialdemokratie," *Sozialistische Monatshefte*, II:11, November 1905, 921.
[66] February 12, 1906, 1226.

by the ruling classes. This refusal would make it inevitable that the ever growing proletariat would finally act on its own behalf.[67]

The last plea for political equality was made during the First World War, when many Social Democrats hoped for decisive concessions from the regime for the postwar period. One year before the split of the party in 1917, the leader of the right wing, Friedrich Ebert, expressed the sentiments and expectations of the moderate majority of functionaries and perhaps also of the majority of the rank and file in this forceful plea:

The masses returned from the trenches will be imbued with strong self-confidence. Theirs will be the resolution that the state for which they offered their lives must not become again the administrative machinery of a small privileged class. This new generation of the trench warfare that faced death and danger for long months, death which knows no classes and no exceptions—this new generation will not permit itself to be driven again into the barbed-wire entanglements of the three-class suffrage. This new generation demands freedom and political equality and it will know how to gain it by fighting if necessary. Therefore the hour of peace must be the hour of political equality.[68]

[67] Bebel, *Akademiker und Sozialismus, op. cit.,* 19 ff. Bebel's mistake was not so much a false assessment of the mentality of the upper classes in Imperial Germany as an underestimation of the political consequences of the slowly improving standard of living and especially of the rise of the new middle classes. He emphasized the potentialities of modern technology and large-scale economic organization, but did not take sufficiently into account the impact of their ongoing realization. In the 1905 preface to the second edition of his speech he saw no reason for revising what he had said in 1897.

Also in 1905, von Elm who was slowly moving from the orthodox to the revisionist side expected that the intransigence and implacability of labor's enemies would preserve "the spirit of class solidarity and of socialism." Discussing his views, the orthodox Ströbel considered it possible that the allegiance of the workers might be sought by the employers and the government, but he relied on the "unchangeable developmental tendencies of capitalism . . . to create an ever stronger disposition for the understanding of socialism and, through it, for the proletarian class struggle." H. Ströbel, "Gewerkschaften und 'sozialistischer Geist,' " *Neue Zeit,* 23:2, 1905, 569.

[68] Ebert in the Reichstag, April 5, 1916, see *Schriften, op. cit.,* 315.

Two years later Imperial Germany was destroyed in the wake of military collapse. This was largely due to wartime frustrations, but allegiance to the Empire would probably not have reached the breaking point if millions of workers had not felt a lack of social and political recognition. The second-class citizenship of the workers lasted formally until the end of the war, and the lack of political recognition for the labor movement until 1914.

VI
Counter-Tendencies

Class cleavage pervaded Imperial Germany because the authoritarian state and the liberal bourgeoisie were unwilling to integrate the labor movement into the national community through compromises resulting in far-reaching democratization. This has been my basic thesis. I will show in this chapter that the antagonistic relationship between the dominant system and the labor movement was not basically changed, but only ameliorated by various counter-tendencies. Directly concerned with the amelioration of the class cleavage, or pursuing policies which had this effect, were: (1) the Prussian and Imperial conservative officialdom responsible for the welfare reforms, (2) the academic social reformers (*Kathedersozialisten*) and the *Verein für Sozialpolitik,* (3) the South German governments, state diets and the Social Democratic factions in these diets, and (4) a younger generation of liberals. Furthermore, as time went on, there was more heterogeneity in the public reactions to the Social Democratic labor movement, especially after the turn of the century. I will contrast these counter-tendencies with the predominant trends.

1. The Academic Social Reformers

In 1872, about a decade before the beginning of the welfare legislation, the *Verein für Sozialpolitik* was founded by academicians, politicians and higher civil servants who were interested in welfare legislation and in the "Social Question" generally. The *Verein* became the leading academic vehicle for social reform and published through the decades a very large number of studies on the social implications of industrialization and on democratization.[1] The members of the association adhered to quite diverse points of view, but they shared a strong opposition to laissez-faire liberalism and a conviction that legislative intervention in the class conflicts of the industrializing society was necessary. Prominent as founders and famous as the leading representatives of the two distinct viewpoints within the association were the economists Gustav Schmoller and Lujo Brentano.[2] Schmoller wanted the "Social Question" solved by a monarchy imbued with strong prerogatives and obligations and by a conscientious and intelligent civil service which would be independent of the industrial aristocracy. Brentano emphasized more strongly the importance of countervailing power between capital and labor.

At the first meeting of those interested in taking a stand against laissez-faire liberalism—many of whom were called *Kathedersozialisten* (Socialists of the Chair) by their laissez-faire opponents —Schmoller explained that most of the participants were motivated by a grave concern about

. . . the deep cleavage characteristic of our social conditions, the struggle between entrepreneurs and workers, between the propertied and non-propertied classes, and the distinct possibility of a social revolution in the far-distant future. . . . they never regard the state, as does natural law and the Manchester school, as a necessary evil which should be restricted as much as possible; for them the state is the greatest moral institution for the education of mankind. They are sincerely for the constitutional system, but they do not want an alternative class rule by the various antagonistic economic classes; they want a strong

[1] Cf. Franz Boese, *Geschichte des Vereins für Sozialpolitik, 1872–1939*, Schriften des Vereins für Sozialpolitik, vol. 188 (Berlin: Duncker, 1939).

[2] Cf. Lujo Brentano, *Mein Leben im Kampf um die soziale Entwicklung Deutschlands* (Jena: Diederichs, 1931). See also Werner Barich, *Lujo Brentano als Sozialpolitiker,* Ph.D. dissertation, Frankfurt University, 1936.

state which legislates above the egoistic class interests, administrates with justice, protects the weak and elevates the lower classes; they consider the 200-year-old battle which the Prussian civil service and the Prussian monarchy have waged for equality of rights, for the abolition of all privileges of the higher classes, for the emancipation and elevation of the lower classes as our German state's best heritage to which we must always be faithful.[3]

The solution of the problem of class cleavage was vital for Schmoller since "all higher civilization, like that of the Greeks, the Romans and other peoples . . . perished in class struggles and revolutions caused by the inability to reconciliate the higher and the lower classes." Schmoller demanded the integration of the lower classes into the national community in order to prevent the distant possibility of a social revolution, which could occur "if it proves impossible on the basis of equality of rights, universal compulsory education, universal draft and all other reforms contemplated to elevate the lower classes, to educate and reconciliate them to such an extent that they fit harmoniously and peacefully into the organism of society and state." [4] Schmoller was for constitutional monarchism because he considered parliamentary government, and a democratic republic in particular, more prone to class rule and class struggle. "Parliamentarism and self-government are the high goals of every free people, but in the course of history they have often resulted, after a short period of accomplishments, in a class rule of the propertied . . . the worst class rule has not existed in monarchies but in republics." Schmoller advocated piecemeal reforms of the existing conditions and criticized the Social Democrats for their utopian plans. He could only see in them "the youthful fervor of the great emergent social movement. Our Social Democrats are somewhat different from but scarcely worse than English

[3] Gustav Schmoller, "Rede zur Eröffnung der Besprechung über die soziale Frage in Eisenach den 6. Oktober 1872," in *Zur Sozial-und Gewerbepolitik der Gegenwart* (Leipzig: Duncker, 1890), 5 and 9.
[4] *Op. cit.*, 10 f.

Chartism was in its time." He condemned the appeal of some Social Democratic leaders to hatred, envy and covetousness, but he acknowledged that others were "personally most honorable." [5]

With these views Schmoller expressed the opinions of a small minority. His 1874 speech on "The Social Question and the Prussian State," from which the last quotations were taken, was reprinted by the Lassallean *Neue Socialdemokrat* but attacked by many liberal newspapers; some outraged readers demanded court action. Great public attention was aroused by Heinrich von Treitschke's answer. In his essay "Socialism and Its Patrons" the prominent National Liberal historian and most famous panegyrist of Prussian glory and German greatness vigorously attacked the *Kathedersozialisten* and the Social Democrats. He was sympathetic toward state intervention, but the "Social Question" was for him first of all a "showy term of neo-Napoleonic derivation" and Social Democracy a French export, bankrupt in its country of origin. Social Democracy was an expression of noxious ideas and desires: "The guiding principle of the whole movement is unmistakably naked sensuality, the fundamental denial of all that raises man above animal." [6]

Because of his belief in the paramount cultural importance of the state, Treitschke also directed his venom against laissez-faire liberals, but he agreed with them that the emergence of the "Social Question" was due not so much to social development as to political factors, such as the introduction of equal suffrage for the Reichstag. Democrats of the year 1848, like Bamberger, Oppen-

[5] Id., "Die soziale Frage und der preussische Staat," *op. cit.,* 49 and 53.

[6] Heinrich von Treitschke, *Der Sozialismus und seine Gönner* (Berlin: Reimer, 1875), 3; first published in the *Preussische Jahrbücher*, Vol. 34, 1874. Treitschke yielded great influence not as a parliamentary deputy, but as editor of the *Preussische Jahrbücher* from 1866 until 1889; before him the journal was edited by Rudolf Haym (cf. Ch. II, 32) and after him by Hans Delbrück for three decades (cf. p. 146 of this chapter). On the character, influence and distribution of the journal, see Annelise Thimme, *Hans Delbrück als Kritiker der Wilhelminischen Epoche* (Düsseldorf: Droste, 1955), 12.

heim and von Unruh, who by then belonged to the left wing of the
National Liberals and adhered to laissez-faire, long ago had revised their earlier positive views on universal and equal suffrage.
Bamberger went so far as to consider the problems arising from
industrialization "not a consequence of misery, but of the improvement of the general condition of mankind," and H. B. Oppenheim,
who had coined the term "Kathedersozialist," denied that there was
a "Social Question" or even a "housing question"—meaning that
conditions had been worse in earlier times.[7] For these laissez-faire
liberals, welfare politics meant socialism. They charged the *Verein
für Sozialpolitik* with producing an artificial class gap between the
liberal bourgeoisie and the working class. The majority of the educated and propertied middle classes sided with their position
against the academic social reformers.[8]

[7] Quoted in Gagel, *op. cit.,* 80.

[8] Schmoller described in 1897 the changing relationships over 25 years of the
Verein to various political groups and the changing perspectives of the public.
Between 1872 and 1875 the adherents of laissez-faire in business and government were the strongest critics, while the conservatives and Bismarck took a
benevolent attitude. In the eighties, after the beginning of the welfare legislation, the Social Democratic attacks mounted. With the end of the *Kulturkampf* in the second half of the eighties, a *rapprochement* between the Center
Party and the *Verein* materialized. Because of the *Kulturkampf* it could not
be accomplished earlier, despite the fact that both "were friendly towards
labor for similar ethical, religious and humane reasons." A sympathetic relationship developed also with the "Protestant-Social movement . . . since
most of us are Protestants." From 1892 until 1895 the progress of welfare
legislation was arrested and the *Verein's* relationship with the government
was again strained. "Zur 25jährigen Feier des Vereins für Sozialpolitik,"
September 23, 1897, in *Zwanzig Jahre Deutscher Politik, op. cit.,* 31. See
p. 32 for other changes in the attitudes of the parties toward the association.
A few examples of the early Social Democratic attacks on the academic social
reformers may be given. In 1872 the *Volksstaat* (87) lashed out against their
welfare plans, condemning them as completely insufficient; it spoke of the
intellectual superiority of Western bourgeois thinkers like Sismonde Sis-
mondi and John Stuart Mill. "The Socialists of the Chair labor with a pair of
spectacles and hemorrhoids—this is the way all German scholarly work is
done" (82). In two other Eisenacher journals the academic social reformers

The Protestant Schmoller thought that despite his affirmation of Prussia's historical role he had "basically remained a South German liberal," just as Chancellor Prince Hohenlohe believed himself to be.[9] Lujo Brentano was, like Hohenlohe, a Catholic and a liberal, but in contrast to Schmoller and Hohenlohe, he was not a partisan of Bismarck and Prussia. He looked to England for his political model. Brentano held the view that the workers were fighting the economic and political order because the state had refused them the chance to defend their interests within the established order. Since the workers were considered "insubordinate" when they fought for their interests, they had come to see themselves as rebels. Brentano condemned the persecution of beliefs which were not expressed in action. As usual, he referred to English examples in order to show that labor leaders allowed to represent labor interests would act with moderation, although they would still adhere to their old radical creed. In fact, their adherence to their radical beliefs made it psychologically possible for them to become moderate in practice. Any attempt at forcing them to abjure their old beliefs would only radicalize them.[10]

Neither the government and the employers nor the public were ready to accept such a view when Brentano made this statement in 1890. Significant but not decisive changes had occurred since 1874, when Schmoller and Treitschke clashed over the problem of integrating the labor movement into the nation. In the meantime

---

were called "Royal Prussian Social Humanists," timid and incapable of stopping the advance of socialism. The Lassallean *Neue Sozialdemokrat* stated simply: "Incurable idiocy . . . the mountains labor, and a mouse is born" (1872, 119). Quoted in Schuster, *op. cit.,* 104 f, 80, 70. About the turn of the century, the Social Democratic attitude toward the *Verein für Sozialpolitik* had become rather conciliatory.

[9] Schmoller, "Die preussische Wahlrechtsreform," *op. cit.,* 65.

[10] Cf. Lujo Brentano, "Arbeitseinstellungen und die Fortbildung des Arbeitsvertrags," report presented at the proceedings of September 1890, *Schriften des Vereins für Sozialpolitik* (Leipzig: Duncker, 1890), Vol. 47, 124 ff.

the great imperial social welfare legislation had been instituted.[11] This meant a triumph for the academic social reformers over the laissez-faire liberals. But the class cleavage that the academic reformers wanted to diminish continued unabated because the antisocialist law of 1878 preceded the welfare legislation. Then, in 1890, the antisocialist law lapsed, and the public accepted the welfare legislation and for the first time showed some sympathy for workers during a major strike, the great miners' strike. Even William II made a benevolent gesture by receiving a delegation of striking workers. The basic difficulty of the "positive" attitude of the Emperor, the reformist bureaucracy, the public and most academic social reformers was their insistence that, in gratitude for the welfare legislation and the relaxation of political repression or just for the demonstration of benevolent paternalism, the workers should recognize the dominant system explicitly and abandon the Social Democratic labor movement, unless its leaders radically changed their intransigence. Therefore, Brentano's call to accept the Social Democrats as they were appeared unjustified. The Social Democrats were at best to be tolerated. At the same meeting where

[11] I will omit details about the Imperial social welfare legislation; whatever positive short-range political effect it might have had was cancelled by the antisocialist legislation. Furthermore, the welfare legislation stopped short of what was considered most important by many workers: protective laws which would go beyond accident, disability, sickness and old age insurance. In the long run the legislation passed helped to prevent an aggravation of the class cleavage. The literature on the welfare legislation is large. I will cite only a few outstanding writings by or about those who carried it through: H. Berlepsch, *Sozialpolitische Erfahrungen und Erinnerungen* (München-Gladbach: Volksvereinsverlag, 1925); Hans Rothfels, *Theodor Lohmann und die Kampfjahre der staatlichen Sozialpolitik* (Berlin: Mittler, 1927); on the resumption of welfare legislation after 1900 under Count Posadowsky, see Johannes Penzler, *Graf Posadowsky als Finanz-, Sozial-und Handelspolitiker* (Leipzig: Weber, 1907 and 1908), 2 vols.; Leopold von Wiese, *Graf Posadowsky als Sozialpolitiker* (Cologne: Christlicher Gewerkschaftsverlag, 1909); on the Social Democratic reactions to the welfare legislation, see Hertha Wolff, *Die Stellung der Sozialdemokratie zur deutschen Arbeiterversicherungsgesetzgebung von ihrer Entstehung an bis zur Reichsversicherungsordnung,* Ph.D. dissertation, Freiburg University, 1933.

Brentano spoke, Bueck, the secretary general of the powerful *Zentralverband Deutscher Industrieller,* argued that the requirements of efficiency and profitableness within the plant and within the capitalist economy could not be met if the workers and their organizations were given equality in relation to the employers. He added that the employers would not resist the organization of the workers, but that "they will never, in as far as 'never' can be said at all, be willing to negotiate with representatives of workers' organizations on the basis of equality as it is understood here." [12] Big business stuck to this policy until 1918 by steadfastly refusing to deal with unions and thus greatly contributed to the perpetuation of the class cleavage.

2. *Trends and Counter-Trends in the Liberal Parties*

Despite the relaxation of political repression after 1890 and despite the gradually increasing cooperation of party and union functionaries in the federal insurance administration, labor courts, municipal parliaments and agencies, some of the lines drawn sharply during the antisocialist legislation persisted. One of the abiding legacies of the antisocialist legislation was the establishment of the liberal parties as mere middle-class parties. The liberals had always been bourgeois, but believed themselves the representatives of the whole people. This belief was now shattered. The old belief that education would make the masses more "enlightened," meaning moderate, was also abandoned. To many liberals it appeared that the workers had been captured, in Unruh's words, by Social Democratic appeals to "selfishness, the desire for other people's property, for the easy life without strain, even for the rule over the well-to-do and educated people" and that they had been taken

---

[12] *Schriften des Vereins für Sozialpolitik, op. cit.,* 151.

in "by the continuous assertion that capital exploited the working class." In complete resignation Unruh concluded: "At best, generations will pass before the most numerous electoral class will see through the sophisms in the seductive speeches and writings, if it ever manages to do so." [13]

The loss of working class support had more direct consequences for the Progressives than for the National Liberals. The Progressives had claimed to be a people's party. But in 1878 Virchow, the famous pathologist and a vocal opponent of Bismarck, declared that

> . . . in fact we do not want to have the real Social Democrats among us. The Social Democrat who purposively pursues his aims is our direct enemy . . . even more than the conservatives. They may come to us voluntarily and join us, but we will not woo them. We must be independent of the government above and of the masses below, who threaten society. . . . Therefore I think that we must look to the right for support among independent men: the industrious people, the propertied, the good old German *Bürgertum.* . . . A particular Social Question does not exist for us, we are concerned with the totality of all cultural issues.[14]

Thus Virchow and Richter, Bismarck's most intransigent liberal foe, led the Progressive party to the right and made it explicitly a middle-class party. The shift was completed when the party fused in 1884 with the strong faction of laissez-faire liberals who had left the National Liberal party. The left wing of the Progressives was either silenced or left the party. The new party was greatly weakened because the bourgeoisie had ceased to be a broad social basis for progressive liberalism. Progressive judges and higher civil servants were eliminated during the Puttkamer era (1878–88) or died

---

[13] Quoted in Gagel, *op. cit.,* 87 f. The survivors of the old liberal generation, with their commitment to an abstract humanism, also felt pessimistic or helpless toward the population growth and other incisive changes brought about by industrialization. Cf. letters of Rümelin to Rudolf Haym in 1879 and of Roggenbach to v. Stosch in 1893, *op. cit.,* 154 f.

[14] Quoted in Gagel, 97 f.

out. The aristocratic style of life was increasingly imitated in the bourgeoisie; to be an officer of the reserve was a dominant aspiration, widespread and important for social mobility and civilian self-esteem.[15] Major reasons for these changes can be seen in the conservative recognition by the eighties of the constitutional regime and the Reich as Bismarck had set it up, and in the bourgeois satisfaction with the achievement of national unification and major constitutional goals. The way for a *rapprochement* between aristocracy and bourgeoisie was open and resulted in the lasting, though sometimes precarious, alliance of Western big business interests and East Elbian agricultural interests. This alliance formed the core of what came to be called Miquel's *Sammlungspolitik,* a policy of allying conservative and liberal, Catholic and Protestant, middle and upper class groups in one great coalition for the defense of the existing order.[16] This alliance dominated the domestic political scene until the First World War, though it was weakened by the breakdown of Bülow's liberal-conservative coalition in 1909.

Johann von Miquel was Prussian Minister of Finance from 1890 until 1901.[17] He had been a democrat in 1848. Thirty years later he was instrumental in leading the National Liberals to the right. In the early nineties he introduced progressive income tax legislation, but this attempt at social justice had the political effect of diminishing the voting power of the lower income groups since the right to vote in one of the three classes was now dependent on the income tax paid by an individual. After the great Social Demo-

[15] Cf. Eckart Kehr, "Zur Genesis des Kgl. preussischen Reserveoffiziers," *Die Gesellschaft,* 1928:2, 492–502; Schücking, *op. cit.,* 24–29, and Karl Demeter for a general appraisal of the impact of the officers' corps and the reserve officers on German society, *Das deutsche Offizierskorps in seinen historisch-soziologischen Grundlagen* (Berlin: Hobbing, 1930).

[16] The alliance of Western big business interests and Eastern agrarian interests led to foreign policies which antagonized England as well as Russia and contributed to the diplomatic isolation of Imperial Germany. Cf. G. W. F. Hallgarten, *Imperialismus vor 1914* (Munich: Beck, 1951), 2 vols.

[17] On Miquel see Hans Herzfeld, *Johannes von Miquel* (Detmold: Meyer, 1938), 2 vols.

cratic electoral success in 1890, Miquel was the most energetic National Liberal advocate of a *coup d'état,* to abolish universal suffrage for the Reichstag, but within the liberal camp he found resistance among the Progressives and the South German National Liberals. His subsequent *Sammlungspolitik* was successful, but at the same time new ideological counter-currents arose within liberalism.

Rudolf von Bennigsen, the leader of the National Liberals from 1866 until 1898, and his South German successor Ernst Bassermann were basically in favor of extending more rights and responsibilities to the working class. However, ideologically more important for the development of right-wing liberalism was the editorial victory of Hans Delbrück, a Free Conservative Reichstag member, over Treitschke, whom he succeeded in 1889 as editor of the very influential *Preussische Jahrbücher.* Within his party Delbrück lost out to Stumm-Halberg, after whom the second half of the nineties was called the "Era Stumm," when welfare legislation came to a virtual standstill.[18] Delbrück left the party at the beginning of this

---

[18] The definitive biography on Bennigsen is Hermann Oncken, *Rudolf von Bennigsen* (Stuttgart: Deutsche Verlagsanstalt, 1910); on Bassermann see Theodor Eschenburg, *Bassermann und die Blockpolitik,* Ph.D. dissertation, University of Berlin, 1929; on Delbrück, see Annelise Thimme, *op. cit.;* Stumm-Halberg, who was elevated into peerage, was the most powerful figure in the Saar industry and dominated its welfare schemes no less than the area's political climate; cf. Hellwig, *op. cit.,* on "Era Stumm" esp. 506–56. German big business instituted extensive private welfare programs, but insisted on absolute managerial authority, on being, as the phrase had it, "master in its own house" (*Herr im Hause*). On private welfare measures of industry see Alexander von Brandt, *Zur sozialen Entwicklung im Saargebiet* (Leipzig: Duncker, 1904); Adolf Günther, *Die Wohlfahrtseinrichtungen der Arbeitgeber. Schriften des Vereins für Sozialpolitik,* Vol. 114, 1905; Julius Post and H. Albrecht, *Musterstätten persönlicher Fürsorge von Arbeitgebern für ihre Geschäftsangehörigen* (Berlin: Oppenheim, 1893), 2 vols.; Richard Roesicke, "Über das Verhältnis der Arbeitgeber zu ihren Arbeitnehmern," *Jahrbuch für Gesetzgebung,* Vol. 7, 1893, 1–22; Rudolf Schwenger, "Die betriebliche Sozialpolitik in der westdeutschen Grosseisenindustrie," *Schriften des Vereins für Sozialpolitik,* Vol. 186, 1934. Relevant for the position of the minority of more liberal employers are

era. He was almost as nationalistic and monarchical as Treitschke, but he advocated a balance between crown and parliament. Delbrück did not want further democratization, as did his friend Friedrich Naumann.

Before turning to Pastor Naumann's important role in German liberalism I will deal with Max Weber, who influenced him greatly. Weber, the son of a National Liberal Reichstag deputy and, at the time, a brilliant young scholar of law and economics, was to remain much more of an outsider in German liberal politics than Naumann. He was very active in the *Verein für Sozialpolitik,* but he held no political office and was, moreover, incapacitated for political and academic activities for half a decade after 1897. From the beginning of his career in the early nineties he was not much concerned with liberal humanitarian reform, conservative welfare legislation or the Marxist problem of alienation; decisive for him was the assertion of the nation's welfare in a world of power politics. In his 1895 inaugural speech at the University of Freiburg on "Nation State and Economic Policy," which greatly impressed Naumann, Weber argued that economic policy had to serve the power interests of the nation.[19] The nation state was nothing mystical for Weber; it

---

Heinrich Freese, *Die konstitutionelle Fabrik* (Jena: Fischer, 1922) and Werner von Siemens, *Lebenserinnerungen* (Berlin: Springer, 1904). For a debate between a liberal and a paternalist manager, see Heinrich Freese, "Empfindsame Sozialpolitik," and J. Vorster, "Die Sozialpolitik des Herrn Heinrich Freese in Berlin," *Preussische Jahrbücher,* Vol. 85, 1896, 135–48, 371–79 and 379–81. The standard textbook in the field was Heinrich Herkner, *Die Arbeiterfrage* (Berlin: Guttentag, 1908), 5th edition.

[19] Cf. Max Weber, "Der Nationalstaat und die Volkswirtschaftspolitik," *Gesammelte Politische Schriften* (Tübingen: Mohr, 1958), 1–25; on the political significance of this speech, see Arnold Bergsträsser, "Max Webers Antrittsvorlesung in zeitgeschichtlicher Perspektive," *Vierteljahrshefte für Zeitgeschichte,* 5:3, 1957, 212 ff. A brilliant study of Weber's political ideas and activities is Wolfgang J. Mommsen, *Max Weber und die deutsche Politik: 1890–1920* (Tübingen: Mohr, 1959); see esp. Chs. III–V. It supersedes J. P. Mayer, *Max Weber and German Politics* (London: Faber and Faber, 1943). All quotations from Weber and Mommsen are by permission of the publisher.

was a concrete entity whose interests had to be safeguarded realistically. Affirmation of this kind of *raison d'état* did not imply advocacy of systematic state intervention at home or abroad. It also was not identical with the contemporary Social Darwinist exaltation of the struggle for existence and the survival of the fittest. Indeed, Weber criticized the evolutionary fallacy of assuming that economically superior classes somehow represented a superior type of man. Economic power and the capacity for political leadership were not necessarily identical. Weber's criterion for evaluating the political claims of social classes was their ability to provide political leadership for the whole nation. Neither the economically declining *Junkers* nor the economically rising working class appeared to qualify for this political leadership; Weber tried to invigorate the liberal bourgeoisie's will to power and to national leadership that had been stunted by the events of 1848 and of 1871.

Weber advocated the "social integration and unification of the nation, which have been destroyed by modern economic developments, in order to prepare it for the severe tests of the future." [20] He was fully in favor of permitting the working class to fight legally for its economic interests, but he contended its claim to political power:

Politically the working class is infinitely more immature than a clique of journalists, who wants to monopolize its leadership, would like to make the workers believe. These circles of declassed bourgeois like to play with the memories of a century ago; they have indeed managed to evoke the impression in timid minds that they are the spiritual heirs of the men of the Convention. But they are infinitely more harmless than they appear to themselves. There is not a spark of that Catilinarian energy of the deed in them, and no trace of that tremendous national passion which permeated the halls of the Convention. They are miserable political tinkers—they lack the great power instincts of a class called upon to take over political leadership. [21]

[20] Weber, *op. cit.*, 23.
[21] *Op. cit.*, 22.

Given his contempt for the powerlessness of the Social Democrats, Weber did not tire of berating the bourgeois public time and again for its fear of the "red spectre" and for its resistance toward integrating them into the political process. He understood well the ideological and organizational advantages which the Social Democrats derived from their isolation, and he expected that their political participation in municipalities and in the state would discredit them quickly if they followed doctrinaire rather than reformist lines.[22] He was willing to accept a Social Democratic domination of municipal and other administrations as long as they did not gain control over the decisive institution: the military.

Weber made Naumann aware of politics as a struggle for power and made him realize that welfare legislation was not an isolated problem of domestic politics. Naumann was originally a follower of the Christian-Social movement of former Court Chaplain Stoecker and accepted its patriarchal conservatism.[23] At first he opposed parliamentarism and debunked the importance of parties, being in favor of corporate representation. But under Weber's influence he recognized that vocational associations as political bodies were inferior to political parties, which could pursue welfare politics as

[22] Cf. Max Weber's address on the occasion of the 1907 convention of the Verein für Sozialpolitik; see *Schriften des Vereins für Sozialpolitik,* Vol. 125, 295–300.

[23] On conservative Protestantism, see William O. Shanahan, *German Protestants Face the Social Question: The Conservative Phase, 1815–1871* (University of Notre Dame Press, 1954), Vol. I. On Naumann, see id., "Friedrich Naumann: A Mirror of Wilhelmian Germany," *The Review of Politics,* 13:3, July 1951, 267–301; id., "Friedrich Naumann: A German View of Power and Nationalism," in E. M. Earle, ed., *Nationalism and Internationalism* (New York: Columbia University Press, 1950), 352–98. The major biography on Naumann is by his disciple and friend Theodor Heuss, later the first president of the Federal Republic of Germany: *Friedrich Naumann* (Stuttgart: Deutsche Verlagsanstalt, 1957). Cf. also Richard Nürnberger, "Imperialismus, Sozialismus und Christentum bei Friedrich Naumann," *Historische Zeitschrift,* 170:3, 1950, 525–48. Not available to me was F. Sponsels, *Friedrich Naumann und die deutsche Sozialdemokratie.* Ph.D. dissertation, University of Erlangen, 1952.

well as take responsibility for the national interest. Naumann wanted the progressive bourgeoisie to lead the working class and to reconstruct socialism to fit the requirements of both welfare politics and foreign politics. He affirmed liberalism as the protector of the individual vis-à-vis the state, and socialism as the protector vis-à-vis any large-scale organization. In 1896 he founded his own political party, the National-Social Association, which Weber joined with reservations. In the program discussions Naumann pushed through a demand for equal suffrage in municipalities in order to accord full political recognition to the workers and to force the Social Democrats to take civil responsibilities.

Naumann worked out his position in successive editions of his book *Demokratie und Kaisertum.*[24] He demanded that Germany have a government better equipped to cope with the needs of a rapidly industrializing nation. He hoped that long-run structural changes in the fast growing population would swell the left-wing vote and strengthen parliament. However, the Social Democrats and the left-wing liberals would have to abandon their old stance of democratic negativism toward the government. He believed that without sacrificing principle a Social Democratic declaration in 1890 to support the government would have reduced the conservatives and National Liberals to a parliamentary minority and facilitated Chancellor Caprivi's attempt to lean on the left-wing liberals. He understood well the Social Democratic reasons for remaining intransigent, but he considered it imperative that the Social Democrats now abandoned their old radical rhetoric and utopianism. A people's monarchy was feasible only if the left supported national defense. Naumann favored a strong fleet capable of protecting Germany's international trade interests, which were vital for improving the standard of living. He called William II an "industrial emperor" (*Industriekaiser*) because he vociferously supported a large pro-

[24] Friedrich Naumann, *Demokratie und Kaisertum* (Berlin: Hilfe, 1900). I used the fourth edition of 1905.

gram of naval expansion. This vision of a fusion of democracy and monarchy (*Kaisertum*) did not convince voters either to the right or left of Naumann. In the 1903 elections his party polled only 30,000 votes compared to the three million votes for the Social Democrats. Subsequently Naumann and most of his followers joined the Advanced Liberals; a minority went over to the Social Democrats.

Men like Friedrich Naumann and Max Weber or the industrialist Walther Rathenau—another brilliant outsider—were not free of biases and misconceptions, but they recognized better than most contemporary liberals the problems and probable direction of industrialization and democratization.[25] These men were of great importance for the advancement of new ideas in an age of large-scale and rapid industrialization, but their influence as ideological pioneers could not be as broad and effective as that of Treitschke and others before them, who served as mouthpieces for prevailing public trends. Naumann's journal, the *Hilfe,* could not compete with the *Preussische Jahrbücher* in terms of public influence. But his ideas did facilitate an eventual policy revision of the liberal left-wing parties. Such a revision was difficult to accomplish because it was likely to weaken the parties numerically, at least for some time; any move toward the left would alienate many bourgeois voters without winning over many workers.

After 1904 Theodor Barth spread Naumann's new ideas in his journal, *Nation,* an advanced liberal magazine. Naumann's ideas

[25] On Naumann's views on the problem of large-scale economic organization and his idea of "the constitutional factory," see Abraham Shuchman: *Co-determination: Labor's Middle Way in Germany* (Washington: Public Affairs Press, 1957), 15 f. Naumann believed that conflicts over property rights would be resolved by the emergent split of the functions of management and of property holders; these conflicts would be replaced by conflicts over internal control and organization. Naumann envisaged corporations owned and managed by the employees. Such arrangement would pose new problems which socialism would have to solve. However, such a "constitutional factory" would be superior to the autocratic factory.—For a synopsis of Naumann, Weber and Rathenau see Knoll, *op. cit.,* 128 ff.

first found some sympathetic reaction in the *Freisinnige Vereini-gung,* one of the two Progressive parties. After the death of the dogmatic and intransigent Eugen Richter, the three left-wing liberal parties (the South German People's party being the third) could effect a *rapprochement.* However, the Progressive shift toward the left was arrested by Bülow's "bloc" of 1907, which established a parliamentary coalition of conservatives, National Liberals, and progressives against the Center party and the Social Democrats. The trend toward the left continued after the "bloc" fell apart in 1909. The three liberal left-wing parties merged into the Progressive People's party in 1910.

Another consequence of the breakup of Bülow's coalition was the foundation of the *Hansabund,* established in 1910 as a rally-ing center for all forces of industrial society—from big business to labor—against the East Elbian aristocracy, whose conservative Reichstag representatives had refused the introduction of inheritance taxes for armament purposes.[26] Characteristic of the rigidity of the domestic political structure was the fact that labor organizations re-fused to join the association and big business deserted it within a year, preferring its old alliance with the big agrarian interests. The result of the Social Democratic and Progressive alliance in the 1912 Reichstag elections was also indicative of the strength of the class cleavage. Such an alliance was nothing new; Richter had concluded it in 1887 and 1890, although he had always remained intransigent toward the Social Democrats; now the Progressive leadership took a relatively positive attitude toward the Social Democrats. How-ever, the run-off results showed that a large part of the Progressive electorate preferred ultimately to vote for a conservative rather than for a Social Democrat—except in Bavaria, where the common

---

[26] On the Hansabund see J. Riesser, *Der Hansabund* (Jena: Diederichs, 1912). A leading figure of the association was Gustav Stresemann, later for six years foreign minister of the Weimar Republic. Cf. Franz Miethke, *Gustav Stresemann der Wirtschaftpolitiker* (Dresden: Sächsische Verlagsan-stalt, 1919).

antagonism toward the Catholic party united the voters of the two parties.[27]

Thus, no decisive realignment of the parties occurred on the federal level before 1914. However, democratization progressed in southern Germany and was even viewed favorably by some members of the younger generation of National Liberals, especially the so-called *Jungliberalen,* who gradually became advocates for the integration of the Social Democrats. The chairman of the federal association of National-Liberal youth groups said at its 1910 convention that

. . . our government's treatment of the Social Democrats does not appear to me to be opportune. You do not stop the expansion of Social Democratic organizations by turning against the individual worker who follows the Social Democrats. . . . Equal rights for all parties, also for the Social Democrats, seems to me the best means of fighting the Social Democrats as a party.[28]

[27] For a detailed analysis of the terms and results of the alliance, see Henry S. Sloan, *The German Social Democrats in the Reichstag Elections of 1912,* M.A. thesis, New York University, May 1952, esp. p. 69. When the secret terms of the alliance became known to the Social Democratic party members, a sharp reaction occurred since it turned out that the Social Democratic leaders had conceded more to the Progressives than vice versa. Many Social Democratic workers were no less averse to vote for a Progressive, than Progressive voters were to vote for a Social Democrat. Only some revisionists were unequivocally in favor of a "great coalition" (*Grossblock*) of Social Democrats and liberals. Cf. Ludwig Frank, *Aufsätze, Reden und Briefe,* Hedwig Wachenheim, ed. (Berlin: Verlag für Sozialwissenschaft, 1924), 185 f; see also articles by Wolfgang Heine. Wilhelm Kolb and Max Schippel in the *Sozialistische Monatshefte,* XV, April 20, 1911, 481–86, September 7, 1911, 1160–64, and December 21, 1911, 1639–44.

[28] Address of Dr. Fischer, chairman of the *Reichsverband der national-liberalen Jugendvereine,* at the Cologne convention, October 22, 1910, cited in August Erdmann, ed., *Die Sozialdemokratie im Urteile ihrer Gegner* (Berlin: Vorwärts, 1911), 142. Erdmann reprints a series of Catholic, conservative, and liberal press statements recognizing the accomplishments of the Social Democratic labor movement or pleading for the renunciation of political repression and personal attacks. On the increasing public recognition, see also Tönnies, *op. cit.,* 472.

Even more outspoken was the National Liberal *Kölnische Zeitung,* which advocated the adoption of the South German example:

The Social Democrats are such a large party that we must take them into account; they will not disappear in one day; no Social Democrat will become a conservative or liberal within a short time. Therefore, we must ask ourselves whether the conditions could not be improved in Prussia if the East Elbian approach were replaced by one more similar to the South German. The system does not have to be changed, we only ask for a less exclusive treatment of persons and issues. If it is true that the South German conditions are preferable to the Prussian ones, then the desire to achieve results in Prussia similar to those achieved in southern Germany is legitimate. Therefore, it should be made easy for every Social Democrat actively to cooperate in economic affairs; this cooperation should not only be tolerated, but elicited, in order to weaken the utopian theoretical demands. Such a consideration does not merely derive from a liberal position, it should be the viewpoint of all those parties which realize that, for the time being, we must accept the existence of a strong Social Democratic party.[29]

It was only after the turn of the century that the Social Democrats and the Advanced Liberals sufficiently lessened their ideological commitments, especially with regard to economic policies, to cooperate in some South German state parliaments. The Social Democrats did so under the strong influence of South German revisionism, which was more democratic than that in northern Germany, where its spokesmen were more nationalist and imperialist. This split was partly due to the different historical legacies of the two regions.[30] Bavaria, Württemberg and Baden introduced equal suffrage in 1904, and in Baden and Bavaria the Social Democrats even voted for the state budget, in violation of established national party policy. The historical roots of the ongoing South German

[29] *Kölnische Zeitung,* November 6, 1909, cited in *op. cit.,* 140 f.
[30] Cf. Boris Goldenberg, *Beiträge zur Soziologie der deutschen Vorkriegssozialdemokratie,* Ph.D. dissertation, University of Heidelberg, n.d. (between 1930–33), 37.

democratization can be traced far into the past. In the 16th and 17th centuries a dualism existed between the territorial princes and the estates, especially in the cities, in southern Germany. When the South German state parliaments came into being after 1820, their members often conceived of them as a loyal opposition to the government and followed the spirit of Montesquieu in their advocacy of the division of power. The most renowned liberal representative of this trend before the 1848 revolution, Rotteck, whose *Staatslexikon* was very influential in bourgeois circles, championed a dualism between government and popular representation. He believed that an enforced unity created between them would inevitably produce despotism. After the revolution the great political scientist Robert von Mohl recommended that the dualism be overcome by giving parliament institutional predominance.[31] Half a century later the South German states did approach this stage, but the historical decision of 1850 favoring the Prussian principle of monarchic constitutionalism remained dominant for the Reich as a whole until its bitter end. Chancellor Hohenlohe's famous verdict on the basic weakness of South Germany in relation to the North was true. The aged prince, South German, Catholic, and liberal in his own way, wrote in his diary on the occasion of a hunting visit with high-ranking Junkers at Jagdschloss Springe on December 15, 1898:

When I sit between the Prussian Excellencies, the contrast between northern and southern Germany is clearly impressed upon me. South German liberalism cannot assert itself against the Junkers. They are too numerous, too powerful, and they have on their side the monarch and the army. The Center party, too, goes along with them. Everything that I have experienced during these four years [as Chancellor] can be explained from this opposition. The Germans are right when they consider my presence in Berlin a guarantee of German unity. As I worked for the unification of North and South from 1866 until 1870 [as Prime Minister of Bavaria], so too must I see that Prussia remains

31 Cf. Hintze, *op. cit.,* 390.

with the Reich, because all of these gentlemen here, including Miquel, do not care about the Reich and would rather abandon it today than tomorrow.[32]

Over the decades, the public image of the Social Democratic labor movement as represented by the press slowly improved. In 1874 a man like the economist and sociologist Schäffle, a former Austrian minister of finance, could express the view of a tiny minority, largely academic, when he credited the Social Democrats with having

. . . rendered an essential service, namely, by critically and politically suggesting the "positive social reform" which has been taken in hand by the government in Germany. . . . To the legitimate demands of Social Democracy—that there shall be furnished even to the proletariat of industry, as a result of their labor, *a position worthy of manhood,* and something more than the barely necessary share of the produce of the national labor community; that the abuse of the superiority of capital and of credit shall be averted; that a sense of joint responsibility in relation to poverty and misfortune shall be awakened; that a public economic management shall be introduced, in so far as the capitalist

[32] Hohenlohe, *op. cit.,* 474. It may be added that neither Bismarck nor Bülow were typical Junkers and made a point of being different. See Bismarck, *Reden,* Kohl, ed., *op. cit.,* Vol. 13, 107, where he refers to his background as evidence that he was not *verjunkert.* After Bülow's downfall in 1909 August Stein, representative of the very influential left wing *Frankfurter Zeitung* in Berlin from 1883 until 1920, who had intimate contact with chancellors, wrote that he had not been a typical Junker even though he had once characterized himself as an agrarian chancellor. Bülow himself expressed a similar qualification in December, 1914, to Theodor Wolff: "I am a Junker myself, but not the perfect Junker; I have seen other countries besides Germany. Jagow [secretary of state] has all their pettiness, all their bad qualities." However, Bülow characterized himself to Wolff, without qualification, as a Prussian: "Every man has his toquade, his obsession. Mine is that I am an enthusiastic Prussian. I feel it—every time soldiers march past, down below." See Irenaeus (pseudonym for A. Stein), *Aufsätze* (Frankfurt: Frankfurter Societätsdruckerei, 1921), 65–77; Theodor Wolff, *op. cit.,* 19 and 17. Wolff was another very prominent Berlin newspaperman.

economy becomes actually useless—to this demand the most complete satisfaction can be given in the way of positive gradual reform, without suppressing capital in the shape of private property, but rather by generalizing it.[33]

Two decades later such voices were more numerous, though they still came predominantly from academic circles. In 1897 the conservative welfare politician Rudolf Meyer acknowledged the contribution that the Social Democratic workers in Germany, Austria and Switzerland had made toward the rise of industry. In their struggle they have developed "the best intellectual qualities, . . . the really good workers . . . are all Social Democrats." [34] The relationship between intelligence, efficiency, and Social Democratic membership was increasingly accepted in the public. Elaborating on this theme the liberal professor Niebergall wrote in 1909 that the Social Democratic labor movement is "now widely recognized as the great liberator of the intellectual life of the people." [35] In the same year a pastor maintained, on the basis of personal observations, that the Social Democratic labor movement had noticeably bettered the character of the common people wherever it had exerted its influence and that it had truly become the church of the poor, as much by its own influence as by the default of the Christian church.[36]

The public recognition of the Social Democrats often had tactical overtones, but even then it could contain genuine admiration. For example, the old Theodor Mommsen wrote acidly in Barth's *Nation* that the Social Democrats are

[33] Albert Schäffle, *op. cit.,* 126 f, my emphasis. The book was originally a series of articles in a religious magazine. It was the first academic treatise on Marx's *Capital* and received considerable public and academic attention.
[34] Rudolf Meyer in Maximilian Harden's anti-Wilhelminian *Zukunft,* March 1897, quoted in Erdmann, ed., *op. cit.,* 49.
[35] Professor Niebergall in the monthly, *Nord und Süd,* August 1909, reprinted in Erdmann, *op. cit.,* 73 f.
[36] See Pastor Liebster, Leipzig, in "Kirche und Sozialdemokraten," reprinted in *op. cit.,* 72.

. . . the only great party which has claim to political respect. It is not necessary to emphasize its talents. Everybody in Germany knows that with a mind such as Bebel's, a dozen East Elbian Junkers would be equipped to shine among their peers. The dedication and the willingness to sacrifice of the Social Democratic masses impresses even those persons who do not share their aims. Our liberals should take as a model the discipline of the party, which asserts itself despite the tremendous difficulties apparent in the party conventions. On the other hand, it cannot be denied that the Social Democrats are to a large extent responsible for the present, nearly desperate political situation.[37]

Mommsen's qualification remained decisive for the majority of the public, while the octagenarian himself came to embrace the demand of the young generation to effect a *rapprochement* with the Social Democrats.[38]

Thus, the counter-tendencies could not obliterate the character of the Empire as an authoritarian state nor the political class cleavage of German society. However, they mitigated the authoritarianism of the state and ameliorated the class cleavage.

[37] Theodor Mommsen in the *Nation,* Dec. 1902, reprinted in *op. cit.,* 169.
[38] On Mommsen's changing attitudes toward the Social Democrats, see Alfred Heuss, *Theodor Mommsen und das 19. Jahrhundert* (Kiel: Hirt, 1956), 212–20; for the text of Mommsen's moving testament of 1899, in which he repudiates the historical course of the nation and the uncritical attitudes of the general public, see p. 282, *op. cit.*

VII

The Role of Marxism in the Social Democratic Subculture[1]

1. The Labor Movement as a Subculture

After 1890 the Social Democratic labor movement contributed to the continued national polarization by rapidly expanding into a large self-contained mass movement and by embracing a Marxist ideology which was no less aggravating to the public because it was attenuated deterministically. The labor movement came to offer to masses of workers a way of life which was significantly different from that of other groups, especially those explicitly supporting the prevailing political and social system. The vehicle for this way of life was a proliferating network of political, economic and cultural organizations. I will call the complex of Social Democratic beliefs and organized activities a subculture in order to indicate the separateness of the labor movement from the dominant system and also their inherent connection.[2] As a political subculture, the labor

[1] The main arguments of this chapter as far as they pertain to the seeming paradox of radical ideology and moderate practice were first presented in my paper on "The Radical Ideology of a Moderate Labor Movement," *Transactions of the Fourth World Congress of Sociology* (Louvain: International Sociological Association, 1959), IV, 9–24.

[2] In Professor Milton Yinger's ideal typical terms, the labor movement was a contraculture as well as a subculture. See his essay on "Contraculture and Subculture," *American Sociological Review,* 25:5, Oct. 1960, 625–35. Yinger distinguishes between a subculture, as a normative system of subsocieties, and contraculture, as emergent norms that appear in conflict situations; he is aware that he is dealing with a continuum. His theoretical distinction is useful as an orienting perspective. My analysis is concerned with the intricate interrelationships of both tendencies in most of the activities of the labor movement.

movement was a permanent factor of instability for the Reich, but it was unable to transcend major political and nonpolitical values of the dominant system.

The labor movement before 1890 was, of course, also a subculture, but for convenience the term will refer here to the large legal mass movement which arose in the nineties. Party historians, too, like Eduard Bernstein and Eugen Prager, distinguish two stages in the development of the labor movement, with 1890 as the dividing mark. Bernstein denotes the development with the phrase "from sect to party," which he chose as the title of one of his writings.[3] Prager distinguishes the era of propaganda of a small party from the era of expansion into a parliamentary mass party, and relates this distinction also to rapid industrialization which furthered the rise of the unions and the growth of the party.[4] At the end of the period, in 1914, the party had 4,100 paid functionaries and 11,000 salaried employees, and its membership rose between 1906 and 1913 from 384,000 to 982,000.[5]

The trade union movement, which counted by that time about two and a half million members, came to occupy an intermediate position between the dominant system and the Social Democratic subculture. It was thoroughly reformist, in contrast to the French and Spanish situation in which anarchist and syndicalist influences tended to make many unions more radical than the socialist parties. In contrast to England, where the reformist unions established the Labour party as their political instrument long after they had arisen, most German unions were created by Social Democrats who appealed to the workers primarily by offering concrete economic benefits. The unions were first of all friendly societies and only secondarily collective bargaining agencies. Collective bargaining

[3] Eduard Bernstein, "Von der Sekte zur Partei," *Zeitschrift für Politik,* Vol. 3, 1910, 498–551.
[4] Eugen Prager, *Geschichte der USPD* (Berlin: Freiheit, 1921), 16.
[5] William Maehl, "The Triumph of Nationalism in the German Socialist Party on the Eve of the First World War," *Journal of Modern History,* XXIV, 1952, 25.

existed in small and medium-sized industries, but not in heavy industry. The mining industry in the Rhineland tolerated a union movement, but did not bargain with it. Some big steel manufacturers did not even permit the organization of workers in unions. The Social Democratic unions, customarily called Free unions because they had no connection with the liberals or the Center party, had only one major competitor in some industries such as mining: the much smaller Catholic unions, which differed on many issues only in their religious emphasis. After the turn of the century, the Free unions were also "free" from party pressures. In the nineties many Social Democrats looked with some misgivings at their purely ameliorative activities. As the economic resources of the unions became stronger than those of the party, the Social Democratic union leaders quickly moved to establish themselves as the full equals of the party leaders and soon began to apply pressures on the party to curb its left-wing radicals.

The Free unions can be considered only in part as a component of the Social Democratic subculture: many of the rank and file were not party members and did not even read party papers—the minimum condition for affiliation. Therefore, only limited attention will be given to them in the subsequent chapters which are concerned with the relative strength and weakness of the subculture in relation to the dominant system.[6]

Facilitating the spectacular growth of the Social Democratic subculture was a permanent organization of extra-parliamentary functionaries who addressed themselves almost exclusively to the working class, thereby gaining an advantage within their own realm over

[6] Basic for the understanding of the unions' differentiation from the party is Heinz Josef Varein, *Freie Gewerkschaften, Sozialdemokratie und Staat: Die Politik der Generalkommission unter der Führung Carl Legiens, 1890–1920* (Düsseldorf: Droste, 1956); for the nineties see also Gerhard Ritter, *Die Arbeiterbewegung im Wilhelminischen Reich: Die Sozialdemokratie und die Freien Gewerkschaften 1890–1900* (Berlin: Colloquiumverlag, 1959); for the following period, see Carl Schorske, *German Social Democracy 1905–1917* (Cambridge: Harvard University Press, 1955).

the parties of notables. The only other party in serious competition for the labor vote was the Center party because it had the ideological and organizational support of the Catholic church. These two parties became the first political mass organization in Imperial Germany. But in the late eighties and the nineties other mass movements emerged, nationalist, agrarian and anti-Semitic, which permanently blocked the Social Democratic expansion into the agrarian and petty-bourgeois strata.[7] The Social Democratic failure to expand significantly into these strata was also due to the inability of the predominantly urban functionaries to support policies which appealed to more of the population than the proletarian electorate. This inability, in turn, was in part conditioned by the official ideology of the Social Democratic subculture, a deterministically articulated Marxism.

In the following section I will deal with the view that deterministic Marxism "corresponded" to the authoritarian structure of the Reich. However, it also was, paradoxically at first sight, compatible with the moderate practice of the labor movement. Moreover, its adoption was not at all inevitable and was, in fact, very slow. Since this involves the qualification of an older, widespread view about the Marxist tradition of the Eisenachers and the Marxist character of the united party after 1875, the reasons for and the quality of the adherence to Marxism will be elaborated in some

---

[7] Cf. Gerhard Ritter, *op. cit.,* Ch. 5, on the rise of these interest groups and mass movements and on the inherent limitations of the Social Democrats; Emil Ritter, *Die katholisch-soziale Bewegung Deutschlands im 19. Jahrhundert und der Volksverein* (Cologne: Bachem, 1954); Lothar Werner, *Der Alldeutsche Verband: 1890–1918. Historische Studien,* Vol. 278, 1935; Alfred Kruck, *Geschichte des Alldeutschen Verbandes, 1890–1939* (Wiesbaden: Steiner, 1954); Massing, *op. cit.;* Wilhelm Treue, *Die deutsche Landwirtschaft zur Zeit Caprivis und ihr Kampf gegen die Handelsverträge,* Ph.D. dissertation, University of Berlin, 1933; Alexander Gerschenkron, *Bread and Democracy in Germany* (Berkeley and Los Angeles: University of California Press, 1943), "Peasant and Industrial Labor," 28–32; this is a study on agricultural protectionism and the *Junkers.*

detail (in section 3).[8] Once adopted, Marxism had positive as well as negative consequences for the dynamics of the labor movement. The rise of right- and left-wing groups will be treated as indicators of internal strain connected with the adoption of deterministic Marxism and the pursuit of a reformist practice (section 4).

2. Radical Theory and Moderate Practice

During the first three quarters of the 19th century, there was much awareness within and without Germany of her "backwardness" in political, economic and social respect. However, after national unification had been achieved and especially during the Wilhelminian period (1890–1918) the image of backwardness rapidly faded in Germany. In the 1920's it was a provocative perspective when Hendrik de Man analyzed Imperial and Weimar Germany in terms of political and economic underdevelopment. He compared Germany with more democratic Western countries and concluded that

[8] In the literature the Eisenachers and the united party of 1875 are often called Marxist. This view seems to go back to Mehring's highly ambivalent 1878 history, *op. cit.;* for him, the Eisenachers were "Communist" because of their tenuous connection with the First International. Mehring, intellectual partisan of Lassalle, temporarily turned against the united party because its class consciousness and internationalism were not balanced by the pro-Prussian legacies of Lassalle and Schweitzer, which the Lassalleans had abandoned even before the merger. In his Lassalle biography, Hermann Oncken, *op. cit.,* 487, recognized that Marx's theoretical influence among the Eisenachers was insignificant. Marxist theory became important only from the eighties on. Perhaps because of its later undisputed predominance the two stages of Marxist influence have been blurred by party and academic historians; see, e.g., the party historian Wilhelm Schröder, *Geschichte der sozialdemokratischen Parteiorganisation in Deutschland* (Dresden: Kaden, 1912), 22 f; and the academic historians J. H. Clapham, *The Economic Development of France and Germany: 1815–1914* (Cambridge: University Press, 1936), 327 f, and Kurt F. Reinhardt, *Germany: 2000 Years* (New York: Ungar, 1961), rev. ed., II, 559 and 613.

Germany, "politically speaking (current Marxist theory notwithstanding), appears rather as a young and backward country than as an advanced country," and Marxism "as a typical form of proletarian socialism in countries without democracy, or at any rate without a democratic tradition." [9] Imperial Germany was "backward" for two reasons: the dominance of an authoritarian state and the social and political consequences of a relatively late but very rapid industrialization. The first factor explained the labor movement's fight for political power, the second the mushroom growth of an industrial ruling class which imitated, in the fashion of the *nouveaux riches,* the military values of the Prussian aristocracy rather than traditions of compromise as did the English bourgeoisie in responding to the legacies of the aristocracy. The general impact of rapid economic change and the acquisitive drive and recklessness of the entrepreneurial class made the workers receptive to an ideology which maintained the paramount importance of economic factors. All of these circumstances intensified the militarization of political and economic conflict and the belief in the effectiveness of "blood and iron" politics.[10]

[9] Hendrik de Man, *The Psychology of Socialism* (New York: Holt, 1927), 428.
[10] Cf. de Man, *op. cit.,* 436 ff. The belief in power politics was not only adopted by industrialists, but also by the majority of the educated and propertied middle classes as the result of historical developments which made for significant differences between Germany and Western Europe. German idealism contributed greatly to the exaltation of a "state of power, culture and law" above religion and society. Marx shared the belief of German idealism in ultimate cultural values which were largely individualist, and in the use of power in any form for realizing these ideals. For an excellent discussion of these developments, see Hajo Holborn, "Der deutsche Idealismus in sozialgeschichtlicher Beleuchtung," *Historische Zeitschrift,* Vol. 174, 1952, 359–84. Holborn mentions briefly that the adoption of Marxism was not at all an inevitable result of industrialization, despite some affinity between socialist demands and the aspirations of the working class. He argues that the rise of the German labor movement as a class movement that was strictly separated from the rest of society consummated the split within the German people, the product of the long development toward the *Obrigkeits-und Machtstaat* of the civil servants and the military. This state was

The turning of the Social Democrats to Marxism can indeed be considered, as de Man suggests, a response to the rigid power and class structure of the Empire and the isolation and powerlessness of the labor movement: "There was hardly any other possibility open to Social Democracy in the Prussianized Germany of prewar days." [11] But this raises the question of the seeming lack of "correspondence" between the radical ideology of the Social Democrats and their moderate policies. The answer must be sought in the mixture of repressive and permissive conditions within Imperial Germany. Joseph Schumpeter agreed with de Man that the national cleavage made the adoption and retention of Marxism understandable. He pointed out that the leaders, all honorable men, had to carry on an intransigent opposition in view of the complete isolation of the movement. However, he also emphasized, in contrast to de Man, the moderate aspects of the Empire. For him, Germany was in some respects not even "backward" in comparison with England, especially as far as the government's response to the social consequences of industrialization was concerned. He pointed to the very substantial welfare achievements of the monarchy, the bureaucracy, and the academic social reformers, which seemed to him superior to the English accomplishments until Lloyd George.[12]

On balance, the sheer repressive power of the dominant system, stressed by de Man, was great enough to make the labor movement embrace Marxism and, at the same time, to discourage extremist activities as long as another way seemed open; because of the attenuated authoritarianism, emphasized by Schumpeter, another way did seem open.

---

inherently handicapped in integrating the old and new classes into a common value system after industrialization had begun. This is in line with the reasoning presented in this chapter.

11 de Man, *op. cit.,* 429.

12 Cf. Schumpeter, *op cit.,* 341–47. Schumpeter uses here, with some modifications, Gustav Schmoller's arguments. Cf. Schmoller, "Die englische Gewerkvereinsentwickelung im Lichte der Webbschen Darstellung," *Jahrbuch für Gesetzgebung,* Vol. 25, 1901, 313.

Before turning to the specific reasons for the seemingly para-doxical relationship between theory and practice of the labor move-ment, it is necessary to identify at least briefly the dialectics of voluntarism and determinism in the "Marxism" of Marx and Engels. The Marxian theory of the proletarian revolution is deter-ministic in so far as capitalism is doomed to destruction for in-herent reasons. The voluntarist element consists in the expectation that the proletariat will overthrow capitalism in a crisis situation, after it has fully developed a revolutionary class consciousness. The communists have the task, according to the *Communist Manifesto,* of spreading this class consciousness. They also have to support all developments leading to the bourgeois revolution which would establish an unfettered capitalism capable of industrializing a country and, at the same time, running full course toward its own destruction. After the failure of the revolution of 1848, Marx toned down his revolutionary phraseology, since, as he wrote on his in-augural address to the First International in a letter to Engels on November 4, 1864, "time is needed until the reawakened move-ment will allow the old audacity of language. It is necessary to be *fortiter in re, suaviter in modo.*" [13] By that time Marx was writing the first volume of *Das Kapital,* which embodied his deterministic search for the proof of the inevitable downfall of capitalism. As the letter indicates, Marx returned to political life with an aware-ness of the limitations imposed upon him as the theoretician of the proletarian revolution. However, he did not like to recognize that the times were essentially nonrevolutionary. He continued during most of these years to expect bourgeois revolutions as a precondi-tion for the fulfillment of his prophecies. However, the second half of the 19th century was without great revolutionary upheaval, and central Europe, in particular, was tranquil in this respect.

A number of Marxist writers in the 1920's and 1930's applied a Marxist approach to this situation and concluded that the deter-

---

[13] *Marx-Engels-Gesamtausgabe, op. cit.,* III:3, 199.

minist component of Marxism was bound to become more prominent than the activist component. Thus Arthur Rosenberg held that the absence of a revolutionary situation made it impossible for the labor movement to adopt Marx's theories in their revolutionary intent.[14] Karl Korsch expressed in strictly orthodox terms that "from the standpoint of materialist dialectic, it is very well understandable that this first Marxist theory could not exist unchanged during the long and practically nonrevolutionary epoch of the second half of the 19th century in Europe." [15] These arguments may explain why Marxism had to become more deterministic, but they do not explain why deterministic Marxism was adopted.

Its adoption by the German labor movement was actually a corollary of the power distribution between the labor movement and the dominant system. The inability of the labor movement to break out of its isolation, on the one hand, and its seemingly inexorable advance within a large isolated realm, on the other, made a deterministically accentuated Marxism a particularly fitting ideology for the Social Democratic subculture. The labor movement was committed to the humanitarian goal of a materially and spiritually richer life for the lower classes. Marxism held out the image of a better world to come. It promised ultimate victory brought about by the combination of the masses against a system that seemed inevitably doomed because of its inherent contradictions and the resulting growth of the labor movement. It gave "scientific" meaning to the frustrations and resentments of the workers toward

[14] Cf. Arthur Rosenberg, *A History of Bolshevism* (London: Oxford University Press, 1934), 18 f. Rosenberg pointed out that the revolutionary component of Marxian theory rooted in the revolutionary communism of 1848 could be utilized theoretically and practically only in one major country, Russia, because there the middle-class revolution appeared imminent. It may be added that today variations of Leninism based on a voluntaristic interpretation of Marxism have, among the traditional left wing ideologies, the greatest appeal in newly developing countries because of the Bolshevik example and the good chance of success for small, determined revolutionary elites.

[15] Karl Korsch, *Marxismus und Philosophie* (Leipzig: Hirschfeld, 1930), 77.

society at large. The belief in the scientific character of their creed contributed much to the strengthening of the confidence of the workers. Given the actual stability of Imperial Germany during more than four decades of peace, Marxism sustained the belief that the future would belong to the proletariat and provided a great deal of encouragement for perseverance in the everyday political operations against the powerful dominant system. Thus, psychologically, the superiority of the opponents and the discrepancy between theory and practice was often not felt.[16] "You hide your powerlessness behind the intransigence of your theoretical formulae with which your excellent comrade Kautsky will provide you until the end of his life," Jean Jaurès told Bebel at the Amsterdam congress of 1904.[17] Indeed, Marxism was a radical creed that did not demand active preparation for a revolution since it relied on the "objective" forces of history; it provided a convenient defense for parliamentary inactivity if this was desired, but it also could be comfortably combined with a reformist practice. Thus it served as an aggressive as well as a defensive instrument against the ideologies of the dominant groups.

Marxism was officially adopted in the theoretical section of the Erfurt program in 1891. Since the labor movement became more and more involved in reformist activities from that time on, there is an apparent paradox to which Karl Korsch pointed when he said that the Social Democratic party was *"volksparteilich* democratic, Lassallean and Dühringian, but only very sporadically Marxist" during the period before 1890. During this time it came nearest to being imbued with revolutionary sentiments; while after the relaxation of repression and the improvement of the economic situation in

[16] Cf. Rudolf Hilferding (pseudonym: Richard Kern) "Revolutionärer Sozialismus," *Zeitschrift für Sozialismus,* I:5, February 1934, 147.

[17] Quoted in Sombart, *op. cit.,* 363. Sombart points out, however, that the leaders, who had to preserve the allegiance of the masses despite the powerlessness of the movement, sometimes explained the lack of direct success with the very superiority of the enemy, and they derived from this the necessity for further exertions (282).

the nineties, Marxism was adhered to as a "kind of theoretical defense and metaphysical consolation." [18] For Rosenberg,

> Marxism now served, above all else, to enable the proletariat to differentiate itself ideologically from the middle class. In other words—to secure for itself an independent class existence within capitalist society. . . . Thus Communism changed from a revolutionary doctrine used by the extreme Radicals among the middle-class intellectuals to drive the working masses onwards, to a professional ideology with whose help the class-conscious workman defended and improved his position within the middle-class order of society.[19]

This defensive function of Marxism derived from the overwhelming power of the opponents. The Marxian conception of politics as a matter of all-out struggle rather than of compromise fitted the situation of a proletariat that was denied social recognition and the opportunity to participate meaningfully in the higher decision-making agencies of the dominant system. The public glorification of *Realpolitik,* which characterized the period following Bismarck's triumphs, may have contributed to a simplification of the perception of power relations. To many Social Democrats, "power appeared," Rudolf Hilferding observed, "concretely embodied in the army, police, capital." He related this to Bismarck's blood and iron politics and concluded that German Marxism had the tendency to develop into a kind of "Bismarxism." This resulted, however, in a hesitation to fight for major political goals which were supposed to be attainable only after the final clash of the opposing forces,

[18] Karl Korsch, *op. cit.,* 14 f. In Germany the last quarter century before the First World War was extraordinarily tranquil: "There were no food riots and street fighting, as in Italy in the 'terrible year' 1898; no nationalist convulsions, such as shook the Hapsburg empire; no crisis comparable to France's Dreyfus affair. There was nothing, of course, to match the Russian revolution of 1905, no labor struggles of the scope and violence of the Homestead or Pullman strikes in the United States, nor even a constitutional crisis such as that occasioned in England by Lloyd George's budget of 1909." Harry Marks, *op. cit.,* 334.

[19] A. Rosenberg, *loc. cit.*

and "the rigid and at the same time transparent power conditions" also weakened the will to fight for political objectives which seemed to have no direct relationship to the long-term goals of the movement.[20]

In conclusion it may be said that both the deterministic character of the radical ideology and the moderate practices of the labor movement were largely shaped by the peculiar combination of repressive and permissive policies in Imperial Germany. Thus the apparent incongruence between theory and practice becomes less of a logical inconsistency than it at first appears. It was of great importance for theory and practice that the authoritarian state did not completely repress the labor movement, but that it permitted a parliamentary framework within which the movement could achieve tangible success. This provided a strong incentive to pursue moderate policies and an equally strong interest in legal status, though moderation appeared, of course, also advisable in view of the overwhelming power of the state. In fact, the repressive power of the state became so great after the establishment of the Empire that it indefinitely postponed all chances of realizing ultimate social and democratic goals. Therefore, the most influential leaders of the labor movement turned to a deterministic theory of history and of industrialization, which seemed to point a way out by offering

[20] R. Hilferding, *loc. cit.* Between the adherence to a rather abstract set of long-range goals and the pursuit of cautious moderation and piecemeal reform lay an area of political action in which important advances could perhaps have been made. During the Weimar Republic, the Social Democrats continued to be plagued by this gap, when they were a pillar of the Republic as well as an opposition party with the aim of large-scale social reconstruction. Even the English labor movement was afflicted with this problem in 1929–30, when its sincerely socialist leaders maintained that nationalization could not be carried out because of the slim labor majority; without nationalization the economy would have to be run along laissez-faire lines, and no large-scale manipulation of the economy, in whatever form, was considered feasible. See Arthur M. Schlesinger, Jr., "Sources of the New Deal: Reflections on the Temper of a Time," *Columbia University Forum,* II:4, Fall 1959, 8.

"scientific" proof that the contemporary society was, for inherent reasons, doomed to destruction, leaving the proletariat to become the founder of a millennium. Any actively revolutionary version of this radical ideology appeared unrealistic because it invited complete repression. Conversely, the actual attempts at suppression did not appear severe enough, especially after 1890, to suggest that the setting up of a small party of professional revolutionaries was opportune, as Lenin came to think in 1903. Thus, the strategic situation in which the labor movement found itself made it embrace as well as mitigate the radicalism of Marxist theory.

3. The Gradual Adoption of Marxism by the Leaders

Marxism was adopted by the leaders of the Social Democratic party, but its adoption was not inevitable. Its reception was dependent on personal, situational, and organizational factors unrelated or only indirectly related to the political structure and the economic development of society at large. The role of Bebel and Liebknecht was paramount; if they had been defeated within the party, Marxism probably would not have been adopted. Without the antisocialist legislation Marxism might have found serious ideological competition. Since these personal and situational factors favored Marxism, the organizational requirements for safeguarding the survival and the growth of the labor movement were also defined in terms favorable to its adoption.

In the early years of the movement the Social Democrats considered themselves revolutionary because they wanted a new type of society, not because they adhered to the Marxian theory of revolution. Many of Lassalle's ideas on socialism were unchallenged during the first decade of the labor movement. Some Marxian ideas were diffused through Lassalle's writings, but there was little awareness of their origin or their systematic meaning. When Schweitzer retired from politics in the early seventies to become a successful playwright, it seems that no one among the Lassalleans retained much understanding of or much interest in Marx's work. Even for Liebknecht, who felt personally close to Marx (with whom he had shared exile in London), and for Bebel the Marxian ideas about the inevitable breakdown of capitalist society became of great psychological and tactical importance only when they had to realize that the triumphs of Bismarck and the Prussian army constituted giant obstacles to their democratic and socialist aspirations. They retained their own confidence by relying heavily on the "objective" tendencies of capitalist society. For decades to come, Bebel stressed those tendencies which, as he used to argue, had created the Social Democratic labor movement to begin with and which would insure its ultimate victory by continuously increasing the working class and strengthening its political organization.[21] Liebknecht and Bebel also embraced Marx and Engels' conviction that German unification would at first enable the full development of capitalism as well as of the proletariat and then bring about the ruin of the former and the triumph of the latter. They were encouraged, furthermore, by Marx and Engels' anticipation that Germany's military victory would result in a shift in the leadership of international socialism from the French to the German workers and in a victory of Marxian theory over that of Proudhon.

Liebknecht and Bebel accepted a good deal of Marx's assumption about the mechanisms of capitalist economy and his psychological assumptions about the reactions of an exploited working class, which was to develop a class-conscious and revolutionary mentality. They propagated class consciousness, but they denied that this would result in revolutionary conspiracy. In an 1869 brochure about the goals of his party Bebel explicitly refused to make any concrete statement about a future revolution because

[21] The theme was, e.g., repeated pointedly in a Reichstag speech which he used to commemorate the 45th anniversary of the labor movement in 1908. See *Reichstag Protocols,* March 27, 1908, 4350.

of the interest of the public prosecutor in this topic, but he added thoughtfully that "the various forms of state and society generally came into being through iron force." [22] Later, he would be even more restrained about the crucial problem of how the Social Democrats could come to power without a revolutionary upheaval. This policy was largely due to tactical considerations of self-preservation, but it furthered a deterministic interpretation of Marxism.

Marxism was still extremely weak when the unification of the two Social Democratic parties took place at Gotha in 1875.[23] In fact, the first Marxist propaganda drive originated as a defensive move. Marx and Engels were shocked into action by Dühring's success within the party, which threatened their precarious theoretical influence. Eugen Dühring (1833–1921) was a *Privatdozent* at the University of Berlin who wrote prolifically in the fields of philosophy, political science, economics, art, literature, mathematics, mechanics and chemistry. He was a positivist and a relentless opponent of Christianity, Judaism and Marxism. In 1871 he published a *Critical History of Political Economy and Socialism* and in 1873 a *Course of Political and Social Economy*. He considered them a whole, with the first volume providing the historical dimension to the systematic analysis of the second.[24] Dühring championed a revolutionary socialism which considered political and not economic factors as primary. Thus he could write that "the actions of the Commune reálly pointed in the direction of revolutionary progress." [25] He regarded economic emancipation as an appendix to political emancipation, and he opposed the anarchy of capitalist production, praising Louis Blanc's idea of the "social ateliers," which would be run by workers on their own account under a public law and with the initial support of state funds.

[22] Bebel, *Unsere Ziele*, 1869, 19 f, quoted in Goldenberg, *op. cit.,* 13 ff.
[23] Cf. Bernstein, *Sozialdemokratische Lehrjahre, op. cit.,* 46
[24] Eugen Dühring, *Kritische Geschichte der Nationalökonomie und des Sozialismus,* 1871, cited after the fourth revised edition (Leipzig: Naumann, 1900); id., *Cursus der National-und Socialökonomie* (Berlin: Grieben, 1873).
[25] Dühring, *Geschichte, op. cit.,* 498.

Dühring placed Louis Blanc and, to a lesser extent, Proudhon above Lassalle and Marx. He accused Lassalle—always spelling his name Lassal in order to identify his Jewish ancestry—of having started his socialist agitation only because he had no role to play among the Progressives and charged him with having taken Blanc's program without acknowledgment. The only positive aspect of Lassalle's work he recognized was the demand for universal suffrage, intended to prepare the way for producers' cooperatives: "This bridge of universal suffrage is one of the more positive elements of the Lassallean program because it implicitly concedes that all of socialism has political preconditions." [26] Lassalle and Marx continued the worst tradition of the French socialists in their adherence to the notion that economic developments are more decisive than politics proper. Thus, in Germany "the sense for political freedom, so powerful in the French Commune, was blunted. . . . The alienation of socialism from its political origins and from all political dignity has made it despicable in this [German] form to all of those who regard the degradation of the goals of mankind, in favor of the principal predominance of animal instincts, as the most extreme retrogression of all cultural progress." [27]

Dühring delivered a bristling attack on Marx and his main work, *Das Kapital*. He ridiculed his concepts of capital and value, the dialectical necessity of the transition from private property to communal property through the expropriation of the expropriators, the blurred Marxian vision of the future state of the working class, and the idea of the total revolution. Only the Marxian description of the historical development of exploitation was accorded some positive comment, whereas the Hegelian dialectic and Marx's use of it encountered his utmost contempt.[28] Some of Dühring's arguments scored well and perceptively exposed some of the basic flaws in the Marxian construction of the world. But since most Social Demo-

[26] *Op. cit.*, 532.
[27] *Op. cit.*, 499.
[28] Cf. *op. cit.*, 502 ff.

crats could not judge the intrinsic value of Marxian and anti-Marxian arguments, Dühring's success must be attributed partly to his emphasis on political activism and partly to his rhetorical skills. He impressed many Social Democrats with his seemingly encyclopedic mind, his apodictic stance and the assertion of his own strictly scientific approach. He repeated this assertion and the hints of his own superiority on page after page, whereas about three-fourths of the sections on Lassalle and Marx consist literally of nothing more than deprecatory statements and vehement invectives. Marx, he said, was a "semi-scholar," a "Jewish Jesuit," vain, confused, dishonest, immoral, etc.; his *Kapital* consisted of "fragments betraying a lack of ability for concentration and exposition." [29]

Dühring's considerable initial success, despite his very strong attack on Marx both personally and theoretically, is indicative of the weakness of Marxian influence in the mid-seventies. At first, Liebknecht, Bracke, Bebel, the young Bernstein, and other prominent Eisenachers welcomed Dühring. In 1872 Bernstein considered Dühring's *Critical History* highly effective propaganda for the socialist movement and sent copies to several persons: among them were the editorial staff of the Social Democratic *Berliner Freie Presse;* Bebel, who reviewed it favorably in Liebknecht's *Volksstaat* in 1874; and Most, one of the most popular leaders in Berlin. In his memoirs Bebel recalls that most Berlin leaders were greatly impressed by Dühring, including Fritzsche, who, after Vahlteich, had been the second proletarian labor leader in the sixties to advocate class-conscious organization.[30]

Marx and Engels finally complained to Liebknecht and agreed with him on a counterattack. It was carried on in the *Anti-Dühring,* which Engels wrote for serialized publication in Liebknecht's *Vorwärts,* the new official journal of the united party in 1877/78. Engels, who, like Marx, could be no less polemical and

[29] *Op. cit.,* 499, 516, 501 and *passim.*
[30] Bebel, *Aus meinem Leben, op. cit.,* II, 317 f.

vitriolic than Dühring, reciprocated in kind and, in the process, wrote the first comprehensive exposition of Marxism available to the public. The *Anti-Dühring* became the first major Marxist work to exert significant influence, though at first it met great opposition. Ex-worker Fritzsche attacked Liebknecht at the Gotha convention of 1876 for suppressing an article by Most on Dühring only because the latter had written against Marx.[31] At the third Gotha convention in 1877, Most first won a majority of the delegates for a motion which would have discontinued Engels' articles on Dühring in the *Vorwärts* because they were for most readers without interest or even offensive. On April 11, 1877, Marx complained to Bracke that Most was one of those ex-workers who overestimated their powers of comprehension. And ex-worker Vahlteich, who was by then, like Most and Fritzsche, also a member of the Reichstag, said at the same convention that the *Vorwärts* made a mistake in publishing Engels' articles. He termed the theoretical differences between Marx and Dühring a dispute between professors; in a public meeting he pleaded for the coexistence of the sympathizers of Marx and Dühring. Among Social Democrats the latter's cause was temporarily strengthened when he was dismissed as instructor from the University of Berlin in the spring of 1877. The Social Democratic press arduously defended him in his conflict with the University. His theoretical opponents also sided with him for tactical reasons. However, he gradually lost most of his personal and ideological support because his attacks on adherents of other theories became more and more offensive. Among those attacked were the *Kathedersozialisten,* whom he accused of having

[31] For the following, see the documentation, especially the letters between Marx, Engels and their Social Democratic friends, in the editor's introduction to the *Anti-Dühring* in the *Marx-Engels-Gesamtausgabe* (Moscow: Marx-Engels-Verlag, 1935), XIX–XXXII, and Engels' introduction, 5 ff; Bebel, *loc. cit.,* Bernstein, *Lehrjahre, op. cit.,* 52 ff; id., *Geschichte der Berliner Arbeiterbewegung* (Berlin: Vorwärts, 1907), Vol. 2, 336.

stolen his ideas. Bernstein, too, who had personal contact with him and who had tolerated his rapidly worsening anti-Semitism for some time, finally turned away.

Although Engels and Liebknecht had barely managed to hold their ground, their defensive campaign was decisive for the further advance of Marxism because the *Anti-Dühring* convinced Bebel, Bernstein, Kautsky and a few others of the superiority of Marxism as a coherent system of ideas. Marxism succeeded partly because of the personal bonds of Liebknecht and a few other Social Democrats to Marx and Engels and partly because of Dühring's personal inadequacies. Furthermore, its deterministic emphasis suited the party far better on the eve of the antisocialist legislation than an ideology of revolutionary activism. From now on the theoretical interest in Marxism was sustained by a small group which grew very slowly. The Austrian Karl Kautsky began to study *Das Kapital* in 1875.[32] In 1881 Bernstein took over the official party paper in exile, *Der Sozialdemokrat;*[33] in 1883, Kautsky, backed by Liebknecht, Bebel and a few theoretically interested members, started the new theoretical journal of the party, *Die Neue Zeit,* in Stuttgart. Soon the advance of Marxism was threatened by bitter controversies among the few theoreticians of the party. Bernstein relates the case of C. A. Schramm, who had the reputation of

---

[32] Cf. Karl Kautsky, "Natur und Gesellschaft," *Gesellschaft,* 1929:2, 482. Fortunately, Karl Kautsky's early memoirs have now been published, edited by his late son Benedikt Kautsky: *Erinnerungen und Erörterungen* (The Hague: Mouton, 1960), 586 pp. However, they became available only after this chapter had been written. For the decisive impact of the *Anti-Dühring* on Kautsky, see B. Kautsky, ed., *Friedrich Engels Briefwechsel mit Karl Kautsky,* 2nd ed. of *Aus der Frühzeit des Marxismus,* enlarged with Kautsky's letters (Vienna: Wiener Volksbuchhandlung, 1955), 4.

[33] The party paper was published in Zürich and later in London; it appeared for the first time on September 28, 1879. Its name had been decided upon by the cautious Reichstag faction which tried repeatedly to get complete control over the paper and maintain its moderate tone in order to avoid an embarrassment to the suppressed party.

being "the most competent authority on the Marxian doctrine" until the early eighties.[34] Schramm, a former insurance clerk, had gained this reputation primarily for his *Grundzüge der National-ökonomie,* which was considered an apt popularization of the first volume of *Kapital.* In 1883 differences of opinion between Schramm, on the one hand, and Bebel, Bernstein and Kautsky, on the other, came to a head. Schramm maintained that Karl Rodbertus, a prominent conservative welfare economist, had provided a scientific base for socialism even before Marx. Although he had been a member of the anti-Lassallean Eisenachers, he extolled Lassalle as a realistic statesman in contrast to that armchair theorist, Marx. The prominent Social Democratic publisher of the *Neue Zeit* and member of the Reichstag J. H. W. Dietz refused to accept a pamphlet by Schramm on *Marx, Rodbertus und Lassalle.* It was, however, accepted by another publisher and member of parliament, Louis Viereck, the owner of the *Süd-deutsche Post.*[35] According to Bernstein, Schramm employed in-

[34] Bernstein, *Lehrjahre, op. cit.,* 147.

[35] Louis Viereck, a former Prussian civil servant (*Referendar*) headed the Berlin *Mohrenklub,* an association promoting socialist theory and engaging in fund raising. It was founded after Dühring's initial success in the mid-seventies when students became interested in socialism. Half of its members were students, half non-academic Social Democrats with theoretical interests. On Viereck, see Bernstein, *op. cit.,* 55 ff, 151, on Schramm, 146–52. Schramm, Viereck, Vahlteich, Most, and Hasselmann eventually left the party; Schramm went to Switzerland, the others to the United States. A comparative note on the differential impact of socialism in the United States and Central Europe may be added. Vahlteich, who was one of at least four former Social Democratic Reichstag members emigrating to the United States, complained in his memoirs about the phenomenon of indifference or contemptuousness of many formerly convinced and loyal German Social Democrats toward Social Democratic activities in the United States. Since there was vigorous agitation for socialism in America, in which the former Reichstag members participated, the differential success of socialism in America and Central Europe was not due to this factor. The more equalitarian conditions in the United States, especially the absence of a military aristocracy and the heritage of universal suffrage, may account for much of the change of attitudes among former German Social Democrats. Be-

vectives against his party opponents and Marx because of his frustration that others excelled him in their understanding of Marx.[36]

Prior to the Schramm controversy, Bernstein and Kautsky had made further progress in their study of Marx by translating together his treatise against Proudhon, *La misère de la Philosophie.* After this, both continued their Marxist studies in London. Engels, Kautsky and Bernstein and some other Marxist theoreticians slowly gained the upper hand during the eighties. Some early and some more recent writings of Marx and Engels were published, and their theories were popularized for the members by the party workers.

As important as the rise of Marxian theoreticians in the labor movement was the fact that deterministic Marxism was furthered because it became tactically relevant for the party leadership during the antisocialist legislation. The intensive repression from 1878 to 1890 had the effect of strengthening both the moderate policies of the labor movement and the contribution of Marxism to the external and internal defense of the party's very existence. The party had to abandon, in popular agitation, its self-identification as a revolutionary body and to emphasize its character as a parliamentary reform party. In 1878 Liebknecht told the Reichstag that "if the [anti-]socialist legislation is accepted we will of course comply with it, because our party is a reform party in the strictest sense of the word"; he denied "most emphatically that our inten-

---

yond differentiating factors such as the higher American standard of living (especially in comparison with the country of origin) and the success of job-conscious unionism, other factors may have weakened socialist allegiance among immigrants: the preoccupation with personal survival and advancement in a foreign country and the realization that the combination of ethnic minority and social underdog made political success impossible. Cf. Vahlteich, *op. cit.,* 47, and Charles Gulick and Melvin Bers, "Insight and Illusion in Perlman's Theory of the Labor Movement," *Industrial and Labor Relations Review,* XI:4, July 1953, 510–31.

[36] This may be indicative of the stress involved for socialist autodidacts in the study and propagation of Marxian theories. Not only did they have to overcome a lack of formal education but they were also confronted with a doctrine which claimed to be both scientific and a guide to political action.

tions are directed toward the overthrow of the existing political and social order." [37] The official party journal in exile, *Der Sozialdemokrat,* assured the public in 1884 that "we will not be so tactless as to harass the Reichstag with motions which, under the given conditions, cannot be acted upon." [38] In the last year of the antisocialist legislation, when there was still the possibility of a renewal, Liebknecht again repeated in the Reichstag the argument that the Social Democrats were abstaining on principle from using force. Marx, he said, had shown that "political forms are not arbitrary, but are the necessary products of economic conditions." Therefore, the Social Democrats who act according to this "scientific recognition" cannot be legitimately accused of aiming at the violent overthrow of the existing society. Marx showed that "today's economic system" cannot last, but will necessarily become more and more socialist. "A natural law, an organic law of development" can neither be changed by the party nor by the ruling groups. There will be a revolution: the only question is whether it will be legal or violent. [39]

It is important to realize that these were not only tactical arguments used vis-à-vis the government and the public. Bebel, Liebknecht and their followers strove hard to instill these views into the members in order to diminish the pressures toward radicalization. Among the top leaders, Hasselmann and Most were enraged enough about the antisocialist legislation—the latter partly because of a harsh two-year sentence he received in the seventies—to advocate a more aggressive policy toward the government. They also began to turn to anarchist ideas. The party, without official leadership, no longer formally existed; it had been dissolved by the executive in October 1878. This was not a tactical maneuver intended to permit clandestine party operations; rather, the executive hoped

[37] Quoted in Kurt Brandis, *op. cit.,* 56.
[38] Quoted in Rose Laub, *An Analysis of the Early German Socialist Movement,* M.A. thesis, Columbia University, 1951, 26.
[39] *Reichstag Protocols,* November 5, 1889, 136 f.

that compliance would result in the speedy repeal of the antisocialist laws and thereby save the party apparatus.[40] In this situation it was possible that Hasselmann and Most might manage to push some of the disappointed members, who were accustomed to quasi-revolutionary rhetoric and incensed about the repression, into actions resulting in complete suppression. Bebel and Liebknecht succeeded in getting the two expelled in 1880, at the secret party convention at Schloss Wyden near Zürich, by appealing to the increased importance of party discipline and by arguing that a *rapprochement* with anarchist doctrines would invite the complete destruction of the party. It must be remembered that the two lunatic attempts at the life of William I which had produced hysterical demands for legislation were indiscriminately associated by the public with anarchism and the socialist movement. Hasselmann and Most had been influential in shaping a good deal of the revolutionary rhetoric of the time. They were popular with the masses, but they lost popularity when they tried to turn the party into a revolutionary action group. In their fight against the more radical elements, Liebknecht and Bebel resorted not only to deterministic arguments, but also claimed the direct support of Marx and Engels, who were dismayed about the opportunistic course of the party. However, Marx and Engels sided with them, recognizing that the Bebel-Liebknecht group made, after all, fewer concessions to tactical expediencies and petty-bourgeois appeals than did other party groups. It may also be assumed that they did not want to break with the only group open to their influence. Indicative of the strength of Bebel's Marxist convictions is an incident which Bernstein relates in an account of his trip to London with Bebel to appease the anger of Marx

[40] The party apparatus had the following extension in the late seventies: In 1876, 22 agitators and 46 officials (editors, distributors, etc.) were employed. In 1877 there was one major newspaper with 12,000 subscribers, 49 smaller newspapers and 14 trade union papers with Social Democratic tendencies. Most of the newspapers were printed in 14 party printing shops. Apart from the newspapers, several hundred thousand brochures were distributed. Cf. Brandis, *op. cit.,* 52 f.

and Engels about the opportunistic course of the party. Bernstein recalls that Bebel assured Marx of the good prospects for the breakdown of capitalist economy in Germany in the near future. On his private business trips, Bebel heard many businessmen complain about the bad economic conditions and interpreted these complaints as a confirmation of Marx's prognosis of capitalism.[41]

It is true that deterministic Marxism gained importance for the top leaders as an antidote for pressures toward radicalization, but its adoption was also directly facilitated by the very process of radicalization resulting from the antisocialist legislation. The radicalization affected especially the lower-ranking functionaries, who became for the first time very influential in internal party politics because they had to rebuild the organizations from the bottom.[42] An efficient underground organization was set up to keep the party alive; illegal distribution of propaganda was the most radical activity involved. Often card and smokers' clubs were actually Social Democratic organizations enabling members to sustain contact within an apparently harmless front. According to the party historian Schröder, the underground organizations were carried on most energetically by the geographically mobile workers in the wood, metal and tobacco industries. By 1883 a few big cities had a tightly knit network of underground cells. At the end of the eighties between 5,000 and 6,000 persons may have been secretly organized in the heavily industrialized area of the Free City of Hamburg, which was kept under permanent martial law.[43]

The mood of the lower-ranking functionaries and the rank and file participating in these activities was, of course, aggressive and defiant. Bebel, who slowly rose above Liebknecht during these years, adjusted himself skilfully, if only rhetorically, to the more radical tendencies. Thus, the period of the antisocialist legislation

[41] Cf. Bernstein, *op. cit.,* 133 ff.
[42] Cf. Schröder, *op. cit.,* 33.
[43] For a detailed description of underground operations and organizations, see *op. cit.,* 34 ff.

did end in radicalization, in the sense that the antagonism between the hard core of the labor movement and the government and other parties was made permanent and that the radical posture was consequently perpetuated. In the seventies, just when the party had become receptive toward reformist tendencies, the antisocialist legislation greatly strengthened the old feelings of intransigent opposition.[44] Twelve years of police and court interference by a dominant system committed to the suppression of the labor movement created a much greater number of intransigent Social Democrats than would have existed without such a period. This prepared the ground for the acceptance of a more radical program in 1891.

4. Consequences of the Adoption of Marxism

The Erfurt program of 1891 was adopted because there was general agreement that the party needed a more sophisticated program than the old Gotha program had been. Despite many similarities between Lassalleans and Eisenachers at the time of their merger in 1875, the latter had made compromises, especially with regard to the demand for state-supported producers' cooperatives. After the experience of the antisocialist legislation, this demand appeared outdated even to many former Lassalleans. Though the drafts for the new program were circulated among the top leadership they were actually prepared only by Bebel and Liebknecht, with the help of Kautsky and Bernstein. Finally, a version approved by Engels was adopted with some modifications. Thus the program had the blessing of one of the two founders of "scientific socialism." In its theoretical part, the program openly accepted the worsening class struggle between the proletariat and the bourgeoisie as the political basis of the labor movement, and it emphasized more than the

[44] Cf. Bernstein, "Von der Sekte zur Partei," *op. cit.,* 524.

Gotha program the international character and commitment of the movement. In some contrast to this Marxist emphasis was the change of the party's name from the "Socialist Workers' Party of Germany" to the "Social Democratic Party of Germany"; this change recognized the new legal status of the movement and indicated the hope of being a "people's," no less than a proletarian, party.

Some party historians date the "complete" victory of Marxism from this time, without making sufficiently clear the nature of this victory.[45] For the top leadership it meant that a different version of socialism was no longer acceptable. During the antisocialist legislation, when the very life of the movement was at stake, the ideological competition of non-Marxist radicals had been easily eliminated on organizational and disciplinary grounds. After 1890, all opposition arising on the right or the left, if it had any theoretical pretensions at all, came to accept Marxism as the common starting ground. It was strengthened by a sense of the importance of unity, which the antisocialist legislation had impressed on the functionaries, both old and young. The conviction of the paramount importance of a united labor movement kept the party together until well into the First World War. Therefore, there was no institutional basis for radically different protest ideologies within the socialist labor movement.

The adoption of a Marxist program appeared to many members and to the public as a step toward greater radicalization, but the moderate practice remained unchanged. During the months before and after the fall of the antisocialist legislation, the party leaders moved with particular caution, and through the nineties they considered its renewal possible. In this sense, the threatening rhetoric of William II was successful in restraining the leaders, although the two major attempts to introduce new legislation, the *Umsturzvorlage* of 1894–95 and the *Zuchthausvorlage* of 1898–99, failed.

[45] See, e.g., Kampffmeyer's introduction to Friedrich Ebert, *Schriften, op. cit.,* 24.

Another reason for the moderation of the party leadership was that a continuous over-all increase of votes, which might one day provide the party with a parliamentary majority, appeared as the only long-term chance to break through the "iron ring" that fettered the labor movement. This situation demanded that nothing be done to jeopardize legal freedom while an aggressive rhetoric was sustained, especially at election times, to appeal to widespread dissatisfaction. Many Social Democratic votes were cast by dissatisfied voters who were not interested in or even averse to socialist doctrines proper. There was no clear idea what might happen if a majority was won, because the government was responsible to the emperor and not to parliament. Concern about the legal status of the movement discouraged any specific discussion of solutions for this problem. The unions, which rose again in the nineties, and the emergent regional organizations in southern Germany, which developed around the party representatives in the state diets, were outright reformist. Furthermore, reformist tendencies were encouraged by the slow increase of opportunities for party and union functionaries to gain influence in municipal parliaments, labor exchanges, sickness funds and labor courts. Many reformist Social Democrats did not challenge the prevailing Marxist ideology—either because they had little interest in theoretical issues, or because they quite practically did not want to strain the unity of the party.[46]

The dualism of theory and practice entailed some lasting advantages—but also increasing disadvantages. It was bound to mobilize against the leadership those who wanted either the party's

---

[46] Typical of such a "practical" reformism were the Bavarian Social Democrats under the very able leadership of Georg von Vollmar, a retired professional officer who had been permanently disabled during the Franco-Prussian war. Vollmar was at first a radical, but after 1890 he took skilful advantage of the community of interests of liberals and Social Democrats in a predominantly Catholic state and he even managed, for a time, to invade successfully petty-bourgeois and peasant strata in the industrially "underdeveloped" country.

policies to conform to its radical creed or its creed to the moderate policies. Within a few years a permanent right and left wing developed, which made the top leadership "Centrist"; this meant that it continued its attempt to strike a balance between radical rhetoric and moderate practice. Bebel, Liebknecht, the members of the Reichstag faction and other prominent leaders had always been spokesmen before the members as well as before the government and the public. After 1890 they had to deal as well with two articulate wings. This explains much of the contradictory and ambiguous nature of the views expressed by them.[47] The Centrist policies also contributed to the phenomenon of driving a member first to the left and then to the right. Bebel used to say that left-wing radicals often would move toward the extreme right within a short time; but, as Michels writes in his necrology, he failed to understand how much the discrepancy between his verbal radicalism and his cautious practice contributed to making young members, especially intellectuals, first radical and then, after their disillusionment, opportunistic.[48]

[47] Indispensable for an understanding of the top leaders' reactions to the internal and external strains and pressures is Friedrich Adler (1879–1960) and the Austrian Socialist party, eds., *Victor Adler: Briefwechsel mit August Bebel und Karl Kautsky* (Vienna: Volksbuchhandlung, 1954), 680 pp. The volume includes letters to and from Ignaz Auer, Eduard Bernstein, Adolf Braun, Heinrich Dietz, Friedrich Ebert, Wilhelm Liebknecht, Hermann Müller and Paul Singer. Victor Adler (1852–1918), a medical doctor, was the brilliant and undisputed leader of the Austrian labor movement before the First World War.

[48] See R. Michels, *op. cit.*, 697 f. Michels criticized Bebel's speeches for "indecision and unevenness" and detected ominous similarities to the writings of the "opportunist" Italian professor Enrico Ferri. He quoted Hellmuth von Gerlach (a Junker who became a left-winger) on Bebel: he always pursued either "the farthest long-range policy or a policy as nearly oriented towards the present moment as was possible" (*allerfernste Zukunftspolitik oder allernächste Augenblickspolitik*). He added: "This is correct. But this shortcoming was no caprice. It was rooted in the character of the man and the character of the German labor movement after 1870." *Op. cit.*, 691.

The first Marxist opposition against the leadership may be briefly described as an illustration of the tendency of believers to make the party's policies conform to its radical creed. It arose in 1890, the time when the Erfurt program was prepared. The lower-ranking functionaries and active party workers had become more radical, primarily because of the antisocialist legislation, but also because of an increasing exposure to Marxist rhetoric. Furthermore, the fall of the antisocialist legislation greatly strengthened the belief in the imminent breakdown of the capitalist system. The opposition fully accepted the concept of the class struggle and explained the moderate policies of the party as the result of the influx of petty-bourgeois elements and of gradually acquired petty-bourgeois attitudes on the part of the older leaders. One of the intellectual representatives of the opposition even used a "vulgar" Marxist argument against the party leaders, pronouncing that "party programs don't prove anything about the character of a party";[49] the social composition of the party was decisive. He also maintained that the complex new program was not understood by party members, that it was the work of the top leaders and was not derived from the radical mood of the masses. The opposition insisted that state reform could not help the working class, and it feared the impact of reform on the fighting spirit of the masses. It demanded that the party pursue a policy of absolute opposition, the Reichstag faction limiting itself to purely propagandistic moves. The opposition hoped for the support of Bebel and Engels and suffered the bitter disappointment of finding both vigorously against them. Bebel was willing to speak in a more radical vein, but was not interested in a further radicalization of urban members. Radicalization of urban districts could not improve the chances of gaining seats in parliament, but might very well induce the government and the bourgeois parties to enact new repressive legislation.

[49] Hans Müller, *Der Klassenkampf in der deutschen Sozialdemokratie* (Zürich: Verlags-Magazin, 1892), 10.

Bebel and the majority of the functionaries fought the opposition with the argument that the party had become more radical—because of its new program.[50]

Although this first organized Marxist opposition was easily crushed, the radical sentiments did not subside. In fact, the Centrist leaders had no interest in suppressing such sentiments because they provided much of the driving force of the movement. However, radicalism in the ranks and the parliamentary goals of the party forced a conflicting pattern upon the leadership which prescribed, on the one hand, a specific radical rhetoric at the party conventions and, on the other, moderate demands and a more diffuse rhetoric in parliament and during election campaigns. As a legal movement the labor movement had to adhere to moderate practices. Because of the strength of the dominant system, the leaders used only the possibilities for political action which would not jeopardize the survival of the movement. On the other hand, considerations of organizational self-maintenance made the leadership stick to its radical rhetoric which had become "infused with value" (Selznick) for the members.[51] Once Marxism had been accepted on various levels of comprehension, any sacrifice of principle could easily have disorganized the followers without improving the strategic position of the party. And because the external situation of

[50] Bebel and Singer used their charisma to fully crush the opposition at meetings, which turned into great demonstrations of the allegiance of the masses to their long-time leaders. Engels called the opposition "a revolt of literati and students." Bernstein, however, makes it clear that the majority of the opposition indeed consisted of workers and functionaries who rose from the ranks, and that it was quite natural for writers and university-educated members to play a role. While Engels charged them with distorting his views and ignoring the practical interests of the movement, Bernstein points out that some passages in Engels' writings seemed to support the opposition. See E. Bernstein, *Geschichte der Berliner Arbeiterbewegung, op. cit.,* 325 f.

[51] On the concept of self-maintenance and infusion with value, see P. Selznick, *Leadership in Administration* (Evanston: Row, Peterson, 1957), 20 f. Cf. also Ch. X, p. 257.

the movement, particularly its isolation within a powerful dominant system, did not basically change over the years, there was no compelling reason to change the ideology.

The Centrist position of the leadership was, by and large, bolstered by a theoretically sophisticated, deterministic interpretation of Marxism, which became known as orthodox Marxism and which was elaborated by Kautsky and his group.[52] As the caretaker of Marx and Engels' literary remains, he did much to make their work accessible to the party. As a party theoretician he was forced to pay greater attention to practical problems than they had needed to. Marx and Engels had purposively refrained from spelling out concrete solutions for the problems of the transition from capitalism to socialism. Kautsky, on the other hand, addressed himself to these problems, but he did so by fusing radical images with reformist meaning. An example is his definition of the dictatorship of the proletariat; as early as 1893 he wrote to Franz Mehring that he could think of no better form for the dictatorship of the proletariat than a powerful parliament, after the English pattern, with a Social Democratic majority and a strong proletariat backing it.[53] He considered a violent revolution possible but visualized as its aim the establishment of parliamentary democracy. Still, this was only a relative moderation. It continued to antagonize the ruling groups, but it also left many persons dissatisfied who were opposed to the dominant system. Although the labor movement was the result of a rigid class structure, its own radical ideology prevented it from appealing effectively to other lower-class groups and to sections of the middle class. While the belief in a unique mission

---

[52] For a detailed analysis of the functions of "Kautskyanism" in the labor movement before the First World War, see Erich Matthias, "Kautsky und der Kautskyanismus. Die Funktion der Ideologie in der deutschen Sozialdemokratie vor dem ersten Weltkrieg," in Iring Fetscher, ed., *Marxismusstudien* (Tübingen: Mohr, 1957), II, 151–97.

[53] Cf. letter of July 8, 1893, cited in Boris Goldenberg, *op. cit.*, 15 f.

was perhaps a response to the lack of social and political recognition, it also helped to prevent such recognition.[54]

This was clearly understood by many reformists and the revisionists.[55] Theirs was an attempt to free the party from some of its ideological impediments and to adjust its ideology to its political practice. The strength of reformist sentiment was even taken into account by Engels, shortly before his death, in his preface to the 1895 edition of Marx's *Class Struggle in France*. Engels discussed some strategic changes that had taken place in the more than 40 years since Marx had written his analysis. The advance of industrialization did create a large proletariat, but the latter "must gradually proceed by hard, tenacious struggle from position to position," since technological military developments make victory from the barricades increasingly difficult. However, the German workers have developed "one of the sharpest weapons, by showing their comrades in all countries how to utilize the general franchise." Legal expansion was the road to ultimate triumph, which could only be blocked if the labor movement gave the governments a pretext for military repression. Optimistically relying on the numerical increase of votes, Engels predicted that "if this goes on, we shall at the close of the century win over the greater part of the middle social layers, petty bourgeoisie as well as small peasants, and we shall come to be the decisive power in the land, before which all other powers must bow whether they like it or not." [56]

While the Centrist leaders were quite willing to make ideological

[54] Cf. Massing, *op. cit.*, 204. See also H. de Man, *Gegen den Strom* (Stuttgart: Deutsche Verlagsanstalt, 1953), 201 f.

[55] Revisionism refers to attempts to revise Marxism, not just to reformist activities.

[56] Quoted from a separate printing of the preface under the title, *The Revolutionary Act* (New York: Labor News Company [Socialist Labor Party], 1922), 22, 26, 36. The impact of this preface was considerable among Social Democrats in various countries and strengthened revisionism theoretically. Its effect could not be obliterated by Kautsky's later proof that Engels had meant to make merely a tactical concession. Cf. Robert Michels, *Political Parties* (New York: Collier Books, 1962), 336.

concessions to the exigencies of the party's situation, Bernstein's challenge, three years later, went too far for them. Bernstein returned from his long exile in England, strongly influenced by the Fabians and by English social and political developments in general. He called on the party "to find the courage to free itself from a phraseology which is indeed outdated; and to appear as what it really is today—a democratic, socialist reform party." [57] The executive quickly moved to keep Bernstein in check, because it feared that the morale of the faithful and the unity of the movement would be weakened. The astute Ignaz Auer, who did not rank much below Bebel, retorted to "Ede" Bernstein in a letter:

Do you really think that a party that has a fifty-year-old literature and a nearly forty-year-old organization . . . can change so quickly? The party would be blown to pieces if the leaders would act according to your demands. My dear Ede, your demands cannot be formally agreed upon and cannot be talked about, they are just acted upon. Our whole activity, even under the infamous law [i.e., the antisocialist legislation], was the activity of a Social Democratic reform party. A party which has to take the masses into account can be nothing else. [58]

Kautsky and others seized on weaknesses of Bernstein's revision of Marx. Bernstein attacked the economic necessity of the breakdown of capitalist society and pointed to the continued importance of the middle classes. However, he did not effectively attack the basic Marxist assumption of the falling rate of profit, which was defended by the new Marxist theory of imperialism. This theory maintained that the capitalist exploitation of as yet unindustrialized countries temporarily arrested the secular trend of declining profit and improved the proletarian standard of living, until the limits of imperialist expansion had been reached. Increasingly

[57] Ed. Bernstein, *Evolutionary Socialism* (New York: Huebsch, 1909), 197. In 1898 Bernstein published this collection of articles under the title, *Die Voraussetzungen des Sozialismus und die Aufgaben der Sozialdemokratie*. See also Peter Gay, *The Dilemma of Democratic Socialism* (New York: Columbia University Press), 1952.

[58] Quoted in G. Ritter, *op. cit.*, 201 f.

severe international conflicts between the imperialist powers would be inevitable and would hasten the destruction of capitalism. This theory was embraced by the new radical left, which emerged about the turn of the century and which advocated mass demonstrations and mass strikes in order to enforce further democratization, especially of the Prussian suffrage. Rosa Luxemburg and Karl Liebknecht, the son of Wilhelm Liebknecht, became its renowned spokesmen.

The isolation of the labor movement and the power of the dominant system strengthened Revisionist as well as radical tendencies. Revisionism was a response to both the stability of Imperial Germany and the orthodox line of the party, while radicalism was a response to the same stability as well as to the rise of Revisionism. Revisionism saw the only solution for the party's dilemma in a *rapprochement* with the left wing of the middle classes; the radicals were convinced that the ruling groups could not be defeated with parliamentary methods alone. Each faction could support its case with strong, but not definitely convincing, reasons.

The existence of a Revisionist wing enabled the Centrist party leadership to appear radical and provided it with new opportunities for verbal radicalism, which preserved the allegiance of the orthodox delegates at the conventions as well as of the extreme left-wing minority. However, since both the Revisionists and the Centrists were more genuine supporters of a parliamentary system than the extreme left was, they ultimately had more in common with each other than the Centrists had with the left. The major issue between Revisionists and Centrists was the degree of democratization reached in Imperial Germany, with the Centrists arguing that a nonviolent revolution in one form or another was probably necessary. The orthodox Marxist rhetoric of the Centrists prevented both sides from fully recognizing their specific similarities. Only the events of 1918 revealed to all that the Centrist leadership had actually embraced the theory of "bourgeois revolution," that is, the goal of parliamentary democracy.

VIII

The Meaning of the Labor Movement to Its Members

Inversely corresponding to the class cleavage in Imperial Germany and the alienation of the Social Democratic workers from the dominant system was the extraordinary personal importance of the labor movement for many of its members. Therefore, I will now turn from the level of the explicit democratic and socialist ideology to the level of the more diffuse meaning of the labor movement for its members, especially the less articulate grassroots attitudes. This will also involve a consideration of the understanding of Marxism by the masses. The major purpose of this chapter is to show that the labor movement came to mean for many workers the enrichment of a life which offered relatively few satisfactions on the industrial job and little social recognition by the dominant system. Equally important is that acceptance of this exalted meaning did not generally lead to a revolutionary attitude.

The leaders considered themselves the spokesmen for the masses, and they indeed verbalized a good deal of what the movement meant to many workers. However, they took the personal meaning of fighting for the movement so much for granted that they said little about it. Furthermore, they were not interested in all aspects of the movement's significance for the masses of members, especially those aspects that did not seem to be in the ideological and tactical interest of the movement. For the functionaries in the lower and middle echelons, various meanings can be derived from the emphasis of their activities. Some aspects of the meaning for the rank and file were verbalized little or not at all, but they can be deduced from the autobiographies of a few lower-ranking, part-time functionaries. There are also a few autobiographies by men who rose from the ranks of workers to become teachers or writers, men who had only a temporary connection with the labor movement. And something can be gleaned from the observations of outsiders. On the whole, the evidence for the meaning of the labor movement to the rank and file is inevitably fragmentary.

1. Leaders and Followers

At the 1890 party convention Bebel said, "We possess the tremendous following and the trust of the working masses only because they see that we are working practically for them, that we do not merely refer them to the indefinite future of the socialist state." [1] Two decades later, the interrelationship of ideological appeals and "practical work" was clearly stated by Ludwig Frank, the most brilliant Revisionist parliamentarian of the years before the First World War.

The propaganda for our future socialist goals has awakened millions of people, orienting them toward goals which transcend their narrow existence. But at present it is the practical work which we have done and want to continue to do that makes us great, that gives us a secure place in the hearts of the masses.[2]

From the sixties until his death in 1913, Bebel came to symbolize above all others the wishes and ideals of the masses. He was recognized by them as one of their own and thus belonged, as Robert Michels pointed out in his necrologue, to the few middle-class persons who attained such a position in the German labor movement. Social Democratic newspapers even claimed him to be

[1] *Parteitag Protocols*, Halle, 1890, 102.
[2] *Parteitag Protocols*, Leipzig, 1909, 340.

a proletarian genealogically.[3] In an un-Marxist fashion, he qualified as a proletarian because in his childhood he had lived in poverty. The elective affinity between Bebel and his followers went so far that Franz Mehring applied to him the Swabian phrase about Ludwig Uhland, the popular poet and liberal members of the 1848 Constituent Assembly: "Every word he ever spoke was right for us." [4] Bebel's apodictic way of stating his views seems to have helped rather than handicapped his relations with the masses even when he made a turn-about.[5] They liked his rhetoric in so far as it expressed their aspirations and resentments, but many workers seem to have had ambivalent feelings toward its radical and utopian aspects.

When the theologian Paul Göhre went to work in a factory in the early nineties, he found that for the majority

. . . especially of the more intelligent, thoughtful, practical, experienced and mature men, neither the official republicanism nor the economic communism were really popular. These were things for which most of them had no real understanding and enthusiasm. They accepted this, along with so many other things, as part of the Social Democratic movement; indifferently they left it to the leaders to deal with these incomprehensible problems, often secretly convinced or at least prepared that these prophesies would never be fulfilled. Thus a relatively well-situated, childless worker, an older, good-natured and polite man once told me: "Things will never be the way Bebel wants them to be in the future. He has already changed his mind, and he will continue to do so." . . .

3 Cf. Michels, "Bebel," *op. cit.,* 674. A difference between English and German labor spokesmen with middle-class backgrounds seems to be that the English leaders also remained spokesmen for their own class although they sometimes emphasized, in their appeal to workers, that they or their ancestors had risen from the ranks of labor. But they did not completely identify with the workers as did Bebel, nor were they recognized to the extent he was. Cf. Reinhard Bendix, *Work and Authority, op. cit.,* 115.

4 Quoted in Pinson, *op. cit.,* 209 f.

5 Cf. Michels, *op. cit.,* 677 and Eduard David, "Die Eroberung der politischen Macht," *Sozialistische Monatshefte,* 1904, 16.

A very intelligent, thoughtful and convinced Social Democrat once told me in a long conversation: You know, I scarcely ever read a Social Democratic book and seldom a newspaper. I used to be unconcerned about politics, but since I have been married and have five big eaters at home I must be concerned about it—not for myself. I am not in favor of red ties, big round hats and similar things. This does not matter to me. Nor do we want to be equal to the rich and distinguished people. There must always be rich and poor people. This we do not want to change. But we want a more just and a better order in the factory and the state. My thoughts about these things I will tell to everyone, whether he likes it or not. However, I will do nothing unlawful.[6]

This self-conscious emphasis on moderation and respectability served a defensive purpose vis-à-vis the government and the public, but there can be little doubt that it was genuine. The self-made astronomer and writer of best-sellers, Bruno Bürgel, supports Göhre's impressions of the majority of Social Democratic followers in the early nineties. Their beliefs were largely based on a secularized Christian equalitarianism, as it was expressed in the great slogans of liberalism and socialism.

It may be of some interest for those of my readers who are not familiar with the world of the working masses to learn something about the feelings and thoughts which moved us at the time. I do not speak of the leaders, the politically trained functionaries who had more intensively studied politics and sociology, but of the broad masses as they were at the time. In no way was there any violent inclination; we were glad not to be molested by the police; we were afraid to cause the slightest provocation for police intervention, because every incident was used to scare the bourgeois public. In a peaceful way the worker hoped to

[6] Paul Göhre, *Drei Monate Fabrikarbeiter* (Leipzig: Grunow, 1891), 112 f. In the early nineties Göhre was secretary of the *Evangelisch-Soziale Kongress,* a group of Protestant clergymen and academic men brought together by the former Court Chaplain Stoecker after he was fired in 1890. Later Göhre and Friedrich Naumann founded the Christian-Social party. After a clash with Naumann, Göhre joined the Social Democratic party in 1901 and became a Reichstag member in 1903. After 1918 he was secretary of state in a federal and a Prussian ministry.

reach his goals. And what were his arguments? Work is the source of all wealth and of all culture. We who do the greatest part of the work share least in the fruits of labor. We are brothers, by birth equal one to another. The existing cultural differences are due to the unfavorable social conditions of the great masses. Nobody can or should be the master of anybody else. Equal rights, equal duties, equal share in the material and cultural blessings of work! We merely want the right to pursue these goals in a peaceful way until the majority of the people has joined us and until a transformation of the capitalist into the socialist society is possible in a peaceful fashion.[7]

Another description of grassroots sentiments for the same time stems from Carl Severing, Prussian Minister of the Interior during most of the Weimar period. He maintains in his autobiography that millions of workers joined the labor movement because they wanted to improve their living conditions and win more freedom, not because of the activities of a few agitators or the propagandistic appeals of Marxist theories. These were his own reasons for joining the trade union and party about 1890, when he was still very young: [8] Severing plays down somewhat the role of agitation and ideology in order to counter the old argument so often hurled at the labor movement that it arose not from genuine but from artificial needs of the workers. It is true that the tenacious activities of a very small number of paid and unpaid functionaries would have been unsuccessful if in responding to their appeals the workers had not felt that their own needs were being met. But eventually the efforts of this nucleus afforded to hundreds of thousands of workers participation in "great issues" of the working class and of mankind as well as meaningful everyday activities

[7] Bruno Bürgel, *Vom Arbeiter zum Astronom* (Berlin: Druckhaus Tempelhof, 1929), 64. The phrase "Work is the source of all wealth and all culture" was the first sentence of the Gotha program of 1875.

[8] Cf. Carl Severing, *Mein Leben* (Cologne: Greven, 1950), I, 34. On the primary interest of many trade union members in concrete economic benefits, see Adolf Braun, "Realismus und Utopismus in den Gewerkschaften," *Der Kampf,* VIII, 1915, 46.

which provided satisfactions denied by the dominant system. Many of these activities looked shallow to radicals, but this did not diminish their importance to those pursuing them. This meaning and the intensive identification of common members with the leaders were eloquently described by Eugen Prager, after he had left the old party during the World War to help establish a new one which would preserve the old spirit:

Have respect for the hundreds of thousands of Social Democrats who worked indefatigably year after year, nameless and without external recognition, though the fruits of their labor were to ripen only for the coming generations. Let us not lightly pass over this period with the assertion that it was a shallow period of the embourgeoisement of the party. Who does not remember what the party meant to him during the long or short span of his membership? Not only the hope for a happier future, but the fulfillment of the present, too: the rescue from the political depression of the time, the belief in the creativity of the proletariat, the recognition of the emergence of a new world. In all of this we shared: in the details of everyday activities as much as in the great battles; the party newspaper was a part of our self, the organization, down to the smallest district and dues meeting, was a living community. Bebel, Singer, the great and the little men who spoke for the party: they were not leaders, they were the masses, it was us. Whether it was a matter of a prison sentence against striking workers, of a lock-out, a parliamentary action, or an election, we were always involved with heart and soul because it was our cause, the cause of the party that was at stake. A split was unthinkable at that time.[9]

Göhre, Bürgel, Severing and Prager do not emphasize the considerable appeal of vulgar Marxism which spread after 1890, interested as they are in pointing to the moderation, respectability, sobriety and dedication of the workers. Because of its complex attractions, simplified, vulgar Marxism became a constitutive part of the labor movement's meaning to many followers. Some of the explanations for these attractions are less flattering for the workers than the preceding accounts of their mentality.

[9] Prager, *op. cit.*, 14 f.

2. The Appeals of Vulgar Marxism

The deterministic component of Marxist ideology was apparently meaningful to both moderate and radical active party members, as well as to the passive followers of the movement. Relating Bebel's popularity to his pronounced Marxist phraseology, Michels explained "the suggestive effect which Marxism in particular exerted on the masses" as a resultant of their strong desires and their passive tendencies. The worker "need only pay his party dues and at election time deliver his Social Democratic ballot. The rest will be taken care of by the 'development.' "[10] Irrespective of whether there was a modal proletarian personality characterized by strong desires and passive tendencies—a theory which Michels took over from the psychologist and democratic politician Wilhelm Hellpach (1877–1955)—deterministic Marxism was indeed attractive to those who were relatively passive supporters.[11] However, it could also motivate many party workers to great exertion in order to facilitate the "inevitable" development in accordance with Marx's dictum that it is possible "to shorten and lessen the birth-pangs of the new society."[12]

For the workers to understand Marxism, it had to be vulgarized. The "Austro-Marxist" Otto Bauer, the leading theoretician of the Austrian party and its leader after the First World War, accepted this in 1907.

Deterministic Marxism is for the masses of workers not only a tremendous advance of knowledge, but also a motive power of their will . . . the reception of a new science by the masses is an historical proc-

[10] Michels, "Bebel," 692 f.
[11] Cf. Wilhelm Hellpach, *Nervenleben und Weltanschauung* (Wiesbaden: Bergmann, 1906).
[12] Karl Marx, *Capital*, 15.

ess in the course of which the masses adapt the thoughts they want to understand to their capacity for comprehension at a given moment. From the history of the natural sciences and of philosophy many examples could be provided which show that the simplification and vulgarization of a new doctrine is nothing but a stage of its victorious advance, of its rise to general acceptance.[13]

The low level of comprehension had advantages as well as disadvantages. It handicapped the functionaries and the ordinary party members when greater knowledge would have made it easier for them to convince more workers or to defend more aptly the socialist position against bourgeois critique. Lack of knowledge combined with great enthusiasm for the new creed many times resulted in frustrations and antagonisms between the believers and their fellow workers.[14] But the firmness of the naive belief in vulgar Marxism also afforded protection against the disillusioning realization of the theoretical difficulties of Marxism and of the complexity of political and social processes. When Joseph Buttinger, who cooperated and finally clashed with Otto Bauer in the Austrian underground movement of the nineteen thirties, was appointed at the age of 24 to the very responsible position of a local party secretary, he delivered 12 carefully outlined lectures on the overambitious topic, "From the Primordial Nebula to the State of the Future"—a farewell address to the youth group he had led. Marxism, as he understood it, gave him more certainty than Catholic dogma had previously given him, and he set out unhesitatingly to explain to his audience problems which he himself did not adequately understand.[15]

13 Otto Bauer, "Die Geschichte eines Buches," *Neue Zeit,* 26:I, 1908, 26 f. This article was written on the 40th anniversary of the publication of the first volume of *Das Kapital.*

14 Cf. the memoirs of Wenzel Holek, *Lebensgang eines Handarbeiters* (Jena: Diederichs, 1930), 212 f. First published in 1909.

15 Cf. Joseph Buttinger, *In the Twilight of Socialism* (New York: Praeger, 1953), 407 f. This is perhaps the most perceptive extensive description by a former Social Democrat of the Social Democratic subculture. Buttinger grew

Of what did vulgar Marxism consist? In his memorial article on
Das Kapital, Otto Bauer enumerates the various disjointed components of vulgar Marxism separately believed in by the masses,
but considered to have scientific connection beyond their understanding:

The mode of production of material life determines the social, political and cultural process of life. It is not the consciousness of men
which determines their existence, but their social existence which determines their consciousness.

The history of all hitherto existing society is a history of class
struggles.

The value of a commodity is determined by the labor socially necessary for its production.

The wealth of the propertied classes derives from the surplus value
produced by the workers, from the unpaid labor of the working class.

Capitalist society tends to increase more and more the misery of the
workers.

Small business will be destroyed; the control over the means of production falls into the hands of a continuously decreasing number of big
capitalists.

Monopoly capitalism has become a fetter on the mode of production which arose under it and with it. The centralization of the means
of production and the socialization of labor will reach a point where
they will be incompatible with the external capitalist form. The final
hour of capitalist private property is approaching. The expropriators
will be expropriated.[16]

Bauer did not explain the appeal of the disjointed propositions
to the workers. This was done later by de Man, who proposed an

---

up at the end of the period under investigation. He became a socialist when
the Social Democratic subculture was reaching its peak in the nineteen-
twenties. Since the basic structure of this subculture emerged long before the
First World War, it seems to be legitimate to consider those of his experiences
pertinent which are not definitely time-bound. Again, as a Social Democratic
subculture, the Austrian labor movement does not appear to be significantly
different from the German.

[16] Otto Bauer, *loc. cit.*

explanation of why and in what fashion key concepts of Marxian theory changed their original meaning in the process of adoption by large numbers of people. He contrasted the differential reactions of workers and of intellectuals to what they considered the iniquitous effects of industrialization. Their affects are similar, but the intellectuals attempt to arrive at valid theories while the masses transform these theories "by a regressive evolution . . . into symbols of affects." [17] He argued that vulgar Marxism was successful because it corresponded to the everyday feelings and perceptions of the masses:

For instance, the concept of exploitation, which Marx based upon scientific argument, acquires a symbolical significance . . . in the minds of the masses. Millions of workers believe that Marx proved that the employers unjustly appropriate part of the value which they, the workers, create—namely surplus value. Among these millions, you will hardly find a few hundred who are capable of understanding Marx's arguments. The immense majority never attempt to get acquainted with them. Besides, the arguments have no bearing upon the symbolical use of the concepts "surplus value" and "exploitation." The symbolical use is entirely based upon the feeling the worker has, born out of experience, that he is being exploited. . . . the masses regard as fundamental that which Marx intentionally left in the shade, or tacitly assumed to be already proved, namely the moral stigma which attaches to the employing class for an unjust appropriation of surplus value. . . . Marxism is that which the labor movement, regarded as a totality of trends of emotion and will, has made of the theoretical system of Marx. Nothing else is alive in Marxism, for nothing else is able to create life, new social life.[18]

However, de Man was aware that the beliefs of many workers, even if they seemed to coincide with their everyday experience, could often easily be disturbed when they had to face members of

[17] De Man, *op. cit.,* 414–16.
[18] *Loc. cit.* On the transformation of the concepts: expropriation of the expropriators, scientific socialism, class struggle, dictatorship of the proletariat, revolution, see *op. cit.,* 419 ff.

higher strata and were told, for example, that the top managers in industry were hard-working men and very important for economic progress.[19] The class distance of workers from middle-class persons and especially the political distance of Social Democratic workers from members of higher strata impeded or made impossible effective political communication. This had advantages for the labor movement and for vulgar Marxism because it decreased the competition from the ideas of the dominant system.[20]

De Man's thesis that vulgar Marxism lent itself as an expression of desires, aspirations, resentments and everyday experiences of the workers may be accepted, but the ideological propositions and prescription alone would not have meant much if the labor movement had not offered the concrete experience of solidarity and of social recognition within a group of like-minded peers. Of course, Marxism provided a good rationale for the solidarity of the working class, but the collective experience was primary.

3. Solidarity and Collective Action

The attractions of solidarity and collective action can be illustrated in three different contexts: at the time of joining the movement, while doing lower-level party work, and during extreme political crises. A few examples, covering the whole period under investigation, may be mentioned. Anton Weiguny described in his memoirs the first attempts to organize journeymen tailors and garment workers (*Schneidergehilfen*) of small businesses in upper Austria in the

[19] Cf. *loc. cit.* For similar observations, see Georg Maercker, *Vom Kaiserheer zur Reichswehr,* 2nd ed. (Leipzig: Koehler, 1921), 161.

[20] Holek's break with the labor movement was in part due to the continuous influence of an educated person who enabled him to rise into the lower middle-class stratum by making him the director of a Protestant youth program. See Wenzel Holek, *Vom Handarbeiter zum Jugenderzieher: Lebensgang eines deutschtschechischen Handarbeiters* (Jena: Diederichs, 1921).

1870's. The thrill of involvement in "serious" collective action for one's own economic group was so strong it enabled a radical break with past clique behavior and rivalry among different vocational groups of journeymen. The young workers suddenly became quite serious at the prospect of responsible group action. Weiguny's colleagues, each in his turn, sacrificed an hour's wage in order to read aloud during work hours, a practice previously observed by the tobacco workers.[21]

When Buttinger was a 15-year-old boy, forced by his proletarian family's poverty to work on a farm, he experienced "the most sublime feeling" of his young life as 400 workers poured into his village to demonstrate against the mistreatment of a Social Democratic health insurance official: "Their appearance . . . awakened a sense of forces that would lift a man above the personal selfishness that, in the village, had shaped his outlook on life." [22]

The "workers' poet" Karl Bröger (1886–1944) at first resisted demands to pay union dues, preferring to be forced off a job. Finally, he yielded to pressures. The conversion, with the experience of solidarity and the renunciation of individualism, came when he listened to the speech of a functionary who threatened a strike if a fired worker was not rehired:

> He who yelled loudest and applauded most was [Bröger]. He was glowing with zeal and conviction. He nodded again and again and searched for the reflection of his own agitation in the faces of the others. Everywhere he found it. . . . He suddenly grasped the value and power of community and was anxious to support this newly found recognition. He began to talk about trade union problems, read what was worthwhile in this field, although he found it strange at first, and passionately accepted the socialist doctrine of salvation.

[21] Cf. Anton Weiguny, *Erinnerungen eines Alten aus den Anfängen der oberösterreichischen Arbeiterbewegung,* 17, quoted in Richard Wagner, *Geschichte der Kleiderarbeiter in Österreich im 19. Jahrhundert und im ersten Viertel des 20. Jahrhunderts* (Vienna: Gewerkschaft der Kleiderarbeiter Österreichs, 1930), 122.
[22] Buttinger, *op. cit.,* 403 f. By permission of the publisher.

He had known that there were the rich and the poor and that there were more, infinitely more poor people. But he had been satisfied with this knowledge and derived from it the incentive to become rich himself. He had not been concerned with the goals of his own life sphere. Indeed, he had rejected his world, he had painfully tried again and again to transcend it spiritually. When he looked back, in the light of his socialist wisdom, on his youthful struggles, they appeared to him like the hopeless fighting of a soldier who, cut off from his troops, desperately carried on his own war. He believed the new order of life would come for all the poor, not just for one alone. It will come for everyone or it will not come at all. His difficult attempts during all those years were bound to end in defeat, for he had desired betterment only for himself; he had dreamed of millions of Marks to give him the good life in harmony with his tastes and capabilities. He had no thoughts for other people or only those of a rich man handing out alms. There is no right to personal happiness, there is only the duty to further the general welfare.[23]

Sons of Social Democrats were likely to join the labor movement, but not merely because of their fathers' example. A case in point is William Bromme.[24] He joined after the fall of the antisocialist legislation because of the appeal of "serious" collective pursuits.

At first Bromme did for the party only what his father demanded. He carried socialist pamphlets and newspapers and shouted slogans during an election campaign. For a while he sympathized, for reasons not given, with the Advanced Liberals. He also spent much time with a nonpolitical group of friends who had formed a regular "table group" (*Stammtisch*) in 1889, unimaginatively called *Frohsinn,* as many of the hundreds of German glee clubs were named. When he first attended socialist meetings at the age of 16, he was much impressed. Even the cheerfulness after the meetings

[23] Karl Bröger, *Der Held im Schatten* (Jena: Diederichs, 1930), 135 f. This autobiographical novel covers the period from the nineties until 1914.
[24] Cf. William T. Bromme, *Lebensgeschichte eines modernen Fabrikarbeiters,* Paul Göhre, ed. (Jena: Diederichs, 1905). The following refers especially to 128–32, 233–39, 326 and 334.

appeared to him different from the boisterousness of his glee club friends. At first, his positive reaction may have been primarily due to the appeal of seriousness and adulthood. But he gradually came to understand, as his father had before him, that the combination of the workers was the only means to improve their conditions. As isolated individuals they could neither change their immediate nor their wider social environment. The labor movement offered a solution. As the father became a victim of his political activity, the direct and indirect achievements of the labor movement began to benefit his son. When the son was dismissed for political reasons and indicted for political blackmail in 1898, the organizations which the father had helped to build supported the son. Under the impact of the labor movement's growth, the state accepted some responsibility for securing improved working and living conditions. Bromme's mother died of tuberculosis; his tubercular condition was treated under the provisions of the sickness insurance. However, Bromme was incapable of further physical work at the age of 33—the year that he finished his autobiography.

When Bromme writes that his political attitude and innermost conviction made him continue to work for the party, despite his ill health and his wife's opposition, he bares only one part of the meaning of the labor movement for him. His memoirs clearly reveal his personal need for sociability and self-respect. Party work was the most meaningful activity of his life. To give it up would have made him just a party member or voter, no longer belonging to the in-group of the local party organization.

This raises the problem of the meaning of the labor movement for the more active members, the lower-ranking functionaries in particular. A relevant example here is Adelheid Popp, who became one of the most prominent women of the Austrian labor movement. Her case shows that material deprivations alone were not usually enough to make a worker turn to the labor movement. Adelheid Popp paints a picture of her youth exposing fully the physical and psychical mutilation inflicted on many men and women of the first lower-class generation recruited for large-scale indus-trialization.[25] However, extreme suffering made her no more favor-able to socialism than it made the thousands of other women at work in Viennese factories during the eighties. She believed the anti-Semitic propaganda and the characterization of Social Demo-crats as anarchists. But when she was without a job for several weeks her Catholic faith was shaken. Trials of Social Democrats aroused her compassion and interested her in the labor movement. After meeting her first Social Democrat in the eighties, she ex-pected the revolution within a short time. Gradually her grasp of socialist ideas improved, and the party speakers and newspapers formulated for her those ideas she was unable to develop on her own:

I heard clearly and convincingly expressed that which I had instinc-tively felt but had never been able to think out. . . . The more con-sciously I became a socialist, the more free and strong I felt to meet all opponents.[26]

Reading pulp magazine fiction had kept her for several years in an imaginary world. Socialism, on the other hand, was concrete in a double sense: it was a theory explaining her material living con-ditions and promising a millennium, and a political movement to which she could belong. The labor movement provided her with meaningful work and an articulate class consciousness. Absorbed in everyday party work, she completely identified with the move-

[25] Adelheid Popp, *Autobiography of a Working Woman* (London: Unwin, 1912). Popp's family came from Bohemia. As industrialization progressed in Austria, many non-German citizens of the Double Monarchy migrated to Vienna, the industrial center of the country. Thus, there was a development similar to, though not as pronounced as, the development in the United States where the lowest social group was to a large extent made up of the most recent wave of immigrants. "Undesirable" workers could be deported from Vienna to their native villages. For her political activities Popp was threat-ened with deportation to Bohemia although she could not speak Czech.

[26] *Op. cit.*, 99 and 34.

ment. This is what it meant to her to become a full-time functionary:

> I was now endlessly happy. I had a sphere of work which satisfied all my longings but which I had considered quite unattainable for myself. It was to me the Promised Land.[27]

The intense identification with the labor movement and the great sense of personal satisfaction were shared by both moderate and radical functionaries. Both groups were equally interested in efficient organization, but the radicals, such as Buttinger, were also concerned with the Marxist indoctrination of the workers, particularly those who were already followers. The more radical functionaries could afford such concern because they did not carry the responsibilities, sustained by the top leaders, for the survival of the movement and for dealing with the government and the public; they could operate nearly exclusively within the classbound and isolated realm of the Social Democratic subculture. Many moderate functionaries, too, immersed themselves completely in this realm. Typical of them was Bromme. He was very useful as a member of a party which aimed primarily at increasing the number of its parliamentary seats and at expanding its organization.[28] The considerable material sacrifices he made for the party were partly borne by his wife and children, who could not share the emotional gratifications which compensated him. He tried to avoid provocations, but was not deterred from party work by the ever present possibility of dismissal for political reasons, criminal prosecution on *ad hoc* pretexts or the danger to his health through overexertion. This is no mean record, but he was not the kind of man likely to impress the more radical functionaries. His absorption in administrative work, membership drives and electoral campaigning, to the more or less tacit exclusion of theoretical interests, placed

[27] *Op. cit.,* 120.
[28] Cf. Bromme, *op. cit.,* 240 f.

him clearly in the ranks of the moderates, among whom the editor of his autobiography, Pastor Göhre, was prominent.[29]

Just as the reasons for joining the labor movement and the activities to which an individual devoted himself shed light on the movement's meaning to each person, so the personal meaning became visible in those moments that threatened the very life of the movement. The events of 1933 proved that the beliefs of the Social Democratic and Communist functionaries and rank and file were not functioning to produce mass resistance against the destruction of the labor movement in Germany. Both movements collapsed when they were outlawed and confronted with totalitarian methods of suppression. But this is no argument against the assumption that the labor movement was the life center of masses of workers. Whenever suppression was not totalitarian, the importance of the labor movement for many members made them try to perpetuate its organizational life. There is a striking parallel between the events of 1878 in Germany and 1934 in Austria: Many members refused to give up what meant so much to them. The leaders, with few exceptions, lost much prestige and control when the confused members turned to them only to be disappointed. The descriptions by Auer, Vollmar and Mehring of the events after the outlawing of the German party in 1878 and Buttinger's account of the suppression of the Austrian party by the clerical fascists are very similar. The failure of the German leadership was cautiously acknowledged in 1889 by Ignaz Auer, who conceded that "the executive com-

[29] In his composite portrait of a middle-aged, female proletarian party worker, Buttinger described one consequence of uncritical immersion into the Social Democratic subculture, namely, the unrelatedness of routine activities to their object: To her "anything written in a book or pamphlet issued by the party was the Gospel truth, sight unseen. Her job was not to read the party literature but to circulate it. It did not occur to her to doubt the contents. To do so would have seemed silly and unjust as if the 'leaders and theoreticians' at the top had questioned the accuracy of her accounting for party buttons and publications. Frau Meier's faith in the party did not rest on its doctrines but on its life." *Op. cit.,* 64. By permission of the publisher.

mittee of the party lost touch with the majority in an exceedingly short time." [30] Vollmar and Mehring were more outspoken. Vollmar agreed with those who accused the leaders of having abandoned the masses, and Mehring wrote in his history of the party that the masses and not the leaders saved the movement. The passage was later eliminated at the insistence of Auer and Bebel.[31]

After 1878 and 1934 many members were soon rallied by energetic organizers willing to use more radical methods, who established an underground movement spreading outward from the big cities.[32] Buttinger's description of many members' reactions to the suppression can probably be accepted for both situations. It clearly reveals the meaning of the movement for them:

To the faithful members and organizers of Social Democracy, the party ban amounted to brutal interference with their personal lives even if it failed to affect their economic existence. The possible loss of a few shillings a week meant nothing to those who now feared for the essence of their lives. The flags and symbols, the badges and pictures, the songs and legends of the "fight for freedom of the working class" had served many as substitutes for a lost religion and for . . . national patriotism. . . . . For tens of thousands, party work was a self-evident duty, gladly performed. The very annoyance attached to all social activities seemed to tie them to it. Often—in choir singing, at giant rallies of the party, in admiring their leaders, and under the magic spell of the great incantations of their "world struggle for freedom"—they had lost their own sense of insignificance. A wonderful, self-surrendering mood would seize them and lend them a greater dignity, more self-assurance, more courage, and a stronger socialist faith. Those were the hours of their ultimate bliss—and of the knowledge that all beauty in their lives came from the better sentiments that had brought them to the socialist movement. There, by their unselfish, satisfying endeavors, they were tied up with greater ends—with the harmony the party preached between their daily political activities and a higher destination of man. To

[30] Ignaz Auer, *Nach zehn Jahren* (Nuremberg: Fränkische Verlagsanstalt, 1913), 95.
[31] Cf. Brandis, *op. cit.,* 56 f.
[32] Cf. Ch. VII, 182 and Buttinger, *op. cit.,* 64 ff.

lose the party was nothing less to them than to lose home, fatherland, and religion.[33]

The fact that the labor movement became "home, fatherland and religion" to hundreds of thousands points up their great alienation from the dominant system. But nearly all of the multitude of activities that made up the Social Democratic subculture were no direct threat to the dominant system.

The resurrection of the labor movement in 1878 in Germany and in 1934 in Austria was largely the result of the refusal of many members to give up inherently nonrevolutionary activities. In Austria, these exasperated and hampered the minority, which aimed at a revolutionary uprising.[34] Thus, though the labor movement was the life center of many workers, this exalted meaning did not in itself constitute a revolutionary force. This was due in part to the moderating factors previously analyzed, but it was due as well to the fact that the Social Democratic subculture remained tied to the dominant culture in relevant respects, despite the depth of the class cleavage.

[33] Buttinger, *op. cit.,* 67 f.
[34] Cf. *op. cit.,* 70 ff. See also my Ch. IX, 231 n.

IX

The Social Democratic Subculture and the Dominant Culture

1. The Impact of the Socializing Agencies of the Dominant Culture

The influence of elementary education, nonsocialist newspapers and literature and of service in the military remained pervasive during the whole period. In contrast, the control of the Protestant state churches over adult workers was largely formal. Like the Anglican church in England, the Protestant German state churches did not energetically fight for the allegiance of the working class; there was no parallel to Methodism.

The power of the socializing agencies of the dominant system was acknowledged by Liebknecht in 1872 and again at the end of the period, in 1915, by Adolf Braun, the perceptive Revisionist labor editor.[1] In between it was often overlooked by Social Democrats, who were proud of their propagandistic and educational efforts. In his famous speech, "Knowledge Is Power—Power Is Knowledge," Liebknecht attacked the class differences in education, the pernicious influence of commercial newspapers on taste and political attitudes, and cheap popular literature (*Kolportage*). He charged that until very recently German classical literature had been completely withheld from the people and concluded that what

[1] See Wilhelm Liebknecht, *Wissen ist Macht—Macht ist Wissen.* Address on the occasion of the anniversary of the Dresden Workingmen's Educational Association on February 5, 1872, and of the Leipzig Workingmen's Educational Association on February 24, 1872. (Leipzig: Genossenschaftsbuchdruckerei, 1873); Adolf Braun, "Bildungsprobleme in der Arbeiterbewegung," *Der Kampf,* Vol. 8, 1915, 241 ff.

grammar school and army barracks started was finished by the bourgeois newspapers. He complained of an increasing preoccupation with military and religious affairs in the newspapers:

> Religious questions have not been treated so zealously for 200 years. One might think we were back in the wildest times of the Reformation, but none of the contending parties is really serious about it—they are only serious in their efforts to secure exclusive control over the minds of the benighted masses. . . . in Prussia, the "leading" state of Germany, the "state of the intelligentsia," the budget for elementary education is 2 million *thalers* compared to 60 million for the army and navy.[2]

Despite such budgetary proportions, Liebknecht accepted the popular stereotype that was to persist for decades that the German workers appeared better trained in the three R's than did English and French workers, but he added, in Lassallean fashion, that the latter were in his opinion "superior to the German workers on the average with regard to political and economic comprehension (*Bildung*)." [3] He also approvingly quoted Buckle to the effect that no other nation suffered from such a split between its highly educated classes and the common people as did Germany; in contrast, the United States was the country with "the least number of men of great erudition and the least number of men of great ignorance" (Buckle).

Even after the end of the Empire, only pupils attending a secondary school could go on to a university, and scarcely any working-class child entered secondary school. The early starting age,

---

[2] Liebknecht, *op. cit.,* 13 f.
[3] *Op. cit.,* 23 f. In his Frankfurt speech of May, 1863 (the "Arbeiterlesebuch") Lassalle had drawn a comparison which became famous and was used for many years as an exhortation and spur for the workers: "You German workers are strange people. Before French and English workers, one has to plead improvement of their dreary condition, but to you one must first prove that you are living under sad conditions." Lassalle, *op. cit.,* III, 227 f.

ten years of age, and the tuition fees were effective deterrents, besides the other social handicaps and biases involved. This perpetuated the class cleavage between the working class and the upper and middle classes, but because elementary education was used as a means of political and social control, the dominant system continued to exert a considerable influence on the disaffected part of the working class and its offspring. Dual loyalty was a resultant of the contending influences.

When the Austrian chancellor, Count Rottenhan, reorganized the educational system shortly after 1800, he considered it the purpose of the elementary school "to make thoroughly pious, good, tractable, and industrious men of the laboring classes of the people." [4] More than 80 years later, the control function of elementary education was emphasized even more strongly when Bismarck said that the primary school should merely teach the three R's and not convey "superficial" knowledge in history, geography and the natural sciences. This was a critique of the insistence on more knowledge by the higher civil servants in the Prussian ministry of cultural affairs and implicitly a critique of the whole liberal attempt to encourage more general education. Many liberals hoped that this would counteract socialist agitation and enable the workers to comprehend the unchangeable laws of economic life. [5] These liberal expectations were, of course, idle, and Bismarck clearly recognized this. When he instituted the "Era Puttkamer," education and religion were more vigorously and perhaps more effectively used as a means of political control than they had previously been. "Puttkamer," explained Eckart Kehr, "was not reactionary

---

[4] Quoted in Charles A. Gulick, *Austria from Habsburg to Hitler* (Berkeley and Los Angeles: University of California Press, 1948), I, 546.

[5] See Bismarck's conversation with H. R. von Poschinger, in Poschinger, *Fürst Bismarck und die Parlamentarier* (Berlin: Trewendt, 1894), 224. For the liberal and mainly laissez-faire position on education see, e.g., editorials in the *Deutsche Industriezeitung*, 1871, 430, and 1877, 262. This was the weekly of the chambers of commerce and trade in the important industrial cities of Chemnitz, Dresden, Plauen, and Zittau in Saxony.

in the sense that he handed back elementary education to the church; rather he used church and religion for his policy of fighting Socialism." [6] In reaction to the attempts on the life of William I school children had to learn more religious texts by heart.[7] It was during this time that William I demanded that "religion must be preserved for the people." William II took a personal hand in re-organizing the teaching of history, first introduced as a separate subject in Prussian schools in 1872. "For some time now," he informed the ministry of education, "I have been occupied with the idea of making the school in its various grades useful in combating the spread of socialistic and communistic ideas. In the first place, it will fall upon the school to lay the foundation for a healthy conception of political and social relations, through the cultivation of fear of God and love of country." [8]

[6] Eckart Kehr, "Das soziale System der Reaktion in Preussen unter Putt-kamer," *Gesellschaft*, 1929:2, 255 f. Puttkamer's religiosity was peculiarly suited for his job. He seems to have believed sincerely that Prussia was "the special favorite of God" (letter of May 1859, quoted in Kehr, *loc. cit.*).

[7] Cf. Philipp Scheidemann, *Memoiren eines Sozialdemokraten* (Dresden: Reissner, 1928), I, 14. Severing (*op. cit.*, 8 and 12) remembers that he had only one school book and the Bible and complains that religious instruction was furthered at the expense of material knowledge.

[8] Thereupon, the Prussian ministry of cultural and religious affairs issued an edict in 1890 which explained the new regulations: they "do not need special justification. German patriots, and in particular citizens of Prussia, are so fortunate as to have a country and a ruling dynasty of whose history they may well be proud. . . . It would be a sin against the coming generation if we were to delay familiarizing it with the blessings which accrue to it by virtue of its connection with the Prussian state. It would be an equally great injustice to the state itself if an unpatriotic generation were reared." Both quotations are cited in Walter Consuelo Langsam, "Nationalism and History in the Prussian Elementary Schools under William II," in Edward Mead Earle, ed., *Nationalism and Internationalism* (New York: Columbia University Press, 1950), 242 f.

Bromme describes how such instruction was followed in the class rooms. One of his highschool teachers explained: "There is now a species of men who call themselves Social Democrats; they want to destroy marriage and family life, to abolish the state and the monarchy, and do away with private property. Therefore, all intelligent propertied people must fear that one day

Elementary school education succeeded in attaching many working-class children to nationalist and monarchic institutions. Such loyalty due to early attachment was an appropriate basis for the political outlook of middle- and upper-class offspring, but it was an obstacle for the labor movement. To exemplify the difference, both Oldenburg-Januschau, who became famous as a prototype of the Prussian *Junker,* and the Social Democratic leader Scheidemann recall their enthusiasm when they saw William I during their childhood. The eleven-year-old Oldenburg-Januschau saw the king of Prussia, with Bismarck, Moltke and Roon, on horseback during the 1866 victory parade in Berlin: "This sight overwhelmed me. It made me the Prussian who belongs with body and soul to his king and his fatherland." [9] Scheidemann had to overcome his early attachment and enthusiasm for the crown before he could embark on a career which reached its climax when he declared Germany a republic in November 1918 and became its first chancellor.[10] When Severing was 14 "the monarchist attitude inculcated by the school had not yet been weakened. When I was asked in the vocational school to recite an appropriate poem on the occasion of the Emperor's birthday in 1890, I did not then have the slightest hesitation to comply with the request." [11]

Another example of the handicaps which childhood impressions constituted for the later susceptibility to socialist agitation is given in Adelheid Popp's autobiography. During her childhood her parents were not yet followers of the Social Democrats; she was preoccupied with the Austrian court and the aristocracy. Her

---

they might be forced to load manure and to push sand carts in the place of servants, that these uneducated men might take their places." Bromme, *op. cit.,* 60.

[9] Oldenburg, *op. cit.,* 14.

[10] Scheidemann, *op. cit.,* I, 14 f; for his only one-sided conversation with William II, in 1917, see II, 53.

[11] Severing, *op. cit.,* 19. Severing's attention was first directed to the Social Democrats as a result of the ambivalent reaction of William II to the miners' strike of 1889.

poverty was so great she was occasionally helped by a duchess and other aristocratic ladies, who continued to play an important role in her daydreams for years.[12] As she grew older, her enthusiasm for the established powers continued. She followed with keen interest the events in royal circles, admired her brother's three-year service in the Imperial army, and was deeply impressed by kind manufacturers. She felt resentment only against the direct oppressors of herself and her working companions: their foremen and masters.[13]

Books about, and pictures of, royal persons, military heroes, and Bismarck were widespread among all social strata and captured the imagination of the young. Bröger describes the power which a simple colored print of Bismarck in uniform on horseback exerted over him during his childhood.[14] Göhre found patriotic biographies of Frederick III and William I, "though in the form of the notorious, mostly inferior *Kolportage* pulps," in the libraries of several families whose heads were openly Social Democratic.[15] A rather picturesque example for the coexistence of opposite symbols in a working-class home is given by Bromme.[16] In his parents' home portraits of the following persons hung in one room: several saints, William I, Field Marshal Moltke, Bismarck, Bebel, Liebknecht, Marx and Lassalle. Bromme does not make clear who had brought

---

[12] Adelheid Popp, *op. cit.,* 34 ff. Heavy daydreaming became her protective device since she was compelled to work around the clock at an age when other children were attending school. She worked illegally from her eighth to her fourteenth year after which working was allowed. Before she was fourteen she had been taken to a hospital, a work house, and an insane asylum. More than ten of her sixteen brothers and sisters died at an early age.

[13] *Op. cit.,* 71, 92. Women in a factory where she had to work were forced into intimate relations by foremen, and they were persecuted or fired if others were chosen as favorites. Popp considered factory work degrading (67) although she was better off there than she had been in the small-scale enterprises of lower middle-class employers.

[14] Cf. Bröger, *op. cit.,* 11.

[15] Göhre, *op. cit.,* 124 ff.

[16] Cf. Bromme, *op. cit.,* 71 f.

together the exponents of the existing order of society and its most renowned opponents.[17] The saints probably hung there at the insistence of the mother; the father was not religious. This incident calls attention to another kind of dual allegiance within the families of workers: the men were more dedicated to the labor movement, the women remained committed to, or at least more influenced by, the dominant culture.

The majority of Social Democrats and certainly of the voters had an ambivalent attitude toward the Empire and frequently a positive attitude toward the rulers of the principalities. Military service, military anniversaries, and military symbols retained many attractions for the workers. Göhre found in 1890 that the majority of Social Democratic followers had a positive attitude toward the Emperor, the king of Saxony and military service, and that only those influenced by "elite Social Democrats" were torn between affection and disaffection.[18] The positive attitude toward the monarchs was often linked with opposition against Bismarck or with the idea that the Emperor might do better if only those around him would not vitiate his good intentions.[19] Göhre made his obser-

[17] Bromme mentions another typical instance in which the influence of the dominant culture asserted itself. When he attended his first political meeting the workers sang songs of the labor movement for hours. But when they marched home toward morning, carrying improvised red flags through the darkness, folk and patriotic songs were also sung. The earlier cultural experience persisted.

[18] Göhre, *op. cit.*, 117–26, 129 f.

[19] This belief was particularly strong among liberals and many common people with regard to Crown Prince Frederick III, partly because there was never a realistic test of his liberal inclinations. For decades he remained in the role of the crown prince, and he died after 99 days of reign in 1888. On the reactions of workers to him, see Göhre, *op. cit.*, 125. With regard to the popularity of William I, it must be remembered that he attained it only through the unification of 1871. Before that he encountered considerable hostility among the middle and the lower classes. This hostility dated back to his role as the *Kartätschenprinz* in 1849, when he used his artillery against the Republican volunteer army in Baden, and it was aggravated during the Prussian constitutional conflict of the early sixties.

vations at a time when William II attempted to gain popularity among the workers by pushing social legislation far beyond the limits considered feasible or desirable by Bismarck. William II soon suffered disappointement; the workers did not desert the labor movement, and he antagonized them by calling Social Democrats, among other things, *vaterlandslose Gesellen* (fellows without a fatherland) in 1895.[20]

Despite William's loss of prestige among the workers in the nineties, the attitudes toward national interests underwent a gradual but positive change. In the same decade a slow *rapprochement* with the prevailing nationalism actually began. The old guard had been patriotic in its own way; however, it had been frustrated by the

20 The "sympathetic, popular image" of William II, as depicted by Göhre, clashes violently with the absolutist self-image of the Emperor, as a letter of 1892 to Chancellor Caprivi reveals in which he spurned popularity, termed the Social Democrats a "gang," and hinted obliquely at the eventual use of military force against external or internal enemies:

"My will is rocklike, and what I have recognized to be right I adhere to, and no devil, not even Prince Bismarck, can make me abandon it. . . . Furthermore, we Hohenzollern are used to making slow progress, laboring under pains, struggles, party cleavages, and want of appreciation. How often have my ancestors and, as the last one, my grandfather, who rests in God, been forced to fight against the will of the imprudent multitude for policies which were first opposed, then criticized, and finally praised. I don't care for popularity. The only guide for my conduct is the precept of my duty and my good conscience in relation to my responsibility toward God. Dear Caprivi, think that I was prepared for bullets and dynamite when I ascended the throne, and I am still alive. Yes, even the Socialist thinks that he can get along with me. You cannot expect more, two years after Bismarck left and the anti-socialist law disappeared. Our time will come as it comes for every man. Let us be patient and do our duty steadfastly; whether or not the people take offense does not matter. Respect will come, it is already 'advancing' in view of your distinction and my trust in God. Trust my leadership and fence courageously where I show the way. Then we will manage to finish the gang and will succeed later in *rebus militariis*. Your very affectionate king William I. R." The occasion of the letter was William's rejection of Caprivi's proposal to hold a world exhibition in Berlin, which could have been used to enhance his popularity. Reprinted in Hans Herzfeld, "Berlin als Kaiserstadt und Reichshauptstadt, 1871–1945," *Jahrbuch für die Geschichte des deutschen Ostens* (Tübingen: Niemeyer, 1952), I, 168 f.

political, social and economic backwardness of Germany. The generation which entered the party after 1890 took pride in the achievements of German industrialism as well as in the power of Imperial Germany. The organizational and particularly the financial strength of the party and the trade unions were greatly enhanced by the economic rise of the country. More and more Social Democrats came to realize that military defeat might prove disastrous for the labor movement and the standard of living of the workers. This rational consideration was increasingly paralleled by a more or less conscious desire to break out of the long political isolation and to reconcile the dualism of loyalties. Furthermore, the perpetual agitation against the "unpatriotic" position of the party gained force when international conditions deteriorated at the turn of the century.[21]

These developments and the continuous influence of the "popular institutions of education," as Liebknecht had called the schools, the press and the military, combined in 1914 to produce enthusiastic support for the war efforts. Then Adolf Braun realized, to his own surprise, that the level of comprehension and the quality of education of the masses were determined by these powers of popular education. He considered the pride in the tremendous Social Democratic efforts to educate the masses justified, but he concluded that even if all these efforts had been completely successful, they would still weigh lightly in comparison with the mass impact of the educational agencies of the dominant system.

---

[21] From 1904 on this agitation was reinforced by the "National Association Against Social Democracy." In its appeals to the public and the workers in particular, the association called upon all "bourgeois" or "state-supporting" parties—to quote one of its favorite phrases—for "united action against the red enemy." Cf. Ferdinand Tönnies, *op. cit.,* 479.

2. Cultural Activities: Opportunities and Limitations

As the labor movement grew in sheer size, it also organized more intellectual, educational and recreational activities which summarily may be called "cultural." Such activities were always pursued by the labor movement; in fact, its beginnings lay in the educational clubs of the 1860's. The Social Democratic subculture was small before 1878, compared with the expansion after 1890, and it did not reach its peak until after the First World War.[22] Still, the multitude of political and cultural activities seemed startling to outside observers during the seventies.[23] These activities were pursued with such vigor because the party offered to the workers the only major means of participating in the political process and in the culture at large.[24] To be sure, workers could sometimes join political and cultural organizations, but they had no influence on their political and administrative direction. By setting up their own organizations they could share cultural and social middle-class activities without being subject to middle-class control. A vicious circle of boycotts developed among the cultural organizations of the labor movement and those of its opponents. It was, for example, incompatible to belong to both a veterans' and a Social Democratic

[22] Democratization then resulted in economic concessions such as the eight-hour day and paid vacations. On the remarkable expansion of the Austrian Social Democratic subculture after 1918, see C. Gulick, *op. cit.,* Ch. 18.
[23] Cf. F. Mehring, *op. cit.,* 163.
[24] There is a significant difference between the cultural organizations of the Social Democrats and what Lipset called the "occupational community" of the printers of the American International Typographical Union. Cf. S. M. Lipset et al., *Union Democracy* (Glencoe: The Free Press, 1956), 102 ff. The "occupational community" of the Social Democratic workers was not separate from the party and the unions. Professor Lipset's main point is the actual independence of the printers' associations from the union. Thus they provide alternative leadership and support a democratic mechanism within the union.

organization. At the 1893 party convention, a motion of the Berlin Reichstag District No. 1 was adopted which stipulated that "all members of the party and Social Democrats in the unions must participate fully in agitation and should not neglect their party duties through membership in *Landsmannschaften* or so-called entertaining associations, clubs, etc." [25]

The whole effort of creating a subculture within the larger culture presupposed a high degree of self-confidence within the nucleus of the party. Like the political organizations, the cultural organizations became vehicles for creating self-confidence and self-respect among the masses of workers.[26] But for the Social Democratic leaders cultural activities remained secondary to political activities. Early proletarian leaders such as Vahlteich and Fritzsche argued from the time that the workers' educational associations began for a clear dominance of politics over education. Liebknecht exhorted his listeners in his 1872 address, "Knowledge Is Power," to realize that learning alone would not liberate the workers.[27] This may have been a warning to members of the two workers' associa-

---

[25] *Parteitag Protocol,* 1893, 22 and 151; see also Schröder, *op. cit.,* 41. When in the sixties and seventies the liberals lost control of the workers' educational associations, liberal educators tried to compete with them by establishing a comprehensive neutral adult education program: "For this reason there was established in 1871 the Society for Adult Education (*Gesellschaft für Volksbildung*). The founders, who included Schulze-Delitzsch, bearing in mind the introduction throughout Germany of universal male suffrage through the new constitution, were provoked into action, as an inaugural proclamation stated, by the 'success which a few unscrupulous men achieved with their socialistic efforts.' This society developed a wide field of activity and by 1910 it had more than 7,000 affiliated organizations throughout Germany." R. H. Samuel and R. H. Thomas, *Education and Society in Modern Germany* (London: Routledge, 1949), 135. For policy pronouncements of church leaders which aimed at the boycott of all Social Democratic organizations before and after the First World War, see C. Gulick, *op. cit.,* 649.

[26] Cf. Andries Sternheim, "Zum Problem der Freizeitgestaltung," *Zeitschrift für Sozialforschung,* Vol. 1, 1932, 337.

[27] Cf. Liebknecht, *op. cit.,* 3.

tions he addressed in Dresden and Leipzig not to overestimate learning at the expense of political exertion. The leaders hoped that cultural interests and gratifications would strengthen the adherence of the followers to the political cause of the movement. They wanted to raise the level of knowledge for political and organizational purposes. Furthermore, they were ideologically committed to the fight for a better life.

The leaders' apprehensions toward the distractive effect of the involvement in cultural affairs on the part of the masses were paralleled by radical charges against the functionaries that they were showing petty-bourgeois traits. With regard to cultural interests, this meant that they could not transcend the cultural attitudes, preferences and tastes of the middle-class groups from which they came or those of the middle-class groups to which they aspired. Especially older leaders adhered to the traditional middle-class standards of idealism in art and literature at a time when the bourgeois avant-garde was naturalist. An example of this cultural preference of leaders and, apparently also, on a lower level of comprehension, of many workers was the attitude toward naturalist literature which may be taken as an index of cultural tendencies within the labor movement. The publication of naturalist literature in the entertainment magazine of the party encountered opposition from workers as well as from veteran leaders and ascending younger leaders. A controversy ensued at the party convention of 1896.[28] The veteran leader Frohme attacked the editor of the Social Democratic home journal, the twenty-year-old *Neue Welt*,[29] for disregarding the entertainment needs of working people and for offending their sense of propriety in sexual matters. He and others asserted that many, if not the majority, of the party members were

[28] For the following, see *Party Protocol*, 1896, 78–85, 93–96, 103, 108–10.
[29] The *Neue Welt* was distributed weekly together with the party papers and therefore had a distribution of 200,000 copies. It was subsidized in 1896 with 48,000 Marks. In the seventies Höchberg had subsidized it with the substantial sum of 100,000 Marks.

against the kind of naturalism presented in the *Neue Welt,* especially the overdrawn description of misery. Less prominent delegates took the floor in order to agree or disagree with the emphasis on naturalist literature in the *Neue Welt.* Its editor, Steiger, defended his educational policies with the same pathos exhibited by his opponents. The "courage to be truthful" which was characteristic of the "new art," as naturalism was called, necessitated the reproduction of the dark as well as the bright sides of life. The minute descriptions of naturalism, he suggested, were a result of advances in the natural sciences, especially those introduced by the microscope.

Our comrades who insist on their Darwinian and materialist world view [can] now show whether they really believe it. . . . Art has become democratic, we no longer need kings on the stage, we no longer need dukes, barons and counts in the novels; now the worker, or whoever it may be, is an equally interesting object irrespective of his social position.

Steiger attacked the old position evident in the arguments of his opponents that art existed "either for instruction or, in the common sense, elevation." He agreed that a pedagogic approach was necessary because the workers, especially in the countryside, were not yet able to absorb all of modern art and literature, but he polemicized in particular against the view that art was only for women. "When I hear this objection, it seems to me that I listen to a real bourgeois: 'Well, for women it is still good enough.' This is an insult to the fair sex to whom you always accord equality in theory." He ended with a plea to make the working class the leader "in all fields of life" and emphasized that "we do not want to accomplish this through the destruction of earlier culture . . . we do want to take over all the Good and the Beautiful and the ability to enjoy it . . . so that the working class, the great fighter for culture of our time, . . . will be prepared for the great tasks of the future."

Frohme replied that he was not against naturalism, but only against its immoral abuses. He quoted an example from *Mutter Bertha,* a novel serialized in the journal, where a young woman is embarrassed because she has to relieve herself. Exclaimed Frohme: "If naturalist art believes it can justify the presentation of such absolute, stinking obscenities in novels, then this tops everything." Molkenbuhr, one of the rising administrators in the party, supported Frohme by asserting that workers who live in misery cannot be expected to enjoy descriptions of more misery and might be driven into a suicidal mood. No other journal of the party, he added, has provoked so many complaints. On the other hand, he said, many workers like to buy the cheap editions of the classics and to attend inexpensive performances of classic plays.[30] Another delegate advised Frohme to go into a cloister if he reacted so strongly, but he also hoped that the *Neue Welt* would be open from then on to "moral idealism . . . which elevates us in our hard struggle." The Revisionist intellectual and Reichstag member Dr. Schoenlank called Molkenbuhr's opinion basically identical with that "which the petty-bourgeois have of art" and told Frohme that his praise of art was not different from "the praise of eternal truth by bourgeois society."

Frohme, Molkenbuhr and the many working-class readers of the *Neue Welt* who were supposedly dissatisfied with this kind of realism were firmly supported by the aging Liebknecht, who himself was under concealed attack for the editorial weaknesses of the *Vorwärts.* He argued that the decline of capitalist society produced a literary decadence which could morally threaten the children of proletarian families, to whom the *Neue Welt* was delivered. Under applause and opposition he said of Hauptmann, reacting to Steiger's uncritical exaltation, that much in his writing was "flat, tactless and

---

[30] According to Göhre, Goethe and Schiller's works were promoted only after the late eighties on a wider scale within the labor movement. Cf. *op. cit.,* 95. According to Severing, Molkenbuhr particularly liked Goethe, Heine, Reuter, and Hebbel. Cf. Severing, *op. cit.,* 33.

ugly . . . and above all not revolutionary, but rather petty-bourgeois-reactionary."

The party members of the Social Democratic strongholds and Reichstag districts Hamburg I, Hamburg II, Altona and Wandsbeck each submitted a motion to the convention concerning the *Neue Welt*. The demands ranged from abolishment of the *Neue Welt* as a free supplement to replacement of the contents to produce "a popular journal of entertainment, rather than an arena for literary experiments." [31] The conflict was neutralized by Bebel, who skilfully took a detached but conciliatory position, which saved Steiger's job as editor of the *Neue Welt*. Bebel turned the literary policy issue into an administrative one by pushing through a motion of his own that a committee should study ways of decreasing the deficit of the home journal.

This debate at the party convention of 1896 cannot be read today without its bringing to mind the Bolshevist and Nazi cultural policies. Some of the most "principled" and "idealist" leaders, like Wilhelm Liebknecht or, within the Russian party, Lenin, also proved to be rather conservative in cultural affairs and accepted the older esthetics of bourgeois idealism and realism. However, within the German Social Democratic subculture, "encircled" as it was by the dominant culture, no dictatorship of taste could be successfully exercised without endangering the unity of the movement; furthermore, during the Weimar period fairly pedestrian Social Democrats who held high municipal and state offices generally had a much more permissive or even encouraging attitude toward the literary and artistic avant-garde than office-holders of different political persuasion.

The culturally progressive wing of the German labor movement could only advocate the assimilation of the works of the bourgeois avant-garde. There were simply not enough men of literary and artistic sophistication in the labor movement to take a more critical

[31] *Parteitag Protocols,* 1896, 14.

approach to the values of the dominant culture or to create new styles and art forms. Some naturalists briefly affiliated themselves with the labor movement, but they were soon disappointed by the strength of conservatism in matters of art. Prominent among them was Wilhelm Bölsche, the founder of the *Freie Volksbühne* (Free People's Stage) in Berlin in 1890.

Thus, while separate cultural activities were a constitutive part of the Social Democratic subculture, most of these activities were not different from those of the culture at large. Since many educators within the isolated labor movement attempted to impart as much of recognized *Kultur* as possible to the workers, this increased the influence of at least parts of the dominant culture among workers, although these components were not necessarily closely related to the central values of the dominant political system.[32] The relatively uncritical acceptance of *Kultur* can be seen in the

---

[32] Some generic reasons for the inability of a subculture to transcend the dominant culture were spelled out by James Baldwin in the context of the relation of American Negroes to American society: "The oppressed and the oppressor are bound together within the same society; they accept the same criteria, they share the same beliefs, they both alike depend on the same reality." More often than not the oppressed cannot create a "new society" even if they win great battles; in reality they fight for a change of the ruling groups or for "elevation of status, acceptance within the present community." See J. Baldwin, *Notes of a Native Son* (Boston: Beacon Press, 1955), 21. The Social Democratic press before the First World War and the Negro press are specific examples for the imitation of the dominant culture as well as for the preoccupation, on a different level, with the realm of the subculture. Baldwin shows that Negro newspapers not only imitate other newspapers but also try to cover "any news, however trivial, concerning any Negro or group of Negroes who are in any way unusual and/or noteworthy" (*op. cit.,* 62). Similarly, the Social Democratic provincial newspapers tried to cover as many events, preferably noncontroversial, within the movement as possible. The major Social Democratic paper, the *Berlin Vorwärts,* imitated the techniques which were used by a bourgeois paper to expand its circle of readers. The theoretical journal of the party, the *Neue Zeit,* criticized in 1905 the *Vorwärts* for having brought its subscription up to 92,000 by modeling itself after the *Berliner Morgenpost.* Cf. Otto Geithner, "Zur Taktik der Sozialdemokratie," *Neue Zeit,* 23:2, 1905, 656.

phraseology used in Liebknecht and Bebel's program for the Saxonian People's party of 1866 no less than in that used by the Social Democratic Program of 1921. The programs speak of "raising the physical, intellectual and moral education of the people," of "making accessible to everybody the cultural values" (*Allgemeinwerden der kulturellen Werte*), and of the "right of all *Volksgenossen* to share the cultural goods."[33] Even the foremost orthodox Marxist, Karl Kautsky, exhibited these uncritical tendencies: The "coming happiness" would be rooted in the "gratifying effects of scientific work," the "appreciative enjoyment in the fields of science and art, in nature, sport, and play." The "masses shall have at their disposal all of culture that has been created up to now. To conquer all of this culture for themselves" is their task.[34]

Since even Steiger's programmatic statement at the 1896 convention and Kautsky's views do not show much critical distance from the "purer" aspects of the dominant culture and toward the cultural limitations of the labor movement, the Social Democrats exposed themselves to the later critique of an esthetically refined Marxism which held that

. . . the history of German Social Democracy should be a warning against such a love of culture. Instead of a critical attitude toward the dominant culture, which would have provided the only chance for the future preservation of its elements, the endeavor often prevailed to wear as a showpiece the bourgeois wisdom of bygone days, just as the peasants put on the outmoded fashions of their overlords.[35]

There was indeed a tendency to split the dominant culture into two parts, one indissolubly associated with the values of the oppo-

---

[33] Quoted in Herbert Marcuse, "Über den affirmativen Charakter der Kultur," *Zeitschrift für Sozialforschung*, VI, 1937, 90 f.
[34] Quoted in Marcuse, *loc. cit.* The Kautsky phrases are from his book, *Die materialistische Geschichtsauffassung*, Berlin, 1927, II, 819, 824 and 837.
[35] Max Horkheimer, "Die Philosophie der absoluten Konzentration," *Zeitschrift für Sozialforschung*, VII, 1938, 380.

nents and one to be appropriated by the masses. The labor movement could, after all, legitimately consider some of the values of bourgeois culture and their literary expressions as a main spring of its inspiration. Given the social origin of most Social Democrats and the educational handicaps under which they had to labor, it was inevitable that even the most sophisticated among them did not have much critical detachment from seemingly desirable parts of the dominant culture. This resulted in relatively indiscriminate efforts to expand the cultural organizations of the subculture. For this lack of discrimination the labor movement was also criticized from a reformist perspective. In his 1915 review of the educational ambitions and activities of the labor movement, Adolf Braun acknowledged that the movement was "the greatest cultural force of the late 19th and early 20th century." [36] But he concluded that it tried to undertake too much in cultural affairs: history, art, natural science, philosophy, etc., were offered in an unrealistic way. He complained that the labor movement was uncritical toward its cultural capabilities vis-à-vis bourgeois society and did not differentiate between what was really of benefit to workers and the movement and what was only satisfying curiosity and the desire for entertainment, however legitimate these might be. He pointed out that often persons dedicated themselves to workers' education who were inexperienced with regard to pedagogics in general and in dealing with workers in particular, even if they were themselves of proletarian origin. He went on to say that he never saw any recognition in the labor movement for the difficulty of introducing knowledge to "a group of adult persons who through their age, experience, and education differed greatly one from another and who were burdened by monotonous work and everyday problems." [37]

A decade after the controversy on naturalism and classics at the 1896 party convention, the sombre reformist Friedrich Ebert drew

[36] Braun, *op. cit.,* 242.
[37] *Loc. cit.*

some conclusions from the inherent organizational limitations of the movement when he became embroiled, along with Hermann Müller, another of the capable administrators of the party, in a controversy with the orthodox editor Heinrich Schulz, one of the educational experts of the labor movement.[38] Object of the controversy was the participation of the Social Democratic *Verein für Volkskunstabende* in Bremen and of trade unions in the *Goethebund,* a neutral middle-class institution for adult education. Schulz maintained that the class struggle would be weakened if the workers satisfied their educational needs indiscriminately. Müller agreed with him that lectures on Lessing, for example, could not really offer much to the workers and were mere entertainment. He advocated more vocational and general education (*Fortbildung*). Müller was careful to point out that "education for the class struggle is indeed the major task," but he immediately added that "we do not always engage in the class struggle . . . we also want to enjoy life." [39] Schulz criticized in particular, in the *Bremer Bürger-Zeitung* (one of the best Social Democratic papers), an invitation extended by the *Goethebund* to Werner Sombart. Müller defended this, arguing that the workers' convictions could not be shaken by the address of a bourgeois professor. Ebert disagreed with Müller on Sombart's lecture because he considered it a partisan address before a politically neutral association, but he defended neutral adult education because intellectually interested comrades had a right to acquaint themselves with fields of knowledge to which the party gave them no access except in the biggest cities, such as Berlin, Hamburg, Munich and Dresden. Therefore, he said, the

[38] Soon afterwards they were to take over leading positions in Berlin, Müller became a secretary of the Berlin Central Workers' Secretariat in 1905. Ebert followed in 1906 and reorganized the party headquarters. On the controversy, see an article of the Social Democratic *Bremer Bürger-Zeitung,* February 2, 1905, reprinted in F. Ebert, *op. cit.,* 251–56. On the general position of Heinrich Schulz, see his official report to the party convention of 1906, "Sozialdemokratie und Volkserziehung," *Protocol,* 323–47.
[39] Quoted in Ebert, *op. cit.,* 252.

party demanded of the "class state" that it further adult education by establishing libraries and museums, by arranging music programs, etc. This did not contradict Vahlteich's demand of forty-four years before that the state, and not the labor movement, carry the burden of general education. It was also compatible with the local Bremen party program, which was drafted by Schulz; but what was essentially an aggressive demand and a challenge in the program derived in Ebert's case from the recognition that the labor movement was unable to appropriate on a large scale even those parts of the dominant culture which were considered desirable.

Still, as long as the dominant system was not shaken, the building of a subculture, with many gratifying cultural and political activities, was the only way to realize at least some of the goals of the movement. However, the many organizations set up for a variety of purposes showed two conflicting tendencies: First, they could bind the members more closely to the political commitments of the party. Second, they could divert, by their inherent satisfactions and difficulties, energies and attention from the political goals of the movement and the crucial problem of power.[40] The expan-

---

[40] When the labor movement was outlawed in Austria in 1934, after its subculture had developed far beyond the prewar levels, many Social Democrats tried to carry on their usual political and cultural activities underground because they could not imagine the destruction of the content of their lives. A struggle ensued between the more militant Social Democrats, on the one side, and the old leadership and the mass of the devoted members, on the other. The militants, who called themselves Revolutionary Socialists, repudiated many of the old policies of the party. They condemned especially its reliance on parliamentary forms of government and the rule of law in the struggle with authoritarian opponents, leading to the final success of these opponents. The Revolutionary Socialists also criticized the party for having given too much attention to cultural activities and drew some conclusions from the insights which Adolf Braun and Robert Danneberg had developed twenty years before as to the relative ineffectiveness of many of these activities. For fifty years, the Revolutionary Socialists argued, the party had tried to achieve socialism through enlightenment according to the old slogan that knowledge is power. Now the socialists had the knowledge and the others the power. The ideals of the "New Men," as the Revolutionary Socialists

sion of the Social Democratic subculture offered increasing opportunities for more and more workers to find social recognition among their peers and thus reduced their dependence, in this respect, on society at large. This was true for the rank and file and even more true for those who utilized the chances of social mobility within the movement. This resulted in an attenuation of the class struggle, as some Marxists correctly charged it would.[41] By helping the workers indirectly to adjust to the society at large, the subculture contributed to the stability of the dominant system.

3. Socialist and Nonsocialist Literature in the Working Class

The relative strength and weakness of the Social Democratic subculture can also be assessed by looking at the distribution of socialist and nonsocialist literature within the working class and the labor movement. In this section I shall deal with literature in general; in section 4, with the nature of the Social Democratic press. Most Social Democratic workers seldom read books, socialist or nonsocialist, but it is worthwhile to review the distribution of literature within the working class because the labor movement made great efforts to bring socialist and "good" nonsocialist literature to the masses. Indicative of the political and nonpolitical reading interests of workers and of favorable and unfavorable conditions for

---

were also called, were mostly those of the old party, but they did recognize that only a successful revolution would accomplish their realization. Cf. Buttinger, *op. cit.,* 70 f.

[41] See, e.g., Goldenberg's argument that the emergence of the labor movement as a society of its own, a "workers' society" with many parallel associations to bourgeois associations, satisfied needs of social recognition and self-respect and thus reduced the movement's capacity to carry on the class struggle. *Op. cit.,* 35 f.

literary receptiveness are the following early examples from the accounts of socialist writers—or at least writers of lower-class origin.

Vahlteich recalls that during the political depression of the fifties scarcely any workers read socialist literature.[42] People with revolutionary and democratic sentiments did not dare to associate with one another for fear of persecution. It was only through a relative that 15-year-old Vahlteich first heard of socialism. His uncle, a tailor, knew Weitling personally, but was unable to secure any of his books in Leipzig. The available socialist literature consisted of Louis Blanc's *Organization of Labor,* Proudhon's books, Engels' *Conditions of the Working Class in England,* and novels by Sue. But nearly all workers and craftsmen who read at all read only bourgeois or governmental papers. Vahlteich's father, a conservative master-craftsman, read the *Königlich Leipziger Zeitung* and the bourgeois *Tageblatt.* Brockhaus' *Allgemeine* was considered radical, that is, liberal. Workers would share one copy of a newspaper, reading it two or three days after publication. In 1857 Vahlteich went to Dresden as a shoemaker's journeyman. He found dissatisfaction with the prevailing conditions, but no understanding for the Social Question and no urge to discuss social problems. Finally he met two old men who had read Weitling; one of them had copied the 314 pages of his *Garantien* by hand.

During these decades reading was the primary means of self-education for interested workers and lower-middle-class persons. Bernstein reports of the early seventies that some workers who lived in the countryside and who were geographically immobile because of their large families tried to widen their mental scope by reading, but they were unable to obtain good literature.[43] Characteristic of the literary interests of workers and craftsmen not yet influenced by the labor movement is Bruno Bürgel's stepfather, a shoemaker, whose "favorite book was a history of Don Carlos, pre-

[42] Cf. Vahlteich, *op. cit.,* 7 ff.
[43] Bernstein, *Lehrjahre, op. cit.,* 20.

tender to the Spanish crown, and the notorious Carlist revolts."[44] He was also fascinated by Napoleon I and often described to his son the retreat over the Beresina. More rare was the case of Andreas Scheu, who later became well known through a political trial; when he began his apprenticeship about 1860 and earned some money, he bought *Schlossers Weltgeschichte* and works by Goethe, Schiller, Börne, Heine, Wieland, Klopstock, Lenau, Uhland and Platen—the best literature, according to the standards of the time.[45]

Carl Severing's working-class parents read the most popular bourgeois home journal, *Die Gartenlaube,* and exchanged with acquaintances copies of the *Buch für Alle* and the *Bibliothek zur Unterhaltung und des Wissens.* The latter was a mixture of entertainment and educational literature, usually read only by young Severing; it became a "guidepost in a land of knowledge which was still ahead of me."[46] Thus, while his parents scarcely read books, they at least did not discourage him. At the age of 15 and 16 (1890–91) Severing received from the vocational school Humboldt's *Kosmos* and *Wissmanns Reisen,* examples of good science

---

[44] Bürgel, *op. cit.,* 16 ff. Apart from reading, the stepfather's hobbies were his glee club and canary birds. Bürgel also describes how he detected, as a young boy, the discrepancies between the moralistic stories of his school book and reality. His father with his family had to move into a large proletarian apartment house in Berlin and worked hard at the age of sixty with no prospect of security in his old age. In contrast, young Bürgel saw on his school outings elegantly dressed young men walking *Unter den Linden,* "enjoying doing nothing."

[45] Andreas Scheu, *Umsturzkeime,* Erlebnisse eines Kämpfers (Vienna: Wiener Volksbuchhandlung, 1923), 38 f. Intellectually his family background was not proletarian. His father was a toolmaker who had failed in a small manufacturing enterprise. His mother ran a tailor shop which employed female apprentices and sometimes female employees. The parents had been on the side of the Revolution in 1848. This is another piece of biographical evidence for the observation that labor leaders partly came from proletarianized homes in which intellectual standards had been preserved. See also Bromme's background, *op. cit.,* passim.

[46] Severing, *op. cit.,* 8; cf. 21 f, 26, 33 f.

and travel literature, as reward for outstanding performance. At the same time and without encouragement from home, he took first glances at the *Metallarbeiterzeitung,* the weekly *Arbeiterchronik,* and the *Volkswacht,* all read in the small shop of his master. He understood little of the content, but greatly sympathized with the intentions of the labor movement. At the age of 18, when he had become a Social Democrat, he tried to read and failed to understand Marx's *Lohnarbeit und Kapital.* For the vast majority of workers he considered it as unintelligible in 1847, when it was first published, as it was in 1893, when he read it.[47]

Adelheid Popp's preoccupation with shilling-shockers (*Kolportage-Romane*) delayed, but did not prevent, her conversion to socialism. She first read dime novels with characteristic titles: *Rinaldo Rinaldini, Katerina Kornaro, Rosa Sandor, Isabella of Spain, Eugenie of France, Mary Stuart, The White Lady in the Imperial Palace, The Heroine of Worth, Emperor's Son* and *Barber's Daughter.* But when she joined the labor movement, she began to read the classical German literature and the prominent party literature, Engels' *Conditions of the Working Classes in England,* Lafargue's *The Right to Idleness,* Lassalle's *Science and the Workers,* Liebknecht's *Knowledge Is Power,* and Bebel's *Woman and Socialism.*[48]

Bebel's book on the misery of women under the system of bourgeois marriage, the bourgeois institution of prostitution, and woman's liberated position in a socialist society was one of the most

[47] There was some Social Democratic children's literature, but it does not seem to have been widely distributed. When Bromme was five years old in 1878, he received at Christmas the first socialist picture book, *King Mammon.* Fairy tales were sometimes rewritten for political purposes, such as the story of *Reinecke Fuchs.* Bromme belonged to the first generation of Social Democrats who were brought up in a socialist home. When he was eleven he had to read socialist pamphlets and newspapers aloud to his family. He understood little of what he read, nor did he know at that time that his father participated in the illegal transport and distribution of socialist pamphlets. See Bromme, *op. cit.,* 32, 51, 60.
[48] Cf. Popp, *op. cit.,* 36, 76, 97–106.

popular socialist writings. It was one of the few great pieces of passionate feminism in German literature. First published in 1879, it was reprinted in several million copies and translated into more than a dozen languages. It was widely read by workers and secretly distributed during the antisocialist legislation. The post-1890 editions were bought mainly by the bourgeois public, as Bebel asserted in the 1895 edition.

Bebel paints the orthodox picture of the future socialist society as characterized by socialized production and consumption and by the absence of the state and money. Woman liberated from the legal and material restrictions of bourgeois society will be the equal of man. Household chores, for example, will be greatly reduced. Society will care for the children and the aged. Marriage will be a "private" contract which can be repudiated by both sides at their discretion. Everyone will be able to choose his occupation. Bebel's description is highly speculative and optimistic. He relies heavily on the spirit of solidarity created under socialist conditions and does not face the problem of authority in the large-scale organizations of modern industrialized society.

The bourgeois public and many of those workers who read bourgeois newspapers encountered in the early nineties two pamphlets by Eugen Richter, the leader of the Progressives, with which he scored a major polemical hit against Bebel. Richter countered Bebel first with a pamphlet *Die Irrlehren der Sozialdemokratie* which appeared first in 1890 with 80,000 copies and then with a parody of Bebel's picture of the future socialist society, *Sozialdemokratische Zukunftsbilder*.[49] Within two years, from 1891 until 1893, more than 251,000 copies of this parody were sold. The newspapers of all nonsocialist parties propagated its distribution, and more than 40 serialized it. Trade and agricultural associations also distributed it. By 1893 it had been translated into eight languages.

Richter's parody starts with the seizure of power by the Social

[49] Eugen Richter, *Sozialdemokratische Zukunftsbilder, frei nach Bebel* (Berlin: Verlag Fortschritt, 1893), 48 pp.

Democrats. All parties except the Social Democratic party are dissolved; the army is disbanded. Money and savings are eliminated. Ration cards replace money. All people must eat in community kitchens and give up part of their furniture. Children are separated from their parents, and people over sixty-five are sent to homes for the aged. Food and dress are standardized. All administrative and production positions are elective—as Bebel had actually propounded. Everyone can apply for a new job. Married people are frequently separated because they must work in different cities. Richter gives a vivid description of the psychological stress and the material deprivations of this situation. Productivity and efficiency are greatly reduced; the Social Democratic government has to resort to severe physical repression; the army has to be restored. Relations with the remaining capitalist countries, England and the United States, as well as with the socialist countries of Europe—all of Europe succumbed to Social Democracy—are strained over economic issues. Finally, Russian and French troops invade Germany, and the Berlin metal workers lead an insurrection against the crumbling Social Democratic dictatorship.

Among Social Democratic followers the attraction of the image of the *Zukunftsstaat* could not be weakened by such polemics. In fact, the success of Bebel's *Woman and Socialism,* probably based on this attraction, and Edward Bellamy's *Looking Backward,* another major piece of literature on future society, was so great that party leaders became apprehensive lest the workers' interest in this topic distract their attention from the immediate problems of the movement.[50] Thus, there was the paradox that Bebel, as a writer, provided the most successful work on the *Zukunftsstaat,* and, as a party leader, could not welcome this aspect of its success. Holek

[50] Wilhelm Keil was greatly impressed by the image of the *Zukunftsstaat* when he read *Woman and Socialism* in the eighties. He also read Bellamy's novel. See *Erlebnisse eines Sozialdemokraten* (Stuttgart: Deutsche Verlagsanstalt, 1949), I, 102–7. Keil went on in his career to become a revisionist; he rose to high parliamentary office in the Weimar Republic and again after 1945.

remembers many discussions with fellow workers on the future state of society and attempts by the most trained Social Democrat in their work group to squelch them. Holek considered the intellectual sluggishness and opportunism of his fellow workers as reasons for their inclination to develop fantasies about the *Zukunftsstaat*.[51]

The interest in the *Zukunftsstaat* was paralleled during the anti-socialist legislation by an even greater interest in edifying literature, such as song books. There was little interest in "enlightening literature." [52] Many lower-ranking functionaries produced an unending stream of edifying literature, much consisting of songs using well-known melodies. Young Severing, for example, was active in providing his local glee club with appealing songs.[53] Andreas Scheu wrote, among many other things, a cantata *An die Arbeit* for a workers' industrial exhibition and a pacifist version of Uhland's famous songs *Der gute Kamerad*.[54]

Those members who were predominantly interested in political and theoretical indoctrination regretted the popularity of edifying literature and the topic of the *Zukunftsstaat*. But this popular interest was an important basis for the growing Social Democratic subculture. Singing songs, listening to poems and indulging in detailed fantasies about the socialist kingdom to come constituted great emotional gratifications for the workers. Indirectly these activities seemed to strengthen the subculture by affirming the allegiance of workers to the movement. It is true that these popular preoccupations did little to further political and theoretical comprehension, and that they could easily detract from more arduous intellectual efforts, but it is also true that the small group of Social Democrats who studied political and theoretical literature did not

[51] Cf. Holek, *op. cit.*, 209 f.
[52] Cf. Schröder, *op. cit.*, 37.
[53] Cf. Severing, *op. cit.*, 30.
[54] Cf. Scheu, *op. cit.*, 141 ff. Buttinger tells a similar story of 1924 when "in spite of all reverence he found the works of the Socialist bards a bit too 'high' for the workers' [i.e., his] understanding, [and] began to write poems and speaking-choruses for the local demand." Buttinger, *op. cit.*, 405.

pursue a course likely to significantly increase the political radicalism of the labor movement. The latter group of Social Democrats pursued two lines of interest: the more or less idealist Lassallean tradition and a materialism composed of Marxist and Social Darwinist elements. For many years there seems to have been more interest in Lassalle and materialist-scientific writers such as Haeckel than in Marx and Hegel.[55] In his polemical account of the Social Democratic agitation of the seventies, Reverend Schuster charged that atheistic-materialist science paved the way for socialism and that the latter endeavored "to transpose its results into the social realm and to translate it into practice."[56] Schuster reprinted an article from the *Volksstaat* (1873, 31) in support of this assertion. Its author suggested that the party give more attention to Darwinism and stop underestimating its power as a weapon. The *Volksstaat* printed the article only with reservations because it could not "side with everything Darwin's adherents write." It appears, however, that then and later most readers were not aware of decisive theoretical differences between Marxist and evolutionary theories.

The great interest in Darwinism and natural science was a trend of the period of the late 19th century, shared by the bourgeois as well as the socialist public. It was accompanied by a de-emphasis of Marxism as a philosophy, inside and outside the labor movement. The Marxist critic Karl Korsch could later justifiably qualify Engels' statement that the German labor movement was "the heir of German classical philosophy" by pointing out that nearly all socialist writers, including Mehring, brushed aside philosophical problems as "immaterial."[57] Marx's philosophical presuppositions were even less well comprehended than his economic theories by his Social Democratic students because they disdained any familiarity with Hegel's philosophy. In 1914 Lenin could, therefore,

[55] Cf. W. Huhn, "Etatismus, 'Kriegssozialismus,' 'Nationalsozialismus' in der Literatur der deutschen Sozialdemokratie," *Aufklärung*, 1952, II:3, 178.
[56] Schuster, *op. cit.*, 193.
[57] Karl Korsch, *op. cit.*, 8 f.

write with some justification into his notebook that "one cannot fully understand Marx's *Capital,* particularly the first chapter, unless one has thoroughly studied and grasped the whole of Hegel's logic. Thus it is that after half a century none of the Marxists have understood Marx." [58] The point is, however, that Marx's *Kapital* did exert great influence by its mere existence, whether it was adequately understood or not, since many Social Democrats believed that it provided a scientific explanation of capitalist society and of its inevitable downfall. This indirect influence of Marx was considerable, but the socialist literature most widely read were Lassalle's *Open Letter* of 1863 and Bebel's *Woman and Socialism* of 1879. Theirs was a direct and non-Marxian influence and, as far as popular agitation and comprehension were concerned, the dominant one. [59]

Few statistics are available on the distribution of socialist and nonsocialist literature within the labor movement. I will draw, for their illustrative value, on some Viennese statistics in order to assess the impact of the Social Democratic subculture at the end of the prewar period. The Austrian labor movement started later than the German labor movement and expanded much more slowly, but Vienna was one of the strongholds of the Second International with about 150,000 German-speaking male and female members organized in the unions and the party. Cultural activities flourished. The lecture system was more extensive than in any other city of the international Social Democratic movement. Each year about 10,-000 persons regularly heard lectures; a smaller number attended lecture courses. Robert Danneberg, who discussed Adolf Braun's gen-

---

[58] W. I. Lenin, *Extracts and Marginal Notes on Hegel's Science of Logic* (Moscow: Marx-Engels Institute, 1932), 99; quoted in Karl Korsch, *Karl Marx* (London: Chapman, 1938), 225.

[59] Overstating his case, F. Darmstaedter even maintained that *Das Kapital* was the most influential socialist work *because* of its indirect impact, i.e., because of the fact that it was not read, that it was difficult to comprehend. Cf. F. Darmstaedter, *Germany and Europe: Political Tendencies from Frederick the Great to Hitler* (London: Methuen, 1945), 95 ff.

eral evaluation of the cultural limitations of the labor movement, considered this, along with the socialist libraries, a great achievement.[60] But he also showed that three-quarters of the trade union members did not borrow books from the socialist libraries in Vienna. Only a fraction of the remaining quarter regularly read books. Even though in one year about one million books were borrowed from all socialist libraries in Austria (200,000 of them in Vienna alone), only two to three per cent were specifically socialist literature. Most of the socialist literature was decades old. In 1913, 83 per cent of the Viennese loans were classified as belles-lettres, five per cent as natural science, and 12 per cent as social science.[61] The latter were mostly inferior books on history. The high percentage of belles-lettres does not indicate the workers' preferences but the fulfillment of the requests of wives and daughters. Before 1918 natural science literature was consistently more popular than socialist literature. Danneberg explains the workers' greater interest in natural science than in social science by citing their usually recent emancipation from religion.[62] If they read history, they were more interested in anti-clericalism than in economic issues.

[60] See Robert Danneberg, "Die Ergebnisse sozialdemokratischer Bildungsarbeit," *Der Kampf*, Vienna, Vol. 8, 1915, 279 ff.

[61] According to Gulick, *op. cit.*, 657, the percentage for 1931 was 73 per cent for poetry and fiction, 16 per cent for social science and 10 per cent for the natural sciences. However, these data are not strictly comparable to those of 1913 because different types of books may have been classified differently although the overall categories are the same. Thus the data do not permit definite conclusions as to the change of percentages involved. It seems, however, that after the First World War the workers' libraries became even less of a direct instrument of political propaganda and concentrated even more on mediating "respectable" literature to workers and their families. The fight against *Kitsch*, though, had always been part of the Social Democratic educational efforts, as Liebknecht's speech, "Knowledge Is Power," shows.

[62] A striking example in support of this explanation is this passage from Keil's autobiography:

"The association owned a little library of natural science works which we used. One of these books gave me a deep insight into the universe and into the origin of the celestial bodies and demonstrated to me the abysmal contrast between scientific explanations and the biblical Genesis. With that, my

In 1914 it was apparent that most workers were not familiar with the socialist theory of imperialism, not even through general agitation.[63] Danneberg observes that interest in socialist literature seems to have decreased in proportion to the expansion of the labor movement, although the evidence presented above would suggest that it was always low. The fact that Kautsky's *Erfurt Program,* Lassalle's writings, and even Bebel's *Woman and Socialism* were scarcely read in 1914 may, however, indicate a further drop of interest in specifically socialist literature. At the end of the period, therefore, it became evident that the results of the educational activities within the subculture fell far short of the intentions and ambitions motivating them. The achievements were, of course, considerable, but they did not seem relevantly to enhance the political effectiveness of the labor movement, beyond attaching a minority of workers and their families more firmly to the educational institutions of the sub-

---

mind was made up not only about the Genesis, but also about all transcendental world views. For me all of this was a new creed, a new gospel through which the old creed was completely abandoned; I thought it was merely necessary to make these books available to the unprejudiced person in order to put him into the same mood." Keil, *op. cit.,* Vol. I, 80. In some cases interest in natural science also seems to have been an attempt to escape from the social reality. This was Bürgel's motivation when, at the age of thirteen, he resolved to become an astronomer even before he was familiar with the word astronomy. He was overwhelmed by his own proletarian experiences and by what he learned from a politically conscious boy, one of the first generation born to a Social Democratic family, whose father was persecuted at the time. Cf. Bürgel, *op. cit.,* 22.

[63] Bauer's *Nationalitätenfrage* had scarcely left the libraries, and other pertinent literature, such as Bauer's *Der Balkankrieg und die deutsche Weltpolitik,* Bernstein's *Die englische Gefahr und das deutsche Volk, Imperialismus oder Sozialismus,* Kautsky's *Sozialismus und Kolonialpolitik, Die Marokkokrise vor dem Reichstag,* and Radek's *Der deutsche Imperialismus und die Arbeiterklasse* was not there at all. Hilferding's *Finanzkapital* was available in only one library. Danneberg attributed the lack of recent socialist literature in part to organizational factors such as the stipulation for local party wards to buy their own books once they were prosperous enough to do so. This stipulation was disliked for its demands on the local treasury, which was presumably used for more "tangible" purposes.

culture. The failure to spread more literature among the working class was not entirely due to the weakness of the subculture nor to the strength of the dominant culture. The environmental handicaps for a reading worker were many. In contrast, it was a failing of the socialist educators, as Danneberg recognized, that a good deal of even the popularizing socialist literature simply demanded too much of the workers' comprehension.

It is impossible to evaluate the impact of socialist literature within the working class without considering the party press, which was more influential than socialist brochures and books; it was the sole means of socialist education for large numbers of workers.

4. The Party Press

The major purposes of the party press were agitation outside the party and internal communication. Its function as a mouthpiece of protest against the dominant system cut across the two purposes. In the beginning the Social Democratic press was purely a means of agitation and "enlightenment." Both the Lassalleans and the Eisenachers insisted on a doctrinaire line, and the press of the united party continued, under Liebknecht's influence, to minimize for a long time all qualities of entertainment since these were considered bourgeois. The differences between the Eisenachers and the Lassalleans referred to tone and strategy, but not to this basic orientation.[64] The Eisenachers sometimes attacked the Lassalleans

---

[64] Lassalle did not yet have a newspaper. His most successful successor, von Schweitzer, ran the *Socialdemokrat* which was replaced in 1871, after his resignation, by the *Neue Socialdemokrat,* edited by Hasselmann. In the first year it supposedly had 3,000 subscribers, in 1873, 18,000 subscribers. The *Volksstaat,* originally a democratic paper under a different name, was the major organ of the Eisenachers. Edited by Liebknecht it was published in Leipzig and had by 1875 about 10,000 subscribers. When the two parties merged in 1875 the labor movement published 29 newspapers and periodicals. Cf. Schuster, *op. cit.,* 10 and 233 f.

for the shrill tone of their agitation. The *Volksstaat,* for example, rejected as ridiculous an attempt by the *Neue Socialdemokrat* to interpret a few cases of typhoid fever in Berlin as a threat to the whole working class, which would therefore have to flock behind the "banner of Lassalle." [65] The Eisenachers favored a decentralized strategy rather than a concentration on one major newspaper as did the Lassalleans. The *Volksstaat* took an evolutionary perspective in arguing that a Social Democratic paper be founded only at a place which already had a newspaper because "the parties we fight are our predecessors; the people have to go through their school and arrive at their level before they will be able to understand the conflict between these other and their own interests." [66]

In contrast to this decentralized approach of the Eisenachers, the Lassallean Hasselmann seems to have hoped that one big paper could achieve an influence similar to that of "the great Marat's weekly," *L'ami du peuple* of 1790 and 1791, which had "more influence on the development of the French Revolution than all the pompous phrases of the deputies and the most refined intrigues of those at the helm of the state." [67] This was certainly revolutionary rhetoric, but no more—precisely because it did not go beyond writing à la Marat.

The revolutionary rhetoric and the doctrinaire line of the Lassalleans and the Eisenachers were accompanied by a vagueness about the concrete tenets of Socialism. To contemporary bourgeois observers like Reverend Schuster, this appeared as a device to trap innocent workers. However, this vagueness was genuine as well as tactical. First of all, there was no common agreement on the

[65] See *Volksstaat,* 1873, 21 and *Der Neue Socialdemokrat,* 1873, 28, quoted in *op. cit.,* 9 ff.

[66] *Volksstaat,* 1874, 81, quoted in *op. cit.,* 13.

[67] Hasselmann in a programmatic article on the purpose of the Social Democratic press, "Was soll die Presse leisten?" *Der Neue Socialdemokrat,* 1872, 100, quoted in *op. cit.,* 144.

tenets of socialism among the leaders in the early seventies.[68] Secondly, in spite of a doctrinaire inclination, the Social Democratic agitation adapted itself to the prevailing mentality of workers in a given region and relied heavily on appeals which were not specifically socialist or which carried only socialistic overtones. And thirdly, caution had to be observed because of the danger of police and court action.[69]

The intra-party function of the press was related from the beginning to the need for self-esteem in view of the frustrated demand for social recognition. "We want to have an organ for critique and complaints," wrote Carl Hirsch in the *Volksstaat* in 1874, "in order to quickly expose mistreatments and excesses on the part of the bourgeoisie and the authorities, to encourage one another, and probably also to amuse ourselves with the stupidity of our opponents. We want to spare ourselves the annoyance of being calumniated in every newspaper we pick up or, what hurts even more, of being paternally advised or held in tutelage." [70]

When the Social Democratic subculture expanded rapidly after 1890, the party press developed into a pure intra-party organ, as can be seen from the fact that its expansion was in no way comparable to the increase in votes. Since many votes were just an expression of opposition against the existing regime, those who cast them were often disinterested in socialist doctrines and internal

[68] Theoretical statements on socialism were infrequent in the newspapers of the two socialist parties during the early seventies. The *Volksstaat* carried quarterly the party program on its front page. This was more an expression of a doctrinaire attitude than of theoretical ambitions. Cf. *op. cit.*, 15. Rather rare seems to have been the kind of sketch of a socialist planned economy as it was presented in the *Neue Socialdemokrat* in 1872, cf. *op. cit.*, 53 f and 75 ff.

[69] See the reply of the *Volksstaat*, 1874, 33, to Dühring's charge of insufficient clarity of the socialist position, quoted in *op. cit.*, 16.

[70] Quoted in Ludwig Kantorowicz, *Die sozialdemokratische Presse Deutschlands* (Tübingen: Mohr, 1922), 33. See also Carl Hirsch, *Die Parteipresse, ihre Bedeutung und Organization* (Leipzig, 1876), 3.

party events and hence did not read the party press. The party press remained an organ for the declaration of faith and for intra-party communications. Gradually more space was given to daily news coverage, although intra-party events still dominated, and entertainment needs were also increasingly considered. But the party press remained unable to attract those readers who fell under the influence of the *Generalanzeiger* press, or to interest intellectuals who were looking for good news coverage.[71] Since newspapers were the only source of printed information for many workers, it mattered a great deal which press they read.

The intra-party orientation of the party press was the subject of a prolonged debate which reached a climax at the party convention of 1913. At the time the party executive wrote in a report to the convention that "our press obviously addresses itself almost exclusively to the organized and trained party member, in relation to whom it can take for granted many things which are still completely unknown to those yet to be won." [72] The failure to appeal beyond the party members to the proletarian or even the middle-class public was partly due to the old fear that the attention of the workers might be diverted if the papers did not focus on party theory and party affairs, and it was partly due to the social composition of the staff of the papers. As late as 1914, 80 per cent of the 241 editors were of working-class origin, and only 28 had academic, though mostly unfinished, training.[73] The social and cul-

[71] The *Generalanzeiger* press gained importance after the turn of the century. These papers, which were usually published by smaller publishing houses, represented the lower middle classes. They were read by many workers and especially their wives who disliked the political character of the party press and its emphasis on the class struggle in articles as well as in novels. Thus these newspapers were a great competition to the party press. However, party functionaries sometimes managed to influence local papers by suggesting that they print specific statements on domestic events.

[72] *Protocol,* Jena, 1913, 8. For Scheidemann's defense of the report, see p. 226. Cf. Kantorowicz, *op. cit.,* 36. For further details on this debate over the years, see *id.,* 10 ff.

[73] For a detailed breakdown of the vocational background, see *op. cit.,* 104 f.

tural background of these editors was generally too limited, even if they had been typographers and printers, to qualify them for more than the coverage of intra-party affairs and the political critique of local events. The doctrinaire tendencies were often re-enforced by more knowledgeable persons among the editors and contributors—belonging to the species of would-be professors (*verhinderte Privatdozenten*)—who had academic or at least schol-arly ambitions but who had been unable to get a higher education or to enter the academic community.

Although the party press could not compete in quality with larger bourgeois journals, it appears to have compared favorably at times with the quality of bourgeois small-town papers. When Göhre worked as a factory worker about 1890, he found that all active Social Democrats read party papers, especially the local party paper which was "quite somberly and, most of the time, better edited than the small-town local press." [74] Quantitatively the Social Democratic press remained dwarfed by the many other papers, neutral and partisan, until the end of the period. Out of about 3,000 dailies, only 79 were Social Democratic,[75] circulating in 1909 about one million copies. Still, they were considered a power-ful force by friend and foe because they were an integral part of the Social Democratic subculture, contributing to the cohesion of the labor movement. But the very emphasis of the party press on indoctrination and intra-party information diminished its appeal to a wider public and thus furthered the self-containment of the labor movement. The party press shared this limitation with the best writers of the party, who addressed themselves nearly exclusively to the labor movement. This limitation was partly self-imposed—party members were not permitted to work for the nonparty press

[74] Cf. Göhre, *op. cit.,* 94 f.
[75] About half of them were non-partisan, 275 conservative, 214 National (i.e., supporting the government), 216 National Liberal, 400 Center, 277 Pro-gressive, 23 Polish, four Danish. See W. Nicolai, *Nachrichtendienst* (Berlin: Mittler, 1920), 168.

—and partly imposed by the general public, which defined these writers as partisan. Thus, it is another index for the depth of the class cleavage in Imperial Germany and the containment of the labor movement.[76]

[76] This is in sharp contrast with the English development where one of the reasons for the success of the Labor Party seems to have been the existence of independent writers like the Fabians who were not isolated from the general public. Cf. Anne Fremantle, *This Little Band of Prophets: The British Fabians* (New York: Mentor Book, 1960).

X
Organizational Strength and Weakness of the Labor Movement

1. Excursus: Robert Michels and Max Weber on Socialist Party Organization

As the Social Democratic subculture expanded, problems of bureaucratization, especially of vested organizational interests, were bound to intensify. A connection between increasing size, bureaucratization and opportunist strategy was suggested by Robert Michels, who illustrated his famous "iron law of oligarchy" with many examples from the German labor movement. In 1911 he published his book, *On the Sociology of Parties in Modern Democracy.*[1] I will deal with Michels' work because his "iron law" and his image of the German labor movement have been very influential in the literature.[2] I will relate it to Max Weber's views, which

[1] Robert Michels, *Zur Soziologie des Parteiwesens in der modernen Demokratie,* Werner Conze, ed. (Stuttgart: Kröner, 1957); this is the second revised edition of 1925. The English edition is from the Italian translation of the first German edition; see *Political Parties, op. cit.;* first published in 1915. In the latest German edition Werner Conze has attempted to correct Michels' bibliographical references, many of which turned out to be faulty.

[2] For an excellent up-to-date account of Michels' academic influence and of political reactions to his work, see S. M. Lipset's introduction to *Political Parties, op. cit.,* 15–39. Gerhard A. Ritter, *op. cit.,* 48 f cites recent German and English literature perpetuating or criticizing Michels' interpretations. Ritter's Ch. II on the organizational and financial practices of the Social Democratic party provides basic information for a qualification of Michels' analysis.

were similar to a degree but which also provided an alternative interpretation; while the friendship of the two men is well known, the nature of their intellectual relationship is not.[3]

Michels' "iron law of oligarchy" maintains that all large-scale organizations inevitably develop oligarchic controls. This is a special dilemma for democratic and socialist organizations. They strive for the emancipation of the masses, but their leaders tend to perpetuate themselves through skill monopoly, control of communication channels and the very gratitude of the masses. Even worse, professional leaders of a democratic party or a labor union ultimately tend to fail the masses by developing an overriding concern with organizational survival. Michels wrote his book from the perspective of Rousseau's ideal democracy, which rejected the principle of popular representation because it involved a diminution, if not a destruction, of popular sovereignty and freedom.

Michels asserted his "iron law" in an apodictic fashion which hid an underlying ambivalence. His career was vacillating. To begin with, his family background was very heterogeneous. His grandfather was a Catholic textile merchant from Cologne, wealthy enough to make each of his nine children a millionaire. His grandmother's first language was French, her family relations French, Dutch and Spanish. By the time Robert Michels had grown up, the family had begun to intermarry with Protestant financiers and aristocratic officers. He was the second member of the family to become an active officer, but he soon quit service in the Prussian army. Rejecting his upper-class background and a military career,

---

[3] The closeness which Michels felt for Weber was expressed in the dedication of his *Political Parties* (first German edition) "to his dear friend Max Weber, that upright man who does not shy away from vivisection if it is in the interest of science, with greetings from a kindred soul." In the foreword to the second edition, Michels again acknowledged Weber's influence and mentioned that for its revision he took into consideration a lengthy critique by Weber; he added that he did not learn much that was new from Weber's posthumously published treatment of parties in *Wirtschaft und Gesellschaft*. Cf. *Zur Soziologie des Parteiwesens, op. cit.*, xxviii f.

he became a socialist with syndicalist and anarchist predilections.[4] However, he retained his family's Franco-German orientation and traveled often to France and Italy, becoming well acquainted with George Sorel. His upper-class origin, syndicalist inclinations and "objective" scholarly work impaired his relations with the German Social Democrats. In 1906/7 he engaged in socialist agitation in the university town of Marburg; this made impossible a regular academic career in Germany. He chose Italy as his *Wahlheimat* (elective country) and became a lecturer at the University of Turin in 1907. He joined the syndicalist wing of the Italian labor movement, but soon withdrew from it. In 1914 he accepted a chair at the University of Basle in Switzerland, from which he observed the seeming triumph of the "iron law of oligarchy" in the First World War. A disappointed idealist, who despaired about his own "iron law" and about the permanent political crisis in Italy, France and Germany, he came to consider authoritarian regimes historically inevitable and finally accepted a professorship from Mussolini in 1928.[5]

When Michels' book appeared, the radical socialist left benefited from its arguments, often built on its own testimony. Yet it was also part of the academic critique of the Marxist belief that administrative and political problems of large-scale organization would be easily manageable under socialism. A major representative of this critique was Max Weber, who tried to save Michels' academic career in Germany and who made him coeditor of the famous *Archiv für Sozialwissenschaft*. The two men agreed that the German labor movement as it was could not offer a radically different form of social organization; it constituted no revolutionary threat; the movement tended to become an end in itself and its leaders "conservative." However, their basic premises and final evaluations differed.

---

[4] Compare his own pertinent description of the young bourgeois enthusiast turning to socialism in *Political Parties, op. cit.,* 241.
[5] These biographical details rely on Werner Conze's thoughtful postscript to the 1957 German edition of Michels, *op. cit.,* 384 ff.

For Weber the basic premise was the national welfare, for Michels, an internationalist syndicalism which Weber called an "apolitical ethos of brotherhood."

Since the nineties, Weber had been strongly under the influence of M. Ostrogorski's monumental volumes on *Democracy and the Organization of Political Parties,* which analyzed the rise of modern party organization in England and the United States.[6] Ostrogorski showed in detail how mass suffrage and industrialization resulted in the creation of party machines mobilizing the masses in quasi-military fashion. Oligarchic controls and mass manipulation were the inevitable outcome. Ideological differences between parties tended to become blurred under the identical pressures of organizational requirements. Weber pointed out to Michels that the German Social Democratic party was, "outside the Anglo-Saxon realm, the only one which is technically fully developed," although it has "by contrast . . . something like a *Weltanschauung*" and thus is "not just a technical machine," as are the parties in the United States.[7] In a similar vein he explained to a distinguished audience at the 1905 convention of the *Verein für Sozialpolitik* what would happen to the Social Democratic party

under the pressure of compelling conditions, particularly under the pressure of the feeling of powerlessness which predominates in the ruling circles . . . , as everybody knows who looks behind the scenes. Of course, its representatives would deny this, but this does not change matters. The party cannot become anything else but a party of the American *genre,* committed . . . to a few slogans . . . , a party which exists for its own sake and that of its office-holders. Just as the workers in the factories are supposed to knuckle under according to the theory

[6] M. Ostrogorski, *Democracy and the Organization of Political Parties* (London: Macmillan, 1902), 2 vols. The book was first published in French in 1893.

[7] Letter of March 26, 1906, quoted in W. Mommsen, *op. cit.,* 124. As is the case with all other correspondence, Michels' letters were not preserved in Weber's *Nachlass.* Mommsen tried unsuccessfully to get hold of them elsewhere.

of the lords of the big business syndicates, and just as these gentlemen and all of us are supposed to bow before the State, everybody in the party is supposed to do so before the ruling bosses. The workers have acquired this lack of character in our State . . . and in our quasi-military factories.[8]

Weber urged the empirical study of basic problems of leadership, organizational structure, social composition and ideology. Michels was understandably interested at first in the role of the intellectuals and especially of the reformists, but eventually he took up these broader problems, at least in part under Weber's influence.[9] How-

[8] *Verhandlungen, Schriften des Vereins für Sozialpolitik,* Vol. 116, 1906, 389 f. Weber purposively exaggerated such statements. He replied to Michels' protests against his similar address at the 1907 convention that he had addressed "the cowards of his own class as a 'class-conscious bourgeois.'" He wanted to diminish their fears of the Social Democrats. Cf. letter of Nov. 6, 1907, quoted in Mommsen, *op. cit.,* 123.

[9] In the 1905 issue of the *Archiv für Sozialwissenschaft,* in which he published the first part of the "Protestant Ethic and the Spirit of Capitalism," Weber outlined some research topics as a postscript to R. Blank's "Die soziale Zusammensetzung der sozialdemokratischen Wählerschaft Deutschlands," Vol. 20, 1905, 507–50, a study which received widespread attention as one of the first empirical studies, including comments from Bebel. Cf. Michels, *Political Parties, op. cit.,* 256. Weber published Michels' studies from 1906 on. Weber's catalogue of research topics (550–53) included: 1. The relationship between the organized elite of the labor movement and the masses of followers; 2. The impact of non-proletarian groups within the party versus the necessity to appeal to non-proletarian groups outside the party during election campaigns; 3. The character and the background of the elements controlling the local organizations and the party newspapers; 4. The professional politicians who live "off" or for the party—explicit comparisons to be made with American parties despite the ideological differences; 5. Difference between academically trained members and those who, due to the class barriers, could not acquire higher education; 6. Universal tendencies of parties to become an end in themselves for their followers; 7. Resulting tendency of Social Democratic office-holders (*Parteipfründner*) to oppose a radical course no less than a clearly reformist one—comparisons to be made with the conflicts of liberal and orthodox theologians on Apostolic writings; 8. Interest of the trade unions in "conservative" party tactics; trade union dependence on the party, due to the need for having the voice of a large party in parliament to fight the chicaneries of the officials and the police—the

ever, he did not link his analyses directly with Ostrogorski's work, to which he refers only occasionally. His *Sociology of Parties in Modern Democracy* supplemented Ostrogorski's study of liberal and conservative parties in the Anglo-Saxon democracies with an analysis of labor movements in semi-authoritarian Germany; in Italy, which did not have a genuine parliamentary monarchy; and in the French Third Republic, which suffered from a persistent crisis of legitimacy.[10] However, in contrast to Ostrogorski and Weber, Michels did not pay much attention to the political systems under which these movements operated; given his premises of the "iron law," such differences appeared fairly immaterial—a perspective which influenced until recently the French, German and American literature on the sociology of parties.

Similarly to Michels' wavering between the affirmation of syndicalist ideals and the skeptical recognition of organizational realities, Weber—to use his own distinctions—vacillated in his evaluation of the Social Democrats between an "ethic of absolute values" (*Gesinnungsethik*) and an "ethic of responsibility" (*Verantwortungsethik*—i.e., a pragmatic ethic. Weber well understood the organizational dilemma of the Social Democrats, but he had little sympathy for the Social Democratic dualism of radical rhetoric and moderate practice. He criticized the party's lack of revolutionary enthusiasm no less than its refusal to declare itself openly a reform party; [11] for him this dualism was "petty-bourgeois" timidity.

---

real cause of the proletarian class consciousness; drawback of this dependence: other parties not interested in wooing labor; relatively small material gains for labor are the result; 9. Extent to which the trade unions are likely to take over the party; possible irrelevance of trade union domination in view of strategic position of the party, especially the need to appeal to unorganized masses; 10. Importance of everyday operations and tactical questions, such as the mass strike, over program demands and theoretical issues.

[10] It may be speculated that the misnomer of Michels' book was perhaps due to its being a parallel to Ostrogorski's broad title.

[11] Cf. letter to Michels of Feb. 1, 1907, quoted in Mommsen, *op. cit.*, 122 and 149.

Weber attended the important 1906 party convention in Mannheim and reported to Michels in disgust:

> Mannheim was a miserable affair. . . . Ten times at least I heard Bebel and Legien emphasize "our weakness" [i.e., the movement's weakness]. On top of it, there were all the extremely petty-bourgeois attitudes, the self-satisfied physiognomies of innkeepers, the lack of *élan,* and the inability to move to the right if the road to the left is blocked or appears to be so—these gentlemen no longer scare anyone.[12]

While Michels still believed in 1907 that the political emancipation of the working class could be derived from its economic indispensability, Weber argued:

> Indispensability in the economic process means nothing, absolutely nothing for the power position and power chances of a class. At a time when no "citizen" worked, the slaves were ten times, nay a thousand times as necessary as is the proletariat today. What does that matter? The medieval peasant, the Negro of the American South, they were all absolutely "indispensable." . . . The phrase contains a dangerous illusion. . . . Political democratization is the only thing which can perhaps be achieved in the foreseeable future, and that would be no mean achievement. . . . I cannot prevent you from believing in more, but I cannot force myself to do so.[13]

Michels did not deny that the German labor movement was a vehicle of democratization, but this was not enough for him. For Weber democratization held out the promise that the coalition between big business and the *Junkers* might be destroyed, enhancing Germany's prestige and power in the world. The basic difference between Michels and Weber eventually came to be the interpretation of the very organizational phenomena on whose existence they agreed. For Michels the "iron law of oligarchy" left no way out. Weber overcame his original exasperation with the bureaucratiza-

---

[12] Letter of Oct. 8, 1906, quoted in Mommsen, *op. cit.,* 122.
[13] Letter of Nov. 6/7, quoted in Mommsen, *op. cit.,* 97 and 121.

tion of political parties and recognized positive consequences. He believed that bureaucratization resulted in a lessening of radical ideology and revolutionary spirit. Party machines with a system of patronage and cooptation could devote themselves realistically to problems of party and national leadership. In his discussion of charismatic authority he compared English and German party developments and concluded that

in a certain respect the chances of charisma are greatest in "unprincipled" parties [*Gefolgschaftsparteien*] made up of a loyal mass following and patronage seekers. These parties make it easier, *ceteris paribus,* for impressive personalities to win the necessary following than do the petty-bourgeois organizations of notables of the German parties, particularly the liberal ones with their "programs" and *"Weltanschauungen"* which are forever the same.[14]

Although Weber did not foresee the Fascist and Communist combination of bureaucracy and extremist ideology and was by no means detached about the Social Democrats, his general approach to party organization appears to me superior to Michels' because it was more concerned with alternatives rather than "iron laws." In later decades, however, Michels' book became more influential than Ostrogorski's stout volumes and Weber's massive fragments; paradoxically, Ostrogorski was eclipsed in the United States despite the fact that Michels did not focus on the Anglo-Saxon realm. American social scientists were stimulated as well as handicapped by the pessimistic orientation of Michels' thesis, which produced much repetitive confirmation and some incisive qualification; the latter contributed fruitfully to the development of theories of institutionalization.

[14] In contrast to Michels' tendency to absolutize generalizations, Weber added cautiously: "But it is probably impossible to generalize successfully. The internal dynamics of party techniques and the social and economic conditions of each concrete case are all too intimately interwoven in any given situation." Weber, *Wirtschaft und Gesellschaft* (Tübingen: Mohr, 1956), Vol. 2, 678.

In the following account of the Social Democratic party organization I will use, for the purpose of broad classification, Philip Selznick's categories of institutionalization, which refer to four recurrent processes in the life history of associations: formalization, self-maintenance, development of a distinctive social composition and social base, and infusion with value.[15] I will deal in some detail with Michels' interpretations and in particular with the extent to which bureaucratization weakened the labor movement beyond its inherent strategic limitations.

2. *Social Composition and Social Base*

The German labor movement had from its very beginnings a delimited social composition and base: the nominally Protestant, relatively skilled working class supplemented by a small number of middle-class intellectuals. There are no representative national statistics, but there is enough evidence to establish the point.[16] The prevalence of these workers was in part due to the fact that a large sector of German industry, especially the manufacturing industry, was of moderate size and required relatively skilled labor. Furthermore, skilled workers have traditionally tended to have a higher level of self-confidence and aspirations as well as of defensive power than unskilled workers have. The organization of masses of

[15] I will not employ the latter category since much of Chs. VII and VIII can be subsumed under it. Cf. P. Selznick, *Leadership* . . . , *op. cit.,* 20 f, and L. Broom and P. Selznick, *Sociology* (Evanston: Row, Peterson, 1955), 237 ff. On the persistence of pessimistic value assumptions in organizational analysis from Michels to Selznick, see Alvin Gouldner, "Metaphysical Pathos and the Theory of Bureaucracy," *American Political Science Review,* Vol. 49, 1955, 496–507.

[16] Cf. Michels, *op. cit.,* 255 f; *id.,* "Die deutsche Sozialdemokratie: Parteimitgliedschaft und soziale Zusammensetzung," *Archiv für Sozialwissenschaft,* Vol. 23, 1906, 471–556; on working-class elites, 514–18.

unskilled and semi-skilled workers was held back because big business extensively blacklisted Social Democratic workers and refused to deal with established unions.[17] Big business also effectively controlled foremen and skilled workers by making long service mandatory for securing supervisory jobs.

Industrialization had a twofold influence on the labor movement, positively by increasing the number of blue-collar workers, negatively by proliferating white-collar jobs. Many working-class parents, even if unionized, often seem to have discouraged their sons and daughters from joining labor organizations so as not to interfere with their chances for occupational mobility.[18] Such mobility was particularly pronounced in the case of printers, who were considered the aristocrats of labor and whose union was the most reformist.[19]

Much has been made of the embourgeoisement of the labor movement. It is true that the party had many lower-middle-class

[17] Cf. Gustav Schmoller, "Der Weltkrieg und die deutsche Sozialdemokratie," *Schmollers Jahrbuch*, XXXIV, 1915, 1111. On the persistence of the elaborate system of supervision of skilled and unskilled workers, see Theo Pirker *et al., Arbeiter, Management, Mitbestimmung* (Stuttgart: Ring-Verlag, 1955), Part III:1. Religious and ethnic differences within the work force handicapped the Social Democratic labor movement in the heavy industry areas of the Ruhr and Silesia. Immigrants from the East Elbian provinces, whose numbers substantially increased late in the period, were hard to organize because of their economic insecurity, their religious affiliation (if they were Catholic), and perhaps also because of their "authoritarian heritage."

[18] Cf. Toni Sender, *The Autobiography of a German Rebel* (New York: Vanguard, 1939), 25.

[19] Cf. S. M. Lipset and R. Bendix, *Social Mobility in Industrial Society* (Berkeley and Los Angeles: University of California Press, 1959), 35. On the expansion of the new middle classes and the personnel problems of both Social Democrats and bourgeois parties, see Adolf Braun, "Die Intellektuellen und die Politik," *Neue Zeit*, 27:2, 1909, 847–53. Industry offered more and more opportunities to the social groups from which the bourgeois parties recruited their parliamentarians and journalists. For the old middle classes, it gradually became socially acceptable to join the administrative and technological hierarchies of commerce and industry.

voters and that its strategy had to take them into account. However, Michels correctly rejected the charges of "anarchizing socialists" and "bourgeois radicals," who decried the role of petty-bourgeois businessmen within the party.[20] He attributed the embourgeoisement to the social and psychological effects of becoming a salaried functionary, although he acknowledged that the latter was usually not much better off than the skilled worker and, in fact, often completely overburdened with work. The functionary, however, was no longer engaged in manual work and had a great job stability, secured at the price of his dependence on party or union. Michels conceded that as "ideologues" the thinking of ex-workers did not necessarily correspond to their social position, but he believed that in the passage of generations the families of ex-proletarian functionaries would be absorbed by the middle classes.[21]

The issue of the embourgeoisement of the functionaries was exaggerated, inasmuch as the majority of the Social Democratic workers had themselves many petty-bourgeois traits. In fact, Michels used this phenomenon, on the occasion of Bebel's death in 1913, in order to explain the elective affinity between the Social Democratic workers and Bebel, the radical petty-bourgeois politician.[22] Michels did not spell out the historical legacies which produced these characteristics. They were the "semi-feudal" but also "semi-bourgeois" institutions and traditions of Germany. The growth of the grand bourgeoisie was slow, but the petty-bourgeoisie, made up of shopkeepers, craft masters, teachers and lower-ranking civil servants, was large and exerted a pervasive influence downward. Many skilled workers retained the two petty-bourgeois strains of moral restraint: a sense of the painstaking fulfillment of duty, work discipline, habits of frugality and "good citizenship" on the one hand, and a tendency toward abstract moralism, "principled" po-

---

[20] Michels, *op. cit.*, 256.
[21] Cf. *op. cit.*, 264 f.
[22] Michels, "Bebel," *op. cit.*, 674.

litical affirmation or opposition, and cultural conservatism on the other.[23]

Michels' analysis of the petty-bourgeois transformations of the functionaries, beyond the petty-bourgeois tendencies of the skilled workers, remains politically inconclusive. The only concrete example of political influence provided by Michels is that exerted by innkeepers, by definition petty-bourgeois businessmen, who were party members and often persecuted ex-proletarians. The privately owned party restaurants were a mainstay of local organization in many small communities until after 1900. Frequently, the innkeepers were informal local party leaders; their role had been particularly important during the antisocialist legislation. Michels charges this petty-bourgeois group with retarding the temperance

[23] A striking example of the adherence to the older bourgeois values of the German middle classes is the following remark by the trained saddler, Friedrich Ebert, then President of the Weimar Republic, on the occasion of his daughter's marriage: "If our young married couple always accepts the principle of the devotion to duty (*Pflichttreue*) and the straight-forward and simple spirit of the burgher (*den geraden schlichten Bürgersinn*) just as they learned it in their parents' home, then it is my belief that they will be prepared to face the storms of life." Ebert, *Schriften, op. cit.*, 356.

When the strains of industrialization were first felt within petty-bourgeois strata, the insecurity and resulting protest often took the direction either of pervasive negativism or of assertive over-identification with the dominant system. Anti-Semitism was one of the results. While the larger part of the non-Catholic working class was attracted to the Social Democrats, a large part of the lower middle class became nationalist, *völkisch* and anti-Semitic. The weakness of anti-Semitism in the labor movement was extraordinary, but there was considerable vote fluctuation between the Social Democrats and other opposition groups. Many Social Democratic votes were a protest against specific elements of the prevailing system, without being cast by adherents of socialist ideas. "Petty-bourgeois negativism strongly influenced the attitudes of the masses," wrote Eckart Kehr in his analysis of the Social Democratic opposition to naval armament (*op. cit.*, 332). He referred also to figures calculated by G. Decker which showed that after 1918 about 20 per cent of the vote in the big cities shifted from the Social Democrats to the *Deutschnationale Partei*, the largest right-wing party. Cf. Georg Decker, "Krise des deutschen Parteisystems," *Gesellschaft*, 1926:1, 12 f.

movement within the party.[24] However, it is probably realistic to assume that masses of rank and file members lacked enthusiasm for this movement of largely younger members, just as the small number of innkeepers did.

Thus, there seems to be no significant evidence that the embourgeoisement of the leaders created any mass conflict between leaders and led. In contrast, there was sometimes conflict between proletarian functionaries and Social Democratic intellectuals. The intellectuals were often as doctrinaire as they were unsuited for the routine tasks of lower-ranking positions; but they were needed for expert functions. Because of their generally superior rhetorical and journalistic abilities and their higher education, intellectuals were met with a mixture of admiration and resentment. Often the resentment was justified, considering their overbearing sense of superiority, their theoretical preoccupations, or simply their middle-class manners; but often they were also believed to have superior wisdom in every field. Consequently, young students were sometimes elected into positions for which older proletarian functionaries with greater practical experience were much better qualified. More often, however, intellectuals were lost to the movement because their job chances were too precarious; they were forced to accept professional careers occupying most of their time or positions which allowed no open profession of sympathy for the movement. Outside the movement they could earn an adequate bourgeois living, but within the movement only a few could do so.

There was an undercurrent of anti-intellectualism, ethnocentrism, and anti-Semitism among the body of lower-ranking and, even more rarely, higher-ranking functionaries. But apart from some expression of it in the last years of the Lassallean party, anti-Semitism was not a part of the ideology or practice of the movement. Given the rise of political anti-Semitism in the eighties and

[24] Cf. Michels, *op. cit.*, 266–70.

nineties and considering what is known today about lower-class attitudes toward minorities and civil liberties, this is a remarkable record.[25]

An example of a clash between proletarian functionaries and intellectuals that was to some extent also a controversy between party and union may be given in order to illustrate the extremes of such controversies and at the same time their basically rhetorical character. In 1905 the unions took a negative stand during the debates on the feasibility, under German conditions, of political mass strikes in favor of democratization.[26] Such strikes had recently occurred in some European countries, especially during the Russian revolution. Some delegates at the 1905 union convention representing the more militant interests criticized the majority. One of them said about the prevailing mentality:

The union executive committees which are represented here have above all an interest in tight control of the funds. The result is a decline of the dynamics of the movement. Their concern is not shared by the masses

---

[25] Even the anti-Semitism within the Lassallean movement was not yet programmatic. But anti-Semitism grew progressively more vulgar as it descended from Lassalle (and Marx) to J. Baptist von Schweitzer and finally to Hasselmann. Despite this, there were many Jews among the Lassalleans, although many of them went over to the Eisenachers in 1869. Bernstein who described these early events makes it clear that "it would be wrong to attribute this split to the stand taken by the old party on the Jewish question. At that time there was as yet no Jewish question in the modern sense of the word." See Ed. Bernstein, "Jews and German Social Democracy," translated from the Yiddish, *Di Tsukunft*, XXVI, New York, March 1921, 146 f, reprinted in Massing, *op. cit.*, 324. Massing's work is an excellent analysis of anti-Semitism in Imperial Germany and of the Social Democratic and Marxist attitudes toward anti-Semitism, as well as toward Zionism.

For a retrospective statement of a representative of anti-intellectual and anti-Semitic undercurrents, see August Winnig, *Das Reich als Republik* (Stuttgart: Cotta, 1928), 97 f; cf. H. Heidegger, *Die deutsche Sozialdemokratie und der nationale Staat: 1879–1920* (Göttingen: Musterschmitt, 1956), 59 f.

[26] See p. 278 below.

of members. It would be enlightening to establish the percentage of salaried officials at this congress.[27]

Orthodox Marxist writers shared this criticism, and a lively controversy ensued between the party and the union papers.[28] The miners' paper protested against the attack on the "personal honor" of the union officials. The "appeal to the callous fist" of the workers, it wrote, was endangering "union discipline" and was no different from bourgeois attacks on "party bureaucrats." The Social Democratic literati would have to stop such insinuations; otherwise it would be made clear to them what was meant by the idea that the liberation of the working class could only be the work of the workers. The newspapers of the woodworkers and of the sculptors agreed with this reply. The papers of the hat and feltware workers and of the painters attacked Kautsky as a man who did not understand the techniques of trade union activities. The hat workers' paper declared that it would be a mistake to consider the political movement as something better than the trade union movement. The paper of the printers, who had the most reformist and Revisionist union, went so far as to threaten union rejection of the party if the "incapable policy of the Jacobin system" was not abandoned, a policy from which even the "fossil Professor" Bernstein had not freed himself; and it demanded a "positive policy" of turning the party into a reformist force. These were certainly angry outbursts from unionists who were also party members, but they did not indicate irreconcilable differences or even serious anti-intellectualism within the party.

On the whole, in Germany, the proletarian functionaries and intellectuals cooperated quite successfully, despite some sporadic

---

[27] *Protokoll der Verhandlungen des fünften Kongresses der Gewerkschaften Deutschlands* (Cologne, May 22–27, 1905), (Berlin: Verlag der Generalkommission der Gewerkschaften Deutschlands, 1905), 239.

[28] The following samples of the newspaper controversy are taken from the summary of an orthodox Marxist writer, Heinrich Ströbel, "Gewerkschaften und 'sozialistischer Geist,' " *Neue Zeit,* 23:2, 1905, 564 ff.

friction, as they also did in England and Scandinavia. The opposite was true in France and Italy, where a lack of balance between intellectuals and proletarian functionaries within the same movement seems to have been one source of anti-intellectualism.[29] Relations in Germany were apparently relatively smooth because the intellectuals who performed staff functions could not, as a group, strongly influence the attitudes and policies of the proletarian functionaries of the line. They were affiliated with the party center as well as with both wings, and only the radical left-wing intellectuals were expressly engaged in the ideological articulation of revolutionary potentialities.[30]

The proletarian women were less inclined to participate in the labor movement than were the men, partly because of their position within a patriarchic family structure and partly because they were fettered to the household and often to solitary labor in the house industry. They were prone to resent their husbands' spending time and money for politico-social activities.[31] For many proletarian families political activity of the husbands involved not only real material sacrifices for the wives, but also prevented them from any political participation of their own, since there was seldom enough income for both to be politically active. In exceptional cases, men withdrew from party activities to allow their more talented wives to work for the party.

There was much resentment among workers against women because they were cheaper labor. Furthermore, Social Democrats for a long time considered them inaccessible to political organization. By 1890, when Adelheid Popp became active as a speaker in Vienna, the Social Democrats had not yet addressed the working women.[32] Popp's success was due to her call for the help of men

[29] Cf. Landauer, *op. cit.*, 489.
[30] Cf. Michels, *op. cit.*, 298.
[31] Cf. Bromme, *op. cit.*, 222 and 240 f, and Holek, *op. cit.*, 212 and 239.
[32] On the Austrian Social Democratic women's movement, see Adelheid Popp, *Der Weg zur Höhe* (Vienna: Frauenzentralkomitee der Sozialdemokratischen Arbeiterpartei Deutschösterreichs, 1929).

to organize women. She herself was proof what a woman could achieve within and for the labor movement. The class consciousness of Social Democrats was made more consistent as they learned to see women as objects of an exploitation similar to or worse than their own. In Germany the Social Democratic women's organization, which flourished after the turn of the century, became part of the most class-conscious and Marxist wing of labor; by 1913 the party had 141,000 female members compared to 841,000 male members. The radicalism of the women's organizations may have had something to do with the fact that Imperial Germany and Austria refused the suffrage to women; in several states women could not even be members of political associations. However, their radicalism seems to have been brought about largely by a self-selective mechanism. Radical women like Clara Zetkin fought hard to expand their organizations and managed to isolate them to a considerable extent from the male reformist bureaucracy.[33]

Similarly radical was the socialist youth movement, which suddenly emerged outside the party in 1904. Since political associations of young people were not legal in northern Germany, the youth movement became the first socialist group after 1900 to employ underground tactics. In southern Germany it was legal until 1908; there it was guided by the young lawyer Ludwig Frank, who fought for reformist goals with radical means. The youth movement attempted to combine trade union and party functions; its major political activity was the fight against militarism. Government and

[33] On the women's movement, see the party executive's report in *Party Protocols*, 1913, 14–17. Clara Zetkin, a former teacher from a lower-middle class family, later became one of the most famous figures of the Communist International. Cf. the memorial volume on *Clara Zetkin* (Moscow: Verlagsgenossenschaft ausländischer Arbeiter, 1934). On the strains between reformist upper- and middle-class and radical lower-class women within the old Social Democratic party and especially the clashes between the aristocratic Lily Braun and Clara Zetkin, see Julie Vogelstein, "Lily Braun: ein Lebensbild," in Lily Braun, *Gesammelte Werke* (Berlin: Klemm, 1923), Vol. I, LVX, and id., *Memoiren einer Sozialistin* (Munich: Langen, 1909 and 1911), 2 vols.

party and union leadership all turned against it—the former by suppressing the independent movement with old and new statutes and the latter by incorporating it legally. Party radicals patronized it and party conservatives like Ebert fettered it. During the war the youth movement again broke away from the party.[34]

3. Formalization: Increasing Complexity and Control

As associations develop they tend to formalize their operations. Increasing size typically leads to more division of labor, hierarchical differentiation and formal controls. Specific historical factors, however, can retard or propel such a development. The mushrooming of the labor movement after 1890 made large-scale organization technically necessary, but formalization proceeded faster in the unions, which were primarily administrative bodies, than in the party, which was not "rationalized" until after 1905. Michels wrote his *Political Parties* during these years without making it clear that from a purely technical viewpoint the party's organization was relatively "outmoded."

The reorganization was rather belated, but it was a major change from the tradition of formally loose organization. The Lassalleans had emphasized tight-knit organization and strict discipline, but despite their class consciousness they were troubled by discord and splits. The Eisenachers, too, did not excel in well-kept discipline and efficient financial management.[35] In the three decades after the merger, the party was financially unstable; its correspondence and bookkeeping techniques were rudimentary, originally because of the antisocialist legislation, later because of ingrained habit. During the repressive period legal opportunities of organiza-

---

[34] Cf. Schorske, *op. cit.*, 97–108, and Karl Korn, *Die Arbeiterjugendbewegung* (Berlin: Arbeiterjugend-Verlag, 1922).
[35] Cf. Schröder, *op. cit.*, 17 f.

tion were limited to some mutual funds of the outlawed unions and, in the more lenient second half of the eighties, to some occupational associations; the only really important legal opportunity was provided by the temporary electoral district organizations. Much ingenuity went into the organization of an underground network whose most radical activity was the distribution of the imported party newspaper, the only means of communication from the leaders to the followers. The remarkable feature of these activities was that they were accomplished without any possibility of enforcing decisions from above. The party was led by the Reichstag faction's executive; election campaigns were directed by a committee of the Reichstag faction.

Between 1890 and 1900 the party remained decentralized because of laws forbidding the national organization of local political associations. For legal reasons, a party member was defined as anyone who affirmed the principles of the program and supported the party according to his abilities. Not until 1909 did party dues become mandatory. A consequence of decentralization was the party executive's lack of knowledge of the size of local membership; for 30 years no census was taken. This condition was corrected only after 1906.

The electoral district organization was the major unit; until 1900 it was not a party, but a public institution in the sense that its leadership had to be elected by public assembly. The functionary closest to the rank and file, the *Vertrauensmann,* also was elected annually at nonparty public meetings as the man in whom the assembly was willing to put its trust, an arrangement instituted during the reorganization of the party in 1891 in order to avoid legal obstacles. The *Vertrauensmänner* had to establish contact with the party executive and be responsible to it.[36] Loyalty and dedication substituted for formal controls. In literal translation *Vertrauensmann* means "confidence man," but the English mean-

[36] Cf. *op. cit.,* 39.

ing is the opposite of the German one. These "confidence men" proved to be very trustworthy; corruption, whether embezzlement, bribery, or similar temptations, was extremely rare.

Only in 1905 was the local party organization, with elected and salaried officials, introduced by statute as the normal form of organization. Until the end of the period there was great local and regional variation, largely due to differences in legislation. Centralization, however, was greatly furthered by the right, accorded to the party executive in 1904, to appoint salaried regional and local party secretaries. Such rights could be granted by the annual party congress, the highest formal party authority, which had paramount importance in approving policies and resolving differences. Throughout the nineties, delegates to the congresses, too, had to be elected in public assemblies, which were exposed to the vagaries of accidental attendance. The centralized regional organizations in southern Germany developed earlier than those of Prussia and Saxony, the main centers of Social Democracy and also of state resistance to it.

When the unions were legally able to reestablish themselves in the nineties, they soon took a stand against the party's claim of being the dominant leader of the class-conscious proletariat and especially against its inclination to overestimate the effectiveness of agitation. At the party convention of 1896 the leader of the unions, Legien, considered it wrong to make the workers believe that mere agitation could bring about the eight-hour day: "Meetings, agitation, protests are of no avail. Organization is everything."[37] He drew this conclusion from the isolation of the party and from the uncompromising attitude of the ruling groups: "In our society, everything is a matter of naked force. The power of the workers lies in their organization. If they strengthen their organization, they increase their power."[38] Legien's rationale was a strong one. Since the centers of national decision-making remained inaccessible, con-

[37] *Party Protocols,* 1896, 157.
[38] Legien in his *Correspondenzblatt,* 1898, 270; quoted in Varein, *op. cit.,* 38 f.

centration of energies on sheer organizational strength was a reasonable alternative for the unions.

In contrast, the party's only hope of overcoming its isolation was the ballot box, and this meant continued attention to agitation. This tactical consideration also led the party to strengthen small-town and rural districts rather than big cities; the latter were underrepresented at the party conventions, in the state organizations and in the Reichstag. The rise of the new bureaucratic institutions sometimes benefited left-wing groups in the cities, but more often it worked in favor of reformists in city, town and village. This embittered the extreme left in the last years before the war. However, in the absence of a body of local and regional studies—a major task, still to be accomplished by students of the German labor movement—it is difficult to decide definitely how much grassroots support the radical resurgence had in the cities; indications are that it had very little mass support until the latter part of the war.[39] This certainly was the belief of the party majority, as it was expressed by a delegate at the 1913 convention:

Comrade Luxemburg said that the party executive does not know anything about the dissatisfaction which is expressed in countless party meetings. If Comrade Luxemburg would not merely read reports, but frequently attend such meetings, she would know that these "revolutionary" meetings are often only attended by a hundred men or women in districts with thousands of members. There a small number of phrasemongers, who are not taken seriously by the party, make their speeches. [Strong agreement in the audience.] . . . This is just about how the spirits look who are intoxicated by Luxemburgian revolutionary phraseology. They are not the masses.[40]

[39] Schorske presents a detailed analysis of the party's reorganization after 1900 in the context of the conflict between radicals and reformists (*op. cit.,* Chs. V and X). These conflicts were mainly carried on among a very small number of functionaries. We may assume that both groups had their publics, but the subsequent radicalization of urban masses of workers during and after the war is probably not a good measure of their prewar involvement in these conflicts.

[40] *Party Protocols,* 1913, 298.

The rapid expansion of the Social Democratic subculture, which called for an enlargement of the organizational apparatus, accentuated recruitment problems after the turn of the century. A conspicuous age gap appeared among the functionaries: the higher-ranking leaders were advanced in age, while many lower-ranking functionaries were very young. The mere persistence of older leaders simply indicated the increasing age of the labor movement and the workings of some of the oligarchic mechanisms described by Michels, who made at this point one of his rare positive proposals:

The practice of choosing an entirely new set of leaders every two years ought long ago to have become general in the socialist party, as prototype of all democratic parties. Yet, as far as the German socialists are concerned, not merely does no such practice exist, but any attempt to introduce it provokes great discontent among the rank and file.[41]

The age gap itself was partly due to external factors, such as the preoccupations of members between the ages of 24 and 30 with raising their families; partly it was due to internal reasons.[42] Many young Social Democrats who had seemed to be embarking on promising or even brilliant careers either disappointed their superiors or withdrew on their own in disappointment. A major reason seems to have been the overburdening of many a promising man with administrative work that left him no time to get more education and political experience. In view of this shortage of manpower, Michels' proposed system would have created even more difficulties, although it may perhaps be argued that the rotation of suitable positions might have alleviated some pressure on younger functionaries.

[41] Michels, *op. cit.*, 121. By permission of the publisher.—Michels makes it clear that he is not concerned with practical suggestions in his book (368). To my knowledge, he never addressed himself to practical proposals in any of his writings.

[42] The following draws on Braun, "Die Intellektuellen . . . ," *op. cit.*, 247 f, and Danneberg, *op. cit.*, 285 f. Braun also maintains that not only at congresses, but also at general workers' meetings all over Germany older workers were predominant.

One effect of the increasing organizational burdens seems to have been the limitation of active grassroots participation in ideological discussions. The Viennese party organization was one of the best in the Second International, but its mere maintenance, Danneberg explained, absorbed the energies of the lower-ranking functionaries and made even higher-ranking functionaries primarily administrators. "Work, don't twaddle" was the motto; consequently many lower-ranking functionaries did no more to educate newly recruited members politically than to deliver the *Volkstribüne* to them and to hold meetings including them. This state of affairs promoted the tendency to debunk political and intellectual interests in favor of efficient organization work and thus accentuated reformist to the detriment of radical tendencies.[43]

Since the lower-ranking functionaries were responsible for efficient operations, or simply because they were best at it, many came to regard major policy changes and ideological revisions or even intense political debate as unwelcome disturbances. At first a general tendency seems to have developed to discourage discussion after lectures and speeches as being just a nuisance; this tendency was more specifically directed toward political discussion as the labor movement's difficulties mounted just before and during the war.[44] Important party declarations were often forgotten by members, al-

[43] Many *Vertrauensmänner* looked down upon those "who were only active as lecturers." Danneberg suggested to the party that some workers, instead of burdening themselves with the function of a *Vertrauensmann,* might be much more useful as socialist literature teachers to their class comrades. *Loc. cit.*

[44] Göhre and Braun remember a more democratic atmosphere in the fortnightly meetings of the electoral district association about 1890. Participation in discussion was elicited with the assurance that no one would be ridiculed for rhetorical inadequacy. Göhre found much ignorance and narrow-mindedness, but also—for him—a surprising amount of intelligence and prudence. He concluded that quite a few workers were on a par or superior to the average educated man with regard to poise and clarity of thinking, but he does not say to what extent a discussion of basic premises was really tolerated. Cf. Göhre, *op. cit.,* 89 ff and Braun, *op. cit.,* 245.

though they appeared in the newspapers, because they were not discussed at party meetings. Reviewing prewar trends, an anonymous member wrote in a letter from the front in 1917:

> The great mass of Austrian workers is indifferent to basic questions (*Prinzipienfragen*); this is perhaps even more valid for . . . the *Vertrauensmänner,* the "practitioners" of the organization. For them any discussion on basic questions always appears as a disturbance. Many *Vertrauensmänner* argue that the workers will turn away from the organizations if they see that the members and even the leaders do not agree, that they fight among themselves. They consider it their task to tirelessly build their organizations, unconcerned about theoretical quarrels; it is the task of the leaders "higher up" to resolve conflicts about basic problems.[45]

This attitude of the lower-ranking functionaries should not be mistaken for subservience. The intermediary position of the lower-ranking functionaries made the top leaders greatly dependent on them. First of all, it was the responsibility of the functionaries in the lower and middle echelons to realize much of what the labor movement could achieve in the short run; then, the leaders needed the subleaders to make the followers accept the party line, especially major policy changes. As Carl Landauer, a one-time participant, suggests, Michels did not sufficiently take into account the control over the party leaders that the lower-ranking functionaries exercised by virtue of being their most important link with the rank and file.

Whenever political strategy required steps contrary to tradition, the national party executive and the socialist members in parliament would take the subleaders into their confidence, either by way of a conference or through consultations between the deputies and the local party officers of their districts. The subleaders would critically examine the proposed course of action, and if they approved of it, they would ac-

[45] H. H., "Parteibetrachtungen eines Frontsoldaten," *Der Kampf,* Vol. 10, 1917, 165.

cept the task of assuring the membership that the interests of the party were well served by the change. In an extreme case, when they could not see through the intricacies of political strategy, the subleaders might accept the word of somebody in whom they had special confidence—not necessarily a Bebel or a Jaurès, but more often a man of far lesser renown, whose devotion and good judgment they had learned to respect. The party members were, as a rule, willing to rely on the opinion of their section leaders and of their local executives—not without grumbling, however, and not without asserting their right of criticism, so that the party machine did not run without many minor jerks. Only in very rare cases, however, did the chain of confidence which connected leaders, subleaders, and members suffer a real break.[46]

The party conventions of 1894 and 1895 were major examples of the inability of the top leaders to impose their policies upon the subleaders. Bebel's centralistic conceptions did not prevail in his great clash with the Bavarian leader Georg von Vollmar at the Frankfurt convention of 1894. A majority of the delegates was unwilling to really dispute the right of the Social Democratic factions in the state diets to follow their own policies. One year later, in Breslau, a majority of the delegates destroyed any future chance of adopting an agrarian program which would have included the advocacy of the interests of small farmers, although Bebel this time strongly supported the reformists. The ideological inclinations of the urban proletarian functionaries, who were vigorously supported by Kautsky's Marxist argument about the inevitable decline of small business and the small peasant, predominated over the executive's and the reformists' attempt to appeal to other social strata.[47] These incidents demonstrated the persistent effects of ideology and social composition in relation to organizational tendencies of centralization and expansion.

Michels analyzed the struggles among the leaders (see his Part II, ch. 6) in acid terms of "human, all too human" antagonisms

---

[46] Landauer, *op. cit.*, 486. By permission of the publisher.
[47] Cf. G. Ritter, *op. cit.*, Ch. V.

incidental to the struggle for personal advancement and power. He played down the influence of the masses no less than that of the subleaders. He went to great length to illustrate the apathy and incompetence of the masses; they were radical only in crisis situations precipitated by a failure of the dominant system. He mentioned in passing that the leaders must always keep in touch with the attitudes and sentiments of the masses, but he did not admit that this could be an effective check.[48] He discounted the "rule of anticipated reactions," to use Carl Friedrich's phrase.[49] The democratic structure of the labor movement meant that, despite the tendencies toward the perpetuation of the leaders and despite the gradual bureaucratization, the social composition of the party and, with that, the direct needs of the workers had to be taken into account by the leaders.[50] Again, Michels strongly tended to neglect the operational level of checks and balances by juxtaposing the extremes of ideal and real. In contrast to the relatively democratic German party, the organizational setup of the Bolshevik party made it easier for the Communist leaders to impose policies without close consideration of the everyday needs of the masses. In fact, from a Leninist perspective, Michels' thesis was countered with the argument that the German party was not oligarchical enough to resist grassroots pressures, as witnessed by the party's policy at the beginning of the First World War.[51]

[48] Michels, *op. cit.*, 172.
[49] Cf. Carl J. Friedrich, *Constitutional Government and Democracy* (Boston: Little, Brown, 1941), 589 ff.
[50] R. Blank, *op. cit.*, argued in 1905 that the Social Democratic party more than any other party was influenced, because of its democratic constitution, by its social composition rather than by the theories and ideals of individuals. The social composition could make itself felt in two ways: In industrial districts it could radicalize some locals; elsewhere it was more likely to favor the moderates.
[51] See the perspective of Karl Ackermann, *Organisatorische Streitigkeiten in der deutschen Sozialdemokratie. Ein Beitrag zur Soziologie des 4. August 1914.* Ph.D. dissertation, Heidelberg, 1946, 2 f and 29 f, as mentioned in G. Ritter, *op. cit.*, 49.

In conclusion, it may be said that the increasing organizational complexity of the party—i.e., its "formalization"—had definite consequences for the relationship between leaders and led: it increased bureaucratic controls, vested organizational interests developed, and grassroots revolts were made more difficult. The latter, however, had not been easy, at least since the seventies, because the repressive legislation and its legacies put such a great value on unity. Furthermore, grassroots sentiment had to be taken into account by the party as a legal opposition facing a powerful dominant system and as a mass movement aiming at strengthening parliamentarism. In fact, the "conservatism" of the leaders, Michels and Weber recognized, was not just a consequence of internal bureaucratization, of increasing "red tape"—it was basic to the movement's strategy under the given conditions of legality and political isolation.[52] The reorganization of the party in the first decade of this century strengthened the movement considerably, but not decisively, since the leaders could do little more than expand it and try to protect it against all-out attack. It is here that the principle of "self-maintenance" can be observed.

4. Self-Maintenance

Associations tend to intensify their concern with self-preservation in the course of formalization and infusion with value, the latter referring to the change of meaning of activities which originally were mainly instrumental. Eventually, concern with self-maintenance may deflect from original goals and commitments, especially from ideological prescriptions. It may be suggested that this aspect of institutionalization is a particularly critical problem for a radical political movement. By definition such movements aim at large-

[52] Cf. Michels, *op. cit.*, 336 f.

scale social reconstruction and usually encounter strong resistance from the dominant system. The leaders must face the possibility of severe restrictions or total suppression.

Michels charged that the labor movement had "suddenly" become "responsible" in its stage of maturity and compared Bebel's rhetoric on the Paris Commune in 1871 with the later "conservatism" of the leaders.[53] There was certainly a difference in tone and mood, but Bebel and Liebknecht were always careful to safeguard the survival interests of their party. They became centrist after 1890 not so much through a change of views but because of the rise of a right and left wing. The right-wing reformists and Marxist Revisionists devoted themselves to the expansion of the organizations and to the piecemeal representation of material interests in state and municipal parliaments, labor courts, and public welfare agencies. The centrist leaders did not give up their intransigent opposition to the dominant system because the isolation of the movement on the national level and in Prussia continued, but they recognized that such a representation of material interests was the only opportunity for positive reformist activity. Perfecting their art of adhering to a radical rhetoric and a moderate practice, they adamantly opposed the reformists only to the extent that they feared for the unity of the movement. The left-wing functionaries, many of whom were very capable organizers and administrators, wanted mass actions such as political strikes in addition to election campaigns and general propaganda. Even Bernstein and Ludwig Frank advocated political strikes, although with firm reformist rather than radical intentions.

As long as the party grew and industrialization seemed to favor the labor movement over its opponents, the Centrist leaders could keep the right and the left within the fold. Radicals and reformists could develop a division of labor.[54] Furthermore, the party could control its internal dissensions because, unlike the French socialist

---

[53] *Loc. cit.;* for Bebel's speech see Ch. IV, 87 above.
[54] Cf. Massing, *op. cit.,* 191.

party, it was never confronted with the decision whether to accept or reject governmental responsibility.[55]

In the last decade prior to the First World War, the labor movement continued to grow in votes and members and substantially improved its organizational and financial condition, but it also suffered a number of important defeats at the hand of the governments, the government parties and big business. It is true that the party triumphed in the Reichstag elections of 1903, a victory which seemed to vindicate the centrist executive's policy of radical rhetoric and moderate practice. Three million votes were cast for the party and 82 seats taken by it. One out of every four voters had cast his vote for the party. It had again shown a vote-getting power which could not be matched by all foreign socialist parties together, and it was only this achievement that counterbalanced the criticism of the party's nonrevolutionary attitudes, a criticism which was widespread among socialist parties of other countries.[56]

The election results of 1903 spurred the government and big business to check the progress of the party and the unions. Although the Social Democrats trusted the general development to work automatically to their advantage, a view seemingly confirmed by the election of 1903, their opponents changed the "inevitable" course of history. The power of big business increased faster than that of the Social Democratic unions and of the other unions,

[55] The first time a socialist entered a national government was in 1899 when the French deputy Alexandre Millerand became Minister of Commerce in the cabinet of Waldeck-Rousseau. This was the cause of prolonged disputes within socialist parties in various countries. The French situation was different from that in Germany in that there was not just one united socialist party with one firmly entrenched credo, but several groups embracing different beliefs. Millerand's group exposed itself to the pressures inherent in the sharing of responsibility within a bourgeois coalition government, while the French Marxists faced sharp competition from other socialist and working-class ideologies. See Ernst H. Posse, *Der Marxismus in Frankreich 1871– 1905* (Berlin: Prager, 1930), 82 ff.

[56] Cf. Robert Michels, "Die deutsche Sozialdemokratie im internationalen Verbande," *Archiv für Sozialwissenschaft,* Vol. 25, 1907, 218 ff.

which altogether had organized about one third of the industrial work force by 1906; by comparison, about two thirds of the employers were organized in employers' associations, which greatly improved the individual employer's ability to fight the unions. The Saxonian textile workers lost a costly strike in 1903. During the 1905 miners' strike, as well as in later years, the mining companies successfully adhered to their established policy of refusing to deal with the unions. In 1905 the government tried to mediate but failed. The employers' intransigence forced the government to introduce legislation in order to remedy some of the misuses of which the miners had complained. But the very fact of government intervention allowed the employers to remain intransigent and to refuse recognition to the unions.[57]

When the Russian revolution of 1905 broke out, the left stepped up its campaign for mass demonstrations and a political mass strike against the Prussian three-class suffrage, but the centrist leaders and the unions were much more impressed by the internal domestic situation than by the Russian example. The set-backs of the labor movement strengthened the position of the unions vis-à-vis the party and of the Revisionists within the party.[58] The unions acted first by repressing discussion of the general strike within their organizations and by openly disavowing it at the Fifth Congress of the Trade Unions, held at Cologne in May 1905. Their spokesman, Bömelburg, made a statement which was to become famous—that even if the unions were outlawed, the cause would not be lost:

Tremendous sacrifices were made to arrive at the present state of organization, and tremendous sacrifices will be necessary to reach a still higher stage. In order to expand and solidify our organizations, we need peace and calm in the labor movement. Our literati sit down and write

[57] Cf. Max Koch, *Die Bergarbeiterbewegung im Ruhrgebiet zur Zeit Wilhelms II* (Düsseldorf: Droste, 1954), 108. On the textile workers' strike, see Massing, *op. cit.*, 192.
[58] For a detailed analysis of this interrelationship, see Schorske, *op. cit.*, 108 ff.

and write. [Interjection: Very true.] The literati may do what they will, but they render a disservice to the labor movement. . . . The strengthening and expansion of the organization is the best weapon against Reaction. The stronger the trade union organizations become and the more we educate the workers to be class-conscious, the more we sharpen our arms against the Reaction. Nobody wishes more than I that the [Prussian] suffrage be improved . . . *but even if the Reaction takes away the suffrage . . . and the right of coalition, we are not yet through.* [Interjection: Very true.] Today the idea is rooted in the working class that an injustice has been done to it; the workers know what human rights [*Menschenrechte*] they have, and no Reaction is capable of suppressing this idea in the people.[59]

In February 1906 the party executive reached a secret agreement with the unions in which it pledged to squelch enthusiasm for the political mass strike as much as possible. But news of the agreement leaked out, and at the convention of 1906 the party executive was forced to consent, against its will, to a new discussion of the general strike in order to secure equal suffrage. The centrist leaders continued to accept the general strike in principle, in order to prevent a further alienation of the left wing, but made the strike dependent on the consent of the unions which had rejected it.

In the "bloc" Reichstag of 1907 the Social Democrats held only half of their previous seats, even though they received more votes than in 1903; a "bloc" of liberal and conservative parties united to defeat Social Democratic candidates in the run-off elections. This defeat reemphasized the ability of the dominant system to successfully manipulate nationalist sentiments in an all-out campaign. The party reacted by pushing its reorganization ahead and by modifying its stand on nationalism. Since its major weapon was

[59] *Union Protocol, op. cit.,* 221 f, my emphasis. The protocol is much less colorful than is that of the party conventions. The discussions are more openly controlled by the executive. They concern the interests of the unions versus the employers, the state and the Social Democratic party. Lip service is paid to the close relationship with the party, but the specific interests of the unions are emphasized.

the increase of its vote, it was forced to adjust to the stronger nationalist trends in public opinion. At the beginning of the new "bloc" Reichstag the Revisionist agrarian expert Dr. David, invoking the authority of the humanist philosopher Eduard Zeller, still adhered to the old abstract-humanitarian position—the nation's moral obligation to humanity—as his party's "national creed."[60] A few weeks later, however, Gustav Noske, who later was to become the first Reichswehr Minister of the Weimar Republic, created a public sensation and a major clash at the 1907 party convention with his first speech in the Reichstag. The speech did not deviate substantively from the older Social Democratic position, especially Bebel's affirmation of a defensive war and his demand for the best possible military equipment; however, the particularly emphatic endorsement of every German's military duties made the difference.[61]

The Reichstag elections of 1912 were the last triumph of the Social Democrats, who emerged as the largest faction in parliament. But at the same time the labor movement reached a critical stage, and the end of its expansion within its large isolated realm seemed to be in sight. The unions continued to be on the defensive against the employers, and there was no prospect of collective bargaining in the heavy industries. The increase of the party's votes had brought it no nearer to forcing the government into an abandonment of the Prussian three-class suffrage. Internal problems mounted as the differences between right and left wing became more acute. The left proposed the general strike again during the last convention of the united party in Jena in 1913. Scheidemann spoke on behalf of the majority against Rosa Luxemburg's resolution.[62] He maintained that the necessary conditions were not given, and

---

[60] *Reichstag Protocols,* March 4, 1907, 231.
[61] Cf. Noske's own account in his autobiography, *Erlebtes aus Aufstieg und Niedergang einer Demokratie* (Offenbach: Bollwerk-Verlag, 1947), 26 ff. See also William Maehl, "The Triumph of Nationalism in the German Socialist Party on the Eve of the First World War," *Journal of Modern History,* XXIV, 1952, 15–41.
[62] *Party Protocols,* Jena, 1913, 230–35.

he warned against the attempt to play the masses off against the leaders and to glorify spontaneous mass action. Bernstein's concern for the welfare of the movement became so great that he came near to embracing Bömelburg's position of 1905. Said Bernstein:

We have erected organizations in the most diverse areas, which through toilsome work have made of our movement a state within a state. This has turned out to be much more uncomfortable for our foes than if we had run the risk of a gamble. We dare not hazard the destiny of the movement; we have built too much, and what has been built is too valuable.[63]

The centrist leadership concentrated increasingly on the preservation of the unity of the party and thus tried to forestall the split which was predicted to be inevitable by a writer whose observation received much attention at the time.[64] In his last years, Bebel

[63] *Op. cit.*, 286. This statement can also be considered an application of his famous credo: "That which is usually called the ultimate goal of socialism means nothing to me, the movement means everything." Bernstein did not take the movement literally as an end in itself, but he understood movement to mean "the general movement of society, in other words, social progress, as well as the political and economic agitation and organization necessary to bring about this progress." Ed. Bernstein, "Zusammenbruchstheorie und Kolonialpolitik," *Neue Zeit*, XVI, I, 1897–98, 548 ff. See also Bernstein, *Die Voraussetzungen des Sozialismus und die Aufgaben der Sozialdemokratie*, *op. cit.*, 169. Bernstein's statement of 1913 should be understood in the same way. His position was not as unorthodox as it might appear when it is compared to the following Marx quote: "Communism for us is not a condition that is to be established nor an ideal to which reality must adjust itself. We call communism the actual movement which abolishes present conditions." Quoted in Karl Mannheim, *Ideology and Utopia* (New York: Harcourt, a Harvest Book, n.d.), 126.

[64] See Robert Brunhuber, *Die heutige Sozialdemokratie: Eine kritische Wertung ihrer wissenschaftlichen Grundlagen und eine soziologische Untersuchung ihrer praktischen Parteigestaltung* (Jena: Fischer, 1906), 208–12. Brunhuber, a member of the editorial staff of the *Kölnische Zeitung* and lecturer at the Business University of Cologne, was an ethical socialist but not a party member.

During peacetime a split would probably not have increased the revolutionary threat to the dominant system because the moderate majority would

fought with all his skills for the salvation of the work of his life, the united party, and sided with the right or the left, whichever appeared necessary in order to preserve the unity of the party or to forestall governmental interference. At the 1903 party convention in Dresden, he made his famous attack on the Revisionists, but a few months later he sided with them. At the Jena convention of 1905, he praised the general strike, and at the Mannheim convention of 1906, he denounced it because he had probably realized in the meantime, as Michels suggests, that

even a declaration of sympathy for the general strike would strongly irritate the government. . . . A hundred times Bebel—not unlike William II—threatened his enemies with disaster and death. He declared that he would crush the Revisionists and made the state afraid of its overthrow . . . [but] the welfare of the party, understood primarily in organizational terms, was the center of his concern.[65]

For Michels this implied an opprobrium, although he understood that the "conservatism" of the leaders was identical with the long-range strategy of the isolated and militarily outclassed movement. Given his value premises, Michels had to disapprove of this identity at the same time that he tried to explain its "inevitability." Ambivalent as he was, he granted to the leaders in 1911 that

they have not yet lost contact with the masses . . . and that the executive committee of the party, and also (perhaps less perfectly) the parliamentary socialist group, still represent the average opinion of the comrades throughout the country. . . . The manner in which the masses entrust their interests to the leaders is, *historically* at least, legitimate and explicable.[66]

---

have become even more reformist and the radical minority would have been even more isolated. But in case of a military catastrophe of the dominant system, the revolutionary intentions of a very radical minority party, even if suppressed, might perhaps have been turned into a more serious threat than that which occurred in 1918.

[65] Michels, "Bebel," *op. cit.,* 688.

[66] Id., *Political Parties, op. cit.,* 133, my emphasis.

In the given historical context this appears to me a significant attenuation of Michels' thesis. The movement's crisis was not due to any betrayal of the masses through the strategy of "self-maintenance." The movement's dilemma was, in essence, due to the fact that the proposals of the two wings could not really improve upon the center's strategy and that no strategy or tactic appeared capable of facilitating democratization in the near future.

> The dilemma of Social Democracy lay in the fact that the tactic required for winning middle-class support was in contradiction with the tactic required to extract concessions from the conversatives. The demonstrations and mass actions of the Social Democrats would frighten the middle classes back into the arms of the Junkers; but without strong action supported by the middle class as well as the workers the Junkers could not be moved to make concessions. . . . There was in fact no right tactic for Social Democracy to pursue in terms of the constitutional issue alone. The constitutional issue was one which, in the long run, was solved only by the revolution; and it is difficult to see how, whatever the tactic of Social Democracy, it could have been otherwise.[67]

I agree substantially with Schorske's reasoning, but I will leave it to my conclusions to assess the argument that only a revolution could solve the constitutional issue. It was certainly true that only through a military defeat of Imperial Germany could a revolutionary change of the constitution be accomplished. Such a defeat was either feared or not anticipated by most Social Democratic leaders. Only Rosa Luxemburg and a few others included the possibility of military defeat in their strategy.

When the Empire was founded in 1871 all the rhetoric of Liebknecht and Bebel could not turn the movement into a revolutionary threat. On the eve of the First World War the vast Social Democratic subculture constituted the most important domestic, even if "dormant," problem for the government. The centrist leaders' basic

[67] Schorske, *op. cit.*, 168. By permission of the publisher.

strategy and their moderating role between the right and the left wings at least succeeded in perpetuating a massive class opposition by maintaining the unity of the movement. Unexpectedly, the war became the great test for Social Democracy and the Empire.

XI
The Unanticipated Showdown

1. The Split of the Labor Movement and the Downfall of the Empire

Imperial Germany approached the First World War with an impressive record of internal stability despite her rapid and spectacular industrialization: No constitutional change had occurred in the Reich and Prussia; there had been crises of personnel and prestige, but none of them had seriously shaken the constitutional defenses of the Emperor, his government, his army and "his" conservatives, who affirmed their monarchist loyalty at the same time that they put their own political and economic interests over national interests. Democratization had made some advance primarily in southern Germany, but on the federal level it was not more than a tendency and in Prussia not more than a possibility for the future. When Otto Hintze wrote his analysis of monarchic constitutionalism in 1911 he was aware that

a tendency toward the transition from the monarchic to the parliamentary system is noticeable in Germany, although it cannot be considered to be strong; it extends from the radical left far into the ranks of the moderate liberals and the Center. . . . After Bülow's resignation [in 1909], the new chancellor energetically opposed the interpretation that Germany was in the process of moving toward a parliamentary system of government.[1]

[1] Hintze, *op. cit.*, 382.

Hintze was in favor of making the system of monarchic constitutionalism unequivocal in the constitution and seems to have had some very cautiously expressed apprehensions about the tendency of William II toward personal government.[2] The majority of public opinion remained in favor of monarchic constitutionalism, and the belligerent rhetoric and personal regime of the Emperor were also popular.

Yet there were some countertrends. In 1913 a Prussian colonel arrested a few civilians in Zabern, a little community in Alsace-Lorraine, and locked them up for a night. This illegal action provoked an extraordinary public protest and resulted in a remarkable condemnation of the government by the Reichstag majority. Liberals, Center and Social Democrats voted 293 to 54, with four abstentions, criticizing the government's self-conscious defense of the colonel's action. The army absolved the officer. The Reichstag was powerless to do more than express its displeasure, but in the same year its budgetary power slightly increased and a very slow development toward a stronger parliament appeared possible. No one, however, knew when and how it would come about.[3]

[2] Hintze observed a certain regularity in the phenomenon that self-governing monarchs have a tendency to appear after the great self-governing ministers: Louis XIV after Richelieu and Mazarin, the Great Elector (Frederick William of Brandenburg) after Count Schwarzenberg, Emperor Ferdinand II after Cardinal Klesl, and Georg III after the elder Pitt. But, Hintze added, the last example also shows that the attempt of a monarch to rule personally is not always successful. Cf. *op. cit.*, 407.

[3] The late Ludwig Bergsträsser, the author of the *Geschichte der politischen Parteien in Deutschland, op. cit.*, who was a member of the Young National Liberals before the First World War and a federal parliamentary deputy after the First and the Second World War, told me in 1959 that he believed then and now that parliament would have continued to grow stronger even if the war had not come and the Empire had not fallen. More questionable is the belief of Arthur Rosenberg, a Communist Reichstag member in the nineteen twenties, that even without the war the polarization between government and Reichstag would eventually have created a revolutionary situation; however, he did not underestimate the military power of the state in peacetime. Cf. Rosenberg, *The Birth of the German Republic, op. cit.*, 58. Rosenberg's book which first appeared in 1928 provides a brilliant description of the major underlying reasons and the specific chain of events which resulted in the dis-

Since the Social Democratic party was dependent on further democratization, its sense of malaise over the impasse was particularly acute when the limits of its own organizational expansion seemed to be approaching. The party had polled 34 per cent of the votes for the Reichstag in 1912 and had a million members by 1914; it held 110 of the 396 seats in the Reichstag, more than 220 in the state diets, more than 2,800 in the city parliaments and councils and more than 9,000 in rural communities.[4]

The outbreak of the war confronted the leaders suddenly with the direct integration of the movement into the national community. Up to the last days before the declarations of war, the party carried on a peace campaign and tried to arrange some common action with socialist parties abroad. When the mobilization began, the party had to face its utter inability to influence either the government or the masses. The radical posture of the labor movement dissolved overnight. At first fears of repression were so great that at the end of July no less a man than Ebert was sent to Switzerland to save party funds. As a legal mass organization, the party was nearly defenseless against the government's possible raiding of its organizations and funds: twenty million Marks, for example, were tied up in business investments, making the party a nation-wide corporation.[5]

Many members were afraid of the foreign military threat, in particular of the Russian "steamroller." Some radicals, like Paul Lensch in the important left-wing *Leipziger Volkszeitung,* took the Marxist theory of imperialism to mean that Germany's economic interests on the world market had to be defended against Britain's capitalist predominance, for the benefit of the German

integration of the Empire. For a case study of the Social Democrats during the war and its aftermath, see A. J. Berlau, *The German Social Democratic Party: 1914–1921* (New York: Columbia University Press, 1949).

[4] Cf. Ernst Drahn, "Sozialdemokratie," *Handwörterbuch der Staatswissenschaften,* Vol. 7, 1926, 533.

[5] Cf. Maehl, *op. cit.,* 25.

working class. More important was the hope of the right wing and of many centrists that through the support of the war efforts the labor movement could break out of its isolation and exact major concessions from the government in the postwar period. Even before the war, Chancellor Bülow and Bethmann-Hollweg, his successor, had been in favor of some modification of the Prussian suffrage, but they had done nothing about it in view of the determined conservative resistance in the Prussian Lower House.

Most important, however, for the Reichstag faction's famous vote for the war credits on August 4, 1914, was the frenzied enthusiasm and the urge of fraternization which overcame many a Social Democratic functionary and masses of workers.[6] This emotional outburst was indicative of the strength of national sentiment and of pent-up political frustration, although the simple thrill of involvement in "great affairs" and of getting a break from everyday routines was also a part of the elation.[7] To many members the cleavage between the labor movement and the nation seemed to have vanished. They experienced a feeling of liberation; the class barriers seemed to have fallen and the working class to be recognized as part of the nation. A striking example for the change that could overcome even an avowed radical was provided by the labor editor Konrad Hänisch:

[6] Michels interpreted the attitude of the Social Democratic leaders at the beginning of the war as definite proof of his thesis; however, he also acknowledged in 1915 that the masses had not rebelled against their leaders. Cf. Michels, *op. cit.*, 357. Put in positive terms, this means that the leaders did not act against the wishes of the masses. Indeed, the enthusiasm of the masses was one of the major factors that limited the freedom of action on the part of the leaders. It remains true, of course, that the leaders' attitude was also influenced by survival interests. Although Bebel, who died in 1913, had been willing to defend the country, he considered the party's position hopeless in the event of war. The incumbent leaders, however, could not be expected to abandon the movement in such an event.

[7] A good description of the atmosphere of August 1914 and of the fraternization of Social Democratic functionaries and workers with opponents is given by Ernst Gläser in his famous novel, *Jahrgang 1902* (1928).

In this war we have learned anew what we had almost completely forgotten: that apart from the class conflicts within a nation there is something common *to all classes of this nation.* We German Social Democrats have learned to consider ourselves in this war as part, and truly not the worst part, of the German nation. We do not want to be robbed again by anyone, from the right or the left, of this feeling of belonging to the German people. . . . We have become aware in this war that the German idea of the state has stood the test politically, organizationally and militarily despite its more superficial and its more serious faults. We have *given up* this inner resistance, which for decades dominated us, consciously or unconsciously, against the German idea of the state because we could no longer honestly maintain it.[8]

Hänisch claimed to speak for the workers, but he was, like David on the right and Lensch on the left, an intellectual with a middle-class background and may have suffered more from the national cleavage than workers did.[9] It may be assumed that few workers perceived, as he did, an "intimate relationship between the best aspects of the German idea of the state and the best characteristics of the labor movement."[10] But an insistence on discipline and fulfillment of duty was indeed shared by Prussian and Social Democratic ideals and habits.[11] Soon numerous writings which fused nationalism and socialism and pitted German collectivist and socialist ideas against Western individualism received much public attention.[12] This facilitated the ideological integration of the labor

[8] Konrad Hänisch, *Die deutsche Sozialdemokratie in und nach dem Weltkriege* (Berlin: Schwetschke, 1916), cf. Schorske's quotation, *op. cit.,* 290.
[9] Hänisch came from an officer's family, David had a Ph.D., and Lensch an M.D.
[10] Hänisch, *loc. cit.*
[11] The rise of a Communist party state after the Second World War amid the ruins of Brandenburg-Prussia has continued this historical parallel in certain striking respects, which deserve more scholarly attention.
[12] Cf. Eduard David, *Die Sozialdemokratie im Weltkriege* (Berlin: Vorwärts, 1915); for a joint publication of Social Democrats and university professors, see Friedrich Thimme and Carl Legien, eds., *Die Arbeiterschaft im neuen Deutschland* (Leipzig: Hirzel, 1915). For a later analysis, see Karl Pribram, "Deutscher Nationalismus und deutscher Sozialismus," *Archiv für Sozialwissenschaft,* Vol. 49, 1922, 371 f.

movement into the national community. Many Social Democratic workers, however, combined the two loyalties in a relatively uncomplicated fashion. A leader of proletarian origin such as Severing implicitly denied the loyalty conflict altogether. His view was similar to the view of older spokesmen that socialists were as patriotic as or even more patriotic than their adversaries. However, for him this was no abstract declaration; it was the basis of cooperation with the Imperial government during the war, of fighting for the preservation of "order"—that is, much of the old social order—during the revolution of 1918, and of suppressing Socialist left-wing opponents.[13]

At first the integration of the labor movement into the dominant system was little more than subordination. The party and the unions lost their limited independence and all chances of political maneuverability. The enthusiasm of the masses, which gripped all countries as the war began, made it easy for the governments involved to quickly unite most political groups under the national banner. In Germany the Emperor declared that he "no longer recognized parties, only Germans." A public peace (*Burgfrieden*) was established between the government and all the parties. After the unions had established that the government was aware of their value as a disciplining and welfare agency, they pledged abstention from all wage and strike movements. Since the defeats of 1903 and 1905, the unions had been careful not to spend great amounts of money on strikes and had preferred to accumulate funds; this was part of Legien's strategy to build up the union power. Now the same funds were used for the war efforts, as unemployment relief and as support for the dependents of draftees. Union and party functionaries served on many public and semi-public boards; they were no longer solely responsible to the members. This change in their relationship was made easier by the thinning of the ranks; in September of 1914, 30 per cent of the party members had already been drafted.

[13] Cf. Severing, *op. cit.*, 223.

The labor movement was now composed of a greatly reduced body of functionaries and rank and file, the latter consisting mainly of older workers and women.

Many members and followers had vaguely believed that the party and the International might be strong enough to prevent war; but when the war started, their enthusiasm knew no bounds. As it became apparent that the war would be unexpectedly bloody and long, disillusionment with the government and the party began to spread. The Social Democratic masses in the army could not politically express this disillusionment, but at home the prewar tensions between the various party factions were rapidly revived. All party leaders were in favor of a quick and negotiated peace, but a growing number of functionaries and members criticized the majority for surrendering too easily to the powers-that-be and for betraying their old commitments. The emergent opposition was severely handicapped by the army's constant readiness to apply the law of siege. This gave the right much greater power than it could have won on its own strength. The right insisted on abiding by the policy of full cooperation with the government as the best hope for improving the movement's position in the long run. However, many centrists and left-wingers despaired over the government's inability or unwillingness to end the war through compromise and to promise definite domestic reforms. For this reason, they decided to restore the party's old policy of intransigent opposition; only the radical left looked toward a revolutionary solution. The decision to leave the party was very hard for many functionaries and workers to make, irrespective of whether they seceded voluntarily or were expelled. The party had become for them a life center, and now they faced the conflict of loyalty to the organization or loyalty to the old ideology of the movement.

In December 1915, 20 members of the Social Democratic Reichstag faction voted against the war credits and 22 refused to vote at all; in March 1916, 18 members established a separate Reichstag faction after being expelled by the majority. With heavy hearts, a large minority of the party (including Bebel's successor as party chairman, Haase, Kautsky, and Bernstein, who was accused of anglophile attitudes) left the party and formed the Independent Social Democratic party (USPD) in 1917. About 40 per cent of the 430,000 party members who were left in 1916 may have joined the so-called Minority Socialists; in the cities, often more than 50 per cent joined.[14] By 1917 the Majority Socialists had lost 80 per cent of the male membership of 1914.[15]

The numerically weak extreme left was at first uneasily allied with the Independents, who were more pacifist than revolutionary. It had already established its own organization, *Spartakus,* the forerunner of the Communist party. Its most important spokesmen were Karl Liebknecht and Rosa Luxemburg, who were several times imprisoned during the war.[16] They were greatly encouraged by the beginning of the revolution in Russia. In 1918 Liebknecht and many members of the *Spartakus* moved closer to the Bolshevists, as a Leninist splinter group, strong in the big seaports of Hamburg and Bremen, had done before them. Rosa Luxemburg, however, turned against the Bolshevist theory and practice of a centralized revolutionary dictatorship. She wanted to rely on the spontaneity of the masses.

Important for the coming revolution was the break in the strategic Berlin ammunitions industries, destroying the iron hold of the top trade union leaders over the workers. Lower-ranking functionaries of the traditionally aggressive metal workers' union organized major strikes, the first beginning on the occasion of a four-year sentence for Karl Liebknecht in 1916. Even the right-wing Social Democrats had to support these strikes if they wanted to retain grassroots support. In order to cope with the growing unrest

[14] On the varying estimates, see Ossip Flechtheim, *Die KPD in der Weimarer Republik* (Offenbach: Drott, 1948), 28.

[15] Cf. F. Ebert, *Schriften, op. cit.,* Vol. 2, 17.

[16] On Karl Liebknecht, see Karl W. Meyer, *Karl Liebknecht* (Washington: Public Affairs Press, 1957); on Rosa Luxemburg, see Paul Frölich, *Rosa Luxemburg* (Paris: Editions Nouvelles Internationales, 1939).

among workers, especially the unskilled and unorganized ones, the Majority Socialists created the position of factory *Vertrauensleute,* but these positions were also used by the Independents. The *Vertrauensleute* became the forerunners of the soviets or workers' councils.[17]

As the downfall of the Empire approached, the divided Social Democrats found themselves burdened with heavy liabilities from their commitments to support or oppose the government. Neither group anticipated the parliamentary responsibility that would suddenly fall to them, although the united party had always advocated the supremacy of parliament over the authoritarian government. Neither of the two socialist parties was prepared for social and economic reconstruction, especially in a situation of near economic bankruptcy and with the prospect of reparations to the victors. The Social Democrats did not know how to socialize the basic industries and, more important, they had never realistically faced the problem of the seizure of power, and for good reason. Before the war the problem seemed very remote; and since the party was dependent at least on the given level of toleration in order to function as a legal mass organization, open discussion of this problem would have been detrimental to its interests.[18]

During the first half of the war the liberal Progressives, the Catholic Center, and the Social Democrats had even less of a chance than in peacetime to promote greater parliamentary control. Since the army was subordinate to the Emperor only, it easily managed to establish a military dictatorship in 1916, after the military necessity for total mobilization of the national resources had arisen. The increasing powerlessness of the civilian government strengthened

---

[17] On the major opposition groups against the party and union leadership, see Flechtheim, *op. cit.,* Ch. I.

[18] In contrast, Lenin who observed developments from exile in Switzerland was unrestrained by legal and organizational considerations of this kind in drawing radical conclusions as to an effective method of seizing power. Shortly after the beginning of the war, he started a campaign for civil war within the warring countries.

the Reichstag vis-à-vis the civilian government. The third wartime chancellor, Count Hertling, negotiated with the parties before taking office at the end of 1917, although his actual "confirmation" depended on the military. However, when General Ludendorff abdicated as the dictator of Germany in October 1918, conceding military defeat, he thrust responsibility for further political action on parliament. Before the Reichstag could consolidate parliamentary government, the revolution swept away Bismarck's edifice.

Early in November 1918, the sailors of the navy struck spontaneously,[19] and the radical leaders of the Berlin metal workers, who had extended their influence into many of the larger cities, moved deliberately. Decisive was the immediate support of the soldiers at home. The uprising of the masses was directed against any continuation of the war. It was a protest against the failure of the rulers to spare them four years of a senselessly bloody war and to avoid military defeat; it did not aim at the introduction of a specific new form of government. If the revolutionary movement did not go beyond the establishment of the parliamentary republic and a measure of social reform, this was, as far as the labor movement was concerned, largely because of the movement's moderating legacies.

Friedrich Ebert was Imperial Chancellor for one day and tried to save the monarchy. Against his wishes Philipp Scheidemann declared Germany a republic on November 9.[20] The lower-ranking functionaries of the old party, together with the Soldiers' Councils, curbed the influence of the Minority Socialists and of the Sparta-

---

[19] Class lines remained sharply drawn during the war and were ever harder to bear as the war progressed. This was especially true in the navy; since the battle fleet stayed mostly at home the class hierarchy was not attenuated by combat conditions.

[20] When the historian Friedrich Meinecke asked Solf, the Secretary of State in the Foreign Office, on November 18 whether Ebert and Scheidemann had not felt a secret joy about the revolution, Solf answered: "No, not at all. They were deadly frightened." Meinecke, *Erinnerungen: 1909–1919* (Stuttgart: Köhler, 1949), 259.

kists. Scheidemann later extolled their loyalty to the party and declared that "these were the men, above all, to whom Germany owed its rescue from Bolshevism." [21] Thus a majority of the Social Democrats and of their bourgeois allies succeeded in democratizing Germany in the direction of parliamentarism. In the process, no radical reconstruction of the Empire's social structure took place.[22]

According to their old conviction, the Majority Socialists firmly attached themselves to the parliamentary system and accepted their position as one of the major parties, none of which could muster a parliamentary majority. A large number of Minority Socialists, especially of the lower-ranking functionaries and the rank and file, were bitterly disappointed about the establishment of a parliamentary republic that did not significantly change the social structure of the Empire. They came to reject democratic ideals with regard to party organization and the political system at large. In 1920 they decided to join the Third International and thus turned the Communist Spartakists from a small group into a mass organization. The Social Democratic party took back into its fold the minority of the USPD, including most of its top leaders, many of whom had been centrists before the war.

Despite its political integration into the parliamentary system and the considerably improved status of the working class, the labor movement continued to be a subculture. The Communist subculture developing next to it was quite similar, excepting, of course, its political goals and some organizational techniques. Both profited from the opportunities of parliamentary rule and from the new social welfare legislation (eight hour day, paid vacation, etc.) which improved the worker's everyday life and gave him more leisure.

[21] The phrase "Rettung von dem Bolschewismus" was also a right-wing slogan. Scheidemann may have used it in order to argue before the general public the importance of the role of the Social Democratic functionaries and to debunk the role of the right-wing military Free Corps. Cf. Scheidemann, *op. cit.*, Vol. 2, 292.

[22] On the political and economic consequences of the survival of the Junkers, see Gerschenkron, *op. cit.*, Ch. II.

The Social Democratic subculture expanded and flourished despite the severe political and economic crises of the postwar years and despite the greater number of alternatives offered by modern mass culture.[23] However, many cultural activities of the labor movement became increasingly similar to neutral adult education or neutral recreation.[24]

In practical politics the labor movement became a huge interest group, conservative in its commitment to the preservation of the democratic republic. But neither the republic nor the labor movement were recognized as legitimate by large sections of the population. As the new political system proved relatively ineffective in the face of foreign intervention and economic catastrophes, such as the breakdown of the currency in 1923 and the World Depression, millions of people turned to new authoritarian ideologies. The political strength of the Social Democratic labor movement at first was locked in stalemate and then rapidly declined. Committed to the rules of the game of parliamentary democracy and weakened by the disintegration of the democratic system, the labor movement finally succumbed to Nazism.

2. The Government and Max Weber Review the Empire's Course

Before drawing any conclusions, I will contrast the government's and Weber's views of the Empire in peacetime and wartime, as they expressed them toward the end of the war but before the American intervention made them realize that all was lost.[25] The views of one

---

[23] The expansion of the Austrian Social Democratic subculture was facilitated by the absence of a strong Communist movement.

[24] Cf. Andries Sternheim, *op. cit.*, 352 f.

[25] The revolution took by surprise not only most Social Democrats and the vast majority of the population but also the government and Max Weber. They all believed in the ability of the military to prevent a political catas-

of the highest-ranking Prussian officials and those of the most vociferous academic critic of the Empire's authoritarian structure provide a useful review of the Empire's course and of alternatives too late considered. The government's statement is less penetrating than Weber's analysis, but it is interesting as an official review of the prewar policy of isolating the Social Democrats, of the wartime policy of cooperating with them and of the growing awareness of the need for reform; Weber's analysis is particularly pertinent because it argues for the imperative necessity of introducing parliamentary government within the monarchy.

In February 1918, the Prussian Minister of the Interior, Drews, sent a memorandum to William II.[26] Reviewing the government's prewar policies, he pointed out that the Social Democrats had stood outside the "national life," and that "politics"—i.e., to him, the government—had to lead "the various forces in the country with changing methods and means in the fight against Social Democracy." In peacetime the "political leadership" had derived "great tactical advantages" from pitting itself "unconditionally" against the Social Democrats. After the outbreak of the war the Social Democrats became the major problem of domestic politics. They were now "part of the national life" and strengthened the military position of the Reich. Cooperation with them had, however, the disadvantage that "for the duration of the war the attitudes of a radical party have to be taken into account." Right-wing groups would welcome a new isolation of the Social Democrats, but the government, Drews advised, should avoid or delay a break with the party during the war. Even at that late hour the minister believed that, if necessary, the government could defeat the Social Democrats in any open conflict. Less than ten months before the outbreak

---

trophe by avoiding military defeat. The population was victimized by a system of propaganda and censorship which preserved the image of military strength until the very end; this image had a realistic element until the arrival of masses of American troops on the continent by the middle of 1918.

26 Reproduced in the appendix of Volkmann, *op. cit.*, 291–306.

of the revolution, he saw no danger because "civil and military power in Prussia-Germany rests on solid foundations, and the sound, order-loving sense of the German bourgeoisie is not as susceptible to revolutionary infections as is the case with our eastern and western neighbors."

The developments within the labor movement during the war, Drews continued, made the government's policy of cooperation increasingly difficult. The Social Democrats resumed the "demands which the government and the parliamentary majority had successfully resisted for decades." Had the war been short, the Social Democrats would have continued their policy of cooperation undisturbed. However, the party was more than any other party dependent on the mood of the masses; their enthusiasm had determined the party's attitude on the fourth of August, 1914. But the mounting dissatisfaction of the masses slowly weakened the party's patriotic stand and resulted in a split in which the minority adopted the old Social Democratic program. Drews explained to the Emperor that the Social Democratic leadership was convinced it could hold the party on a "positive national" line if the government were willing to make concessions in domestic politics and would clearly show its willingness to make peace. However, the split of the party forced the Majority Socialists to compete with the radical minority for the allegiance of the masses. For the government, the split of the party meant that dormant problems of social and political reform had to be faced once more. Drews argued in favor of a reform of the Prussian three-class suffrage because the Social Democrats would have to be able, after the war, to justify their patriotic policy to the masses. Drews realized that the abolition of the three-class suffrage, which had been a major aim of the party for decades, linked the masses and the party. He charged that the right-wing parties were responsible for the delay in the introduction of reforms, which had to be pronounced if consensus on foreign policy were to be preserved. Apart from the issue of electoral reform, he considered food shortage to have the most serious effect on the masses.

Food shortage was the primary reason for the people's urgent desire for peace. The problem was particularly grave in Berlin, but Drews considered it unlikely that the Berlin workers would riot or stop work spontaneously—again, only a few months before it happened.[27]

In the summer of 1917 Max Weber exposed the Empire's weaknesses in a series of articles in the influential liberal *Frankfurter Zeitung*.[28] His views sharply contrasted with the government's and Hintze's belief in the viability and superiority of monarchic constitutionalism under the given German conditions. Weber's critique proceeded from his basic belief that the bureaucratization of modern life was universal and inevitable, at the same time that politics would always be a struggle for power. The supreme challenge, then, was the preservation of individual freedom and, related to it, the continuous regeneration of capable political leadership. The viability of a political system was dependent on its ability to produce political leaders. Therefore, the survival and power interests of Germany had to be more important than any commitments to specific political forms. The gravest weakness of the German political system was government through conscientious and competent bureaucrats, who failed as political leaders. German bureaucracy could proudly point to great administrative achievements, but the victories of the military bureaucracy during the war could at best only compensate for the political weakness of government by bureaucrats. Bureaucratic government, and not rule by autocracy, was the basic flaw of the German system. In fact the modern con-

---

[27] Bebel was more perspicacious: he predicted in the Reichstag on Dec. 7, 1905, that in case of a war of Germany against France and England food shortage would drive the people into rebellion. In the same speech he also presaged the downfall of the prevailing political order if Germany engaged in a war which included the United States. See *Reichstag Protocols*, 158 B.

[28] Max Weber, "Parlament und Regierung im neugeordneten Deutschland," *Gesammelte politische Schriften* (Tübingen: Mohr, 1958), 294–431. This book-length essay is an enlargement of the articles and one of Weber's most important political writings. The essay was published in the summer of 1918.

stitutional monarch could not be an autocrat in the strict sense of the word, since he was unable to control the powerful bureaucracy. He was no specialist and no politician. And yet, in Germany, the temptation for the monarch to enter the political arena was great, for he was only confronted by the bureaucracy and not by a strong parliament. Despite the "personal regime" of the Emperor, the actual ruler was the bureaucracy—uncontrolled and responsible to no one, since it justified its power with the legitimacy of the monarch, just as Bismarck had done. "Monarchic government" in Germany and Russia descended to the level of perpetual departmental struggles, with personal intrigues abounding. In a parliamentary system these struggles are more open to inspection and control.

Rule by bureaucrats was a legacy of Bismarck, who had suppressed all political talents. He left Germany without political education; the level of public political sophistication was lower in 1890 than in 1870. Contrary to customary accusations that parliament was powerless because of its incompetence, it could not raise its level because it was powerless. Under "monarchic government" the qualified leaders were driven elsewhere to seek a realm of freedom for their energies and capabilities—in particular, to industry. Contrary to prevailing prejudice, parliament actually had had quite a few outstanding leaders and still had potential leaders. Weber relates from his personal experience that the older leaders accepted Caesarism as long as a politician of Bismarck's magnitude ruled, but that they wanted to strengthen parliament under his successors. They did not succeed largely because Bismarck destroyed the possibilities for a clear majority party. Weber points to a significant generational difference: National unification became of supreme emotional importance for the generation that followed its achievement, more so than for the participating generation that went through the tensions of achieving it. The generation of writers after 1878 extolled Bismarck's shrewdness and brutality, not his better characteristics. The same literati who exalted Bismarck rejected parliamentarism because of its inherent demagoguery and recklessness. However, in Germany there had been demagoguery and mass influence without democracy—because of the absence of institutionalized democracy. Bismarck himself was a master of demagogic and other reckless methods. Even his welfare legislation had a demagogic basis, consisting as it did of a primitive concept of eliciting gratitude. He transposed the Prussian Constitutional Conflict to the Reich level by keeping the issue of military appropriations alive in order to weaken the Reichstag. He manipulated the issue of the tariffs and of the antisocialist legislation. The inappropriate methods used to fight the Catholic church resulted in a devastating defeat for the authority of the state; the antisocialist legislation destroyed the unions, "the only working-class institutions capable of a sombre representation of interests." The workers were driven into the

most extreme radicalism of pure party politics. . . . In the treatment of the unions one point was overlooked, a point that even today some politicians have not yet understood: a state that wants to base the spirit of its mass army on honor and solidarity must not forget that in everyday life and in the economic struggles of the workers the sentiments of honor and solidarity are the only decisive moral forces for the education of the masses. This and nothing else means "social democracy" in purely political terms.[29]

Weber considered parliamentarism indispensable because it was the only means to control the bureaucracy and to produce capable political leadership. He was, therefore, interested in awakening public understanding for the preconditions of effective parliamentarism. The German system of "monarchic government" militated against the selection of capable leaders because the highest positions were subject to bureaucratic advancement and to accidental connections with the court. Some bureaucrats had the capabilities required for political leadership, but the sense of political independence was not encouraged in a bureaucracy. Under mo-

[29] Weber, *op. cit.,* 306.

narchic constitutionalism party politics was merely the representation of local interests and a struggle for subordinate patronage. Even this struggle went on behind closed doors, exemplified by the Center party's patronage system in the federal agencies. Job patronage existed in other political systems as well, but in Germany it did not result in the selection of leaders qualified to lead the nation. Contrary to Hintze, who rejected the liberal view of the Government as being in fact a conservative party rule, Weber pointed out that since 1878 the impartiality of the bureaucracy simply means that only conservatives can be *Landräte* (district heads) in Prussia, that "every government and its representatives must necessarily be 'conservative,' merely tolerating some concessions to the patronage of the Prussian bourgeoisie and of the Center." [30]

In Germany, Weber continues, parliament appears as the natural enemy of the government, as an harassment of the bureaucracy and as a body of "ignorant demagoguery" and "routinized impotence" because the structure of the diet permits only negative or passive politics: critique, complaint, and the rejection, modification and passing of the budget and of bills presented by the government. Party leaders have to abandon their seats and leadership in parliament if they take a position in the federal government or on the Federal Council, representing the states. Thus, both parliament and the leader concerned are weakened. Parliament is further handicapped by its inability to overcome the hurdle of administrative secrecy.

The introduction of parliamentarism not only was resisted by the court, the government and big business, but it also met resistance from the parties and parliament. The parties had been trained by Bismarck to be negative forces and were unable to agree on a positive program to be submitted to the monarch. Party bureaucracies were resentful of strong political leaders. The Center's au-

[30] Cf. Weber, *op. cit.*, 351 and Hintze, *op. cit.*, 382.

thoritarian wing was akin to the spirit of the bureaucracy. The largest party, the Social Democratic party, was the least willing to take on governmental responsibility. However, the willingness to accept responsibility was a precondition of effective parliamentarism.

The Social Democrats were handicapped by "pseudorevolutionary" conventions from the antisocialist period and by "evolutionist" theories. Most important, however, was the fear of the leaders of repudiation by the rank and file if they should openly cooperate with the government. "This situation motivated the leaders to keep the party for decades in a kind of political ghetto, in order to avoid any kind of contaminating contact with the workings of bourgeois state mechanisms. Despite appearances, they do this even now." Weber was aware of the leader's dilemma: On the one hand, the war greatly strengthened syndicalism, "the unpolitical and antipolitical heroic ethos of brotherhood"; on the other, the Imperial bureaucracy might revert to its old policies after the war.[31] Weber agreed with the Social Democratic leaders that the returning soldiers must have the right to participate in postwar political and economic reconstruction. Universal and equal suffrage and a strong parliament were necessary if Germany were to acquire a government with solid domestic support, capable of safeguarding the interests of the nation in a critical world situation.

Max Weber's critique was fortified by a superlative sociological understanding of political systems, their preconditions and their consequences. However, he did not claim the support of social science for his political views. He knew that parliamentary democracy and its recruitment of leaders had their own difficulties and unanticipated consequences, but he was willing to stake the nation's fate on his perception of the relative superiority of parliamentary democracy over monarchic constitutionalism in an age of precipi-

[31] Weber, *op. cit.*, 354.

tous rationalization and aggravated power struggles. He knew very well that empirical arguments cannot decisively influence ultimate values. His reform proposals represented the viewpoint of a distinct minority, which was thwarted by the powers-that-be until catastrophe engulfed defenders and opponents of the dominant system.

XII
Conclusions

When established national communities undergo the early stages of industrialization, they are confronted with the problem of the political and social integration of the emergent industrial work force. Theories of industrialization, whether Marxist or not, have usually stressed its inherent dynamics in creating labor protest; only recently have they given greater attention to the political and cultural context of industrialization and labor protest. This has been owing, in particular, to the impact of events in newly developing countries. However, the same recurrent problems of labor protest had to be faced in one way or another by European countries when they were passing through the early stages of economic development.

In the history of Europe the two extreme solutions for the problem of lower-class integration have been England and Russia. In the former integration was accomplished under a parliamentary system of government which acceded step by step to labor's demand for formal political equality and a greater share in the national product. Class conflict was ameliorated because of this accommodation. In Russia an authoritarian monarchy insisted on the complete subordination of employers and workers. An independent class-conscious labor movement was not tolerated to any significant extent. Popular protest was finally focussed on the very institution of Tsarist autocracy which nominally claimed responsibility for the welfare of the people. An underground organization of professional revolutionaries adhering to a voluntaristic interpretation of Marxism developed. In the wake of external military defeat, this minority of the labor movement succeeded in mobilizing peasant discontent and in launching a total revolution.

Imperial Germany constitutes a complex intermediate case between England and Russia. Labor protest did not develop at first, as in England, into a trade union movement which supported the liberals for a long time and created a parliamentary labor party only after the turn of the century; nor did it evolve in the direction of a revolutionary underground movement as in Imperial Russia. The German labor movement was a response to political conditions turning the movement itself into the major champion of parliamentary democracy and isolating it as a class-conscious subculture.

1. Descriptive Summary

At the beginning of German industrialization, the liberal bourgeoisie strove for a constitutional state with more or less parliamentary prerogatives. However, class consciousness based on property and education made the liberals hesitant about or hostile toward the political participation by large numbers of workers on terms of equality. The vicissitudes of the struggle against the authoritarian monarchy reinforced this inclination of the liberal middle classes. Only by a policy of compromise with the militarily superior monarchy could the liberals participate in the cherished task of national unification and at least indirectly influence the government. The liberal attitudes alienated a small group of politically interested and active workers; their class consciousness was sensitized by the liberal class-conscious policies. An independent class-conscious labor movement came into being when this small group of workers joined its meager forces with isolated radical-democratic, antiliberal intellectuals. (Chapter II.)

Parliamentary government was incompatible with the particular authoritarianism of the monarchy. Under a system of monarchic constitutionalism the government was appointed by the monarch and shared responsibility with him, but not with parliament. Against the liberal and later Social Democratic demand for parliamentary government, this constitutional arrangement was defended with the traditionalist legitimacy of the monarch and, pragmatically, with requirements of military effectiveness and with the heterogeneity of Prussia and the Empire. A large and independent liberal party and, even more so, a rapidly growing Social Democratic labor movement appeared to Bismarck and his successors as a major threat to the balance of power under monarchic constitutionalism. Bismarck's policy of splitting the liberals and of suppressing the Social Democrats was also based on a long-run perspective of revolutionary dangers which the rise of the masses entailed for "civilized" European society. These two perceptions prevented a recognition of the limited revolutionary potential of the Social Democrats and of any realistic attempt at their integration. After Bismarck's attempt at suppression had failed, a policy of isolation helped to preserve the intransigence of the Social Democrats. (Chapter III.)

Two central issues came to characterize the cleavage between the bourgeoisie and the labor movement, the issues of revolution and patriotism. These—and, to a lesser degree, the issue of idealism versus materialism—resulted in high-pitched rhetorical exchanges between the spokesmen for both sides. The rhetorical antagonism was to some extent self-perpetuating, but underlying it was a basic disagreement about national unification through Prussia. The achievement of national unification satisfied what had been for many middle-class persons the most important demand and seemed to entail for others so many benefits as to justify a continued acceptance of Bismarck's setup of the Empire. For the Social Democrats national unification through Prussia appeared to be either outright pernicious or at best a very doubtful advance. The intensity of feelings of exaltation and affirmation, on the one hand, and of resentment and disdain, on the other, was bound to exacerbate the class cleavage. (Chapter IV.)

Given the basic structure of the authoritarian state and the resulting impasse of the Social Democrats, the antagonistic discourse between the spokesmen of the government and the labor movement continued unabated for half a century. The Emperor, his chancellors and high-ranking civil servants did not waver in their public display of hostility toward the Social Democrats, who responded in kind. Both sides clung to their intransigent rhetoric even though the government gradually abandoned all serious attempts at suppression and even though the labor movement became progressively more involved in reformist activities. This habitual rhetoric reflected a basic value conflict as well as the strategic requirements arising for both sides from the structure of the constitutional system. The rhetoric reinforced the immobility of the political dividing line, which, late in the period, was sometimes rigidly preserved less from serious conviction than for tactical expediency. (Chapter V.)

Trends toward the amelioration of the class cleavage did not effect a basic change. A part of the higher-ranking civil service was reform-minded and succeeded in introducing major welfare legislation. The academic social reformers labored to assess the dynamics of an industrializing society and to impress government and public with the necessity of some reforms. However, both groups remained very distant from the Social Democrats, condemning their unwillingness to cooperate with those in power. The evolution of some states toward parliamentarism did not significantly influence power conditions on the federal level and in Prussia. A trend toward recognizing the personal respectability of the Social Democrats and the disciplinary value of an organized labor movement did not extend to the crucial holders of power. A young liberal generation, which was less antagonistic to the labor movement, did not mature before the First World War broke out. Whatever long-run potential for significant political change these ameliorative tendencies may have possessed, they did not come to fruition during the life-span of the Empire. (Chapter VI.)

A major manifestation of the class cleavage was the development of a large and self-contained Social Democratic subculture, embodying a way of life for masses of workers. The mixture of permissive and repressive conditions characteristic of the dominant system made a moderate practice advisable, but it also encouraged the adherence to a radical though deterministically attenuated Marxist ideology. This relative attenuation did not make it less objectionable to the opponents of the Social Democrats. Deterministic Marxism "corresponded" to the prevailing rigid power conditions, but its adoption was very slow; it became important as a means of ideological defense no less than attack. It justified the reliance on "automatic" social developments and on moderate practices in general. However, it involved increasing strains for the movement. It prevented its appeal beyond proletarian strata, and it was bound to create a conflict between those who wanted to pursue a more reformist path and those who demanded a more radical course. (Chapter VII.)

The official Marxism constituted only part of the meaning which the labor movement had for the workers. Many of them absorbed it in an inevitably simplified and vulgarized form, which often protected them against the realization of social and ideological complexities and sometimes exposed them to the frustrations of inadequate comprehension. The rank and file recognized the party leaders as their spokesmen, but vulgar Marxist beliefs do not seem to have overcome a tendency to be skeptical toward the leaders' vision of radical social reconstruction. Many workers were anxious to prove themselves sober and respectable. The Social Democratic subculture gave them an opportunity to experience the moral sentiments of solidarity in collective action; it provided them with many satisfactions not available to them in society. This compensated for their sense of social inferiority and of second-class citizenship. (Chapter VIII.)

However, the influence of the political and cultural norms of the dominant system remained strong and pervasive, especially through the agencies of elementary school, army service and newspapers. A dual loyalty was typical of the Social Democratic workers. The cultural exertions of the Social Democrats were extraordinary, but many cultural activities actually reinforced the workers' adherence to significant components of the dominant culture. The leaders were committed to the improvement of their followers' cultural level; they hoped that cultural activities would strengthen their attachment to the political cause of the movement, yet most leaders were culturally quite conservative. Library and lecture programs were extensive, but interest was often limited to nonsocialist topics. The socialist press was doctrinaire, and since it had a strong intra-party orientation, it furthered the self-containment of the movement. (Chapter IX.)

The labor movement's rapid expansion after 1890 made the organizational maintenance of party and unions more and more complex. The Social Democratic unions, resurrected primarily as mutual insurance societies, very soon concentrated upon organizational strength rather than upon agitation. However, the party reorganized its rapidly obsolescent apparatus only after 1905 according to the technical requirements of a mass movement. Bureaucratization and embourgeoisement do not appear to have caused its growing difficulties in the last years before the First World War. Many leaders and proletarian members had always been culturally petty-bourgeois; the masses of followers were not more radical than the leaders; and the intellectuals got along relatively well with the proletarian functionaries. Contrary to Robert Michels' emphasis, I support the point of view that the party's crisis was not due primarily to the predominance of organizational interests in survival and "self-maintenance" over allegedly older, radical aspirations. Its dilemma was more strategic than organizational: the top leaders' strategy of "self-maintenance" as well as the alternatives advocated by the right and left appeared unable, in the near future, to change the national balance of power. (Chapter X.)

At the beginning of the First World War the labor movement was integrated, in a strictly subordinate fashion, into the national community. Initially the leaders supported the government because they feared its repressive power, considered the war to be defensive, and were confronted with rank and file enthusiasm. Very important was the leaders' hope that the support of the war efforts might overcome the stagnation of democratization. However, disillusionment soon spread and resulted in the split of the labor movement. In order to highlight the internal reasons for the downfall of the Empire, I contrasted the Prussian government's perception of its own peace and wartime policies with Max Weber's wartime critique of monarchic constitutionalism, which required, in his opinion, a no less radical cure than its replacement with parliamentary rule. The latter came about only after the Empire's military defeat, which was aggravated by the legacy of the class cleavage. Labor did achieve a precarious formal equality in the new republic. (Chapter XI.)

2. Negative Integration and Historical Alternatives

In 1913, when Vilfredo Pareto was at work on his *Trattato di sociologia generale,* the Zabern incident occurred.[1] He discussed it as a particular case of the general problem of the use of force. Interested as he was in the stability of social systems and the unintended consequences of social action, he contrasted French and German sentiments and the political systems of the two countries. He observed that under the "Latin condition" the people are always right, the army always wrong, and that under "the Germanic condition . . . people whose nerves are affected by the mere glimpse of a soldier had better stay indoors."[2] The Dreyfus affair polarized French political life and threatened the stability of the Third Republic; the protest of the Reichstag majority about the Zabern incident could not shake the German government. And the French government fell in December 1913 as a result of a belated left-wing revenge over the prolongation of military service.

1 On the Zabern incident, see p. 286, above.
2 Vilfredo Pareto, *The Mind and Society,* A. Livingston, ed. (New York: Harcourt, Brace, 1935), 1489. By permission of the publisher.

French left-wingers were incensed about the Zabern affair as well as about their own government's armament policies. Pareto pointed out that their antimilitarism was unintentionally harmful to the international interests of democracy vis-à-vis the authoritarian interests of Imperial Germany. In contrast, the German militarists strengthened their system by vigorously upholding the army's Zabern action. However, in looking for unintended consequences of their actions, he noticed that they were also weakening their system by creating a crisis of allegiance. Pareto concluded that "both the defenders of the Latin condition and the defenders of the Germanic condition entirely disregard the quantitative problem": Are intermediary conditions (C, instead of A and B) possible?—i.e., instead of the prevailing French and German conditions.[3]

Pareto wanted to make sociology scientific in the quantitative and predictive sense. He believed that a strictly value-neutral, "logico-experimental" approach could establish social laws and social uniformities. Yet complex political systems have remained beyond the grasp of successful quantitative and predictive treatment, and judgments on the degree of social stability and on the extent of unintended consequences are unavoidably subjective and controvertible. However, Pareto's general approach to the stability and flexibility of political systems and to the problem of unintended consequences is pertinent for us. We have to assess the relative viability of monarchic constitutionalism and of conflict regulation through isolation and negative integration. Logically, this also requires a consideration of historical alternatives, a mental projection whose analytical necessity and legitimacy have been established ever since Max Weber and the renowned historian Eduard Meyer carried out their memorable controversy about its methodological adequacy.[4] Max Weber's own option for parliamentary government under the monarchy, for example, was an

---

[3] *Ibid.*, 1494.
[4] Cf. Part III of *The Methodology of Max Weber,* E. A. Shils and H. A. Finch, eds. and transl. (Glencoe: Free Press, 1949).

attempt to establish "an intermediate state, C," in Pareto's words, that "might perhaps better than A or B assure the attainment of the purposes aimed at by defenders of the two extremes." In particular, we must face the question of alternative developments because the First World War and Germany's military defeat cannot be considered historically inevitable, although on hindsight they do not appear to be surprising events.[6]

The authoritarian monarchy was stable as long as it was not defeated externally; its traditional legitimacy and military power were reinforced by the achievement of national unification and rapid industrialization. At the same time monarchic constitutionalism was a concession to the forces of democratization, although it was granted more from a position of strength than of weakness. Bismarck made constitutional compromises in 1867 and again in 1871, when he took his two decisive steps toward national unification.[7]

[5] Pareto, *loc. cit.*

[6] Cf. Robert Kann on the questionable inevitability of the breakdown of the Double Monarchy in 1918: "The last link in the chain of causation that led to the dissolution of the dual empire was unquestionably the First World War. A good deal about the reasons for its outbreak is known of course, including both the active and passive share of Austria-Hungary in bringing about the catastrophe. Yet nobody has succeeded or probably ever will succeed in proving the logical inevitability of the great conflagration. . . . Actually, the World War in itself was not even the last phase of . . . disintegration. The Habsburg monarchy was technically intact until the two last weeks of October 1918. . . . No conscientious analyst of these fateful events is able to eliminate the powerful effect of seeming accidentals on those stormy happenings." *The Habsburg Empire: A Study in Integration and Disintegration* (New York: Praeger, 1957), 23. By permission of the publisher.

[7] Significantly these compromises with the liberals were never made in the spirit of the British upper-class mentality expressed in a remark of Lady Dorothy Nevill to H. M. Hyndman about incipient working-class organization: "The turn of the people will come some day, I see that quite as clearly as you do. But not yet, not yet. You will educate some of the working class . . . and when you have educated them, we shall buy them, or, if we don't, the Liberals will. Besides we shall never offer any obstinate or bitter resistance . . . when your agitation becomes really serious we shall give way a little . . . our object is to avoid any direct conflict in order to gain time." Quoted in Anne Fremantle, *op. cit.*, 25 f.

To this extent monarchic constitutionalism proved flexible. Although its logic did not permit major concessions toward parliamentarism, more basic reasons explain the unwillingness and inability of Bismarck and his successors to modify the system. It is true that a dominant system cannot be expected to prepare for the eventuality of its own military defeat, but after all, a higher degree of integration of the working class, accomplished through appropriate concessions during peacetime, might have saved Imperial Germany altogether in 1918. It may be fair to say that Bismarck's basic assumption—the irreconcilability of parliamentarism with the survival interests of the monarchy and the Empire—proved as fatal for his edifice as it did for his career. Despite his sense for *Realpolitik* his long-range vision was blurred by ideological preconceptions. After 1945, when he became once again particularly controversial, Hans Rothfels conceded his failure to understand the peaceful protest character of the Social Democrats and the complexity of Marxian theory, but reasoned that, after the experience of Bolshevism and Nazism, this failure can no longer be seen as just a natural outcome of a reactionary class bias. Behind the labor movement, Rothfels argues, Bismarck sensed the danger of popular dictators carried into power by the masses, the spectre of totalitarianism—in his words: the union of Jacobins and Cossacks.[8] I agree that Bismarck, as well as many conservatives and liberals, had indeed a premonition of things to come; but theirs was also a self-fulfilling prophecy in that they contributed substantially to the rise of the totalitarian movements of later decades by taking an uncompromising stand against their democratic opponents, especially the Social Democrats. They eventually drove the most radical wing of the Social Democrats to establishment of the Communist party; the hostility and hatred against the labor movement and parliamentarism, instilled over decades into the right-wing middle

[8] See Rothfels, ed., *op. cit.,* XLVII.

classes, became one of the major sources of Nazi sentiment after the fall of the Empire.

The phenomenon of negative integration emerged in a situation in which neither the transition to parliamentarism nor the complete repression of the labor movement appeared feasible. The Reichstag was constitutionally weak, but its mere existence constituted an inherent restraint on the government. This became clear when Bismarck attempted to tamper with his life's work and to precipitate a *coup d'état*. The edifice he had created proved not only resistant to liberal reconstruction, as he wanted it to be, but also to reconstruction along more authoritarian lines. The government did not dare to tear apart the web of reciprocity it had established with the Reichstag over two decades, and without sufficient voting strength in the diet it felt incapable of completely suppressing the labor movement. The compulsion of circumstances dictated a conscious policy of tolerating the labor movement in a state of isolation. Thus a class-conscious Social Democratic subculture based on legal mass organization was free to develop.

The subculture was "negatively" integrated into the dominant system because by its very existence it provided an important means for the controlled expression and dissipation of conflict and thus contributed, for decades of peacetime, to the stability of the Empire. Specifically, the Social Democratic subculture furthered political moderation and industrial discipline in the following way: (a) It gave the workers the political and social recognition which the dominant system denied them. (b) Radicalism was greatly weakened because both the individual Social Democrat in his industrial job and the party as a whole had to be careful not to provoke retaliatory measures or an intensification of repressive policies. Because of the permissive aspects of the dominant system, party and unions had an overriding interest in legality and therefore strove to protect themselves against complete suppression by fighting Blanquist and anarchist tendencies. (c) With the expansion of the labor movement, more and more workers were taught by their own representatives to accept the necessity of authority, discipline, skill and good work performance. Social Democratic workers endeavored to prove to themselves and to others that radical political aims and personal respectability were not mutually exclusive. (d) Indirectly the Social Democratic labor movement enforced better living and working conditions by its mere presence and thus promoted reformist moderation and industrial peace, even though the unions could not negotiate with big business and even though the Social Democrats did not cooperate on welfare legislation.

The peculiar combination of repression and permissiveness resulting in negative integration also had significant consequences at the moment of Imperial Germany's military defeat. It may be suggested that by refraining from any persistent attempt at complete suppression the dominant system encouraged the labor movement to stay on a relatively moderate path; this facilitated the survival of important social, economic and even political components of the old regime—bureaucracy, army, right-wing parties—after its political debacle. During the lifetime of the Empire the labor movement's democratic-parliamentary commitments were reinforced by the advantages of legality. When the Empire collapsed the labor movement had no concrete economic and social alternatives to offer. The long years of isolation within a powerful system had discouraged any concern with social reconstruction after its downfall. When called upon to take responsibility for the country, the old Social Democratic party (Majority Socialists) retained much of the established order, and the Minority Socialists retreated to the old stance of opposition. Only the numerically weak extreme left wanted a total revolution, but had no mass support for it.

If there had been no war, some democratization on the federal level and in Prussia might have occurred in the long run; the fact that the reformist tendencies—analyzed in Chapter VI—were not strong enough to change the basic structure of the Empire as long as it actually lasted, does not exclude this possibility. The Prussian three-class suffrage was a formidable roadblock, and its disappearance was not likely in the near future; symbolically it was the most important indicator of the second-class or, literally, the "third-class" citizenship of the workers. However, this very importance might have heightened the effect of any suffrage concessions. With a modicum of reform, the dominant system might have been able to continue the check on the labor movement long enough to force the greater part of it into abandoning the stance of radical opposition and into adopting a clear position of loyal opposition or even cooperation. Economically, such a development was, of course, dependent on a rising national income, a higher standard of living for the workers, and especially a continuous increase of the tertiary industries and the new middle classes, vitiating the Social Democratic hopes of "automatic" victory. Thus, negative integration might have become positive integration, although on a more unequal basis than in England.

A victorious outcome of the war would have greatly strengthened the dominant system, resulting in substantial material benefits to the working class and probably also in some political concessions granted from a position of benevolent strength; but a peace founded on compromise might have led to even greater concessions. Improvements in the areas of parliamentary rights, collective bargaining, state arbitration of labor disputes, and work and leisure conditions could have resulted at first in a boom for the cultural activities of the labor movement, as was to happen after the First World War despite the continued economic hardships and political convulsions. With the basic political cleavage substantially narrowed, a greater spread of economic wealth and the rise of mass media of entertainment, including spectator sports, might have gradually dissolved the Social Democratic subculture and turned the party into a purely parliamentary one. After another historical catastrophe, this, too, finally happened in the West Germany of the 1950's, the decade of the triumph of middle-class parliamentary democracy.

How should the Social Democrats be adjudged in the light of

these historical developments and speculative alternatives? The socialist millennium never arrived. Many Social Democrats sincerely believed in its imminence, although it is unclear—and possibly beyond historical reconstruction—whether their revered leader August Bebel really did, despite his voluble assurances. At any rate, most Social Democrats, whether for or against Eduard Bernstein, *acted* as if they considered "the movement everything, the goal nothing"; the existence and welfare of the movement, the advancing of material working-class interests and the struggle for piecemeal democratization were concrete goals and realistic values, while the socialist millennium and, even more so, a "glorious revolution" were above all anti-ideals pitted against the official values of Imperial Germany. As an intransigent opposition aiming at the seizure of power, the movement was a failure; as an embodiment of social protest, it was a splendid achievement of the working class; as an instrument of social reform its success was very limited, but the latter role became its major one after the two world wars. Its later successes on the municipal, state and (more limited) federal levels are relevant here in view of the historic continuity of the movement, which is now just 100 years old—older than any other German party.

For half a century the party has represented one-third of the electorate on the federal level but never substantially more. The ideological antagonism of a century ago is still a potent historical legacy, despite all political changes and ideological adjustments.[9] The charges of Max Weber and other liberals are probably correct that through its original self-conscious and class-conscious isolation the Social Democratic movement perpetuated the power of the con-

[9] In the 1961 federal elections in the Federal Republic of Germany, many voters cast a protest vote against the aging "bourgeois Bismarck," Chancellor Adenauer, by supporting the Liberal-Conservative party (FDP), an amalgam of progressive and conservative traditions from the Empire and the Weimar Republic and of former Nazis; many of them did not vote for the Social Democrats, who had considerably modernized and mitigated their program, because they still considered them "Red" and harbored some of the same old stereotypes about the party as were current during the Empire.

servative and the illiberal forces. However, as this analysis has endeavored to demonstrate, the ideological antagonism was fully reciprocal. The Social Democrats and their bourgeois and governmental adversaries were trapped by their ideological pre-conceptions and habitual rhetoric, which thwarted the modicum of give and take that might have prevented the later historical disasters.

The eruption of ideological commitments into mass violence might not have occurred without the international catastrophe of the First World War. The war became decisive for the relations between the German—and the Russian—labor movements and the established political systems, whereas it played a much less important role in England and France. The Scandinavian countries, spared by the First World War, provide perhaps the best vantage point for assessing Imperial Germany on this score. In them the pressures for a large standing army and increasing armaments were considerably weaker. But even under these favorable conditions it took democratization about half a century—up to the end of the First World War—to reach the stage of full universal suffrage and full parliamentary government. In Denmark, for example, a conserv-ative government ruled for two decades, from 1876 on, without parliamentary appropriations, far longer than Bismarck did during the Constitutional Conflict in Prussia. But in a different interna-tional and military context the long-range consequences were less detrimental to democratization than in Imperial Germany. In Nor-way, by contrast, the issue of national independence helped rather than hindered democratization, probably because of the absence of major international complications and military pressures.

For the current theories of industrialization and democratiza-tion a relevant *caveat* emerges from this analysis. The prevailing theories are largely based on the internal developments of sev-eral countries. In the case of West Germany, two world wars "recti-fied" her conformity to the theory that the problem of working-class protest is "best" solved by the integration of the lower classes into the pluralist system of a highly industrialized country. The two wars destroyed the old aristocracy and the *terribles simplificateurs* whom Jacob Burckhardt expected with sad premonition; "middle-class elites" rule undisputed. To an onlooker who did not know that the two wars had interfered, it might seem that the intrinsic forces of industrialization had brought about this result. Sketched broadly and viewed over the full span of a century, the German case fits the theory of an inherent "logic of industrialism" advanced by Clark Kerr and others. With successful economic development, labor protest seems to decline, the "end of ideology" to approach, and bureaucratic skirmishes between big organizations to prevail over the conflict of classes with one another and the state. It is true that at the end of the reviewed period, which comprises only half a century, Germany had barely reached the stage of "economic maturity," in W. W. Rostow's terms, and was far from the "age of high mass-consumption." But it was already clear that labor protest would not pose a cumulative threat and that a very precarious accommodation and very unequal integration of the labor movement were sufficient to diminish the danger of a revolutionary challenge. However, such long-run perspectives tend to lack explanatory power in any given case because they blur the impact of ideologies, institutional legacies and international events. These three factors largely determine the struggle for democratization. Just like industrialization, democratization does not appear to have determinate consequences. The lower-class challenge may be checked by various degrees of national integration on the basis of equality, inequality or isolation; only in case of persistent failure does the likelihood of total revolution increase.

Finally, the relative degree of integration even within a pluralist system should be kept clearly in mind, lest the more obviously unequal forms of integration be misperceived. The two basic conceptions of democracy, which separated the right and left of German Social Democracy and partly also its historians, are relevant here.

Democracy may be defined as a system of institutional arrangements permitting the bloodless change of governments, the assertion and balancing of group interests and the protection of civil liberties. This conception—sometimes called Schumpeterian—is increasingly affirmed among political sociologists. According to it, Weimar Germany and the United States appear as model cases of democratic systems, disregarding the criterion of stability. The other conception of democracy is older and more formal and goes back to Rousseau's "general will," which does not permit organized interest groups and parties. In historical reality there have been, on the whole, only quasi-Rousseauan systems manipulating the "general will"; they have been plebiscitarian, Caesarist and eventually totalitarian in the sense of the *Volksgemeinschaft* and of Stalinism. Communist "democracy" today implies the absence of large landowners, shareholders and corporation managers and the integration of the working class into a system run by a new class of functionaries. From a Communist perspective the Germanies of Bismarck, Weimar and Bonn, as well as the United States, appear as reactionary capitalist countries which repress the working class by spurious forms of integration.

Pluralist theoreticians themselves have not been blind to the dangers of too complete a political integration and have also dealt extensively with the problem of how to preserve individual liberty in the age of the Big Organization with its total claim on the individual. George Orwell and some critics of American corporate mass society have seen the beginnings of a new totalitarianism in their countries which integrated the lower classes on a formally equal basis. As far as many newly developing countries are concerned, the difficulties of national integration—due to a multitude of cultural, ethnic and economic factors—seem to invite authoritarian "solutions." Thus the highly developed as well as the newly developing countries continuously face recurrent problems of national integration and individual liberty. In this context Imperial Germany and her negative integration of the working class should be seen as one important instance of the struggle for democratization in a rapidly industrializing world.

3. *A Personal Postscript*

> In propounding this or that theory an author as a rule wants other people to assent to it and to adopt it—in him the seeker after experimental truth and the apostle stand combined. . . . If one's aim is to inspire or reinforce certain sentiments in men, one must present facts favorable to that design and keep unfavorable data quiet. But if one is interested strictly in uniformities, one must not ignore any fact that may in any way serve to disclose them. . . . We keep open house to all facts, whatever their character, provided that directly or indirectly they point the way to discovering a uniformity.
>
> —Pareto, *Trattato* [10]

In the course of my research I have been as impressed with the difficulties of establishing "uniformities" or generalizations as I have been with the thinness of the line between academic analysis and moral judgment. As the study advanced I began to reflect increasingly upon my own scholarly and political presuppositions and conclusions.

As a member of a generation which was very early forced into political awareness by living through Germany's totalitarian regime

[10] Pareto, *op. cit.*, 44 f.

during an increasingly devastating war, my first questions about German history were inevitably directed toward the search for the causes of the historical catastrophe. I was reared, in my early teens, to respect Ebert and Scheidemann, Rathenau and Stresemann as men who, despite their faults, had been statesmen and responsible politicians in contrast to the rulers of the day. After the war, I intensified my readings in German history; I was particularly impressed by the dire prophecies on Germany's future essayed a century ago by the great poet and critic Heinrich Heine, whose outlawed volumes had remained on the family bookshelves until incendiary bombs destroyed them toward the end of the war. Rejecting wiser family counsel, I began to sympathize, with youthful fervor, with the left wing of the Social Democratic party in Imperial Germany; I believed that the socialist left should have succeeded in 1918/19. I was also convinced that a massive denazification program could prevent a repetition of the right-wing developments that had occurred after the First World War. Eventually, however, I began to comprehend the dictatorial and totalitarian implications of a brand of anti-fascism that would have excluded indefinitely a substantial part of the population from the process of democratic government. Research on the failure of the American denazification program helped me to understand the difference between the requirements of political purges necessary for political reconstruction and moral retribution transcending the realm of mechanical institutional change. Moralistic and legalistic American traditions were in part responsible for this failure.[11]

American writers on the history of the German labor movement have combined a traditionally liberal exasperation with obstacles standing in the way of a democratic society, beyond the Anglo-Saxon realm, with a tendency to be more sympathetic toward the German radical left than toward the convinced Social Democratic believers in

[11] Cf. Guenther Roth and Kurt H. Wolff, "The American Denazification of Germany." *Studies in German-American Postwar Problems.* No. 1, Dept. of Sociology, Ohio State University, 1954, 46 pp. (mimeo.).

parliamentary democracy.[12] Such a view appears to me permissible only if based on the assumption that a left-wing dictatorship in 1918/19—disregarding for the moment its historical impossibility —would have made German history less bloody for outsiders in subsequent years. The facts of Nazism provide a powerful moral perspective for German history, but it is neither fair to past generations nor analytically adequate to view this history solely with the questionable wisdom of hindsight.

When I began my research, my own perspective of the history of the German labor movement was strongly affected by German self-recrimination and conventional American perspectives. But gradually I came to change my views. I tried to arrive at a more balanced and detached view, influenced by the positivistic injunctions of an American graduate education and perhaps also by the soothing atmosphere of the Pacific Coast, far removed from Germany in time and space. Looking over the completed study, I find myself more sympathetic to the right and the center of the Social Democratic movement than to the left. In fact, a historical daydream opposite to the one behind the older literature might emerge from my own work. If the Empire could have been saved and if a major conservative and right-wing liberal crisis of legitimacy could have been averted by establishing parliamentarism within the monarchy rather than a democratic republic, neither Communism nor Nazism might have triumphed. Disregarding many other historical forces and pushing the historical fantasy to its limits, even the chances for a Second World War and a subsequent Cold War might have been slimmer. This is the hopeful "right-wing" utopia —actually voiced in part by British statesmen from Winston

---

[12] Cf. Klaus Epstein's very perceptive review of the works by Joseph Berlau, Peter Gay and Carl Schorske in *World Politics,* XI, 1959, 629–51. Epstein indicates that American historians find it difficult, given the fortunate history of the United States, to empathize with a country that seemed to be overwhelmed with "insoluble" problems. The contemporary plight of France may create the necessary empathy more easily than Imperial Germany.

Churchill to Clement Attlee—[13] which contrasts with the hopeful "left-wing" utopia of other writers. If this could have been "bought" with the continued existence of a distasteful Hohenzollern monarchy, boisterous Junkers and supercilious civil servants (though parliamentarism would presumably have mellowed them), it appears a small historical price.

A skeptic might retort that the heterogeneity of the Empire was so great that Bismarck's Germany, unified with "blood and iron," could perhaps have been preserved without monarchic constitutionalism only by an extremely nationalist appeal to all strata of the population. Imperial Germany, he might concede, could have developed into a parliamentary system, but at the price of intensified nationalism once again subordinating the working class. Or he might point out that a successful national unification under a parliamentary system in 1848 might have created a nationalist and expansionist Germany, compared to which the Germany of Bismarck's policies was relatively restrained. In the worst case, the end effect of such hypothetical developments might have been not too dissimilar from the Nazi *Volksgemeinschaft*.

It is indeed not easy to avoid a deterministic view of social structure and historical legacies, but my study of Imperial Germany and of her Social Democrats has endeavored to preserve a sense for the capacity of individuals and groups to change some parts of their lives as well as for the fateful persistence of social structures and the unpredictable uniqueness of historical events.

---

[13] See Winston Churchill, *The Gathering Storm* (Boston: Houghton Mifflin, 1948), 10 f, and the more indirect remark by Clement Attlee in the House of Commons on July 9, 1952, quoted in Edward Shils and Michael Young, "The Meaning of the Coronation," *Sociological Review*, I, 1963, 64.

Bibliography

1. Protocols

Protokoll der Verhandlungen des fünften Kongresses der Gewerkschaften Deutschlands, Cologne, 1905 (Berlin: Verlag der Generalkommission, n.d.).

Protokolle über die Verhandlungen des Parteitages der Sozialdemokratischen Partei (Berlin: Vorwärts, 1890–1913).

Stenographische Berichte über die Verhandlungen des Reichstag (Berlin: Norddeutsche Buchdruckerei und Verlagsgesellschaft, 1869–1914).

Verhandlungen. Schriften des Vereins für Sozialpolitik, vol. 116, 1906.

2. Autobiographies, Memoirs, Letters, Collected Works Biographies and Monographs on Major Participants

Adler, Victor, *Briefwechsel mit August Bebel und Karl Kautsky*, Friedrich Adler, ed. (together with Parteivorstand der Sozialistischen Partei Österreichs) (Vienna: Volksbuchhandlung, 1954).

Auer, Ignaz, *Nach zehn Jahren* (Nuremberg: Fränkische Verlagsanstalt, 1913).

(Bassermann, Ernst)
   Eschenburg, Theodor, *Bassermann und die Blockpolitik*, Ph.D. dissertation, University of Berlin, 1929.

Bebel, August, *Aus meinem Leben* (Berlin: Dietz, 1946), 3 vols.
   Gerlach, Hellmuth von, *August Bebel: Ein biographischer Essay* (Munich: Langen, 1909).
   Michels, Robert, "August Bebel," *Archiv für Sozialwissenschaft*, vol. 37, 1913, 671–700.

(Bennigsen, Rudolf von)

Oncken, Hermann, *Rudolf von Bennigsen: Ein deutscher liberaler Politiker, nach seinen Briefen und hinterlassenen Papieren* (Stuttgart: Deutsche Verlagsanstalt, 1910).

Berlepsch, Hans Freiherr von, *Sozialpolitische Erfahrungen und Erinnerungen* (Mönchengladbach: Volksvereinsverlag, 1925).

Bernstein, Eduard, *Sozialdemokratische Lehrjahre* (Berlin: Bücherkreis, 1928).

Bismarck, Otto von, *Bismarck und der Staat: Ausgewählte Dokumente,* Hans Rothfels, ed. (Stuttgart: Kohlhammer, 1953), 2nd ed.

Id., *Die gesammelten Werke,* Gerhard Ritter and Rudolf Stadelmann, eds. (Berlin: Deutsche Verlagsgesellschaft, 1932), vol. 15.

Id., *Die politischen Reden des Fürsten Bismarck,* H. Kohl, ed. (Stuttgart: Cotta, 1905), vol. 13.

Id., *Gedanken und Erinnerungen* (Stuttgart: Cotta, 1921), 3 vols.

Braun, Lily, *Memoiren einer Sozialistin* (Munich: Langen, 1909).

Vogelstein, Julie, "Lily Braun: Ein Lebensbild," in L. Braun, *Gesammelte Werke* (Berlin: Klemm, 1923).

Brentano, Lujo, *Mein Leben im Kampf um die soziale Entwicklung Deutschlands* (Jena: Diederichs, 1931).

Barich, Werner, *Lujo Brentano als Sozialpolitiker.* Ph.D. dissertation, University of Frankfurt, 1936.

Bröger, Karl, *Der Held im Schatten* (Jena: Diederichs, 1930).

Bromme, William, *Lebensgeschichte eines modernen Fabrikarbeiters,* Paul Göhre, ed. (Jena: Diederichs, 1905).

Bülow, Bernhard Fürst von, *Memoirs of Prince von Bülow* (Boston: Little, Brown, 1931/32).

Bürgel, Bruno, *Vom Arbeiter zum Astronom* (Berlin: Druckhaus Tempelhof, 1929).

Buttinger, Joseph, *In the Twilight of Socialism* (New York: Praeger, 1953).

(Delbrück, Hans)

Thimme, Annelise, *Hans Delbrück als Kritiker der Wilhelminischen Epoche* (Düsseldorf: Droste, 1955).

Ebert, Friedrich, *Schriften,* Paul Kampffmeyer, ed. (Dresden: Reissner, 1926).

Peters, Max, *Friedrich Ebert* (Berlin: Arani, 1950).

Frank, Ludwig, *Aufsätze, Reden und Briefe,* Hedwig Wachenheim, ed. (Berlin: Verlag für Sozialwissenschaft, 1924).

Hohenlohe-Schillingsfürst, Fürst Chlodwig zu, *Denkwürdigkeiten der*

Reichskanzlerzeit, A. von Müller, ed. (Stuttgart: Deutsche Verlagsanstalt, 1931).

Holek, Wenzel, *Lebensgang eines Handarbeiters* (Jena: Diederichs, 1930).

Id., *Vom Handarbeiter zum Jugenderzieher* (Jena: Diederichs, 1921).

Holstein, Friedrich von, *The Holstein Papers,* Norman Rich and M. H. Fisher, eds. (London: Cambridge University Press, 1955).

Kardorff, W., *Wilhelm von Kardorff,* Siegfried von Kardorff, ed. (Berlin: Mittler, 1936).

Kautsky, Karl, *Erinnerungen und Erörterungen,* Benedikt Kautsky, ed. (The Hague: Mouton, 1960).

Id., *Friedrich Engels Briefwechsel mit Karl Kautsky,* Benedikt Kautsky, ed. (Vienna: Wiener Volksbuchhandlung, 1955).

Keil, Wilhelm, *Erlebnisse eines Sozialdemokraten* (Stuttgart: Deutsche Verlagsanstalt, 1949), 2 vols.

Lassalle, Ferdinand, *Gesammelte Reden und Schriften,* Eduard Bernstein, ed. (Berlin: Cassirer, 1919), vols. 1–3.

Id., *Nachgelassene Briefe und Schriften,* Gustav Mayer, ed. (Stuttgart: Deutsche Verlagsanstalt, 1921–25), six vols.

Footman, David, *Ferdinand Lassalle: Romantic Revolutionary* (New Haven: Yale University Press, 1947).

Lukacs, Georg, "Die neue Ausgabe von Lassalle Briefen," *Grünbergs Archiv für die Geschichte des Sozialismus und der Arbeiterbewegung,* XI, 1925, 414.

Oncken, Hermann, *Lassalle* (Stuttgart: Deutsche Verlagsanstalt, 1920), 3rd ed.

Ramm, Thilo, *Ferdinand Lassalle als Rechts-und Sozialphilosoph* (Vienna: Westkulturverlag, 1953).

(Liebknecht, Karl)

Meyer, Karl W., *Karl Liebknecht* (Washington: Public Affairs Press, 1957).

Liebknecht, Wilhelm, *Karl Marx* (Chicago: Kerr, 1904).

(Lohmann, Theodor)

Rothfels, Hans, *Theodor Lohmann und die Kampfjahre der staatlichen Sozialpolitik* (Berlin: Mittler, 1927).

(Luxemburg, Rosa)

Frölich, Paul, *Rosa Luxemburg* (Paris: Editions Nouvelles Internationales, 1939).

de Man, Hendrik, *Gegen den Strom: Memoiren eines europäischen Sozialisten* (Stuttgart: Deutsche Verlagsanstalt, 1953).

Marx, Karl and Friedrich Engels, *Marx-Engels Gesamtausgabe*, V. Adoratsky, ed. (Berlin: Marx-Engels Verlag, 1931), vols. III:3 and III:4 (Correspondence).

Korsch, Karl, *Karl Marx* (London: Chapman, 1938).

Mayer, Gustav, *Friedrich Engels* (The Hague: Nijhoff, 1934), 2 vols.

Meinecke, Friedrich, *Erinnerungen: 1901–1919* (Stuttgart: Koehler, 1949).

(Miquel, Johannes von)

Herzfeld, Hans, *Johannes von Miquel* (Detmold: Meyer, 1938).

(Mommsen, Theodor)

Heuss, Alfred, *Theodor Mommsen und das 19. Jahrhundert* (Kiel: Hirt, 1956).

(Most, Johann)

Nomad, Max, "Johann Most, Terrorist of the Word," in id., *Apostles of Revolution* (Boston: Little, Brown, 1939).

(Naumann, Friedrich)

Heuss, Theodor, *Friedrich Naumann* (Stuttgart: Deutsche Verlagsanstalt, 1957).

Nürnberger, Richard, "Imperialismus, Sozialismus und Christentum bei Friedrich Naumann," *Historische Zeitschrift,* vol. 170, 1950, 525–48.

Shanahan, W., "Friedrich Naumann: A German View of Power and Nationalism," in Edward Mead Earle, ed., *Nationalism and Internationalism* (New York: Columbia University Press, 1950), 352–98.

Id., "Friedrich Naumann: A Mirror of Wilhelmian Germany," *The Review of Politics,* 13:3, July 1951, 267–301.

Noske, Gustav, *Erlebtes aus Aufstieg und Niedergang einer Demokratie* (Offenbach: Bollwerk-Verlag, 1947).

Oldenburg-Januschau, Elard von, *Erinnerungen* (Leipzig: Koehler, 1936).

Popp, Adelheid, *Autobiography of a Working Woman* (London: Unwin, 1912).

(Posadowsky-Wehner, Graf von)

Penzler, Johannes, *Graf Posadowsky als Finanz-, Sozial-und Handelspolitiker* (Leipzig: Weber, 1907/8), 2 vols.

Wiese, Leopold von, *Graf Posadowsky als Sozialpolitiker* (Cologne: Christlicher Gewerkschaftsverlag, 1909).

Scheidemann, Philipp, *Memoiren eines Sozialdemokraten* (Dresden: Reissner, 1928).

Scheu, Andreas, *Umsturzkeime: Erlebnisse eines Kämpfers* (Vienna: Wiener Volksbuchhandlung, 1923), 3 vols.

(Schweitzer, Johann Baptist von)
Mayer, Gustav, *Johann Baptist von Schweitzer* (Jena: Fischer, 1909).

Sender, Toni, *The Autobiography of a German Rebel* (New York: Vanguard Press, 1939).

Severing, Carl, *Mein Lebensweg* (Cologne: Greven, 1950), 2 vols.

Stein, August (pseudonym: Irenaeus), *Aufsätze* (Frankfurt: Frankfurter Societätsdruckerei, 1921).

(Stresemann, Gustav)
Miethke, Franz, *Gustav Stresemann als Wirtschaftspolitiker* (Dresden: Sächische Verlagsanstalt, 1919).

(Stumm-Halberg, C. F.)
Hellwig, Fritz, *Carl Ferdinand Freiherr von Stumm-Halberg* (Heidelberg: Westmarck Verlag, 1936).

Vahlteich, Julius, *Ferdinand Lassalle und die Anfänge der deutschen Arbeiterbewegung* (Munich: Birk, n.d., ca. 1902/3).

(Max Weber)
Bendix, Reinhard, *Max Weber: An Intellectual Portrait* (Garden City: Doubleday, 1960).

Bergsträsser, Arnold, "Max Webers Antrittsvorlesung in zeitgeschichtlicher Perspektive," *Vierteljahrshefte für Zeitgeschichte*, V:3, 1957, 209–19.

Mommsen, Wolfgang, *Max Weber und die deutsche Politik. 1890–1920* (Tübingen: Mohr, 1959).

Winnig, August, *Das Reich als Republik* (Stuttgart: Cotta, 1928).

Wolff, Theodor, *Through Two Decades* (London: Heinemann, 1936).

3. Contemporary Academic and Political Literature 1848–1918

Anonymous, "Parteibetrachtungen eines Frontsoldaten," *Der Kampf*, vol. 10, 1917, 163–66.

Bauer, Otto, "Die Geschichte eines Buches," *Neue Zeit*, vol. 26:I, 1908, 23–33.

Bebel, August, *Akademiker und Sozialismus* (Berlin: Verlag Sozialistische Monatshefte, 1906), 2nd ed.

Id., *Die Frau und der Sozialismus* (Stuttgart: Dietz, 1910), 50th ed.

Bernstein, Eduard, *Die Voraussetzungen des Sozialismus und die Aufgaben der Sozialdemokratie* (Stuttgart: Dietz, 1909); English edition: *Evolutionary Socialism* (New York: Huebsch, 1909).

Id., *Geschichte der Berliner Arbeiterbewegung* (Berlin: Vorwärts, 1907), 3 vols.

Id., "Von der Sekte zur Partei," *Zeitschrift für Politik,* vol. 3, 1910, 498–551.

Blank, R., "Die soziale Zusammensetzung der sozialdemokratischen Wählerschaft Deutschlands," *Archiv für Sozialwissenschaft,* vol. 20, 1905, 507–50.

Brandt, Alexander von, *Zur sozialen Entwicklung im Saargebiet* (Leipzig: Duncker, 1904).

Braun, Adolf, "Bildungsprobleme in der Arbeiterbewegung," *Der Kampf,* vol. 8, 1915, 240–50.

Id., "Die Intellektuellen und die Politik," *Neue Zeit,* 27:2, 1909, 847–53.

Id., "Realismus und Utopismus in den Gewerkschaften," *Der Kampf,* vol. 8, 1915, 42–47.

Brentano, Lujo, "Arbeitseinstellungen und die Fortbildung des Arbeitsvertrags," *Schriften des Vereins für Sozialpolitik,* vol. 47, 1890, 119–30.

Brunhuber, Robert, *Die heutige Sozialdemokratie* (Jena: Fischer, 1906).

Calwer, Richard, "Englands Absichten und die deutsche Sozialdemokratie," *Sozialistische Monatshefte,* XI, 1905, 919–22.

Daniels, Emil, "Ein vergessenes Dokument zur Geschichte der Freiheitskriege," *Preussische Jahrbücher,* vol. 144, 1911. 256–64.

Danneberg, Robert, "Die Ergebnisse sozialdemokratischer Bildungsarbeit," *Der Kampf,* vol. 8, 1915, 272–89.

David, Eduard, "Die Eroberung der politischen Macht," *Sozialistische Monatshefte,* X, 1904, 9–18.

Id., *Die Sozialdemokratie im Weltkriege* (Berlin: Vorwärts, 1915).

Deutsche Industriezeitung, 1871, 1877, published by the Chambers of Commerce in Chemnitz, Dresden, Plauen and Zittau.

Dühring, Eugen, *Cursus der National- und Socialökonomie* (Berlin: Grieben, 1873).

Id., *Kritische Geschichte der Nationalökonomie und des Sozialismus* (Leipzig: Naumann, 1900), 4th rev. ed.

Engels, Friedrich, *Anti-Dühring.* Special volume of the *Marx-Engels-Gesamtausgabe* (Moscow: Marx-Engels Verlag, 1935).

Erdmann, August, *Die Sozialdemokratie im Urteile ihrer Gegner* (Berlin: Vorwärts, 1911).

Freese, Heinrich, *Die konstitutionelle Fabrik* (Jena: Fischer, 1922).

Id., "Empfindsame Sozialpolitik," *Preussische Jahrbücher*, vol. 85, 1896, 135–48 and 379–81.

Geithner, Otto, "Zur Taktik der Sozialdemokratie," *Neue Zeit*, 23:2, 1905, 656–62.

Göhre, Paul, *Drei Monate Fabrikarbeiter* (Leipzig: Grunow, 1891).

Günther, Adolf, *Die Wohlfahrtseinrichtungen der Arbeitgeber. Schriften des Vereins für Sozialpolitik*, vols. 112–14, 1905.

Hänisch, Konrad, *Die deutsche Sozialdemokratie in und nach dem Weltkriege* (Berlin: Schwetschke, 1916).

Haym, Rudolf, *Die deutsche Nationalversammlung: Ein Bericht aus der Partei des rechten Zentrums* (Frankfurt: Jügel, 1849), 2 vols.

Held, Adolf, *Die deutsche Arbeiterpresse der Gegenwart* (Leipzig: Duncker, 1873).

Hellpach, Wilhelm, *Nervenleben und Weltanschauung* (Wiesbaden: Bergmann, 1906).

Herkner, Heinrich, *Die Arbeiterfrage* (Berlin: Guttentag, 1908), 5th ed.

Hintze, Otto, "Das monarchische Prinzip und die konstitutionelle Verfassung," *Preussische Jahrbücher*, vol. 144, 1911, 381–412.

Lenin, V. I., *Extracts and Marginal Notes on Hegel's Science of Logic* (Moscow: Marx-Engels Institute, 1932).

Liebknecht, Wilhelm, ed., *Der Hochverratsprozess wider Liebknecht, Bebel, Hepner* (Berlin: Vorwärts, 1894).

Id., *Wissen ist Macht—Macht ist Wissen* (Leipzig: Genossenschafts-buchdruckerei, 1873).

Marx, Karl, *Capital* (New York: The Modern Library, 1936).

Id. and Friedrich Engels, *Basic Writings on Politics and Philosophy*, Lewis S. Feuer, ed. (Garden City: Doubleday, 1959).

Mehring, Franz, *Die Sozialdemokratie* (Bremen: Schünemann, 1878) 2nd ed.

Michels, Robert, "Die deutsche Sozialdemokratie im internationalen Verbande," *Archiv für Sozialwissenschaft*, vol. 25, 1907, pp. 148–231.

Id., *Soziologie des Parteiwesens* (Stuttgart: Kroner, 1957); English edition: *Political Parties* (New York: Collier, 1962).

Müller, Hans, *Der Klassenkampf in der deutschen Sozialdemokratie* (Zürich: Verlags-Magazin, 1892).

Naumann, Friedrich, *Demokratie und Kaisertum* (Berlin: Hilfe, 1900).

Id., *Die politischen Parteien* (Berlin: Hilfe, 1910).

Ostrogorski, M., *Democracy and the Organization of Political Parties* (London. Macmillan, 1902).

Pareto, Vilfredo, *The Mind and Society,* Arthur Livingston, ed. (New York: Harcourt, Brace, 1935), 4 vols. This is the translation of the *Trattato di sociologia generale,* first published in 1916.

Post, Julius and H. Albrecht, *Musterstätten persönlicher Fürsorge von Arbeitgebern für ihre Geschäftsangehörigen* (Berlin: Oppenheim, 1893), 2 vols.

Richter, Eugen, *Sozialdemokratische Zukunftsbilder, frei nach Bebel* (Berlin: Verlag Forschritt, 1893).

Riehl, Wilhelm, *Die bürgerliche Gesellschaft* (Stuttgart: Cotta, 1930), first published in 1851.

Riesser, J., *Der Hansabund* (Jena: Diederichs, 1912).

Rösicke, Richard, "Über das Verhältnis der Arbeitgeber zu ihren Arbeitnehmern," *Jahrbuch für Gesetzgebung,* vol. 7. 1893, 1–22.

Russell, Bertrand, *German Social Democracy* (London: Longmans, Green, 1896).

Schäffle, Albert, *The Quintessence of Socialism* (London: Sonnenschein, 1896).

Schmoller, Gustav von, "Der Weltkrieg und die deutsche Sozialdemokratie," *Schmollers Jahrbuch,* vol. 39, 1915, 1–12.

Id., "Die englische Gewerkvereinsentwickelung im Lichte der Webbschen Darstellung," *Schmollers Jahrbuch,* vol. 25, 1901, 291–314.

Id., *Zur Sozial-und Gewerbepolitik der Gegenwart* (Leipzig: Duncker, 1890).

Id., *Zwanzig Jahre deutscher Politik: 1897–1917* (Munich: Duncker, 1920).

Schröder, Wilhelm, *Geschichte der sozialdemokratischen Parteiorganisation in Deutschland* (Dresden: Kaden, 1912).

Schücking, Lothar, *Die Reaktion in der inneren Verwaltung Preussens* (Berlin: Hilfe, 1908).

Schuster, Richard, *Die Social-Demokratie, nach ihrem Wessen und ihrer Agitation quellenmässig dargestellt* (Stuttgart: Steinkopf, 1875).

Stein, Lorenz von, *Geschichte der sozialen Bewegung in Frankreich von 1789 bis auf unsere Tage* (Darmstadt: Wissenschaftliche Buchgesellschaft, 1959), 3 vols., first published in 1848–50.

Ströbel, Heinrich, "Gewerkschaften und 'sozialistischer Geist,'" *Neue Zeit*, 23:2, 1905, 561–69.

Thimme, Friedrich and Carl Legien, eds., *Die Arbeiterschaft im neuen Deutschland* (Leipzig: Hirzel, 1915).

Tocqueville, Alexis, *The Old Regime and the French Revolution* (Garden City: Doubleday, 1955), first published in 1856.

Treitschke, Heinrich von, "Der Sozialismus und seine Gönner," *Preussiche Jahrbücher*, vol. 34, 1874, 67–110 (also published by Reimer, Berlin, 1875).

Vorster, Julius, "Die Sozialpolitik des Herrn Heinrich Freese in Berlin," *Preussische Jahrbücher*, vol. 85, 1896, 371–79.

Weber, Max, "Parlament und Regierung im neugeordneten Deutschland," *Gesammelte politische Schriften*, Johannes Winckelmann, ed. (Tübingen: Mohr, 1958), 2nd ed., 294–431, written in 1917/18.

Id., Remarks on Blank, *op. cit.*, *Archiv für Sozialwissenscraft*, vol. 20, 1905, 550–53.

Id., *Wirtschaft und Gesellschaft*, Johannes Winckelmann, ed. (Tübingen: Mohr, 1956), 4th ed.

Id., *The Methodology of Max Weber*, E. A. Shils and H. A. Finch, eds. and transl. (Glencoe: Free Press, 1949).

4. Post-1918 Literature on the Labor Movement and Socialism

Anderson, Evelyn, *Hammer or Anvil* (London: Gollancz, 1945).

Balser, Frolinde, *Sozial-Demokratie 1848/49–1863* (Stuttgart: Klett, 1962), 2 vols.

Berlau, A. J., *The German Social Democratic Party: 1914–1921* (New York: Columbia University Press, 1949).

Brandis, Kurt, *Die deutsche Sozialdemokratie bis zum Fall des Sozialistengesetzes* (Leipzig: Hirschfeld, 1931).

Drahn, Ernst, "Sozialdemokratie," *Handwörterbuch der Staatswissenschaften*, vol. 7, 1926.

Drexel, E., "The Communist Presence in France," *American Political Science Review*, L:2, 1956, 321–38.

Epstein, Klaus, "Three American Studies of German Socialism," *World Politics*, XI:4, 1959, 629–51.

Flechtheim, Ossip, *Die KPD in der Weimarer Republik* (Offenbach: Drott, 1948).

Freemantle, Anne, *This Little Band of Prophets: The British Fabians* (New York: Mentor Book, 1960).

Gay, Peter, *The Dilemma of Democratic Socialism: Eduard Bernstein's Challenge to Marx* (New York: Columbia University Press, 1952).

Goldenberg, Boris, *Beiträge zur Soziologie der deutschen Vorkriegssozialdemokratie*, Ph.D. dissertation, University of Heidelberg, 1932.

Heidegger, H., *Die deutsche Sozialdemokratie und der nationale Staat: 1879–1920* (Göttingen: Musterschmitt, 1956).

Hilferding, Rudolf (pseudonym: Richard Kern), "Revolutionärer Sozialismus," *Zeitschrift für Sozialismus*, I:5, 1935, 145–52.

Huhn, Willy, "Etatismus, 'Kriegssozialismus', 'Nationalsozialismus' in der Literatur der deutschen Sozialdemokratie," *Aufklärung*, II:3, 1952, 162–79 and II:4, 264–88.

Kampffmeyer, Paul and Bruno Altmann, *Vor dem Sozialistengesetz* (Berlin: Der Bücherkreis, 1928).

Kantorowicz, Ludwig, *Die sozialdemokratische Presse Deutschlands* (Tübingen: Mohr, 1922).

Kautsky, Karl, "Natur und Gesellschaft," *Gesellschaft*, 1929:2, 481–505.

Koch, Max, *Die Bergarbeiterbewegung im Ruhrgebiet zur Zeit Wilhelms II: 1889–1914* (Düsseldorf: Droste, 1954).

Korn, Karl, *Die Arbeiterjugendbewegung* (Berlin: Arbeiterjugend-Verlag, 1922).

Korsch, Karl, *Marxismus und Philosophie* (Leipzig: Hirschfeld, 1930).

Landauer, Carl, *European Socialism* (Berkeley and Los Angeles: University of California Press, 1959) 2 vols.

Laub-Coser, Rose, *An Analysis of the Early German Socialist Movement*, M.A. thesis, Columbia University, 1951.

Maehl, William, "Recent Literature on the German Socialists, 1891–1932," *The Journal of Modern History*, XXXIII:3, 1961, 292–306.

Id., "The Triumph of Nationalism in the German Socialist Party on the Eve of the First World War," *The Journal of Modern History*, XXIV, 1952, 15–41.

de Man, Hendrik, *The Psychology of Socialism* (New York: Holt, 1927).

Marks, Harry J., "The Sources of Reformism in the Social Democratic

Party of Germany, 1890–1914," *The Journal of Modern History*, XI:3, 1939, 334–56.

Matthias, Erich, "Kautsky und der Kautskyanismus: Die Funktion der Ideologie in der deutschen Sozialdemokratie vor dem ersten Weltkrieg," in Iring Fetscher, ed., *Marxismusstudien* (Tübingen: Mohr, 1957), vol. II, 151–97.

Mayer, Gustav, "Der Allgemeine Deutsche Arbeiterverein und die Krisis 1866," *Archiv für Sozialwissenschaft*, vol. 57, 1927, 167–75.

Id., "Die Trennung der proletarischen von der bürgerlichen Demokratie," *Grünbergs Archiv*, II, 1912, 1–67.

Neufeld, M. E., *Italy: School for Awakening Countries. The Italian Labor Movement in Its Political, Social, and Economic Setting from 1800 to 1960* (Ithaca: Cornell University Press, 1961).

Popp, Adelheid, Der Weg zur Höhe (Vienna: Frauenzentralkomitee der Sozialdemokratischen Arbeiterpartei Deutschösterreichs, 1929).

Posse, Ernst, *Der Marxismus in Frankreich 1871–1905* (Berlin: Prager, 1930).

Prager, Eugen, *Geschichte der USPD* (Berlin: Freiheit, 1921).

Pribram, Karl, "Deutscher Nationalismus und deutscher Sozialismus," *Archiv für Sozialwissenschaft*, vol. 49, 1922, 298–376.

Ritter, Gerhard A., *Die Arbeiterbewegung im Wilhelminischen Reich: 1890–1900* (Berlin: Colloquiumverlag, 1959).

Rosenberg, Arthur, *A History of Bolshevism: From Marx to the First Five Years' Plan* (London: Oxford University Press, 1934).

Schorske, Carl E., *German Social Democracy 1905–1917: The Development of the Great Schism* (Cambridge: Harvard University Press, 1955).

Schumpeter, Joseph, *Capitalism, Socialism and Democracy* (New York: Harper, 1947) 2nd ed.

Shuchman, Abraham, *Codetermination: Labor's Middle Way in Germany* (Washington: Public Affairs Press, 1957).

Sloan, Henry S., *The German Social Democrats in the Reichstag Elections of 1912*, M.A. thesis, New York University, 1952.

Sombart, Werner, *Der proletarische Sozialismus* (Jena: Fischer, 1924), 10th ed., 2 vols.

Varein, Heinz Josef, *Freie Gewerkschaften, Sozialdemokratie und Staat: Die Politik der Generalkommission unter der Führung Carl Legiens: 1890–1920* (Düsseldorf: Droste, 1956).

Wagner, Richard, *Geschichte der Kleiderarbeiter in Österreich im 19.*

Jahrhundert und im ersten Viertel des 20. Jahrhunderts (Vienna: Gewerkschaft der Kleiderarbeiter Österreich, 1930).

Wolff, Hertha, *Die Stellung der Sozialdemokratie zur deutschen Arbeiterversicherungsgesetzgebung von ihrer Entstehung bis zur Reichsversicherungsordnung,* Ph.D. dissertation, University of Freiberg, 1933.

5. Background Literature on the Period 1848–1918

Anderson, Eugene N., *The Social and Political Conflict in Prussia: 1858–1864* (Lincoln: The University of Nebraska, 1954).

Bergsträsser, Ludwig, *Geschichte der politischen Parteien in Deutschland* (Munich: Isar Verlag, 1955).

Boberach, Heinz, *Wahlrechtsfragen im Vormärz. Die Wahlrechtsanschauung im Rheinland 1815–1849 und die Entstehung des Dreiklassenwahlrechts* (Düsseldorf: Droste, 1959).

Boese, Franz, *Geschichte des Vereins für Sozialpolitik: 1872–1939. Schriften des Vereins für Sozialpolitik,* vol. 188, 1939.

Briggs, Asa, "The Language of 'Class' in Early Nineteenth-Century England," in id., ed., *Essays in Labor History in Memory of G. D. H. Cole* (London: Macmillan, 1960), 43–73.

Id., *Victorian People* (Chicago: University of Chicago Press, 1955).

Churchill, Winston, *The Gathering Storm* (Boston: Houghton Mifflin, 1948).

Clapham, J. H., *The Economic Development of France and Germany: 1815–1914* (London: Cambridge University Press, 1936).

Craig, Gordon A., *The Politics of the Prussian Army: 1640–1945* (New York: Oxford University Press, 1956).

Darmstaedter, F., *Germany and Europe: Political Tendencies from Frederick the Great to Hitler* (London: Methuen, 1945).

Decker, Georg, "Krise des deutschen Parteisystems," *Gesellschaft,* 1926:1, 1–16.

Demeter, Karl, *Das deutsche Offizierskorps in seinen historisch-soziologischen Grundlagen* (Berlin: Hobbing, 1930).

Id., "Die soziale Schichtung des Deutschen Parlamentes seit 1848, ein Spiegelbild der Strukturwandlung des Volkes," *Vierteljahrschrift für Sozial-und Wirtschaftsgeschichte,* vol. 39:1, 1–29.

Dietzel, Hans, *Die preussischen Wahlreformbestrebungen von der*

Oktroyierung des Dreiklassenwahlrechts bis zum Beginn des Weltkrieges, Ph.D. dissertation, University of Cologne, 1934.

Gagel, Walter, *Die Wahlrechtsfrage in der Geschichte der deutschen liberalen Parteien: 1848–1918* (Düsseldorf: Droste, 1958).

Gerschenkron, Alexander, *Bread and Democracy in Germany* (Berkeley and Los Angeles: University of California Press, 1943).

Gollwitzer, H., "Der Cäsarismus Napoleons III. im Widerhall der öffentlichen Meinung Deutschlands," *Historische Zeitschrift,* vol. 173, 1952, 23–75.

Gooch, G. P., *Germany and the French Revolution* (London: Longmans, 1920).

Gulick, Charles A., *Austria from Habsburg to Hitler* (Berkeley and Los Angeles: University of California Press, 1949), 2 vols.

Hallgarten, G. W. F., *Imperialismus vor 1914* (Munich: Beck, 1951), 2 vols.

Heffter, H., *Die deutsche Selbstverwaltung im 19. Jahrhundert* (Stuttgart: Koehler, 1950).

Herzfeld, Hans, "Berlin als Kaiserstadt und Reichshauptstadt, 1871–1945," *Jahrbuch für die Geschichte des deutschen Ostens,* vol. I, 1952, 141–70.

Holborn, Hajo, "Der deutsche Idealismus in sozialgeschichtlicher Beleuchtung," *Historische Zeitschrift,* vol. 174, 1952, 359–84.

Horkheimer, Max, "Die Philosophie der absoluten Konzentration," *Zeitschrift für Sozialforschung,* VII, 1938, 376–87.

Hughes, H. Stuart, *Consciousness and Society: The Reorientation of European Social Thought: 1890–1930* (New York: Knopf, 1958).

Kehr, Eckart, "Das soziale System der Reaktion unter dem Ministerium Puttkamer," *Gesellschaft,* 1929:2, 253–74.

Id., *Schlachtflottenbau und Parteipolitik: 1894–1901* (Berlin: Ebering, 1930).

Ir., "Zur Genesis des Kgl. preussischen Reserveoffiziers," *Gesellschaft,* 1928:2, 492–502.

Klass, Gert von, *Krupps: The Story of an Industrial Empire* (London: Sidgwick and Jackson, 1954).

Knoll, Joachim, *Führungsauslese in Liberalismus und Demokratie* (Stuttgart: Schwab, 1957).

Kruck, Alfred, *Geschichte des alldeutschen Verbandes: 1890–1939* (Wiesbaden: Steiner, 1954).

Kupisch, Karl, *Vom Pietismus zum Kommunismus* (Berlin: Lettner, 1953).

Langsam, Walter Consuelo, "Nationalism and History in the Prussian Elementary Schools under William II," in Edward Mead Earle, ed., *Nationalism and Internationalism* (New York: Columbia University Press, 1950), 241–260.

Märcker, Georg, *Vom Kaiserheer zur Reichswehr* (Leipzig: Koehler, 1921).

Marcuse, Herbert, "Über den affirmativen Charakter der Kultur," *Zeitschrift für Sozialforschung,* VI, 1937, 54–94.

Massing, Paul W., *Rehearsal for Destruction: A Study of Political Anti-Semitism in Imperial Germany* (New York: Harper, 1949).

Mommsen, Wilhelm, *Stein, Ranke, Bismarck: Ein Beitrag zur politischen und sozialen Bewegung des 19. Jahrhunderts* (Munich: Bruckmann, 1954).

Nicolai, W., *Nachrichtendienst, Presse und Volksstimmung im Weltkrieg* (Berlin: Mittler, 1920).

Pack, Wolfgang, *Das parlamentarische Ringen um das Sozialistengesetz Bismarcks 1878–1890* (Düsseldorf: Droste, 1961).

Pinson, Koppel S., *Modern Germany, Its History and Civilization* (New York: Macmillan, 1954).

Poschinger, H. R. von, *Fürst Bismarck und die Parlamentarier* (Berlin: Trewendt, 1894).

Reinhardt, Kurt F., *Germany: 2,000 Years* (New York: Ungar, 1961), vol. II.

Ritter, Emil, *Die katholisch-soziale Bewegung Deutschlands im neunzehnten Jahrhundert und der Volksverein* (Cologne: Bachem, 1954.)

Ritter, Gerhard, *Der Schlieffenplan: Kritik eines Mythos* (Munich: Oldenbourg, 1956).

Id., *Staatskunst und Kriegshandwerk: Das Problem des 'Militarismus' in Deutschland* (Munich: Oldenbourg, 1954).

Rosenberg, Arthur, *The Birth of the German Republic: 1871–1918* (London: Oxford University Press, 1931).

Rosenberg, Hans, *Bureaucracy, Aristocracy and Autocracy: The Prussian Experience* (Cambridge: Harvard University Press, 1958).

Saitschick, Robert, *Bismarck und das Schicksal des deutschen Volkes* (Basel: Reinhardt, 1949).

Samuel, R. H. and R. H. Thomas, *Education and Society in Modern Germany* (London: Routledge, 1949).

Sartorius von Waltershausen, A., *Deutsche Wirtschaftsgeschichte: 1815–1914* (Jena: Fischer, 1932), 2nd ed.

Schilfert, Gerhard, *Sieg und Niederlage des demokratischen Wahlrechts in der deutschen Revolution 1848–1849* (Berlin: Ruetten, 1952).

Schwenger, Rudolf, *Die betriebliche Sozialpolitik in der westdeutschen Grosseisenindustrie. Schriften des Vereins für Sozialpolitik,* vol. 186, 1934.

Shanahan, William O., *German Protestants Face the Social Question: The Conservative Phase: 1815–1871* (University of Notre Dame Press, 1954), vol. I.

Simon, Walter, *The Failure of the Prussian Reform Movement: 1807–1819* (Ithaca: Cornell University Press, 1955).

Stern, Alfred, *Der Einfluss der Französischen Revolution auf das deutsche Geistesleben* (Stuttgart: Cotta, 1928).

Sternheim, Andries, "Zum Problem der Freizeitgestaltung," *Zeitschrift für Sozialforschung,* I, 1932, 336–55.

Stolper, Gustav, *German Economy: 1870–1940: Issues and Trends* (New York: Reynal & Hitchcock, 1940).

Tönnies, Ferdinand, *Kritik der öffentlichen Meinung* (Berlin: Springer, 1922).

Treue, Wilhelm, *Die deutsche Landwirtschaft zur Zeit Caprivis und ihr Kampf gegen die Handelsverträge,* Ph.D. dissertation, University of Berlin, 1933.

Volkmann, Erich Otto, *Der Marxismus und das deutsche Heer im Weltkriege* (Berlin: Hobbing, 1925).

Werner, Lothar, *Der Alldeutsche Verband: 1890–1918* (Berlin: Ebering, 1935).

6. *Literature on Industrialization, Bureaucratization and Democratization*

Almond, Gabriel and J. S. Coleman, eds., *The Politics of the Developing Areas* (Princeton University Press, 1960).

Baldwin, James, *Notes of a Native Son* (Boston: Beacon Press, 1955).

Bendix, Reinhard, *Higher Civil Servants in American Society* (Boulder: University of Colorado Press, 1949).

Id., "Industrialization, Ideologies, and Social Structure," *American Sociological Review,* 24:5, Oct. 1959, 613–23.

Id., "Social Stratification and the Political Community," *Archives Européennes de Sociologie,* I, 1960, 181–210.

Id., "The Lower Classes in the Age of Democratic Revolution," *Industrial Relations,* I:1, Oct. 1961, 91–116.

Id., *Work and Authority: Ideologies of Management in the Course of Industrialization* (New York: Wiley, 1956).

Blumer, Herbert, "Early Industrialization and the Laboring Class," *The Sociological Quarterly,* I:1, Jan. 1960, 5–14.

Dahrendorf, Ralf, *Class and Class Conflict in Industrial Society* (Stanford University Press, 1959).

Friedrich, Carl, *Constitutional Government and Democracy* (Boston: Little, Brown, 1941).

Gouldner, Alvin, "Metaphysical Pathos and the Theory of Bureaucracy," *American Political Science Review,* vol. 49, 1955, 496–507.

Gulick, Charles A. and Melvin Bers, "Insight and Illusion in Perlman's Theory of the Labor Movement," *Industrial and Labor Relations Review,* XI:4, 1943, 510–31.

Kerr, Clark, Frederick H. Harbison, John T. Dunlop and Charles A. Myers, *Industrialism and Industrial Man* (Cambridge: Harvard University Press, 1960).

Id. *et al.,* "The Labour Problem in Economic Development," *International Labour Review,* LXXI:3, March 1955, 1–15.

Lipset, Seymour Martin, *Political Man: The Social Bases of Politics* (Garden City: Doubleday, 1960).

Id., "Political Sociology," in R. Merton *et al.,* eds., *Sociology Today* (New York: Basic Books, 1959), 81–114.

Id., Martin Trow, James Coleman, *Union Democracy* (Glencoe: Free Press, 1956).

Id. and Reinhard Bendix, *Social Mobility in Industrial Society* (Berkeley and Los Angeles: University of California Press, 1959).

Lorwin, Val, "Working-Class Politics and Economic Development in Western Europe," *American Historical Review,* LXIII:2, 1958, 338–51.

Mannheim, Karl, *Ideology and Utopia* (New York: Harcourt, Brace Harvest Books, n.d.).

Marshall, T. H., "The Nature of Class Conflict," in R. Bendix and S. M. Lipset, eds., *Class, Status, Power* (Glencoe: Free Press, 1953), 81–87.

Palmer, R. R., *The Age of Democratic Revolution* (Princeton University Press, 1959).

Pirker, Theo., *et al.*, *Arbeiter, Management, Mitbestimmung* (Stuttgart: Ring-Verlag, 1954).

Rimlinger, Gaston, "The Legitimation of Protest: A Comparative Study in Labor History," *Comparative Studies in Society and History,* II:3, April 1960, 329–43.

Rostow, W. W., *The Stages of Economic Growth: A Non-Communist Manifesto* (Cambridge University Press, 1960).

Schlesinger, A. M., Jr., "Sources of the New Deal: Reflections on the Temper of a Time," *Columbia University Forum,* II, Fall 1959.

Sheppard, H. L., "Approaches to Conflict in American Industrial Sociology," *British Journal of Sociology,* V:4, 1954, 324–41.

Selznick, Philip, *Leadership in Administration* (Evanston: Row, Peterson, 1957).

Talmon, J. L., *The Origins of Totalitarian Democracy* (New York: Praeger, 1960).

Ulam, Adam, *The Unfinished Revolution* (New York: Random House, 1960).

Yinger, Milton, "Contraculture and Subculture," *American Sociological Review,* 25:5, Oct. 1960, 625–35.

Index of Names